Blended Learning across Disciplines:
Models for Implementation

Andrew Kitchenham
University of Northern British Columbia, Canada

Information Science
REFERENCE

Senior Editorial Director:	Kristin Klinger
Director of Book Publications:	Julia Mosemann
Editorial Director:	Lindsay Johnston
Acquisitions Editor:	Erika Carter
Development Editor:	Michael Killian
Production Coordinator:	Jamie Snavely
Typesetters:	Jennifer Romanchak and Deanna Zombro
Cover Design:	Nick Newcomer

Published in the United States of America by
Information Science Reference (an imprint of IGI Global)
701 E. Chocolate Avenue
Hershey PA 17033
Tel: 717-533-8845
Fax: 717-533-8661
E-mail: cust@igi-global.com
Web site: http://www.igi-global.com

Library of Congress Cataloging-in-Publication Data

Blended learning across disciplines : models for implementation / Andrew Kitchenham, editor.
p. cm.
Includes bibliographical references and index.
Summary: "This book presents a global perspective on blended learning and augments that perspective with examples and applications from leading scholars around the world"--Provided by publisher.
ISBN 978-1-60960-479-0 (hardcover) -- ISBN 978-1-60960-480-6 (ebook) 1. Blended learning--Cross-cultural studies. 2. Educational technology--Cross-cultural studies. 3. Comparative education. I. Kitchenham, Andrew, 1963-
LB1028.5.B566 2011b
371.3--dc22
2010054439

British Cataloguing in Publication Data
A Cataloguing in Publication record for this book is available from the British Library.

Table of Contents

Section 2
Practising Blended Learning

Section 3
Extending Blended Learning

Detailed Table of Contents

growth effectively. Research findings with very large student samples show the impact of blended learning on student achievement, identify predictors of student success, and illustrate correlates of student satisfaction with blended learning when ambivalent feelings mediate student perceptions of the educational environment. By illustrating these principles through a case study in a large metropolitan research university, the authors contend that strategic alignment and evaluation results inform each other in an incremental, transformational process.

This chapter presents three cases where asynchronous video communication was used to help offer students instruction high in fidelity and flexibility. Instructors in a blended learning format struggle to find an effective balance between face-to-face instruction that is high in fidelity and online instruction that is high in flexibility. Although the medium for sharing asynchronous video varied between the three cases, findings indicate that video was a useful tool to improve instructor immediacy and/or social presence with a minimum amount of face-to-face instruction. The instructors in all three cases saw asynchronous video communications as an effective way to communicate with students, and the majority of students responded positively to asynchronous video communications.

This chapter reviews some of the projects the authors have been carrying out in later years, all of them involving the use of Learning Management Systems for different target groups. The universe of blended learning started uncertainly, as all new ventures, amid overt resistance of traditionalist teachers, but boosted by the drive of a few enthusiasts that wanted to bring novel perspectives into education. Everyday practice, together with the growing services it is rendering, has turned blended learning into the mainstay of education. They provide details about students' response, teachers' attitudes and parents' opinions. They also show how their model has grown richer and richer thanks to the feedback obtained from all parts. Finally, future lines of development are suggested, among which, mobile learning stands out. A recently launched mobile learning project is summarized.

fivefold on the success – qualitatively based firstly on a questionnaire completed by learners and secondly on interviews of educators, thirdly, quantitatively on learner performance before and after the intervention. Fourthly, a single school is used as a case study where the mathematics performance of the learners who participated in the ISP is compared to those who did not participate in the ISP. Finally, the scope of blending of this model is evaluated by means of a radar chart, adapted from an existing radar measure. The findings of the study suggest that the use of DVD technology in the blended learning approach impacted favourably on the mathematics learning and enhanced the mathematics performance of these learners.

This chapter describes the role of blended learning in medicine. The teaching of medical students is of paramount importance for society as the goal is to have well-educated and competent physicians that can help address the healthcare issues facing today's society. The pedagogical influences that drive medical education have seen many advances in the past 30 years, but one that is seen as a leader for the future is the use of blended learning. This chapter will highlight how blended learning in medicine allows learners to be flexible in their education, as they are not constrained by time or distance as they move towards developing core competencies needed for their chosen discipline. One of the key drivers of this momentum in medicine is technology and, as we will see, it will facilitate blended learning as the one of the leading pedagogical influences in medical education for the future.

This chapter describes the use of pervasive games. Though not widely researched or implemented in the field of blended learning, pervasive game frameworks in the alternate and augmented reality game genres are highly relevant to education, particularly in curricula seeking to use blended principles. Key characteristics of alternate and augmented reality games are identified, along with specific game examples, and their applicability to various learning theories including situated learning, guided experiential learning, and integrated thematic instruction is discussed. Several learning projects using these frameworks conducted by the Mixed Emerging Technology Integration Lab are described, and the Moving Knowledge Engine delivery system and game engine for pervasive blended learning solutions is outlined. The chapter concludes by discussing future possibilities for implementing pervasive games in blended learning programs to achieve deep, complex learning and high student engagement.

This chapter describes how cloud based computing, the open-source and open-content movements, social networking, and mobile technologies can transform the ways people can work, learn, and communicate in higher education. Educational technologies both enable and require new approaches to teaching, learning, and assessment that transcend hierarchical, industrial-based content delivery models that have characterized the campus experience for the past century. Delicious, Google, Blogger, Moodle, Wikipedia, YouTube, Ning, iMovie, Facebook, Twitter, iPod, iPhone, iPad, all help to map new terrain in instant, interactive, creative, and collaborative knowledge building communities.

This chapter describes how blended learning requirements are increasing, in part because of the population explosion and policies pertaining to the democratization of education. Yet, thousands of students and faculty remain deficient in the use of blended learning to advance technology in developing countries, especially sub-Saharan Africa. This research employed a quantitative assessment design aimed at improving best available practices, processes, and performance in terms of the blended learning offered in a university setting. A six-point Likert-type questionnaire was used to gather data. Multiple statistical procedures were employed in the subsequent analysis—percentage, mean point values, chi-square, and ANOVA. A majority of the respondents to the questionnaire agreed that the teaching of MIS to students is effective and has a positive impact on their academic achievements. This groundbreaking research presents a realistic resource for the practical application of blended learning in university education in Nigeria as well as a comprehensive view of the benefits and problems of the applicability of blended learning.

This chapter comprises an outline of the prototype concept we refer to as Second-Wave Enabled Technology Enhanced (SWETE) instruction. SWETE is positioned to subsume the blended learning concept, which we critique as a categorization that will fade to ubiquity as second-generation e-learning paradigms predominate in digitally-mediated education and training. In this chapter, the operational attributes of the SWETE model are presented via description of second-wave technologies, delineation of recent changes in educational cultures and contexts, and discussion of the principles of effective digitally-mediated education. We highlight the benefits of social media-driven instructional designs and introduce the use of Blackboard LMS/social network site mashups as core tools for online teaching and learning. The chapter ends with a look at the future of mobile and blended learning, and a call for research into the use of social network technology in the delivery of learning opportunities.

This chapter discusses the blending of anonymous short message services (SMS) with a learning management system (LMS) to support non-traditional postgraduate learners in a block release programme at a higher education institution. The personal ownership of the mobile phone, coupled with its being always present and connected, was enhanced through the provision of anonymous communication via SMS. The seamless integration with the LMS optimized the limited access learners had to the LMS with abundant access to the mobile device. The mobile phone enhanced with anonymity created a safe learning environment based on andragogical principles. The postgraduate programme made extensive use of the learning management system (LMS). In block release programmes, learners are distributed in developing countries and have one contact week per module. During both pre and post-contact sessions, learners are located in contexts where mobile connectivity is more guaranteed than Internet access. Most resources are downloaded during the contact week for reading offline. As learners interact with resources, they engage in internal dialogue, and mobile phones can facilitate a way to artifact internal dialogues. Being mature adult learners, anonymous SMS creates a safe and equal socially networked knowledge production environment.

Foreword

Blended learning has become so much a part of our everyday understanding about the integration of technology into teaching and learning activities that it is almost surprising to reflect on its relatively recent coinage. Wikipedia credits Paul Myers of the BBC College of Journalism for inventing the term in 2000, and while it may have other roots, there is little evidence of its usage before that date. As Paul recounts:

"I needed a label for the new techniques I devised to help me train BBC staff. I was doing Internet research training, but I got fed up writing Web addresses on flip charts. I came up with a website to use during the course, a 'course companion.' This allowed trainees to click on links rather than have to read my handwriting. From there, I added exercises, then pre-course and post-course work. Then study material, tools that could be useful back in the work place, audio and video exercises, live examples, online treasure hunts. It became a very dynamic, imaginative way of staging a course, and soon other trainers were asking me help to build their own 'course companions.' This sort of training needed a name, so I thought of 'combined learning' as we used so many different sorts of media and techniques. That didn't sound right, so I came up with 'blended learning." (Paul Myers, personal communication, 2010).

Whatever the provenance of the term, it is clear that it was quickly popularised, in particular in commercial organisations where (unlike the education system) classroom time is an expensive overhead, and supporting learning outside of the classroom affects the bottom line. Not that its adoption was regarded as simply a cost-saving measure, since the new types of learning opportunity that were being offered were also embraced for their educational benefits: "The future direction of e-learning has been defined as 'blended learning,' according to many company executives [who] ...are blending multiple training practices to provide a fuller, more beneficial training experience for their employees." (Mitchell, 2001). It is also clear that academic interest in blended learning grew substantially around 2002-3, with an increasing number of peer-reviewed publications, establishing a tradition of innovative applied research that has continued to this day, as evinced by this volume.

Of course the term itself is just a label for certain types of learning delivery, and those practices had already been emerging for some time; Marsh stated in 2001 that "Blended learning is one of the leading trends in training today. While it is a fairly new term, the concept has been around for decades" (Marsh, 2001). Whilst one might question the idea that blended learning had been around for quite so long, Moodle's online learning history does trace the development of learning technologies from 1960, and refers to Cisco's Networking Academy in 1998 as "the largest blended learning initiative of its time" (Moodle, 2010). Perhaps the timeline is confused by possible definitions of blended learning. As Graham (2005) points out, depending on which definition you choose, blended learning may mean combining instructional modalities (or delivery media), combining instructional methods or combining online and face-to-face instruction. Thus not all definitions of blended learning would assume the use of technology. Further, there are other terms that have been used to refer to similar approaches to teaching and learning, "hybrid learning" being perhaps the most popular, but there have been others. However, it is also clear that the generally accepted concept of blended learning is that it blends some aspects of technology with face-to-face learning, and that its growth really dates from the late 1990s with the emergence of online tools that could readily support it such as Blackboard and Moodle. Its value is of course not just based on using technology but applying it in the most appropriate way for a given context: "Blended learning is balanced learning. This balance is achieved by combining the advantages of two learning modalities" (Voci & Young, 2001). Isakson memorably blogged in 2002 that ideally we should be blending learning like a good scotch whisky, not just tossing it like a salad, so it is not just about throwing any technology into the learning mix, but about choosing the best learning delivery options, both technology based and more traditional. How this is done, of course, will depend very much on the context, the nature of the subject (this volume cover topics as diverse as medicine, MIS, mathematics, chemistry, and teacher training), the geographical distribution of the teachers and learners, the technological environment, the type of learner, and a whole raft of other considerations including cultural, personal, and economic factors. Thus, the chapters in this book address blended learning from a host of different perspectives, from the institutional to the technological, from the national to the global.

Given this complex set of factors, what can we say about blended learning after more than a decade of technological advancement, experiment, and experience? Reading the chapters in this volume gives us an excellent overview of the trends and changes that are driving blended learning today. Obviously the technology has moved on apace, giving us far broader options for blending different types of learning delivery. Some authors underline the importance of new aspects of Internet technologies in blended learning innovation. These include various Web 2.0 technologies, such as social networking and mashups, as well as mobile, cloud, and open source computing. Such technologies have given the opportunity to go beyond inflexible one-way content delivery models to more interactive and creative learning environments. Another important innovation is the use of pervasive games in blended learning. Game based learning has become increasingly recognised as a valuable tool in the educators' kit, as game engines and conceptual designs are increasingly utilised for the "serious" games that can educate as well as entertain.

Mobility is clearly becoming an important part of blended learning initiatives, as reports from Europe, Africa, and the Americas in this volume assert. In 2010, the Open University claimed a world record for being the first to reach 20 million iTunes downloads, and this was all learning material (Coughlan, 2010). The high penetration of consumer broadband and portable digital media players that enabled this record was almost inconceivable a decade ago. Changes in global technology diffusion are also having an impact on the possibilities for blended learning initiatives in developing nations. In particular, chapters in this volume focus on the South Pacific and Africa as two contrasting but informative contexts for blended learning. Several chapters from African authors address the major challenges and opportunities blended learning in the particular circumstances of that continent. As the ITU indicates, Africa has the highest ratio of mobile to total telephone subscribers of any world region (ITU, 2006), so learners are often located in contexts where mobile connectivity is more guaranteed than Internet access. One African initiative, which also seeks to leverage technologies that are widely available, uses DVDs as part of a blended learning system. Indeed, the use of video-based interaction for asynchronous blended learning is also promoted in a chapter from the United States. The main issue that can impact on technology based initiatives in developing nations is, of course the technology itself, but there are other important factors including cultural considerations. These considerations can also be important in developed nations, as shown by the New Zealand study that considers issues of both indigenous (Maori) culture and conservative professional culture.

In addition to technology, we can also learn about broader perspectives of strategy and institutional transformation, of concerns that are universal and concerns that must take account of local conditions. Several of the chapters in this book address blended learning from an institutional, strategic perspective, which attests to the increasing maturity of blended learning as a means of educational provision. Such perspectives acknowledge that blended learning is not only a technological issue but one that also addresses diversity, and wide ranging support for both students and faculty.

As blended learning continues to both mature and embrace innovative technologies and pedagogies, books such as this can help us to reflect on the multi dimensional experiences of teachers and learners in an increasingly complex technological and social environment. By drawing together such a varied range of perspectives, this book makes a valuable contribution to our current knowledge of blended learning and will help us to move forward with a deeper understanding of the important issues and technologies that go into the contemporary educational mix.

Dr. David Parsons, Massey University, New Zealand
Editor in Chief, International Journal of Mobile and Blended Learning

***David Parsons** is the founding editor-in-chief of the International Journal of Mobile and Blended Learning and holds an academic post at Massey University, Auckland, New Zealand. His work on mobile learning has been published in a range of journals, including the International Journal of Mobile Learning and Organisation and IEEE Transactions on Learning Technologies, and he has presented at many major conferences including mLearn, IADIS Mobile Learning and the IEEE International Conference on Advanced Learning Technologies. He acted as Chair for the Conference on Mobile Learning Technologies and Applications (MoLTA) in 2007. He was co-editor (with Hokyoung Ryu) of 'Innovative Mobile Learning: Techniques and Technologies' (Information Science Reference, 2009) and is the author of a number of texts on software development covering Java, C++, and Web-based applications. He is a member of the International Association for Mobile Learning and a professional member of the British Computer Society.*

REFERENCES

Coughlan, S. (2010). Open University claims record iTunes downloads. *BBC News*. Retrieved July 3, 2010, from http://news.bbc.co.uk/2/hi/education/10446141.stm

Graham, C. (2005). Blended learning systems: Definition, current trends, and future directions. In C. Bonk & C. Graham (Eds.) *The handbook of blended learning: Global perspectives, local designs* (pp. 3-21). Pfeiffer.

Isackson, P. (2002). *Learning circuits*. Retrieved July 3, 2010, from http://www.internettime.com/itimegroup/astd/lc_blog.htm

ITU. (2006). ICT World Telecommunication/ICT Indicators Database *Information and Communication Technology (ICT) statistics*. Retrieved July 3, 2010, from http://www.itu.int/ITU-D/ict/statistics/ict/index.html

Marsh, J. (2001). *How to design effective blended learning*. Brandon-Hall. Retrieved July 3, 2010, from https://hhsu.learning.hhs.gov/communities/downloads/0208BWM23533.pdf

Mitchell, L. (2001). *New training methods offer personalized e-learning*. IDG. Retrieved July 3, 2010, from http://www.itworld.com/IWD010416tcelearning

Moodle. (2008). *Online learning history*. Retrieved July 3, 2010, from http://docs.moodle.org/en/Online_Learning_History

Voci, E., & Young, K. (2001). Blended learning working in a leadership development programme. *Industrial and Commercial Training, 33*(5), 157-160.

Preface

INTRODUCTION

Since the term was coined by Paul Myers of the BBC College of Journalism, blended learning has become a mainstay of university and workplace-based teaching and learning, and more recently, in the school system as the Net Generation (Tapscott, 1998) begins to expect alternate methods of acquiring knowledge (Tapscott, 2009). For the purposes of this book, with varying permutations, blended learning is defined as combining face-to-face (f2f) teaching with computer-mediated instruction (Graham, 2006). The idea of combining face-to-face learning with some form of on-line learning made sense a decade ago as it allowed much more flexibility in delivering instruction to diverse groups of learners. In 2010, blended learning has become a mainstay for universities because of that flexibility, to be sure, but more importantly, because of the thousands of dollars that can be saved by changing the mode of delivery so that there is much more online than face-to-face delivery. As Young (2002) pointed out, the President of Pennsylvania State University argued that blended learning was "the single-greatest unrecognized trend in higher education today (p. A33). As it turns out, he was correct. Bates (2000) predicted lucidly that changing from a face-to-face model to a hybrid, or blended learning, model requires more capital up front, but the change would save thousands in as few as three years. As the blended learning applications in this book demonstrate, blended learning not only addresses the needs of the new generation of learners but also saves money for university adminstrators in a time of ever-shrinking budgets.

As the Digital Natives (Palfrey & Gasser, 2008; Prensky, 2010) and Net Generation (Montgomery, 2007; Tapscott, 2009), learn in the school system and enter our undergraduate and graduate programs, we need to address their learning needs. We truly need to re-think education in the age of technology (Collins & Halverson, 2009; Tomei, 2009) since this generation of students expect social media networks, podcasts, wikis, and blogs as the mainstays of education. Their brains are wired differently than previous generations, and they do not sit still for solely face-to-face instruction (Tapscott, 2009). They are multimodal learners who thrive in environments where discussion is encouraged and performing multiple tasks to find answers to problems is standing operating procedure. They prefer to uncover ideas rather than have teachers, instructors, and professors to cover the ideas in class. In an age of cloud-based computing (Babcock, 2010), these learners expect to have access to information 24/7 through the Internet and through their mobile devices. As the chapters in this book show, these students are ready for blended learning and ready to take blended learning to the next stage: mobile learning.

Uniqueness of the Book

It has been five years since Bonk and Graham (2006) produced "the first book to cover blended learning situations and scenarios around the globe" (p. xxxii) and, in a sense, this book continues where they left off. This book is unique in that it is one of the few that presents a global perspective on blended learning and augments that perspective with examples and applications from around the world, written by scholars who are leaders in their countries and in the world. It highlights examples from the school system, from undergraduate classes, and from graduate classes.

This book also blends in androgogical principles as they apply to blended learning situations, an argument I purported some time ago now (Kitchenham, 2005), as well as heutagogical principles as we consider the self-directed nature of the lifelong learner. As Bonk and Graham saw their book as a conversation starter about blended learning, I see this book as a continuation of that conversation. As discussants, we now know more about blended learning, its triumphs and challenges, than we did as few as five years ago. We now see applications in developing countries as they embrace mobile systems in place of the less-reliable Internet connections and witness the explosion of knowledge as avenues for knowledge acquisition open up. In the developed countries, we see that same explosion, but we also see a finetuning of the blended learning framework. Lastly, this book is unique in that it combines the tried-and-tested blended learning models with the potential of mobile learning opportunities. In fact, much of that argument is continued in another edited book of mine, *Models for Interdisciplinary Mobile Learning: Delivering Information to Students*.

Target Audience

The prospective audiences for this volume will be academics and practitioners in the areas of distance learning, e-commerce/e-government, healthcare, business, education, engineering, and science, to name but a few. This volume contains chapters from leading experts in the field which will be immensely helpful for all stakeholders and will aid them in all aspects of teaching and learning.

The potential uses for this publication are vast. The volume could be used as a prescribed text in graduate schools across the world since there is a great deal of information on the latest trends in blended learning. The book can used as a bookshelf book for academics since much of the current research on blended learning is encapsulated in these pages from myriad respected scholars. The book can be a frequently-used library reference book since it contains trends, recent research, and seminal studies on blended learning in an easy-reading style. The volume is pertinent to higher education administrators as both a source for change and for faculty discussion. Lastly, this book is perfect for anyone who is interested in reading about the next stages of blending face-to-face instruction with online learning. Once again, having chapters from leading experts in the field will be helpful and will aid readers in all aspects of teaching and learning in the age of e-learning.

The potential benefits for the reader of this publication are that he or she will have cutting-edge research on blended learning, written by key academics in the respective areas of expertise (see the next section and the Tables of Contents for chapter headings and abstracts). Additionally, the benefit of this edited volume to enhance the available literature is that it would bring together the writers from other books and journals into one volume. It could also lead to opportunities for new and experienced researchers to meet at a common venue based on what is written in the chapters.

The Structure of the Book

The book begins with an informative foreword by David Parsons who outlines the history of the term and explains its evolution. The book itself is divided into three natural sections. The first, *Theorizing About Blended Learning*, includes four key chapters dealing with theoretical and philosophical arguments for blended learning. The second section, *Practicing Blended Learning*, contains four chapters that exemplify blended learning in various contexts. The last, *Extending Blended Learning*, includes five chapters that demonstrate how blended learning can be applied in innovative ways.

Theorizing about Blended Learning

The book opens with a chapter that contextualizes the book and subsequent chapters. In "*Towards a Technology- Enhanced University Education*," Valia Spiliotopoulos argues that learning technologies, such as blended learning methods, can clearly meet the outcomes, objectives, and goals of universities across the world. She outlines several actual examples from universities that have taken the concept of blended learning and created courses and methods that exploit the incredible potential of blended learning. The Canadian context outlined is similar to many post-secondary settings whether the setting is in Florida or Fiji, South Africa or France. Spiliotopoulos makes the argument that blended learning meets the needs at the course or program level, to be sure, but she states that institutional needs can also be met by providing support from the top-down for the individuals and faculties that are building robust blended learning models from the bottom-up. In fact, if universities are meant to be competitive in the 21st century market where walls and mortar are inconsequential, university administrations need to support centres for teaching and learning at the mid-range level, but they also need to support grassroots initiatives that often are unseen beyond a conference presentation or published paper.

The second chapter, "*Blended Courses as Drivers of Institutional Transformation*," augments the argument presented in the first chapter. Charles Dziuban, Joel Hartman, Thomas B. Cavanagh, and Patsy D. Moskal describe innovative projects at the University of Central Florida, a hotbed for both research and practice on blended learning. Many times, the bottom line for organization administrations is whether initiatives such as blended learning have any effect for university or organizational change. The authors provide a convincing argument for the transformational potential of blended learning and the importance of aligning with the outcomes and strategic initiatives of the university. They report that the student enrollment in blended courses at UCF have increased over 450% in ten years. Additionally, using research findings from large student samples of over 86,000, they demonstrate that blended learning has positive impacts on student achievement, can predict success variables, and show correlations between blended learning and student ambivalence. They conclude the chapter of a case study from their institution that shows how strategic aligments and student results inform each other in a gradual process of transformation.

In the third chapter, "*The Use of Asynchronous Video Communication to Improve Instructor Immediacy and Social Presence in a Blended Learning Environment*," Jered Borup, Charles R. Graham, and Andrea Velasquez present three cases in which the instructors used asynchronous video communication to provide high fidelity and high flexibility instruction to the students. In the first case, the instructor used the video feature in Facebook to communicate with the students and created weekly orientation videos that were linked on the course group page; in the second case, the instructor used VideoThread to augment the course content and created weekly orientation videos that were linked on the course wiki; in the last case, the students could access to a group video blog for discussions with all or some students and to an individual video blog to communicate with the instructor alone. In all three cases, the instructors reported that the perceived asynchronous video communication was an effective means with which to communicate to the students and the students themselves reacted positively to the approach.

In the last chapter of this section, "*Blended Learning Revisited: How It Brought Engagement and Interaction into and Beyond the Classroom*," Pablo Ortega Gil and Francisco Arcos García review several projects that used Learning Management Systems (LMSs) for specific groups of learners. They demonstrate that LMSs have had positive impacts on students through e-homework, on struggling students through innovative approaches, and on truant students by providing incentive to come to and stay in school. They conclude their chapter with a project that extends their work on blended learning into the realm of mobile learning and the use of PDAs by their students.

Practising Blended Learning

In Chapter 5, "*Blended Learning Examples in Education and Chemistry*," Robert Hogan describes blended learning from the point of view of a developing nation, Fiji. That is, the chapter describes how blended learning, which has changed the teaching and learning process in developed countries, has just begun to spread in developing countries, arguing that the improved Internet access has enabled students to be part of the blended revolution and has created a new market for universities to offer blended programs in Asia, Africa, and the Pacific. In particular, the chapter outlines instructional design, cultural considerations, technical issues, and initial findings from offering two blended learning courses: an undergraduate course in Chemistry and a graduate course for teachers.

Sue Tappenden, in "*Blended and Mobile Learning: Experiences from a New Zealand Faculty of Law*," focuses on her own blended learning experiences as an instructor in the Law Faculty at the University of Waikato. She provides a solid argument for designing a blended law course with the two key considerations of a conservative profession and the cultural needs of Maori students. Since Law is a conservative profession and is bound by external requirements, mandatory courses need to be face to face; however, elective courses can be delivered online. Additionally, Maori students find it very difficult to take part in a competitive approach to gaining course content but Tappenden points out that the use of blended learning technologies such as podcasts and DVDs, within a constructivist framework, allows these students to take part at their own pace and be a part of a collaborative, rather than competitive, community.

In Chapter 7, "*Towards Alleviating the Post-Apartheid Education Crisis in South Africa*," Pragashni Padayachee and Ansie Harding describe a blended learning model devised at the Nelson Mandela Metropolitan University (NMMU) that incorporates DVD technology into the course content as an affordable and easily-accessible technology for specific secondary school learners in the Eastern Cape of South Africa. Providing evidence from student questionnaires, teacher interviews, pre- and post-test results, a single-school case study, and a radar measure, the authors demonstrate, qualitatively and quantitatively, that the use of DVD technology resulted in students improving in the mathematics learning and performance.

In the next chapter, "*The Role of Blended Learning in 21st Medical Education: Current Trends and Future Directions*," Geoffrey W. Payne describes the role of blended learning in medicine and how blended learning is perceived as a clear leader in the training of well-educated and competent physicians. The Northern Medical Program is unique in that the students study from one of three campuses, the University of British Columbia, the University of Victoria, and the University of Northern British Columbia, and receive their courses via online delivery. They also rotate through the three communities when they take part in the residency requirements. Payne provides a thorough overview of the history e-learning in medicine, a lucid argument for the inclusion of blended learning in the discipline, and a brief discussion of the future of blended and mobile learning in Medicine.

Extending Blended Learning

In Chapter 9, "*Fundamental Design Elements of Pervasive Games for Blended Learning,*" David Metcalf, Clarissa Graffeo, and Luke Read describe pervasive games within the framework of blended learning. The authors present the argument for pervasive game frameworks within alternate and augmented reality game genres as highly relevant to education. They identify key principles for reality games, provide specific game examples and how they are applicable to situated learning, guided experiential learning, and integrated thematic instruction. In particular, they share their findings and experiences conducted by the Mixed Emerging Technology Integration Lab and outline the Moving Knowledge Engine delivery system and game engine for pervasive blended learning solutions.

Michele Jacobsen, in "*A Case Study of a Blended Doctoral Program in Educational Technology,*" describes an online and blended doctoral program at the University of Calgary, a leading Canadian university in educational technology delivery. She outlines the genesis of the program, the development of courses, her own experiences in teaching courses, and the revisions to the program. She also explains the potential of such programs and hardware as Delicious, Google, Blogger, Moodle, Wikipedia, YouTube, Ning, iMovie, Facebook, Twitter, iPod, iPhone, and iPad in the teaching and learning process within a blended learning framework.

In the next chapter, "*Blended Learning in Nigeria: Determining Students' Readiness and Faculty Role in Advancing Technology in a Globalized Educational Context,*" Nwachukwu Prince Ololube outlines a study that examined available promising practices, processes, and performance within a blended learning framework in a Nigerian university. In particular, he discusses the experiences of the students and instructors in Management Information System (MIS) or Business 224, a core course for those in the Department of Business Administration and Accounting. Using a six-point Likert-type questionnaire and 21 research hypotheses, he performed multiple statistical procedures, percentage, mean point values, chi-square, and ANOVA, he demonstrated that blended learning is effective and has a positive impact on student performance.

In Chapter 12, "*Blending In: Moving Beyond Categories in Digitally-Mediated Learning,*" Marvin D. LeNoue and Ronald Stammen outline their prototype blended learning concept, Second-Wave Enabled Technology Enhanced (SWETE) instruction. They present the operational attributes of the SWETE model, highlight the benefits of social media-driven instructional designs, and introduce the use of Blackboard LMS/social network site mashups as core tools for online teaching and learning. In particular, they argue that the SWETE has two key components of Second-wave e-learning which requires maximizing learner independence and freedom, and the realization that technology is an enhancement to, rather than a replacement for, teaching and learning. They conclude the chapter with a examination of the future for blended and mobile learning and with a call for more research into the use of social network technology within blended learning frameworks.

In the concluding chapter, "*Blending Anonymous Short Message Services with Learning Management Systems,*" Dick Ng'ambi discusses his research on blended anonymous short message systems (SMS) with a learning management system (LMS) to address the needs of non-traditional post-graduate students at the University of Cape Town. Among the SMS learning management system and within a blended learning framework, the students use a Virtual Noticeboard, collaborative mobile memos, collaborative-network learning, and podcast-mediated reflection. Ng'ambi argues that the SMS system allows for a safe and equally-social teaching and learning environment for these adult learners in which mobile phone connections are much more reliable than Internet access.

CONCLUSION

This book represents months of hard work from a group of dedicated scholars who are passionate about blended learning. It is truly collaborative and international effort on the part of 25 academics from seven countries and four continents. When I was asked by IGI Global to edit a book dealing with international perspectives on e-learning, I was deeply honoured and rose to the challenge of soliciting chapters from colleagues across the world. In total, there were over 50 submissions from which 28 were chosen. The book chapters were submitted to a double-blind review and the successful authors wrote their final chapters. As it turned out, the quality and quantity of the book chapters were so outstanding that we decided to make the original book into two excellent books. This one, *Blended Learning across Disciplines: Models for Implementation*, represents the blended learning scholars, but much of their content deals with the arguments outlined in the second book, *Models for Interdisciplinary Mobile Learning: Delivering Information to Students*. Although the decision to include a chapter was certainly not arbitrary, many times the decision was difficult. I believe that the end product will provide an extremely valuable resource to those students, researchers, and scholars interested in the topic of blended learning.

In the end, this book has become an excellent resource for any person interested in blended learning: the definitions, the concept, examples from around the world, and applications from secondary school to graduate school. It will be a valuable addition to any person's library.

Andrew Kitchenham
University of Northern British Columbia, Canada

REFERENCES

Babcock, C. (2010). *Management strategies for the cloud revolution.* Toronto, Canada: McGraw-Hill.

Bates, A. W. (2000). *Managing technological change: Strategies for college and university leaders.* San Francisco, CA: Jossey-Bass.

C. J. Bonk & C. R. Graham (Eds). (2006). *The handbook of blended learning: Global perspectives, local designs*. San Francisco, CA: Pfeiffer.

Collins, A., & Halverson, R. (2006). *Rethinking education in the age of technology: The digital revolution and schooling in America.* New York, NY: Teachers College.

Graham, C. R. (2006). Blended learning systems: Definition, current trends, and future directions. In C. J. Bonk & C. R. Graham, C. R. (Eds). *The handbook of blended learning: Global perspectives, local designs* (pp. 3-21). San Francisco, CA: Pfeiffer.

Kitchenham, A. D. (2005). Adult learning principles, technology and elementary teachers and their students: A perfect blend? *Education, Communication, & Information, 5*(3), 285-302.

Montgomery, K. C. (2007). *Generation digital: Politics, commerce, and childhood in the age of the Internet.* Cambridge, MA: MIT Press.

Palfrey, J., & Gasser, U. (2008). *Born digital:Understanding the first generation of digital natives.* NewYork, NY: Basic Books.

Prensky, M. (2010). *Teaching digital natives: Partnering for real learning*. Thousand Oaks, CA: Corwin Press.

Tapscott, D. (1998). *Growing up digital: The rise of the Net Generation*. Toronto, Canada: McGraw-Hill.

Tapscott, D. (2009). *Grown up digital: How the Net Generation is changing your world.* Toronto, Canada: McGraw-Hill.

Tomei L.(Ed.). (2009). *Information Communication Technologies for enhanced education and learning: Advanced applications and developments*. Hershey, PA: IGI Global.

Young, J. R. (2002, March 22). Hybrid teaching seeks to end the divide between traditional and online instruction. *Chronicle of Higher Education*, A.33.

Acknowledgment

I would like to wholeheartedly thank all who were part of the collection and double-blind review process for the chapters contained in this volume. This project would not have been so successful without the help extended by all and the incredible abilities of all to meet the required deadlines. I would like to especially thank Dr. Colin Chasteauneuf for his support as a colleague and a listener, as well as for his reviewing a few manuscripts and copyediting a few more.

Many of the authors in this volume served as reviewers for their peers, and I thank them for their commitment to the high-quality scholarship that emerged. You were constructive and comprehensive and I know that each author appreciated the detailed feedback. This book is yours as much as it mine, and I hope that you have an opportunity to share it with your colleagues at home and further afield.

I would also like to thank Mike Killian at IGI Global for his patience with my myriad of emails and for always having an answer, no matter how mundane the question. You own part of this book as well, and I cannot express my gratitude enough. I also thank IGI Global for the invitation to edit this book and for the chance to edit another as a direct result of this project.

Lastly, I would like to thank my wife, Leah Jackson, for her support and understanding now and in the past for encouraging me to take on more writing projects and my son, Davy, who taught me about miracles and always teaches me something everyday.

Andrew Kitchenham
University of Northern British Columbia, Canada
August, 2010

Section 1
Theorizing About Blended Learning

Chapter 1
Towards a Technology-Enhanced University Education

Valia Spiliotopoulos
University of Victoria, Canada

ABSTRACT

Although Canadian universities have distinct cultures, research strengths, and teaching philosophies, many also share similar values and goals that respond to an increasingly multicultural, diverse, and technologically advanced society. The aim of this chapter is to demonstrate how learning technologies used in a blended learning environment can help to meet the goals of a contemporary university education. An understanding of blended learning as an effective model for meeting goals not only at the course and program levels, but also at the institutional level, is essential for the widespread, mainstream implementation of this model so that it becomes a part of regular practice by faculty from a variety of disciplines and learning contexts.

INTRODUCTION

This chapter will focus on the potential that educational technologies have to support the common goals of a university-level education, specifically in blended learning contexts. Although there is an increasing number of students who take fully online distance courses and programs (Moller et al., 2008), many undergraduate and graduate students still commute to campus and expect flexible, innovative, and engaging learning experiences with technologies that they commonly use or will be expected to use in today's professional, academic, and social environments.

Since definitions of blended learning or hybrid learning abound, it is important to provide as many concrete examples as possible in order to encourage faculty across disciplines to consider the pedagogical merits of this approach and to demonstrate to administrators the relevance of this model in meeting overall institutional goals. A better understanding of blended learning within the context of strategic university goals is impor-

DOI: 10.4018/978-1-60960-479-0.ch001

tant in order to "embed" (Jasinski, 2007) the use of educational technologies at the institutional level and to reinforce the integrated nature of teaching, learning, and technology beyond the distance education context. Much of the literature on blended learning focuses on the integration of digital technologies in face-to-face (F2F) courses for the purposes of meeting learning outcomes at the individual course or program level (Garnham & Kaleta, 2002; Garrison & Vaughn, 2008; Twigg, 2003). Discussions at these levels are an important first step in the effective implementation of educational technologies for blended/hybrid learning; however, understanding how blended learning can support *institutional* goals and values can motivate faculty to use technology as a regular part of their practice and can better involve administrators in making key decisions around educational technology.

The use and management of learning technologies have often been associated with distance education programs and with faculty/students who are "digital natives" participating in virtual environments. In blended learning, the web-based technologies are transferred to the F2F classroom to enhance interaction and student-centered activities (web-enhanced classrooms) or to enhance online education through classroom contact (classroom-enhanced online education) (Dziuban et al., 2004). However, for the purposes of this chapter, blended learning can also refer to both software and hardware or installed devices in physical learning spaces (i.e., DVD players, document cameras, whiteboard capture systems, videoconferencing, web cameras) and mobile devices (cell phones, clickers, PDAs, laptops or Tablet PCs, iPods, iPads, digital cameras, USB drives, and GPS systems) to enhance interaction, flexibility, and to increase student engagement (Milne, 2006). Providing examples of educational technology use beyond the context of web-based distance/online education is an important step towards better understanding and implementing blended learning models across disciplines.

First, this chapter will provide a brief discussion of the rationale behind the goals that are commonly stated in university strategic plans, vision, or mission documents by referring to George Kuh's (2005) work on student engagement and success. Next, blended learning will be promoted as an effective model for engaging instructors and learners with the principles and practices that lead to student success. The bulk of this chapter will focus on examples of blended learning within the context of common university goals that aim to engage students, improve communication skills, support diversity, interdisciplinarity, and inquiry. Finally, challenges to the implementation and embedding of blended learning approaches into regular practice will be discussed, and future research directions to address those challenges will be recommended.

BACKGROUND

Despite unique university cultures, there appears to be common principles and goals shared by many Canadian universities: student engagement, the development of communication, language, and critical thinking skills, internationalization and global citizenship, respect for diversity, interdisciplinary courses and programs, community-based initiatives, and support for undergraduate research. According to Kuh et al. (2005, p. xiii), these goals and values are considered essential for student success and economic independence in an information-driven global economy. Many traditionally underserved students have come to this realization, and the mass democratization of education has created the challenging task of providing high quality post-secondary education to as many as three-quarters of the adult population (Kuh et al, 2005). To demonstrate public accountability, many universities now publish strategic plans or mission documents that include educational goals, policies, and practices that lead to student success (Kuh et al., 2005). Though teaching on the basis of these goals, principles and practices might not necessarily lead to successful student learning, certain strategies, tools, and approaches can maximize opportunities for engaging students and enhancing the learning process.

One such approach is through blended learning, which involves the purposeful inclusion of information and communication technologies, as well as multimedia or mobile devices, in order to meet learning goals (Milne, 2006). According to Kuh et al. (2005), technologies play a large role in enhancing educational environments in universities that are considered models of educational excellence. Technologies have the potential to increase student-to-faculty interaction, student-to-student interaction, as well as time on task, and they also help meet the needs of students with diverse learning styles.

Throughout this chapter, a very broad definition of blended learning is used. It can include blended programs that offer fully online courses and face-to-face (F2F) courses, or a course or program that is accessible by distance and on-campus students simultaneously (supported by videoconferencing, for example). Blended or hybrid learning can also refer to F2F courses that are enhanced by educational technologies, such as clickers, mobile technologies, and learning management systems (LMS). Some of these courses might continue to require regular classroom attendance (without a reduction in "seat time"), whereas other courses might have a F2F component that constitutes 75% or 50% of the course, with the remaining time requiring an online component that is coherently integrated into the course in a purposeful manner.

According to Garrison and Vaughn, "blended learning is more than enhancing lectures. It represents the transformation of how we approach teaching and learning. [...] Blended learning is a coherent design approach that openly assesses and integrates the strengths of face-to-face and online learning to address worthwhile educational goals." (Garrison & Vaughn, 2008, p. x). The inclusion of the technology is not just an add-on; it is there for a specific educational purpose that helps to meet a learning outcome. Also, the technology is not just a substitute for transmission approaches in the face-to-face classroom, for it is this substitution of similar passive learning approaches in the initial attempts at fully online course delivery that has led to limited student success and unfavourable drop-out rates (Dziuban et al., 2004).

Blended learning is also about creating a more flexible learning environment. According to Collis and Moonen (2001), flexible learning has often been understood as distance education. However, this is not necessarily the case. "Flexibility can involve options in course resources, in types of learning activities, in media to support learning" even for full-time, on-campus students (Collis & Moonen, 2001, p. 9). Flexibility requires technologies because they enable students to overcome the limitations of time, location, delivery method, and the communication style offered in many face-to-face courses. Collis and Moonen further argue that universities "can't not do it" (2001, p. 29) – that is, universities must offer flexible learning environments that blend technologies in a variety of educational contexts in order to address the changes in student demographics, learning styles, public expectations, and the economic climate.

The purpose of this chapter is to demonstrate ways in which blended learning can support student success and meet institutional goals expressed in university vision and mission documents. Showing the possibilities that blended learning can provide will help to focus on the important role that learning technologies play in promoting enriching educational experiences beyond the distance education context. Although some institutions are responding, there is still hesitation and resistance to change that entails integrating technology into blended learning environments. Despite the challenges and fears that often accompany technology, many faculty and students are nevertheless taking the leap and discovering innovative ways of learning that are meeting the diverse needs of students and promoting student success.

ACHIEVING UNIVERSITY GOALS THROUGH BLENDED LEARNING: EXAMPLES ACROSS THE DISCIPLINES

Student Engagement

In their book, *Student Success in College,* Kuh et al. (2008) indicate that most of the research on student development shows that the "time and energy that students devote to educationally purposeful activities is the single best predictor of their learning and personal development" (p. 8). Activities that engage students are those that encourage student-faculty contact, cooperation and interaction among students, active learning, prompt feedback, time on task, high expectations, and respect for diverse talents and ways of learning – as described by Chickering and Gamson (1987) in the "Seven Principles for Good practice in Undergraduate Education." Today's universities are aiming to be accountable to parents, students, and the public by offering environments and activities that not only advance research, but that are consistent with these seven principles for the purposes of providing students with enriching educational experiences. Research on engaging students and enhancing their learning experience using a blended learning model suggests that this model can be effective as long as adequate support is provided to faculty and students (Albrecht, 2006; Dzuiban et al., 2004; Holly & Oliver, 2010).

One faculty member in Computer Science at a western Canadian university aimed to engage her students by using these principles while blending mobile and internet technologies in her fully face-to-face classroom (Storey & Trude, 2009). As is the case with many instructors teaching Net Generation students (Oblinger & Oblinger, 2005), this faculty member noticed that many students had their own laptops, cell phones, or PDAs and often used social software, such as Twitter or Facebook, during her class. She supposed that such activities were minimizing the time on task that was required to learn the course content and skills. To better meet the learning needs of these Net Generation students who were accustomed to multitasking with mobile devices and social media, the instructor decided to have them use Twitter for a variety of reflective and interactive activities. In her course, "Computer-Supported Collaborative Work," the students used Twitter throughout the term to form a diary study of experiences using collaborative technology and how it helped (or hindered) their learning. Students were advised to create an anonymous twitter id with fake information to protect their privacy, and they were expected to twitter each week in order to earn a participation mark. Students used Twitter both during the lectures and outside of the lectures to discuss class content (in this case, the content included an analysis of computer-based collaborative tools such as Google Wave, a local learning management system, and Twitter); share resources (mainly links that related to the course content, but that were not part of the required reading); follow administrative updates (announcements regarding assignments, exams, guest lectures); and provide supportive comments from fellow students and the instructor (such as "great job on the presentation").

Although there was some initial hesitation because of concern that the students by using mobile technologies and Twitter would not focus enough time on task, an informal analysis of the short tweet postings indicated that there were practically no "useless" tweets (i.e., tweets that were only done to improve the participation mark and didn't have any relevant content). The number of tweets per student ranged from approximately 5 to140, and there were over 1,000 tweets produced over the course of the term, which might well be indicative of increased participation and time on task. It appears that Twitter provided students with an additional channel during class to communicate with each other and with the instructor – key factors that promote student engagement and success. Predictably, the number of tweets peaked in the days before assignment deadlines and exams, but also during the lectures. Since it is not uncommon for computer science students to bring laptops or cell phones to class, the use of Twitter seemed to give them a way to use these tools to participate in class discussions rather than in non-class related activities. Though some instructors might question students' ability to listen to a lecture and follow a discussion on Twitter at the same time, informal student testimonials revealed that students liked being able to multitask, and they felt more comfortable participating because they were familiar with the technology. The instructor also followed Tweet discussions before and after class, thereby demonstrating teaching presence online. In doing so, she could ensure that issues and questions that arose from the students' postings were addressed, thereby making the technology-based activity an integral part of the teaching that blended coherently with students' learning goals.

Another tool that has been shown to promote student engagement is clickers or personal response systems (Caldwell, 2007). This technology might not be considered by some as traditional blended learning because clickers are used in face-to-face classrooms; however, clickers serve as a learning technology that enhances F2F classes and can be considered as part of the blended learning model, as it provides opportunities for interaction and instantaneous, anonymous feedback – both of which can promote student engagement. Clickers are being used in lecture theaters for large introductory classes such as psychology, biology, or chemistry to quiz students on the accuracy of their knowledge. However, instructors in small graduate and undergraduate classes in business and sociology courses are also using clickers in ways that do not involve expecting students to provide a "right" or "wrong" answer. The anonymity of clickers allows students in the humanities and social sciences to express their opinions on controversial issues through instantaneous polls, and the results can serve as a springboard for further discussion and analysis. Clickers can also be used for anonymous peer review, instantaneous feedback on student presentations, role plays, debates, or as informal feedback on an instructor's teaching. Clickers might soon even be replaced by cell phones, PDAs, or other mobile devices that can download an application for polling. Ultimately, however, it is the student interaction or peer instruction (Mazur, 1997) that occurs before, during, and after the use of these devices that is the real key to the effectiveness of the tool to maximize student engagement in the F2F classroom.

Internationalization/ Global Citizenship

Although the coherent integration of mobile tools and internet technology for fully face-to-face classrooms (as shown above) is a more recent innovation of the blended learning model, more common examples of blended learning have arisen in learning situations that can accommodate learners in remote locations or include students in other countries. Technology is inextricably linked to the processes of globalization and internationalization, and an increasingly interconnected world is changing the demands placed on students (Burbules & Torres, 2000). Students are beginning to explore the broader world through exchanges, study abroad opportunities, international internships, work opportunities, and travel, as well as through the friends and co-workers they meet face-to-face and online. To succeed in diverse contexts, universities need to infuse the curriculum with international perspectives, issues, and experiences so that students can better accommodate to this rapidly changing global world. Information and communication technologies offer opportunities to enhance interaction with students from different cultures by eliminating the barriers of time and space. The next section will demonstrate how the goals of internationalization can be achieved through blended learning approaches, specifically in the fields of health and modern language education.

With the advent of world health issues, such as SARS, HIV/AIDS and, more recently, the H1N1 flu virus, health disciplines have had to include international and global health issues and perspectives as part of the curriculum. In one Western Canadian university, the development of undergraduate and graduate public health and nursing programs has involved the inclusion of students not only from other parts of Canada and the world, but also from non-urban, Aboriginal communities. Adding content about international and cross-cultural health issues and problems through additional readings, though essential, is not considered the only way to achieve better understanding of these areas. Interacting about these issues with students from other regions and countries renders the subject matter more relevant and adds an additional perspective. To bridge the barriers of time and space, instructors in the program blend videoconferencing or Elluminate Live tools, or even Skype, into their F2F courses to facilitate interaction on world and community health issues with students abroad or in remote areas. In this way, students can question, debate, and participate in discussions with students from diverse areas in synchronous (real time) or asynchronous environments, verbally or in writing. The perspectives gained from a diverse student body not only help learners with their communication skills, but also help them to see health issues through a cross-cultural lens, thereby leading to improved interactions with patients. The technology is purposefully blended into the curriculum in order to meet the learning goal of internationalization and to provide an engaging, transformative experience to students that will improve their practice.

Another discipline that is attempting to meet the goals of internationalization and intercultural communication is that of modern/foreign language learning. Although accuracy and fluency in the target language have often been the goals of learning a second language, one area that has been increasingly noted as requiring more attention is the understanding of culture and the development of cross-cultural communication skills (Kramsch, 1998). In many Canadian universities, the use of real-time, voice-over technologies, such as Skype, e-meetings, and discussion forums through LMSs, are being used to encourage students to communicate with students at a distance who are native speakers of the target language in a 'virtual exchange' format. In Canada, for example, instructors from anglophone universities who teach French are coordinating with instructors from francophone universities in Quebec who are teaching English for the purpose of organizing both synchronous and asynchronous communicative activities that allow not only for the development of language skills, but also for the opportunity to discuss cross-cultural issues and to develop an awareness of cultural sensitivities through the respectful expression of differing opinions and ideas.

These virtual exchanges are most effective if activities used with synchronous and asynchronous voice/text tools are clearly structured so that there are specific interactive tasks and goals that students need to accomplish. To achieve this, adequate "scaffolding" in terms of the vocabulary/grammatical structures to be used during the exchange session, as well as the cultural background of the participating students, is needed for productive exchanges. Finally, to maintain motivation and assess learning, it is important that the interactive exchange sessions be included as part of the formal assessment of the students in the course and not considered merely as a "fun", optional activity.

Similar technologies and strategies are being used with other languages, such as German or Japanese, in order to create language/culture exchange environments with students from international universities. Although the communication and Internet technology exists to create a purposeful learning environment that meets the goals of internationalization and cross-cultural competence in a blended context, there are still some challenges to accessing and implementing them to be able to work effectively with an international audience or with remote communities within a region/province. Many Canadian universities are gaining access to videoconferencing and live electronic meeting technologies; however, the cost does serve as a barrier to accessing these technologies, and often only the better funded faculties/disciplines will have access to them, creating inequities within an institution. Skype is an ideal tool to use with students from other countries because it has a broad user base and is free, easy to install, and easy to use. It supports voice and video calls, text chat, file transfers and screen sharing, and conferencing (albeit with no video). However, the U.S. Freedom of Information and Privacy Act bars universities from requiring that their students export personal information to servers outside of Canada. Since the creation of a Skype account entails the possible export of personal information to servers in other parts of the world, an alternative is needed for students who do not wish to create an account. Once the university offering the program has achieved access to the technology, even Net Generation students may need training on how to use the various technologies, and some of the students abroad might experience technical difficulties (due, for example, to insufficient bandwidth or firewalls) and might be unable to connect with the students in the Canadian university. It is also challenging to coordinate sessions across various time zones in ways that are fair to all students participating from abroad. Despite these challenges, Canadian instructors are working closely with university IT departments to smooth out the logistics of using these tools in blended learning environments in order to include international student voices and to enrich the educational experience of domestic students.

Community-Based Initiatives

As previously mentioned, universities are increasingly striving to become more accountable to the public that they are serving by applying and transferring knowledge that serves the community, by including the community in research and curriculum development, and by increasing access to education to remote communities (see *Office of community-based research*). In the latter scenario, in many Canadian universities located in the city centre, the use of mobile technologies, learning management systems, and eLive tools enables teaching and learning to occur with Indigenous students in their home communities.

At one Western Canadian university, a Virtual Learning Lodge (VLL) specifically supports online and mixed mode courses for Aboriginal students in remote communities across British Columbia (Coady & Gibbs, 2009). The VLL is a course management system that gives students access to UVic resources (courses, advisors, instructors), but also allows local community sites to share public events through RSS feeds. For example, the VLL facilitated the inclusion of North Island participants in two conferences held at UVic, supported students in remote island locations in the School of Child and Youth Care, and included two North Island students to participate in a first-year Computer Science course held on campus.

According to Coady and Gibbs (2009), although there is increased participation by remote community members in on-campus events and educational offerings, the technology has not yet met expectations in terms of quality of connections, video, sound, and ease of use. In addition, blended learning that involves off-campus participants with on-campus participants in real time requires the organization of cohort groups as well as the availability of distributed tutored video instruction for these cohort groups. In addition, on campus participants might need to be aware of cross-cultural issues and develop intercultural communication skills when involved in discussion forums or peer review exercises with Aboriginal students who live, work, and learn in their communities outside of the city centre.

As with blended learning initiatives that aim to include international perspectives and experiences, in this case the technology not only provides access to education, but the new possibilities afforded by the technology necessitate the development of a new set of skills – namely intercultural competence and cross-cultural communication skills, as well as the ability to translate knowledge in ways that are understood by communities outside the university. Also, the connectedness and interaction enabled by the technology provide an opportunity to include the knowledge and perspectives of the remote community as part of the knowledge-building process. Technologies help to bridge the gap between the outside community and the university by providing the platform for communication; however, until remote and rural communities receive better access and technical support for the technology, community-based initiatives that blend on-campus students in F2F learning experiences with off-campus students might not be able to maximize their potential for student engagement.

Diversity

As we have seen, blended learning has taken advantage of the mobile and internet technologies traditionally used in fully distance learning contexts and has repurposed them to meet the learning goals of internationalization and cross-cultural competence, as well as to meet the needs of Net Generation learners, in fully F2F courses and blended F2F/online courses and programs. In fact, these technologies have demonstrated their potential to address a broad range of diversity issues in blended learning contexts. For both ethical and legal purposes, these issues are increasingly coming to the forefront in many campuses as institutions are responding to the need to reflect the causes of social equity and social justice expected of an institution within a democratic society.

According to Maher and Tetreault (2007, p. 2), starting at about the 1970's, "students and faculty from underrepresented groups demanded entrance and full acceptance into the academy – as undergraduate and graduate students, as faculty, as scholars, and as institutional leaders." A different profile of the university was being sought – one that would challenge the white, male, heterosexual, and middle-class domination of higher education, and transform it into one that supported women faculty and students, faculty and students from various cultures and diverse sexual orientations, as well as those with disabilities, and diverse learning styles. The previous section demonstrated how values of internationalization and intercultural communication have been enhanced through blended learning environments that included both face-to-face interaction and various communication technologies. This section will demonstrate how various technologies have supported students with different learning styles and disabilities.

In teacher education programs, student-teacher candidates are encouraged to model effective teaching and learning practices that meet students' diverse learning styles, as well as to become familiar with some of the digital learning technologies and social software that many of their own students are using. Dr. Tim Hopper at The University of Victoria encourages his students to experiment with using concept mapping software not only for their own learning, but also as a teaching strategy. Concept mapping can be an effective tool for visual learners, and it can help generate ideas and motivate the writing and thinking process. Though concept mapping can be done with traditional paper and pencil, those who have engaged in this activity often realize that they have to re-organize their map significantly and have to go through many drafts. Digital versions of concept maps make this necessary editing easier and more efficient. Concept maps can be saved in digital format and can be shared with other students through e-mail and course management system, and they can be included in an ePortfolio. In teacher education, they can be used to prepare lesson and unit plans, to write papers and reports, and as a teaching tool.

In addition to supporting visual learners, Dr. Hopper also encourages students to think about their practicum experience or course content through spoken journal reflections. Writing in a journal has been the standard practice for reflective learning in many fields in the humanities and social sciences; however, writing might not be the most effective strategy to promote reflection as many students suffer from writer's block or feel that what they write must be so polished and accurate that it could impede expression. However oral expression that is recorded and podcast through a course site might better meet the needs of more verbal and auditory learners. Some students have informally reported some initial awkwardness in talking to the computer or digital recorder, but many end up preferring this approach, as it is efficient, is consistent with their learning style, and can be a good catalyst for the writing process.

Another area in which technology has made impressive strides in promoting diversity is in assisting or accommodating students with disabilities. According to Dawson and Keenan (2009), universities in Canada have an ethical and legal duty to accommodate people with disabilities – one that is governed by The Charter of Rights and Freedoms. In order to fulfill this responsibility, universities must work with faculty to design instruction, curriculum, and a learning environment that removes barriers for students with disabilities to maximize opportunities for learning (Dawson & Keenan, 2009). By using principles of Universal Instructional Design as well as blending adaptive technologies and mainstream communication technologies or learning management systems, students with disabilities can have equal opportunities for participation and engagement in the learning process. Examples of strategies that faculty are encouraged to use in order to meet the needs of students with disabilities include selecting texts that are available in digital format so that students with vision impairments can use a screen reader to access the readings, or podcasting lectures and uploading the digital audio files on course websites in order to assist students who are hard of hearing. Many resource centres for students with disabilities provide text-to-speech and screen reading software, idea mapping software, speech recognition software, and screen enlargement software. As such, faculty are encouraged to create materials (i.e., lecture notes) in formats that have an accessibility feature, thereby allowing them to be used with the adaptive software available. In addition, the more visual and auditory material that is available in digital format through a course website, the more accessible that knowledge is to students with physical injuries or disabilities, for whom 'coming to class' might not be possible. Purposefully blending even mainstream communication technologies in fully face-to-face courses can help students with disabilities access more easily the education to which they have a right.

Interdisciplinarity

Another goal that often arises in university strategic plans is that of interdisciplinarity. This approach to learning and teaching is similar to interdisciplinary research in that it involves collaboration, real world problem-solving, and applied knowledge from various disciplines (Lattuca, 2001). To begin the process of interdisciplinary teaching, faculty from various disciplines have to share and communicate with other faculty about course syllabi, readings, resources, and assessment practices, at both the course and program levels. This sharing and communication are often facilitated through the use of wikis or document sharing portals. Within a blended learning context, wikis have been used in interdisciplinary courses to create and share content on a topic that is authored and reviewed by instructors and students from different disciplinary backgrounds (Reinhold, 2006). In this way, wikis can promote collaboration through an enriched and shared vision of issues, problems, and solutions, and can create a dynamic course curriculum. Using technologies for interdisciplinary teaching and learning is an area that will become more prominent as the open source movement and free public access to knowledge gain momentum. At the moment, we have seen many learning object repositories, such as MERLOT and SOL*R, where teaching materials and ideas can be re-purposed or modified by instructors from other disciplines or backgrounds. However, many faculty are still hesitant to share freely the resources they have developed for teaching, and this hesitancy hampers the potential for interdisciplinary course or program design.

Interdisciplinary knowledge and teaching is not limited to faculty working only with other faculty from different disciplines. In the field of business, an interactive website called the Utilium Network, created by Dr. Micheal Fern, allows academics to exchange information with managers of private and public sector-organizations. The network includes academics from various fields, such as psychology, sociology, and business from around the world. Utilium enables faculty to post concise, easy-to-read reports of academic research related to organizational issues that managers can view through RSS feeds. Managers can also ask academics questions on a discussion forum or blog or share their perspectives of the research from a practical standpoint. This site not only assists managers in the decision-making process by accessing the latest research, but it also provides a place for academics to demonstrate how their research can be applied and how it can affect society. Furthermore, this site can be accessed as well by students so that they can observe how interdisciplinary research can be applied and be of benefit to a community or industry. Students can also participate in the site, sharing their research, adding and rating resources, and posting their perspectives. Using knowledge from a variety of disciplines to address real-world problems and issues is central to interdisciplinary approaches, and blending on-line open forums, such as Utilium and wikis into on-campus courses supports interdisciplinary curriculum development and makes knowledge relevant, applied, and dynamic.

Undergraduate and Graduate Research

As previously mentioned, one of the key factors that promote student engagement and success is student-faculty interaction as well as the application of knowledge. A student working alongside a faculty member on a research project is an ideal way to promote this interaction as well as to apply and extend the knowledge learned in classrooms (Kuh et al., 2005). Although this opportunity has traditionally been available to graduate students, upper-level undergraduate students are also keen on gaining this experience. Many universities are recognizing the value of undergraduate research to enhance the student experience and are including this as a goal in their strategic plans.

Communication and information technologies, though often used for *teaching* in blended and distance learning contexts, are also great tools for supporting learning through *research*. Increasingly, students and faculty members are using wikis and blogs to write research proposals and publications together and to share findings and insights as well as relevant literature. Students learn to use project management software to understand goals, clarify roles, and set timelines for a research project. Multimedia technologies (digital audio and video recorders) and mobile tools can help to collect and record data. Online repositories are used to store data of various file types, and data analysis software helps to categorize data in an effective, efficient manner. In the final stages of the research process, students use word processing, graphics, presentation and publication software to demonstrate and share findings and to invite peer review. In the area of research, it appears that graduate programs, which typically include more collaborative and independent learning contexts than undergraduate programs, seamlessly blend the use of these tools in the development of various research skills. This purposeful blending of tools and skills can greatly benefit the educational experience of graduate students who wish to pursue both research and professional careers.

More recently, the open, online journaling system has also allowed universities to create their own peer-reviewed research journals that both faculty and students can participate in. At the University of Victoria, undergraduate students are awarded funding to conduct research under the supervision of a faculty member and are invited to submit their research to the online journal *The Arbutus Review.* In this way, an undergraduate student can have the experience of making their knowledge public and participating in the publication process by honing academic writing skills as well as editing and peer-review skills. Faculty can use these open journaling systems in their face-to-face courses by creating as a final class project a mini-conference with published proceedings or an academic journal that includes student papers and is peer reviewed and edited by students as well as the faculty member.

As we can see, blending a range of communication, multimedia, mobile and open source technologies in undergraduate and graduate programs within F2F, collaborative, and independent learning contexts can support the development of research skills and lead to greater student engagement and success in scholarly pursuits.

Communication and Critical Thinking Skills

As we have seen in some examples above, the blending of social software such as Twitter, wikis, discussion forums, as well as ePortfolios into face-to-face courses can provide opportunities for the development of writing skills for interactive communication as well as for individual reflection. The use of these tools is quite common in the humanities and social sciences, but these tools are also being explored in professional schools, computer science, and the trades.

Electronic portfolios have been recognized as providing opportunities for students to build their critical thinking and writing skills and to showcase their work to peers or potential employers (Siemens, 2004). In many post-secondary institutions in western Canada, some professional schools that have a practicum or internship component as part of the program, such as education, nursing, or social work, expect students to develop an ePortfolio as a capstone project near the end of the program as a means of ensuring that their professional competencies have been achieved. One western Canadian university has developed a SSHRC funded ePortfolio system that is being used in the faculty of education and in the schools of nursing and social work (Hopper & Sanford, 2010). In addition to setting personal learning goals, students use the competencies set by professional bodies as the standard they need to achieve upon completion of the program. They select artifacts that demonstrate their learning progress (i.e., papers, reports, role play videos, teaching demo, or lesson plans), post them on their ePortfolio, and reflect on what they learned or on what they might have done differently. The ePortfolio allows students to self-assess their improvement in relation to their goals and competencies. In addition to promoting self-assessment, ePortfolios can be shared with other students for peer review, thereby further enhancing critical thinking as well as discipline-specific communication skills. Blending ePortfolios into professional programs can help students develop the professional communication and reflective thinking skills required for professional development in their careers.

Other programs that have experimented with using ePortfolios are in Computer Science and the Trades. At a western Canadian polytechnic institution, in an effort to promote deep learning and better communication skills, students in a computer science program were challenged to reflect on their work and explain in words, (rather than code), what and how they learned through an ePortfolio (Meyles & Woo, 2007). Although the students were initially hesitant to use this approach, informal feedback indicated that they appreciated the opportunity to see their progress over time and to develop the necessary communication skills required for the workplace.

An ePortfolio was also used by students in the aircraft maintenance program at this same institution for the purposes of documenting and explaining the various stages of building or repairing the wing of an aircraft (Spiliotopoulos et al, 2007). During the F2F workshop, students photographed the wing at different stages of the development process, and after each photograph, they explained what they did, how they did it, and how their approach helped to fix a problem. They had the opportunity not only to express and share their problem-solving skills with the instructor and other students, but also had a venue in which to demonstrate to friends and relatives what they were learning, thereby enriching and developing a sense of pride about their education.

As we can see, technologies such as ePortfolios, synchronous and asynchronous forums, and wikis that are blended into F2F courses have the potential to enhance writing and critical thinking. These technologies bring more opportunities for collaborative writing and peer review, and they open student thoughts and ideas to an audience beyond the instructor. As a result, they can increase interaction, student engagement, as well as academic and professional success.

SOLUTIONS, RECOMMENDATIONS AND FUTURE RESEARCH DIRECTIONS

Some of the challenges involved in using educational technologies in blended contexts to meet strategic vision goals at the post-secondary level include faculty motivation, faculty development, instructional design resourcing for blended approaches, and coordinating academic culture with IT culture across campus (Butler & Sellbom, 2002; Moser, 2007). In some campuses, there is very little reward or recognition for faculty who use blended learning approaches to meet institutional goals, especially for professors who do not teach in distance education contexts. University faculty feel many pressures to meet expectations for high quality research and publication, and if their teaching is good enough, they would much rather spend their time researching and writing than learning how to use a new technology for the purposes of improving the student learning experience. However, according to Bates (2010), institutions not only need to set innovative teaching as a strategic goal; they also need to reward it. If universities were to offer funding or time in order to encourage on-campus faculty to explore blended learning, perhaps some faculty who have an interest in innovation would take the opportunity. Also, some instructors need to be convinced that integrating technology into their teaching would improve student learning. As such, administrators could recognize research in the area of teaching and learning with technology in the discipline or could support inquiry into blended learning approaches through the Scholarship of Teaching and Learning (SoTL). Also, faculty learning communities (Vaughn & Garrison, 2008) could be developed to share insights and experiences with blended learning, and these communities could provide valuable input into the key decisions around access to technology, user support, and infrastructure.

According to King (2003) and Bates (2010), professional development in the effective use of educational technologies in blended or hybrid contexts should be systematic and strongly encouraged or even compulsory. Insufficient support and a lack of faculty development opportunities might lead to blended learning environments that are driven more by technology than by pedagogy. Therefore it is essential that the necessary resourcing and infrastructure for creating blended learning environments be available (Moser, 2007). In many universities, support for instructional design and technology user support have been offered exclusively to distance education technologies, but as blended programs and courses are being created to improve student engagement and to meet university strategic goals effectively and efficiently, more instructional design and technical support will be required for faculty who teach in blended environments. To achieve this, there needs to be greater coordination and collaboration amongst academics and IT departments on campus in order to address the many concerns over privacy and intellectual property that often arise when technology is used for teaching, learning, and research. Also, administrators need to respond to the needs of faculty teaching in blended learning contexts; yet a case-study of educational technology management in North American and European universities (Bates, 2010) revealed that administrators were not adequately prepared to make appropriate decisions about technology. Once administrators receive some orientation to guide their decision-making on educational technologies, blended learning approaches can be adopted, implemented, and embedded as part of regular teaching practice for the purposes of maximizing student engagement and success.

CONCLUSION

This chapter has provided examples of blended learning in a variety of fields in order to demonstrate how this approach can support the goals outlined in many university strategic plans and mission statements. Though more research needs to be done to document the value of blended learning for improving student engagement and student success, the increased attention it is receiving by many scholars, faculty, and students suggests that there is merit in infusing such technologies into programs and on-campus courses in order to maximize opportunities for student learning.

REFERENCES

Albrecht, B. (2006). Enriching student experience through blended learning. *Educause Center for Applied Research, 12*, 1–12.

Bates, T. (2010). *Strategic thinking about e-learning*. Paper presented at BC Educational Technology Users Group, Victoria, BC.

Burbules, N. C., & Torres, C. A. (Eds.). (2000). *Globalization and education: Critical perspectives*. New York, NY: Routledge.

Butler, D. L., & Sellbom, M. (2002). Barriers to adopting technology for teaching and learning. *EDUCAUSE Quarterly, 2*, 22–28.

Caldwell, J. E. (2007). Clickers in the large classroom: Current research and best practice tips. *CBE Life Sciences Education, 6*(1), 9–20. doi:10.1187/cbe.06-12-0205

Chickering, A. W., & Gamson, Z. F. (1987). Seven principles for good practice in undergraduate education. *AAHE Bulletin, 39*(7), 3–7.

Coady, Y., & Gibbs, C. (2009). *The virtual learning lodge: A framework under construction*. Paper presented at the Canadian e-Learning Conference, Vancouver, BC.

Collis, B., & Moonen, J. (2001). *Flexible learning in a digital world*. London, UK: Kogan Page.

Dawson, T., & Keenan, L. (2009). *Universal instructional design: Creating an accessible curriculum at UVic*. Victoria, BC: University of Victoria.

Dziuban, C. D., Hartman, J. L., & Moskal, P. D. (2007). Blended learning. *Educause Centre for Applied Research, 7*, 1–12.

Garnham, C., & Kaleta, R. (2002). Introduction to hybrid courses. *Teaching with Technology Today, 8*(6). Retrieved June 14, 2010, from http://www.uwsa.edu/ttt/articles/garnham.htm

Garrison, R. D., & Vaughn, N. D. (2008). *Blended learning in higher education: Framework, principles, and guidelines*. San Francisco, CA: Jossey Bass.

Holly, D., & Oliver, M. (2010). Student engagement and blended learning: Portraits of risk. *Computers & Education, 54*, 693–700. doi:10.1016/j.compedu.2009.08.035

Hopper, T., & Sanford, K. (2010). Program-wide e-portfolios: Creating new spaces for an inside-out approach to teacher education. *Teacher Education Quarterly*. Retrieved June 14, 2010 from http://teqjournal.org/hopper.html

Jasinski, M. (2007). *Innovate and integrate: Embedding innovative practices*. Brisbane, Australia: Commonwealth of Australia. Retrieved June 14, 2010 from http://innovateandintegrate.flexiblelearning.net.au/docs/Innovate_and_Integrate_Final_26Jun07.pdf

King, K. P. (2003). *Keeping pace with technology: Educational technology that transforms. Vol. two: The challenge and promise for higher education faculty*. Cresskill, NJ: Hampton Press.

Kramsch, C. (1998). *Language and culture*. New York, NY: Oxford University Press.

Kuh, G. D., Kinzie, J., Schuh, J. H., & Whitt, J. E. (2005). *Student success in college: Creating conditions that matter*. San Francisco, CA: Jossey Bass.

Lattuca, L. R. (2001). *Creating interdisciplinarity*. Nashville, TN: Vanderbilt University Press.

Maher, F. A., & Tetreault, M. K. T. (2007). *Privilege and diversity in the academy*. New York, NY: Routledge.

Mazur, E. (1997). *Peer instruction: A user's manual*. Upper Saddle River, NJ: Prentice Hall.

Meyles, S., & Woo, S. (2007). *ACIT/COMP 2101 Portfolio development*. Retrieved June 10, 2010, from http://whileone.ca/download/ePortfolio-intro/ePortfolio-introduction.html

Milne, J. K. (2006). Designing blended learning space to the student experience. In D. Oblinger (Ed.), *Learning spaces* (pp. 11.1 – 11.12). Retrieved June 14, 2010, from http://www.educause.edu/LearningSpaces

Moller, L., Wellesley, R. F., & Huett, J. (2008). The evolution of distance education design on the potential of the Web. *TechTrends, 52*(4), 66–70. doi:10.1007/s11528-008-0179-0

Moser, F. Z. (2007). Faculty adoption of educational technology. *Educause Quarterly, 30*. Retrieved on September 14, 2007, from http://connect.educause.edu/library/abstract/Faculty-AdoptionofEdu/40010

Oblinger, D. G., & Oblinger, J. L. (Eds.). (2005). *Educating the net generation*. Retrieved from www.educause.edu

Office of Community-Based Research. (n.d.). Retrieved June 14, 2010, from http://web.uvic.ca/ocbr/

Reinhold, S. (2006). WikiTrails: Augmenting wiki structure for collaborative, interdisciplinary learning. In D. Riehle & J. Noble (Eds.), *WikiSym '06 Proceedings of the 2006 Annual Symposium on Wikis* (pp. 47-58).

Siemens, G. (2004). *E-portfolios. E-learn space: Everything e-learning*. Retrieved March 23, 2010, from http://www.elearnspace.org/Articles/eportfolios.htm

Spiliotopoulos, V., & Beers, M. (Producers), & Dekkers, P. (Director). (2007). *Teaching, learning, and working with e-portfolios*. Vancouver, BC: British Columbia Institute of Technology.

Story, M., & Truede, C. (2009). *Wikis? Twittering? Facebook? The implications and challenges of Web 2.0 technologies in teaching and learning.* Presented for Learning and Teaching Centre Instructional Technology Series, University of Victoria, B.C.

Twigg, C. A. (2003). *Program in course redesign.* National Centre for Academic Transformation. Retrieved June 14, 2010, from http://thencat.org/PCR.htm

Vaughan, N., & Garrison, D. R. (2008). *Blended faculty community of inquiry: Linking leadership, course design, and evaluation.* EDUCAUSE Learning Initiative (ELI) Annual Meeting, San Antonio, TX.

ADDITIONAL READING

Bates, A. W. (2000). *Managing technological change: Strategies for college and university leaders.* San Francisco: Jossey-Bass Inc.

Bates, A. W., & Poole, G. (2003). *Effective teaching with technology in higher education: Foundations for success.* San Francisco: John Wiley & Sons Inc.

Durham Technical Community College. (2002). *Hybrid classes: Maximizing resources and student learning*: http://courses.durhamtech.edu/tlc/www/html/Special_Feature/hybridclasses.htm

King, K. P., & Lawler, P. A. (2000). *Planning for effective faculty development: Using adult learning strategies.* Malabar, FL: Krieger Publishing.

Mossavar-Rahmani, F., & Larson-Daugherty, C. (2007). Supporting the hybrid learning model: A new proposition. *MERLOT Journal of Online Learning and Teaching, 3*(1), 67-78. Retrieved from http://jolt.merlot.org/

Rogers, E. M. (2003). *Diffusion of innovations* (5th ed.). New York: The Free Press.

Singh, H. (2003, December). Building effective blended learning programs. *Educational Technology, 433*(6), 51–54. Retrieved from http://asianvu.com/digital-library/elearning/blended-learning-by_Singh.pdf.

University of Mulwakee. *Hybrid Courses*: http://www4.uwm.edu/ltc/hybrid/

Voos, R. (2003). Blended learning-What is it and where might it take us? *Sloan-C View, 2(*1). Retrieved June 14, 2010 from http://www.sloan-c.org/publications/view/v2n1/blended1.htm

KEY TERMS AND DEFINITIONS

Blended Learning: A learning model or approach that mixes both web-based, mobile technologies, and classroom technologies for on-campus courses or programs (with or without a reduction in 'seat time'). A rationale for the use of technology should be assumed, and blended environments should be created to promote interaction, inquiry, and collaboration.

Electronic Portfolio: A collection of student work in digital form for the purposes of reflecting on one's learning or showcasing one's achievements.

Embed: "to fix or set securely. It is equated to 'institutionalisation' or the sustained use of an innovation by a critical mass as a routine practice. It is the final stage of an innovation process that starts with an initial decision to engage (adoption), moves to spreading the word (diffusion), consolidates in utilization (implementation), and culminates in embedding (integrate as core practice)." (Jasinski 2007, p. 1).

Net Generation: A demographic cohort born after the 1980's who grew up with the internet and has a strong familiarity with communications, media, and digital technologies.

Student Engagement: The "time and energy that students devote to educationally purposeful activities is the single best predictor of their learning and personal development" (Kuh et al., 2005, p. 8).

Teaching Presence: Denotes the instructor's online participation in terms of establishing curriculum, approaches, and activities, as well as moderating, guiding, and focusing discourse and tasks (Garrison & Vaughn, 2008, p. 24)

Universal Instructional Design: Designing curriculum and delivering instruction by taking into consideration the needs of all learners and removing barriers to learning while maintaining high academic standards.

Chapter 2
Blended Courses as Drivers of Institutional Transformation

Charles D. Dziuban
University of Central Florida, USA

Joel L. Hartman
University of Central Florida, USA

Thomas B. Cavanagh
University of Central Florida, USA

Patsy D. Moskal
University of Central Florida, USA

ABSTRACT

The authors discuss the transformational potential of blended learning and the importance of alignment with strategic initiatives of the institution. They show that key elements for student and faculty support result in numerous positive outcomes, including increased access and the ability to manage growth effectively. Research findings with very large student samples show the impact of blended learning on student achievement, identify predictors of student success, and illustrate correlates of student satisfaction with blended learning when ambivalent feelings mediate student perceptions of the educational environment. By illustrating these principles through a case study in a large metropolitan research university, the authors contend that strategic alignment and evaluation results inform each other in an incremental, transformational process.

INTRODUCTION

Blended courses, or courses in which both traditional classroom and online methods are employed to deliver instructional content and interaction, have proven to be among the most popular choices for students. At first glance, this popularity seems intuitive because blended courses allow a student to take advantage of much of the flexibility and convenience of an online course while retaining the benefits of the face-to-face classroom experience.

Although fully online learning has become well established in U.S. institutions of higher education (Allen & Seaman, 2010), many institu-

DOI: 10.4018/978-1-60960-479-0.ch002

tions appear to be struggling with conceptualizing and implementing blended learning. While both classroom-based and fully online instruction are well understood, it appears that the mixture of the two modalities poses challenges for some institutions.

Yet, where blended courses (also known as hybrid or mixed-mode courses) have succeeded, they have most often done so when strategically aligned with an institution's mission and goals. The development and delivery of blended courses can be used to address a variety of institutional, faculty, and student needs. For universities, blended courses can be part of a strategy to compensate for limited classroom space. For faculty, blended courses can be a method to infuse new engagement opportunities into established courses or, for some, provide a transitional opportunity between fully face-to-face and fully online instruction. For students, blended courses offer the conveniences of online learning combined with the social and instructional interactions that may not lend themselves to distance delivery (e.g., lab sections). If an institution's blended learning strategy can be designed to address the needs and dynamics of all three constituencies (institution, faculty, and student) simultaneously, then the modality can become a powerful force for transformation.

However, the converse is also true. When blended courses do not succeed, it is often the result of a misalignment with institutional, faculty, and/or student needs. An example of an institutional misalignment would be offering a blended course that time shifts face-to-face meetings on an irregular basis (e.g., the first three weeks of the term are in class, the next two meetings are online, followed by two weeks in class, and then every other week online). While possibly making instructional sense, such a schedule would not allow an institution to leverage the blended format to maximize classroom space utilization. Because of the irregular schedule, the classroom would need to remain reserved for the entire term, even during those sessions that are conducted online. A more effective approach might be to schedule blended courses so that they accommodate a regular, predictable meeting schedule. An example of misalignment with faculty needs would be arbitrarily compelling unwilling faculty or inappropriate topics into the blended modality. Forcing a subject best addressed via a different modality into a blended format will create extra work and unnecessary angst for already-busy faculty. For students, the benefits gained by a blended course are realized only if the associated risks are mitigated; for, without careful course planning and design, the blended format could offer the worst aspects of both the live and online modalities instead of offering the best. Students must also possess the self-motivation required to be successful in online learning. If an institution can create a supportive environment for faculty and students to ameliorate these risks, the transformational potential of blended learning can be realized.

In this chapter, the blended learning initiative at the University of Central Florida (UCF) will be used as a case study to illustrate how institutional, faculty, and student needs can be concurrently served through blended learning strategies. This model for blended learning is based on the balance of micro (course) and macro (institutional strategy) requirements. UCF's strategic, transformational model of blended learning is illustrated through data points including the marginal success/withdrawal rates in blended learning programs based on several thousand student registrations; the conditional course success rates based on categories such as generational perspective, discipline, demographic variables, ability, achievement, and course level; and the student rating of instruction of blended learning courses based on prototypes of what students believe comprises excellent instruction. In addition, UCF has developed a student satisfaction model for blended learning based on the notion of ambivalence in a complex environment, showing that such models are dynamic and evolving.

BACKGROUND

The term "blended learning" is most-often applied when describing individual courses. According to the Sloan Consortium (Sloan-C), a leading professional organization dedicated to promoting and supporting online education, a blended course is one in which 30%-79% of the instruction is delivered via technology. Sloan-C further defines this type of course as one "that blends online and face-to-face delivery. A substantial proportion of the content is delivered online, typically uses online discussions, and typically has some face-to-face meetings" ("Sloan Consortium's Definition", n.d.). An example of such an approach is a Chemistry course at Harper College where the instructor "distinguished between lab exercises that teach concepts vs. those that teach techniques, then divided lab activities into three types:

A. Application of concepts (e.g., density) are delivered virtually via online lab exercises.
B. Skills that are important to experience "hands on" (e.g., titration) are practiced in face-to-face labs.
C. Activities that are important to observe but do not require skill practice are demonstrated by the instructor in face-to-face labs" ("Blended Learning", n.d.).

However, limiting the concept of blended learning to a course-level perspective may impede an institution from achieving instructional and organizational transformation because it focuses attention away from a broader strategic vision for blended learning across the entire enterprise. A more strategic approach is to develop a holistic, blended program where students are afforded choices throughout their studies regarding course delivery options. These choices can consist of traditional face-to-face courses, fully online courses, and blended or hybrid courses. An example of this type of blended learning at a programmatic level can be found at Babson College, where approximately 60% of the Fast Track MBA program is online, with 80% of the online portion delivered as asynchronous discussions and the rest delivered via traditional classroom instruction. Going forward, "Babson hopes to be able to investigate how to best tune the percentages between on-ground and online and, as well, understand how to best combine live and off-line asynchronous presentations" (Babson Strategy, n.d.). When institutions expand their strategic thinking to include an academic worldview that considers blended learning at a programmatic level, they can start to realize significant impacts far beyond that possible via individual courses.

Another element of an institutional blended learning strategy is the establishment of a blended support system. It is ideal in a blended program to be able to offer students choices in how they register for courses, receive advising about their degree plans, and interact with the general administrative functions required at every postsecondary institution. A common expression at UCF is "online, not in line," which describes this type of blended service delivery approach. While online choices are available for online payment of fees, for example, students can also choose to make payments in person on either the main campus or one of the many regional campus locations. While "online" functions are offered, "in line" options are always available for those who choose them. The university library offers extensive online resources and services, providing anytime access to a broad spectrum of information. As with the design of a course that must take advantage of the strengths of both face-to-face and online delivery strategies, a blended support infrastructure must do the same.

A useful framework in which to place these intersecting notions of blended learning is the Sloan Consortium's five pillars of quality in online education (Lorenzo & Moore, 2002): learning effectiveness (course level), cost effectiveness (program, infrastructure, and institutional level), access (student, program, and institutional level), faculty satisfaction (faculty and course level), and student satisfaction (while focused at the student or course level, this cuts across all dimensions). In order to truly achieve institutional transformation in the service of a college or university's mission, blended learning must be considered in this broader construct of the Sloan-C pillars as applied to courses, programs, and infrastructure.

MANAGING GROWTH AT UCF

Over the past several years, UCF has experienced rapid growth. As of this writing, UCF stands as the third largest university in the United States with over 53,500 students. This growth has placed unprecedented pressure on the physical campus infrastructure. Although building construction continues when funding is available, the time it takes to complete a construction project can be lengthy. UCF needs to construct approximately 8,000 square feet of classrooms every year to keep up with growth. Each additional classroom seat that does not need to be created saves approximately $6,500 in construction costs and $330 per year in operational costs (Hartman, 2010). Creative scheduling of blended courses in existing facilities is one of several key strategies UCF is employing to address its growth demands (along with a significant commitment to fully online courses). By placing two or three courses in a single classroom, staggered throughout a week, with the rest of the course work conducted online, UCF has been able make much more efficient use of its classroom inventory (Hartman, 2010).

UCF has made an institutional commitment to the development and support of blended learning. At the course level, UCF's Center for Distributed Learning offers a comprehensive faculty development program that helps faculty better understand how to design and deliver courses in this modality. In addition, with ongoing instructional design, media production, and technical support, faculty have a plethora of resources at their disposal. At the program level, the Center for Distributed Learning works with colleges, academic departments, and the university's Regional Campuses system to support programmatic blended learning. At the infrastructure level, the "online, not in line" motif provides students with choices regarding how they interact with UCF's administrative functions. All of this activity is done in a deliberate, strategic fashion in support of the university's broader mission. Among UCF's core goals are student access, the quality of undergraduate education, inclusion, and partnerships. All of these can be directly supported by the blended learning initiative.

Because of this institutional strategy for blended learning, student registrations in blended courses at UCF have increased more than 450% over the past ten years (Figure 1). During the 2009-2010 academic year, blended courses at UCF represented 5% of the university's total student credit hours. Today, blended and fully online courses combined equate to 18% of the university's total student credit hour production. Although the focus of this discussion is blended courses, it is worth including the fully online course offerings at this junction because of the implication for blended learning *programs*, where students may choose from face-to-face, fully online, and blended/hybrid course options.

Faculty members teach a blended course offering at UCF after completing a comprehensive development program called IDL6543. This professional development course models how to teach online using a combination of seminars, labs, consultations, and web-based instruction and is delivered in a blended format, meeting one day per week with the rest of the work online. The program lasts eight weeks and the total time commitment is approximately eighty contact hours. By being placed into a blended course as "students," faculty are able to gain a student's perspective of the experience. Each faculty member is paired with an instructional designer who works with him or her both throughout IDL6543 and beyond to help design, structure, produce, and

Figure 1. Web (fully online) and blended course section growth at UCF

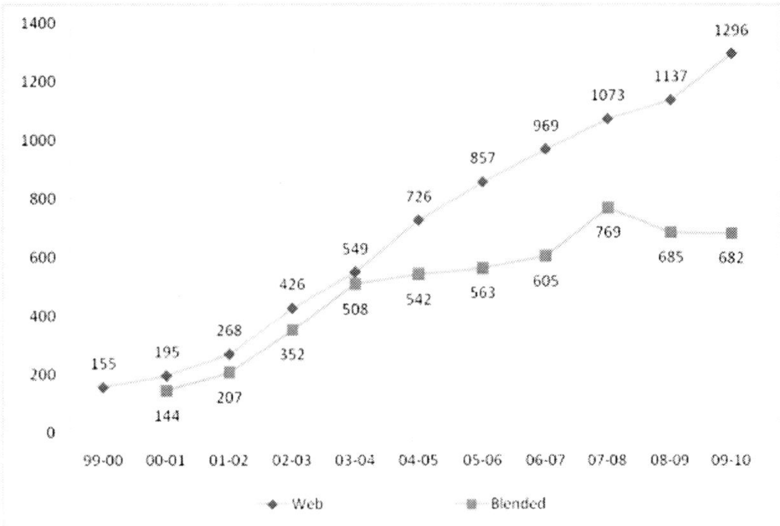

assess each course. UCF has made significant investments in resources and infrastructure to support the university's distributed learning initiative, which includes fully online and blended courses. Working strategically with colleges and academic departments, the Center for Distributed Learning can direct these resources and infrastructure where they will have the greatest institutional impact and alignment with the university's mission and the needs of students and faculty. This holistic, institutional approach has resulted in steady growth, student and faculty satisfaction, and assistance in managing classroom utilization.

Institutional Alignment

One of UCF's most successful initiatives has been the formation of a strategic partnership between Online@UCF and the university's Regional Campuses system. Regional Campuses support eleven instructional locations located throughout UCF's eleven-county service area. Making fully online and blended courses part of Regional Campuses' offerings has allowed Regional Campuses to expand program offerings, as well as enhance flexibility and convenience for area students. Today, Regional Campuses' online offerings are one of UCF's fastest-growing segments (Table 1). A strategic focus on blended courses to meet Regional Campus student demand resulted in a significant spike in those types of courses during the 2007-2008 academic year.

A Sloan Consortium-funded program related to "localness" has helped to accelerate strategic thinking about blended learning in the Regional Campuses, particularly at a programmatic level.

Table 1. UCF regional campus fully online and blended course student credit hours

	Fully Online		Blended	
Academic Year	**n**	**%**	**n**	**%**
2002-03	22,801	27	5,711	7
2003-04	36,840	35	7,699	7
2004-05	33,690	35	7,159	7
2005-06	48,008	41	8,806	8
2006-07	57,393	44	9,946	8
2007-08	64,843	44	17,067	12
2008-09	74,561	46	10,847	7
2009-10	88,834	51	11,383	7

The concept of "localness" addresses the broadest view of programmatic blended learning, wherein students can choose course offerings that are completely online, blended, located at a regional campus, or located on the main campus. Students can customize their course delivery modalities in targeted programs to meet their unique needs and circumstances at any given point in their academic careers. In other words, they can "blend" all of these options to create their degree and certificate programs. In addition, through in-person advising in the regions and an online portal branded "Learning On Demand," the student services requirements of a strategic blended learning model are satisfied.

Faculty Satisfaction

In examining the strategic alignments of successful blended learning initiatives, the second area that must be considered is faculty satisfaction. Faculty research at UCF has shown the benefit of this strategic support (Dziuban, Hartman, Moskal, Sorg, & Truman, 2004; Moskal & Dziuban, 2001). In these studies, faculty members were surveyed after teaching both fully online and blended courses. Their reactions to the associated workload, level of interaction within the course, and willingness to continue teaching in each modality were collected. The results showed that faculty responses to teaching blended courses were overwhelmingly positive.

The results of these studies are consistent with the wider university community. To date, more than 800 UCF faculty members have completed the IDL6543 program. Since 1997, when UCF began offering blended courses, 5,057 individual blended course sections have been delivered. As a course delivery modality, this format has become an ingrained part of how the university facilitates instruction. Faculty adoption and satisfaction with blended learning have contributed to this institutional transformation.

Larger Scale Research on the Impact of Blended Learning

Invariably when a new technology, teaching method, or instructional modality comes onto the educational scene, questions arise about its effectiveness for enhancing educational quality. Certainly, this is true of blended learning even as educational theorists continue developing a workable definition for the construct. Some prominent examples include combining online and face-to-face instruction, value-added approaches to blends (access, incremental pedagogy, and transformation), multiple cognitive modes, place and time, and resolution of learning issues across modes (Bleed, 2001; Bonk & Graham, 2006; Clark, 2003; Garrison & Vaughn, 2009; Graham, 2006; Novak, Patterson, Gavrin, & Christian, 1999; Picciano, 2009; Power, 2008; Williams, 2003). Although there may not currently be a universally accepted operational definition in place, the mental model for blended learning has a well established history of embracing the confluence of several learning approaches (Picciano & Dziuban, 2007).

This section discusses the impact of blended learning as an educational intervention by posing specific questions about the way that it influences student achievement, possible predictors of that achievement, and correlates of student satisfaction. We explore student ambivalence in this environment and examine decision rules for determining what characteristics of classes lead students to perceive their blended environment with a moderate degree of ambivalence, with some degree of ambivalence, or with strong ambivalent feelings about their learning experience.

Statistical Significance

A word about the methods we use in this chapter and our omission of any tests of statistical significance: the reader will see that with the sample sizes reported here almost any difference observed, no matter how trivial, will be statistically significant.

Using such a metric in these circumstances is inappropriate and misleading. Significance is not the issue of import here. We are more concerned with questions such as: what are the success and withdrawal rates in various student demographic categories? Does understanding the demographic profiles of our students help increase certainty about knowing whether they are likely to succeed or withdraw? To what degree do domains such as demographic profiles, ability, and academic performance predict success and withdrawal in blended learning? Are there robust decision rules for determining how students will evaluate their blended learning experiences?

Success

Defining a generally accepted success metric in blended learning courses in an environment such as the University of Central Florida leaves the investigators with relatively few options, grades being the most viable surrogate for measurement. However, utilizing a binary system where achieving a grade of A, B or C signifies *success* and everything else is coded *not success* eliminates many of these problems. One might argue that this process makes no distinction between students who accomplish excellent work and receive an A grade and other students who perform at the average and earn a C. They would be correct; however, from an institution-wide and psychometric perspective we have given up the specificity of grade distributions in favor of reliability gained through transformation. In addition, one can make the case that all of those succeeding students meet the criteria for remaining enrolled. Those ones and zeros constitute the operational definition of success in this study. We reemphasize that not achieving success is not tantamount to failure but rather "*not success*."

In order to assess the relationship of success with the various student demographic profiles we indexed how knowledge of a student's position on several categories would reduce the uncertainty of whether or not they are likely to succeed. The index (uncertainty coefficient) for this aspect of the study is based on information theory (Hays, 1963). The measure is a function of the marginal and the conditional uncertainty of success given any demographic variable. The result is the percentage of reduced uncertainty.

Table 2 presents the results of students' success by demographic factors—gender, generation, ethnicity, and adult status. Overall, females (88%) were more successful than males (81%) and success rates declined with younger generations, with the younger millennial students (born 1981-1994) having the lowest success rate (84%) and baby boomers (born 1946-1964) the highest (94%). Ethnicity indicated similar success rates for Caucasian/White students and Asian students (87%), slightly lower success rates for Hispanic/Latino (84%), and the lowest success rates for African American students (82%). Adult status (age 25 or higher) further showed that the older adults succeed at slightly higher rates (91%) when compared with their non-adult counterparts (83%). The uncertainty reductions for the student demographic factors were 1% for all elements except for ethnicity, which was 0%.

Table 2. Success by student demographic factors

Factor	n	%	Uncertainty Reduction
Female	54,285	88	
Male	32,261	81	1%
Baby Boomer	4,950	94	
Generation X	8,208	92	
Millennial	61,790	84	1%
Am. Indian/Alaska Native	306	83	
Asian	3,630	87	
Black/African American	5,994	82	
Hispanic/Latino	8,564	84	
White	50,475	87	0%
Adult	29,276	91	
Non-Adult	57,270	83	1%

Success rates of students by varying course demographics are presented in Table 3. Overall, students succeeded better in higher level classes. Lower undergraduates had a success rate of 75%, compared with upper undergraduates at 89%, and graduates at 95%. Success rates by college varied widely from an overall success rate of 76% for College of Business Administration courses to a high of 97% for Nursing courses. The uncertainty reduction for both course level and college was 6%. Class size showed a decreasing success rate with an increasing class size, although classes of 31-60 showed the highest success (89%) and those in the largest category (241-480) showed the lowest overall success rate (81%). The reader should be cautioned that success rates vary widely across individual courses and course demographics. We present overall statistics here. The uncertainty reduction for class size was 1%.

Table 3. Success by college demographic factors

College	n	%	Uncertainty Reduction
Lower Undergrad	27,568	75	
Upper Undergrad	44,691	89	
Graduate	14,287	95	6%
Humanities	7,089	84	
Business Administration	19,976	76	
Health & Public Affairs	15,891	95	
Nursing	1,535	97	
Sciences	9,842	87	
Education	13,966	95	
Engineering and Computer Science	2,203	89	
Hospitality Management	4,576	90	6%
1-30 students	31,291	88	
31-60 students	23,823	89	
61-120 students	10,132	85	
121-240 students	7,772	81	
241-480 students	13,528	81	1%

Withdrawal

Indexing student withdrawal from blended classes seems much more straightforward, and indeed it is. However, there are still important considerations here as well. Not surprisingly, there are several classifications for a withdrawing student, some having to do with academic progress and others relating to such things as medical reasons that are not markers of academic difficulties. Therefore, students withdrawing for health reasons were not included in this study. Once again, we calculated the uncertainty reduction in knowledge of withdrawal given the position on any demographic variable.

Examining withdrawal by student demographic factors, Table 4 shows that overall, fewer females withdraw (5%) than males (7%), and once again, those students who are the oldest generation outperform those younger students with 4% of baby boomers and generation Xers (born 1965-1980) withdrawing, compared to 6% of the millennial students. Students who were African American were less likely to withdraw (4%) when compared to their Asian (5%), White/Caucasian

Table 4. Withdrawal by student demographic factors

Factor	n	%	Uncertainty Reduction
Female	54,795	5	
Male	33,126	7	5%
Baby Boomer	4,975	4	
Generation X	8,274	4	
Millennial	74,672	6	2%
Am. Indian/Alaska Native	372	5	
Asian	4,282	5	
Black/African American	7,481	4	
Hispanic/Latino	10,369	6	
White	58,991	5	4%
Adult	29,582	4	
Non-Adult	58,339	6	3%

(5%), or Hispanic/Latino (6%) counterparts. Uncertainty reduction ranged from 2% to 5%. Adult status indicated that those who were adults (25+) withdrew at a slightly lower rate (4%) than those non-adults (6%).

Examining college variables, (Table 5) we see that lower undergraduates had the highest rate of withdrawal (9%), more than doubling that of their upper undergraduate counterparts (4%). Graduate students showed the lowest rate of withdrawal (3%). Withdrawal rates by college varied widely from a low of 2% in the College of Nursing and Health and Public Affairs to a high of 8% in Business Administration and Humanities. Class size showed an interesting lack of pattern with both the two largest (241-480 students—7%, and 121-240 students—6%) and the smallest class sizes (1-30 students—5%) having the greatest number of withdrawals. The lowest withdrawal rate occurred in those classes which had 31-60 students (4%).

Table 5. Withdrawal by college demographic factors

College	n	%	Uncertainty Reduction
Lower Undergrad	28,216	9	
Upper Undergrad	45,411	4	
Graduate	14,294	3	2%
Humanities	7,091	8	
Business Administration	20,331	8	
Health & Public Affairs	16,084	2	
Nursing	1,538	2	
Sciences	9,893	7	
Education	13,961	3	
Engineering and Computer Science	2,857	4	
Hospitality Management	4,610	3	3%
1-30 students	31,649	6	
31-60 students	24,635	4	
61-120 students	10,335	5	
121-240 students	7,772	6	
241-480 students	13,536	7	3%

Uncertainty reduction for class level, college, and class size was 2%, 3%, and 3% respectively.

Correlates of Success and Withdrawal

Earlier we mentioned three domains for predicting success and withdrawal in blended learning: demographics, academic ability and academic performance. Investigating the predictive power of each of these domains presented substantial challenges because we wished to contrast those predicative efficiencies across the domains. Because demographic variables scale differently from Scholastic Aptitude Tests (SATs) and grades, we used various covariance indices that are comparable as they approach zero. For instance, the relationship of gender with success and withdrawal resulted in phi coefficients (Glass & Hopkins, 1995), SAT scores with success and withdrawal yielded point biserial correlations, as did the relationship with grades (Glass & Hopkins, 1995). The relationship with larger demographic tables such as generational membership and class size incorporated Cramer's V (Hays, 1973). All of these indices have a zero point but do not necessarily range from -1 to +1 because for the categorical measures the sign is arbitrary. The same issues apply to the multiple correlations. For some variable sets we derived bona fide multiple correlations while those indices for categorical variables were analogs (Long, 1997).

Table 6 presents the correlations of success and withdrawal with student demographics--age, adult status, generation, ethnicity, and gender, as well as class size and term the course was offered. Correlations for all variables and student success were low indicating very little relationship between the variables and success, with values ranging from a correlation of .03 for term and success and -.03 for the correlation of class size and success to the highest correlation being gender and success at -.09. The squared multiple correlations of .02 further indicate the unpredictability of success when given these variables.

Table 6. Relationship of blended success and withdrawal with student and class demographics

	Success (r2 = .02)				Withdrawal (r2 = .01)	
	n	r			n	r
Age	86,546	.08		Age	87,921	-.03
Class Size	85,326	-.03		Class Size	87,867	-.01
Adult Status	86,423	.06		Adult Status	88,013	-.02
Ethnicity	68,969	.08		Ethnicity	81,495	.04
Gender	85,721	-.09		Gender	87,544	.04
Generation	74,948	-.06		Generation	87,625	.02
Term	85,897	.03		Term	87,955	-.03

Examining the demographics for withdrawal (Table 6) presented a similar picture with correlations approaching zero--with a low of -.01 for the correlation of class size and withdrawal to a high of .04 for both ethnicity and gender. The multiple r^2 of .01 again indicates that these variables are not effective when predicting withdrawal among UCF's blended learning population.

Perhaps surprisingly, we found very little correlation with students' scores on the SAT and ACT with either success or withdrawal. Table 7 presents the results of these analyses with correlations among success and each of the SAT and ACT sections ranging from .01 for the SAT verbal to a high of .03 for either the ACT Total score or English section. Correlations for withdrawal rates and SAT/ACT components were even lower with the highest correlation of .02 for the SAT Verbal section. Once again, r^2 values approached zero, indicating the lack of usefulness of these variables when predicting who will succeed or withdraw from blended courses.

Table 8 illustrates the correlations between various student grade point averages (GPAs) and success and withdrawal rates. While high school GPA was weakly correlated (.16), students' current GPA showed a moderate correlation (.51) with success. Intuitively, this makes sense as it reflects that students who are succeeding in college in general are succeeding in blended courses as well. Cumulative GPA (.42) and UCF GPA (.46) showed slightly lower correlation. R squared for success with these GPAs was .37.

Table 7. Relationship of blended success and withdrawal with SAT and ACT scores

	Success (r2 = .01)				Withdrawal (r2 = .01)	
	n	r			n	r
SAT Total	59,758	.02		SAT Total	60,862	.01
SAT Verbal	59,801	.01		SAT Verbal	60,906	.02
SAT Math	59,798	.02		SAT Math	60,901	.00
ACT Total	36,449	.03		ACT Total	37,852	.01
ACT Math	36,333	.02		ACT Math	36,934	-.01
ACT English	31,276	.03		ACT English	36,871	.01
ACT SCR	36,421	.02		ACT SCR	36,421	.00

Table 8. Relationship of blended success and withdrawal with GPA

	Success (r2 = .37)				**Withdrawal (r2 = .04)**	
	n	**r**			**n**	**r**
HS GPA	86,546	.16		HS GPA	86,823	-.07
Current GPA	84,000	.51		Current GPA	85,352	-.12
Cum. GPA	86,289	.42		Cum. GPA	87,663	-.14
UCF GPA	77,785	.46		UCF GPA	78,470	-.13

Lower correlation was found with withdrawal rates and GPAs, with HS GPA being the lowest correlation (-.07) and Cumulative GPA being the highest (-.14). R squared for these variables was a low .04.

Predicting Student Satisfaction in Blended Learning

We used classification and regression trees (CART) (Brieman, Friedman, Olshen, & Stone, 1984) to develop decision rules for identifying patterns that best depict student evaluation of their blended experience. The tree procedure divides the data into groups that maximize predictability. Through an iterative process of decision rules, CART decides which variable best predicts satisfaction after each one has been examined in turn. The algorithm divides the subjects into homogenous groups based on the best predictor. Then the process begins again by finding the second best predictive variable after the first has been selected and redistributes homogenous groups under the nodes of the best predictor. This continues until all predictability in the system has been exhausted, usually when very small numbers appear in particular categories. The process effectively handles all possible interactions among variables. In practice, the sample under consideration is split, with half used for tree development and the second half of the subjects used for validation. Also, the initially-developed tree goes through a pruning process to protect against over-fitting the data. The final tree produces an if-then, tree-like structure that is intuitive, easily understood, and readily applicable, permitting investigators to examine specific decision rules that produce the likelihood of success, withdrawal or satisfaction.

The Special Case of Ambivalence and Student Satisfaction

The final phase of this study assessed student satisfaction with blended learning mediated though ambivalence—the degree to which they experience mixed feelings about blended learning (Long, 1985; Rapp & Dziuban, 2000). We all experience ambivalent feelings at some time in our lives, simultaneous positive and negative emotions about school, work, friends, family, political issues, and even ourselves (Craig & Martinez, 2005). Students might feel extremely positive about the instructor, but dislike the course material; they can enjoy the course, but dislike the 8:00 a.m. time or the classroom. Most students want access to course materials, but resent what they consider the excessive costs of textbooks. These conflicted feelings extend to broader issues as well. Students worry about not getting an education while at the same time questioning the value of the education they receive. They make every effort to do well, but frankly wonder if the effort is really worth it. Others might be positive about the increased access blended courses afford, but be turned off by a course management system that fails periodically.

Weigert (1991) provides us with perceptive insights about modern society and how it abounds with contradictory structures and experiences that culture fails to resolve, thereby raising our sense of ambivalence. He argues that our contemporary mediated information society leads us to question every idea, value, or concept so that historic beginnings, endings, and closures obscure their boundaries, and resolution of important issues becomes difficult as best. Therefore, in pluralistic societies such as ours, people find themselves positioned among many referent groups that exert pressures for competing actions, emotions, or commitments. Progenitors of ambivalence in modern culture appear as change, complexity, incompleteness, ambiguity, and uncertainty.

Given this background, we assessed students' satisfaction with their blended learning experiences with the end-of-course evaluation response protocol for students in the years 2003-2007 (Appendix A). The resulting data set comprised over 45,000 student responses for that period. The instrument has been in place at the University of Central Florida for a number of years having undergone comprehensive validation work (Wang, Dziuban, Cook, & Moskal, 2009). The survey consists of 16 five-point Likert items where students respond to course aspects such as organization, instructor responsiveness, effective assessment, facilitation of learning, and instructor availability, among other dimensions. The final question is the ubiquitous *overall rating of the course* ranging from poor to excellent. This item provided the benchmark for our study of the interaction between ambivalence and student satisfaction with blended learning. Instead of considering the responses an ordinal ranking of student perceptions of course quality, ranging linearly from dissatisfaction to satisfaction, we considered the scale points nominal categories signifying varying degrees of ambivalence toward the course. Consider this definition of ambivalence from Wikipedia: "Ambivalence is a state of having simultaneous, conflicting feelings toward a person or thing. Stated another way, ambivalence is the experience of having thoughts and emotions of both positive and negative valence toward someone or something" ("Ambivalence," 2004). The system classified the students' overall ratings of their blended courses according to the following rubric in Table 9.

Under the revised scoring procedure, students were sorted into the above categories, producing five binary membership vectors for each stage of ambivalence. From that rescaling, each classification vector becomes a dependent measure in a CART analysis using the following independent variables: class level (lower undergraduate, upper undergraduate, and graduate), college membership, and the first fifteen items on the end-of-course survey instrument.

The Decision Rules for Satisfaction Under Varying Ambivalence Conditions

Table 10 identifies the decision rules for various levels of student satisfaction when each of the five points on the overall rating item becomes an anchor for ambivalence. We assume that as responses migrate from the center where ambivalence reaches its highest level toward the extremes of the scale,

Table 9.

Positive with little or no concerns	**Positive with some concerns**	**Equal proportions of positive and negative feelings**	**Negative with some positive aspects**	**Negative with few or no positive aspects.**
5 Excellent	4 Very Good	3 Average	2 Fair	1 Poor

Table 10.

Rule 1: Overall Positive Non Ambivalent Rating (N=22,107) Marginal p=.48						
	E	VG	A	F	P	Cond. Prob.
Facilitation of Learning	•					
Interest in Learning	•					.93
Rule 2: Overall Positive Ambivalent Rating (N=12,401) Marginal p=.27						
	E	VG	A	F	P	Cond. Prob.
Facilitation of Learning		•				
Interest in Learning		•	•	•		
Organization		•	•	•		.66
Rule 3: Overall Ambivalent Rating (N=7,360) Marginal p=.17						
	E	VG	A	F	P	Cond. Prob.
Facilitation of Learning	•	•	•			
Communication			•	•	•	
Respect			•	•	•	.74
Rule 4: Overall Negative Ambivalent Rating (N=2,542) Marginal p=.05						
	E	VG	A	F	P	Cond. Prob.
Facilitation of Learning			•	•		
Communication				•	•	
Organization				•	•	.74
Rule 5: Overall Negative Non Ambivalent Rating (N=772) Marginal p=.03						
	E	VG	A	F	P	Cond. Prob.
Facilitation of Learning					•	
Respect					•	.82

conflicted feelings will diminish. Of the possible predictor variables—course level, college membership, and the remaining fifteen items on the survey—only the instrument items contributed to the predictive model for overall satisfaction.

Rule 1 specifies that two items on the questionnaire are primary in determining whether or not students will judge their blended courses as an excellent educational experience. If they characterize their instructors as *facilitators for their learning* and feel that faculty show an *interest in learning* for their students, then there is a .93 probability that the overall course rating will be *Excellent*. Note that the response pattern to those two items roughly doubles the chances that students will evaluate their courses as superior. The marginal chance of that happening is .48 while the Rule 1 conditional probability is .93. There appears to be little or no ambivalence in this student response pattern: it simply requires two items to receive "*excellent* ratings" and the rest will follow. Interestingly, excellent blended courses appear to be a function of instructor characteristics rather than organization or structure of the course.

Rule 2 profiles students who are positive toward blended courses but temper that disposition with some mixed feelings. The rule increases the chances of this category happening from .27 to .66—roughly an odds ratio of 2.5:1. Notice that positive but ambivalent course evaluations involve three items and many more possible response patterns, indicating that complexity and ambivalence increase simultaneously. Two of the items carry over from Rule 1—*facilitation* and *interest*--but course *organization* enters the predictive mix as well. In order to fit this positive (but filtered) evaluation, students must assign a *very good* to *facilitation of learning,* but they have much more latitude on *interest in learning,* which can range from *fair* to *very good,* and course *organization,* which also ranges from *fair* to *very good.* Therefore, the possibility exists that this category might range from three *very good* ratings to one *very good* and two *fair* responses. These multiple possibilities resonate with students who might be somewhat undecided about their blended learning experience. One explanation for this is that course organization becomes a factor in contributing to an ambivalent status in some cases. Therefore, we would characterize a very good instructor who has a few organizational issues with the class causing some dissonance in his or her students. Interestingly, *organization* is a factor that can readily improve with staff development.

Rule 3 identifies those students whom we consider genuinely ambivalent—those who are unsure, see both strong positives and negatives, or remain just plain "up in the air" about the quality of blended courses. Note that the marginal probability of this category indicates that only 17% of the respondents will assign this response to blended courses. Contrast this with the combined marginal values that show 75% of students assign positive responses of some level to this instructional mode. However, remember that we are dealing with conditional probabilities in this analysis and estimating what elements cause a student to become ambivalent about blended learning. Rule 3 is even more complex than Rule 2, signifying that as students' ambivalence increases, their decisions have less specificity. The items joining *facilitation of learning* include the instructor's *communication* ability and his or her *respect* for students. This adds a new dimensionality to ambivalence with even more possible response patterns. *Facilitation* can range from *excellent* to *average*. *Communication* and *respect* can range from *average* to *poor*. Actually, this leads to an almost unlimited configuration that will produce an ambivalent (average) rating for a course. Note that conformity to Rule 3 makes a student four times more likely to be genuinely ambivalent about the course than his or her peers. This entire set of items relates to instructor characteristics rather than course structure.

Rule 4 begins a less positive scenario for blended learning. Although the marginal probability indicates that only 5% or less of the student population responds this way, the group represents over 2,500 students in our sample. This is a significant number; therefore, the rule identifies an important student sub-population which may require special attention if they become prone to withdrawal. The pattern makes it almost fifteen times more likely that these students' overall rating will be negative and ambivalent. In this case, *facilitation* may be seen as *average* or *fair* while *communication* and *organization* may be rated as either *fair* or *poor*. Once again *facilitation of learning* appears as a primary consideration but the lesser categories of *communication* and *organization* mediate class evaluations.

Rule 5, like Rule 1, is clear, specific, and non-ambivalent. These students evaluate *facilitation* and *respect* poorly which leads to a *poor* overall rating, the exact opposite of Rule 1. Only 3% of the over 45,000 respondents in the sample responded this way, but the rule increases the chances of identifying them by a factor of approximately 27. Once again, there are only two items, but they carry the day for students who react negatively to blended learning and have very few doubts about their feelings. Just like the positive, non-ambivalent category, it is all about the instructor and not the mode.

What do the Data Tell Us about Success, Withdrawal and Satisfaction?

Some reasonably clear patterns emerge from the larger data set on blended learning. First, very little other than a students' history of sustained academic effort and accomplishment serve to predict whether or not they will succeed in their blended courses. Although in this chapter we have chosen to not to make comparisons with other delivery modes such as fully online, face-to-face, or lecture capture, we hypothesize that this would also be the case in these circumstances as well. This should be verified and is the subject of future research on our campus. Further, demographic profiles do relatively little to clarify the probabilities of success or withdrawal in blended courses. This seems a counterintuitive finding, but knowing a student's gender, ethnicity, generational status, and age or a course's level, college, and class size does little to reduce the uncertainty about the student's accomplishment.

Second, our data clearly support this comment by Martinez, Craig and Kane, (2005): "In retrospect it seems rather simplistic to think of attitudes as always being unidimensional" (p. 1). Student satisfaction with their blended learning environments is not a straight line dimension from dissatisfaction to satisfaction. As Feldman (1995) points out, any point on a survey response probably represents the central tendency of a whole raft of attitudes, many of which are contradictory. In this paper, we suggest that the most important moderating variable in student satisfaction is ambivalence.

Finally, the data suggest that when blended learning aligns itself with institutional strategic initiatives and the proper support infrastructure is in place for student and faculty cohorts, success will be substantial and withdrawal percentages will be minimal. At UCF, this success has manifested in measurable faculty satisfaction and significant growth in the delivery of blended learning courses and programs.

CONCLUSION

Institutional transformation at a university with the size of the scope of the University of Central Florida constitutes an ambitious undertaking. However, when properly managed, blended initiatives reposition the institution for better response to current student lifestyles and educational requirements while increasing the efficient use of classroom space. Outcome data suggest that these benefits enhance learning effectiveness while mitigating infrastructure expansion requirements created by demographic pressures.

The key to realizing continued success with blended learning initiatives involves its alignment with institutional, faculty, and student needs. Hitt and Hartman (2010) summarize those elements as:

- An articulated vision for the institution,
- Specification of the institution's current position and where it is going,
- For what does the institution want to be known?
- What must be accomplished or avoided in order to achieve success?
- What are institutional strengths and weaknesses?
- How can the institution achieve buy-in from key community constituencies?
- How can blended learning be used as an engine for positive change in responding to the institution's vision?

With these organizational components as a backdrop, blended learning can play a key role in the transformation of universities as they become enablers of learning effectiveness in an environment of continuous change.

REFERENCES

Allen, I. E., & Seaman, J. (2010). *Learning on demand: Online education in the United States, 2009*. Retrieved January 26, 2010 from http://www.sloan-c.org/publications/survey/pdf/learningondemand.pdf

Ambivalence. (2010, May 14). In *Wikipedia, the free encyclopedia*. Retrieved May 24, 2010, from http://en.wikipedia.org/wiki/Ambivalence

Bleed, R. (2001). A hybrid campus for a new millennium. *EDUCAUSE Review, 36*(1), 16–24.

Bonk, C. J., & Graham, C. R. (Eds.). (2006). *The handbook of blended learning: Global perspectives, local designs*. San Francisco, CA: Pfeiffer.

Brieman, L., Friedman, J. H., Olshen, R. A., & Stone, C. J. (1984). *Classification and regression trees*. New York, NY: Chapman & Hall.

Clark, D. (2003). *Blend it like Beckham*. Retrieved January 25, 2010, from http://www.epic.co.uk/content/resources/white_papers/blended.htm

Craig, S. C., & Martinez, M. D. (Eds.). (2005). *Ambivalence and the structure of political opinion*. New York, NY: Palgrave Macmillan. doi:10.1057/9781403979094

Dziuban, C., Hartman, J., Moskal, P., Sorg, S., & Truman, B. (2004). Three ALN modalities: An institutional perspective. In Bourne, J., & Moore, J. C. (Eds.), *Elements of quality online education: Into the mainstream* (pp. 127–148). Needham, MA: Sloan Center for Online Education.

Feldman, S. (1995). Answering survey questions. In Lodge, M., & McGraw, K. (Eds.), *Political judgment: Structure and process* (pp. 249–270). Ann Arbor, MI: University of Michigan Press.

Garrison, D. R., & Vaughan, N. D. (2008). *Blended learning in higher education*. San Francisco, CA: Jossey-Bass.

Glass, G. V., & Hopkins, K. D. (1995). *Statistical methods in education and psychology* (3rd ed.). Boston, MA: Allyn & Bacon.

Graham, C. R. (2006). Blended learning systems: Definitions, current trends, and future directions. In Bonk, C., & Graham, C. (Eds.), *The handbook of blended learning: Global perspectives, local designs* (pp. 3–21). San Francisco, CA: Pfeiffer.

Hartman, J. L. (2010). *The promise and practice of blended learning*. Presented at the meeting of the Sloan-C Blended Learning Conference, Chicago, IL.

Hays, W. L. (1963). *Statistics for psychologists*. New York, NY: Holt, Rinehart, and Winston, Inc.

Hays, W. L. (1973). *Statistics for the social sciences* (2nd ed.). New York, NY: Holt, Rinehart, and Winston, Inc.

Hitt, J. C., & Hartman, J. L. (2010). Two views of alignment. *EDUCAUSE Review, 45*(2), 8–9.

Long, J. S. (1997). *Regression models for categorical and limited dependant variables*. Thousand Oaks, CA: Sage Publications.

Long, W. A. (1985). The practitioner and adolescent medicine. *Seminars in Adolescent Medicine, 1*(1), 85–90.

Lorenzo, G., & Moore, J. (2002). *The Sloan Consortium report to the nation: Five pillars of quality online education*. Retrieved July 8, 2008 from http://www.sloanconsortium.org

Martinez, M. D., Craig, S. C., & Kane, J. G. (2005). Pros and cons: Ambivalence and public opinion. In Craig, S., & Martinez, M. (Eds.), *Ambivalence and the structure of public opinion* (pp. 1–14). New York, NY: Palgrave Macmillian.

Moskal, P. D., & Dziuban, C. D. (2001). Present and future directions for assessing cyber-education: The changing research paradigm. In Vandervert, L., Shavinina, L., & Cornell, R. (Eds.), *CyberEducation: The future of long distance learning* (pp. 157–184). Larchmont, NY: Mary Ann Liebert Publishers.

Novak, G. M., Patterson, E. T., Gavrin, A. D., & Christian, W. (1999). *Just in time teaching: Blending active learning with web technology*. New Jersey: Prentice Hall Series in Educational Innovation.

Picciano, A. G. (2009). Blending with purpose: The multimodal model. *Journal of Asynchronous Learning Networks, 13*(1), 7–18.

Picciano, A. G., & Dziuban, C. D. (Eds.). (2007). *Blended learning: Research perspectives*. Needham, MA: Sloan Consortium.

Power, M. (2008). The emergence of a blended online learning environment. *MERLOT Journal of Online Learning and Teaching, 4*(4), 503-514. Retrieved from http://jolt.merlot.org/vol4no4/power_1208.pdf

Rapp Young, B., & Dziuban, E. (2000). Understanding dependency and passivity: Reactive behavior patterns in writing centers. *The Writing Center Journal, 21*(1), 67–87.

Sloan Consortium. (n.d.). *Blended learning Chemistry course.* Retrieved January 25, 2010, from http://www.sloanconsortium.org/node/262

Sloan Consortium. (n.d.). *The Babson Strategy: Blended online education enables localness and geo-localness.* Retrieved January 25, 2010, from http://www.sloanconsortium.org/node/441

Sloan Consortium. (n.d.). *Definition: What is online learning?* Retrieved January 25, 2010 from http://www.fldlc.org/taskforce/pdf/sloan_definition.pdf

Wang, M. C., Dziuban, C. D., Cook, I. J., & Moskal, P. D. (2009). Dr. Fox rocks: Using data-mining techniques to examine student ratings of instruction. In M. C. Shelley, L. D. Yore, & B. Hand (Eds.), *Quality research in the literary and science education: International perspectives and gold standards* (pp. 383-398). New York, NY: Springer Science +Business Media.

Weigert, A. J. (1991). *Mixed emotions: Certain steps toward understanding ambivalence*. Albany, NY: State University of New York Press.

Williams, J. (2003). Blending into the background. *E-Learning Age Magazine, 1*.

ADDITIONAL READING

Bates, M. (1989). The *design of browsing and berrypicking techniques for the online search interface*. Los Angeles, CA: Graduate school of library and information science.

Bauerlein, M. (2008). *The dumbest generation: How the digital age stupefies young Americans and jeopardizes our future*. New York: Tarcher.

Bush, M., Dziuban, C. D., Moskal, P. D., & Wang, M. C. (2005). Student success in online learning. In Nata, R. (Ed.), *Issues in higher education* (pp. 1–14). Hauppauge, NY: Nova Science Publishers, Inc.

Chickering, A. W., & Gamson, Z. F. (1987). Seven principles for good practice in undergraduate education. *AAHE Bulletin, 39*(7), 3–7.

Davidovitch, N., & Soen, D. (2006). Using students' assessments to improve instructors' quality of teaching. *Journal of Further and Higher Education, 30*(4), 351–376. doi:10.1080/03098770600965375

Diamond, J. (1999). *Guns, germs, and steel: The fates of human society.* New York, NY: W.W. Norton & Company, Inc.

Dziuban, C. D., Hartman, J., Juge, F., Moskal, P. D., & Sorg, S. (2005). Blended learning: Online learning enters the mainstream. In Bonk, C. J., & Graham, C. (Eds.), *Handbook of Blended Learning Environment*. Pfeiffer Publications.

Dziuban, C. D., Hartman, J. L., Moskal, P. D. (March 30, 2004). Blended learning. *ECAR Research Bulletin*. Available online at [http://www.educause.edu/ecar/].

Dziuban, C. D., Hartman, J. L., & Moskal, P. D. (2007). Everything I Need to Know About Blended Learning I Learned From Books. In Picciano, A. G., & Dziuban, C. D. (Eds.), *Blended Learning: Research Perspectives* (pp. 265–286). Needham, MA: Sloan Center for Online Education.

Dziuban, C. D., Moskal, P. D., Bradford, G. R., Brophy-Ellison, J., & Groff, A. T. (in press). Constructs that impact the net generation's satisfaction with online learning. In R. Sharpe, H. Beetham, & De Freitas (Eds.), *Rethinking learning for a digital age: how learners are shaping their own experiences*. Routledge, New York.

Dziuban, C. D., Moskal, P. D., Brophy-Ellison, J., & Shea, P. (2007a). Student Satisfaction with Asynchronous Learning. *Journal of Asynchronous Learning Networks*. *11*(1). Needham, MA: Sloan-C. Available online at [http://www.sloan-c.org/publications/jaln/v11n1/pdf/v11n1_10dziuban.pdf].

Dziuban, C. D., Moskal, P. D., Brophy-Ellison, J., & Shea, P. (2007b). Technology-Enhanced Education and Millennial Students in Higher Education. *Metropolitan Universities, 18*(3). Indianapolis: Indiana University-Purdue University Indianapolis (IUPUI).

Dziuban, C. D., Moskal, P. D., & Futch, L. (2007). Reactive Behavior, Ambivalence, and the Generations: Emerging Patterns in Student Evaluation of Blended Learning. In Picciano, A. G., & Dziuban, C. D. (Eds.), *Blended Learning: Research Perspectives* (pp. 179–202). Needham, MA: Sloan Center for Online Education.

Dziuban, C. D., Moskal, P. D., & Hartman, J. L. (2005). Higher education, blended learning, and the generations: Knowledge is power: No more. In Bourne, J., & Moore, J. C. (Eds.), *Elements of quality online education: Engaging communities*. Needham, MA: Sloan Center for Online Education.

Garrison, D. R., & Vaughan, N. D. (2008). *Blended learning in higher education: Framework, principles, and guidelines*. San Francisco, CA: John Wiley & Sons, Inc.

Ginns, P., & Ellis, R. (2007). Quality in blended learning: Exploring the relationships between on-line and face-to-face teaching and learning. *The Internet and Higher Education, 10*, 53–64. doi:10.1016/j.iheduc.2006.10.003

Ginns, P., Prosser, M., & Barrie, S. (2007). Students' perceptions of teaching quality in higher education: The perspective of currently enrolled students. *Studies in Higher Education, 32*(5), 603–615. doi:10.1080/03075070701573773

Graham, C. R., & Dziuban, C. D. (2008). Core research and issues related to blended learning environments. In Spector, J. M., Merrill, M. D., Van Merrienboer, J. J. G., & Driscoll, M. P. (Eds.), *Handbook of research on educational communications and technology* (3rd ed.). Mahwah, NJ: Lawrence Earlbaum Associates.

Hartman, J. L., Dziuban, C. D., & Moskal, P. D. (2005). Preparing the academy of today for the learner of tomorrow. In Oblinger, D. G., & Oblinger, J. L. (Eds.), *Educating the Net Generation*. Educause.

Hartman, J. L., Dziuban, C. D., & Moskal, P. D. (2007). Strategic initiatives in the online environment: Opportunities and challenges. *Horizon, 15*(3), 157–168. doi:10.1108/10748120710825040

Howe, N., & Strauss, W. (2000). *Millennials rising: the next great generation*. New York: Vintage Books.

Kolitch, E., & Dean, A. V. (1999). Student ratings of instruction in the USA: Hidden assumptions and missing conceptions about 'good' teaching. *Studies in Higher Education*, *24*(1), 27–43. doi:10.1080/03075079912331380128

Kuh, G. D. (2001). Assessing what really matters to student learning. *Change*, *33*(3), 10–19. doi:10.1080/00091380109601795

Laumakis, M., Graham, C., & Dziuban, C. (2009). The Sloan-C pillars and boundary objects as a framework for evaluating blended learning. *Journal of Asynchronous Learning Networks*, *13*(1), 75–87.

Lorenzo, G., & Dziuban, C. D. Ensuring the net generation is net savvy. In D. Oblinger (Ed.) (2006) *Educause Learning Initiative*. ELI Paper 2: September 2006. Available online [http://www.educause.edu/ir/library/pdf/ELI3006.pdf].

Lorenzo, G., Oblinger, D., & Dziuban, C. D. (2007). How choice, co-creation, and culture are changing what it means to be net savvy. *EDUCAUSE Quarterly*, *30*(1), 6–12.

Morville, P. (2005). *Ambient findability: What we find changes who we become*. Sebastopol, CA: O'Reilly Media, Inc.

Moskal, P. D. (2009). Dancing with a bear: One university's experience with evaluating blended learning. *Journal of Asynchronous Learning Networks*, *13*(1), 65–74.

Moskal, P. D., Dziuban, C., & Hartman, J. (2010). Online learning: A transforming environment for adults in higher education. In Kidd, T. (Ed.), *Online education and adult learning: New frontiers for teaching practices*. Hershey, PA: IGI Global. doi:10.4018/978-1-60566-830-7.ch005

Moskal, P. D., Dziuban, C. D., Upchurch, R., Hartman, J. L., & Truman, B. (2006). Assessing online learning: What one university learned about student success, persistence, and satisfaction. *Peer Review: Emerging trends and key debates in undergraduate education. Learning & Technology*, *8*(4), 26–29.

Muilenburg, L. Y., & Berge, Z. L. (2005). Student barriers to online learning: A factor analytic study. *Distance Education*, *21*(1), 29–48. doi:10.1080/01587910500081269

Oblinger, D. G., & Oblinger, J. L. (Eds.). (2005). *Educating the net generation*. EDUCAUSE.

Pounder, J. S. (2007). Is student evaluation of teaching worthwhile? An analytical framework for answering the question. *Quality Assurance in Education*, *15*(2), 178–191. doi:10.1108/09684880710748938

Prensky, M. (2009). H. sapiens digital: From digital immigrants and digital natives to digital wisdom. *Innovate, 5*(3), Retrieved 1 July, 2009, from http://www.innovateonline.info/index.php?view=article&id=705.

Renaud, R. D., & Murray, H. G. (2005). Factorial validity of student ratings of instruction. *Research in Higher Education*, *46*(8), 929–953. doi:10.1007/s11162-005-6934-6

Star, S. L. (1989). *Regions of the mind: Brain research and the quest for scientific certainty*. Stanford, CA: Stanford University Press.

Taleb, N. N. (2007). *The black swan: The impact of the highly improbable*. New York, NY: Random House Press.

Tapscott, D. (1998). *Growing up digital: The rise of the net generation*. New York: McGraw-Hill.

Twenge, J. M. (2006). *Generation me: Why today's young Americans are more confident, assertive, entitled — and more miserable than ever before*. New York: Free Press.

Ustunluoglu, E. (2007). University students' perceptions of native and non-native teachers. *Teachers and Teaching: Theory and Practice*, *13*(1), 63–67.

Wang, M. C., Dziuban, C. D., Cook, I. J., & Moskal, P. D. (2009). Dr. Fox Rocks: Using data-mining techniques to examine student ratings of instruction. In Shelley, M. C., Yore, L. D., & Hand, B. (Eds.), *Quality research in literacy and science education: international perspectives and gold standards* (pp. 383–398). Dordrecht, The Netherlands: Springer. doi:10.1007/978-1-4020-8427-0_19

Wendover, R. W. (2002). *From Ricky & Lucy to Beavis & Butthead: Managing the new workforce*. Aurora, CO: The Center for Generational Studies, Inc.

KEY TERMS AND DEFINITIONS

Blended Success And Withdrawal: The proportion of students who have achieved success (on our campus a grade of A, B, or C) or have withdrawn from a blended course before its completion.

Demographic Prediction: Analytic models that use demographic variables for determining student success, withdrawal, and satisfaction.

Faculty Satisfaction: Faculty perceptions toward the blended educational environment.

Institutional Strategies: Systematic organizational planning that involves blended learning.

Student Ambivalence: Conflicting feelings students hold toward their blended learning environment.

Student Satisfaction With Blended Learning: Student perceptions about the quality of their blended learning experiences.

Systematic Blended Learning: Blended learning programs that become part of institutional strategic initiatives.

Trend Analysis: Understanding the sequenced nature of data within specified time periods.

APPENDIX A

Table 11. Student perception of instruction items for the University of Central Florida

Source	Questions
Administration	1. Feedback concerning your performance in this course was:
	2. The instructor's interest in your learning was:
	3. Use of class time was:
	4. The instruction's overall organization of the course was:
	5. Continuity from one class meeting to the next was:
	6. The pace of the course was:
	7. The instructor's assessment of your progress in the course was:
	8. The texts and supplemental learning materials used in the course were:
Board of Regents	9. Description of course objectives and assignments:
	10. Communication of ideas and information:
	11. Expression of expectations for performance:
	12. Availability to assist students in or outside of class:
	13. Respect and concern for students:
	14. Stimulation of interest in the course:
	15. Facilitation of learning:
	16. Overall assessment of instructor:

Chapter 3
The Use of Asynchronous Video Communication to Improve Instructor Immediacy and Social Presence in a Blended Learning Environment

Jered Borup
Brigham Young University, USA

Charles R. Graham
Brigham Young University, USA

Andrea Velasquez
Brigham Young University, USA

ABSTRACT

Instructors in a blended learning format struggle to find an effective balance between face-to-face instruction that is high in fidelity and online instruction that is high in flexibility. This chapter presents three cases where asynchronous video communication was used to help offer students instruction high in fidelity and flexibility. Although the medium for sharing asynchronous video varied between the three cases, findings indicate that video was a useful tool to improve instructor immediacy and/or social presence with a minimum amount of face-to-face instruction. The instructors in all three cases saw asynchronous video communications as an effective way to communicate with students, and the majority of students responded positively to asynchronous video communications.

DOI: 10.4018/978-1-60960-479-0.ch003

INTRODUCTION

A report by the United States Department of Education's National Center for Education Statistics (NCES) found that over 90% of public colleges and universities offered distant learning courses during 2007 (Parsad & Lewis, 2008). University administrations have used online education as a cost-saving tool. Online learning also proves to be beneficial to instructors and students who require an amount of flexibility and access that cannot be found in a face-to-face classroom. However, online education lacks much of the quality of interaction and pedagogy found in a face-to-face environment and many are turning to a blended learning model (Graham, Allen, & Ure 2005). Graham (2006) defined blended learning as any community of learning that combines face-to-face instruction with computer-mediated instruction. In an attempt to improve online education, a growing number of public colleges and universities are combining the two modes of instruction. The NCES documented that nearly half of four year public colleges and universities offered blended learning courses. That percentage rises to 66% when examining two-year public colleges (Parsad & Lewis, 2008).

In addition to increasing cost effectiveness, flexibility, and access, Graham (2008) also cited that blended learning can facilitate more effective pedagogical practices by increasing active learning, cooperative learning, and learner-centered strategies. Rice, Starr, and Spencer (2005) reported that faster Internet along with the availability of hardware and software has allowed blended learning environments to more efficiently incorporate a "media cornucopia" (p. 216) into learning. Rice et al. acknowledges much of the same media can also be incorporated into face-to-face classrooms. However, it is the time and space flexibility of a supportive blended learning environment that can foster more in-depth independent learning. Asynchronous group communications may also include a larger diversity of viewpoints because the nature of the discussion allows time for more people to participate including shy or anxious students who normally do not participate in face-to-face group discussion (Graham, 2006; Rice, Starr, & Spencer, 2005).

Online Communications in a Blended Learning Environment

The nature of online education limits the forms and quality of personal interactions a student has with instructors and peers. All communities of learning have dimensions of interaction in space, time, and fidelity (Graham, 2006). A face-to-face learning environment requires student and instructor to share the same physical space; however, it also allows synchronous communication where ideas and information can be shared with a very short lag time. Also, in this environment there is a high level of fidelity were the senses of sight, audio, touch, and smell are active in the learning process (see Figure 1).

In contrast, in an online environment the student and instructor do not need to share the same physical space. Similarly, the time dimension of interaction is also commonly distributed through the use of asynchronous communication. These qualities of distributed interactions in both time and space are what give online education the flexibility that has made it popular with instructors and students. However, interactions found in an online learning environment have a low level of fidelity with most interaction being text based (see Figure 2). Both models of instruction have their affordances and constraints with face-to-face instruction providing a high level of fidelity but also providing little flexibility and online instruction providing a high level of flexibility with a low level of fidelity (Graham 2006).

By combining face-to-face and online instruction, the level of fidelity will increase as compared to online only learning environments. However, the more face-to-face class time a blended learning course employs the less flexibility it will have.

Figure 1. Dimensions of interaction in a face-to-face environment

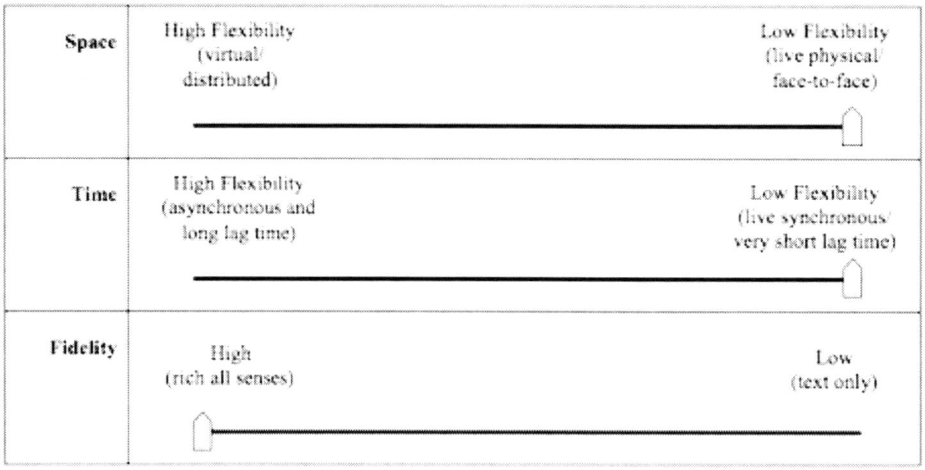

As a result the level of fidelity in a blended learning course can be raised only so much through face-to-face instruction and still retain the flexibility that has made online education popular. Blended learning instructors should also look to improve online interactions with students as a way to increase the overall fidelity of their course. Faster Internet and the advent of Web 2.0 technologies has made the Internet highly interactive, yet much of the interaction found in online learning communities has low fidelity and remains text and content based (LaRose & Whitten, 2000). However, the potential for more meaningful instructor-student and peer-to-peer interaction has dramatically improved. Gunter (2001) commented, "The Internet has shifted from being a communication mode of text-only to a powerful two-way multimedia communication system with applications that have the potential to revolutionizing teaching and training" (p. 196).

Figure 2. Dimensions of interaction in a text based online environment

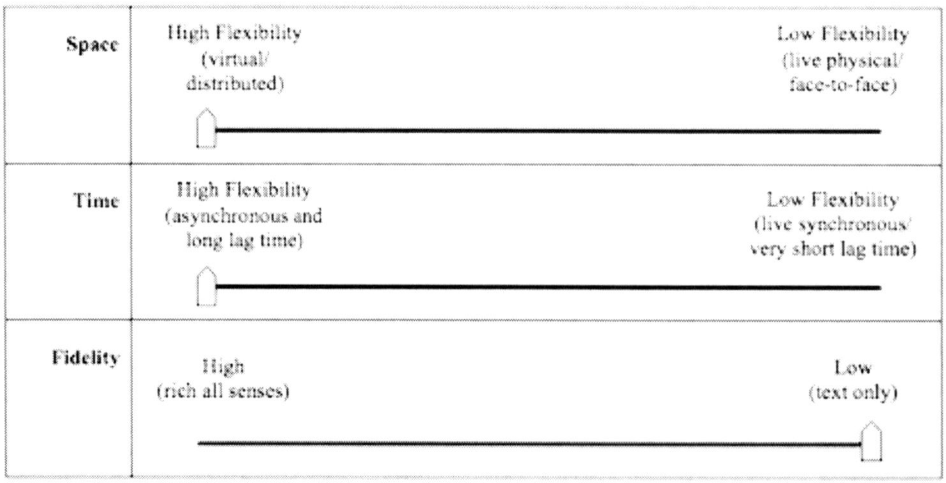

Instructor Immediacy and Social Presence

Learning in a text based online environment may create barriers to establishing a strong sense of instructor immediacy and social presence. Mehrabian (1969) originally defined the construct of immediacy as "those communication behaviors, some visual, other vocal that enhance closeness to and non-verbal interaction with another" (p. 213). These nonverbal communication behaviors can include eye contact, body posture, and facial expression, all of which have the ability to give students a sense of closeness to the instructor. Gorham (1988) added that humor, sharing of personal stories, and encouragement can also improve instructor immediacy. Instructor immediacy has also been found to have a positive effect on student motivation (Christensen & Menzel, 1998; Chistophel, 1990; Christophel & Gorham, 1995). Although, text-based online courses can develop instructor immediacy through the use of humor, sharing of personal stories, and encouragement they cannot include visual and vocal cues that naturally occur in a classroom.

Rourke, Anderson, Garrison, and Archer (1999) claimed the roots of the construct of social presence can be found in the concept of immediacy. Social presence has been defined as the ability of learners to socially and effectively convey themselves as "real people" with emotions, feelings, moods, and senses of humor (Garrison, Anderson, & Archer, 2000; Rourke et al., 1999). Although, Garrison et al. (2000) recognize that social presence can be established in a text-based course, they also believe that the lack of visual cues can be a barrier to establishing a strong social presence. However, they also recognize that asynchronous text-based communication has some advantages over face-to-face instruction, such as providing time to reflect on what has been said and to craft thoughtful responses. Rovai (2002) also acknowledged that it is harder for students to develop social presence in an online learning environment as compared to face-to-face instruction because fewer social cues are present. He goes on to suggest student success in online courses would increase if instructors worked to reduce students' sense of isolation by helping them make connections with peers.

Using the Media Richness of Asynchronous Video

Students and instructors in a low fidelity text based environment can develop social presence (Garrison et al. 2000; Rouke et al., 1999; Rovai, 2002) and instructor immediacy (Gunter, 2007; LaRose & Whitten, 2000). However, Ice, Curtis, Philips, and Wells (2007) indicate that social presence and instructor immediacy may more easily and effectively be established when a high fidelity medium is used. As instructors in an asynchronous online course, Ice et al. (2007) felt they had done everything they could to develop personal relationships with their students given the constraints of text based communication. They introduced audio feedback into their course and found it to be more effective in conveying nuance as compared to the low fidelity text based feedback. They further reported that the audio feedback increased students' perception of the instructor as caring and "revealed an overwhelming student preference for asynchronous audio feedback as compared to traditional text based feedback" (p. 18).

Media richness may help to explain why Ice et al. (2007) found audio feedback to be more effective as compared to text. Rice et al. (2005) defined media richness as "the extent to which a medium can support language variety, feedback, nonverbal cues, and learning" (p. 220). Daft and Lengel (1986) originally ranked the richness of commutation media and placed face-to-face at the top and written documents near the bottom just above numeric documents. They saw face-to-face instruction as the richest medium of communication because of its ability to give clear and immediate feedback and the number of verbal and non

Figure 3. Blended learning models to achieve a high level of flexibility and fidelity

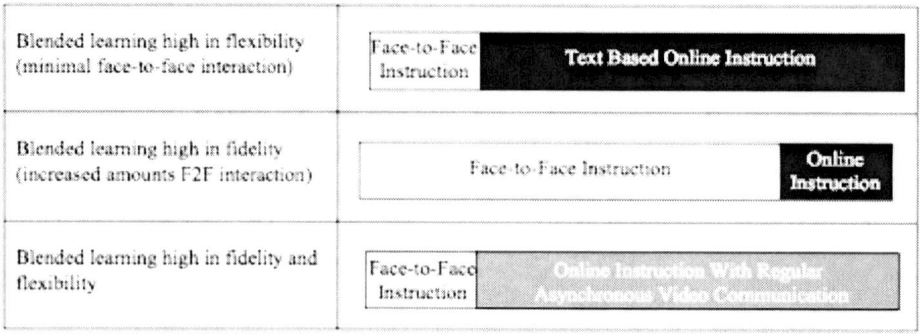

verbal cues it contains. They also wrote that the more media richness the more efficient complex information can be conveyed and understood. Therefore, simple straightforward information can often be understood more efficiently through a low fidelity medium while more complex information is better communicated via a high fidelity medium. Overbaugh and Casiello (2008) reported that when given complex collaborative tasks students in a distributed learning environment will gravitate to high richness media if they are made available.

Griffiths and Graham (2009a) suggested that the blended learning model coupled with the media richness found in asynchronous video communication may bridge the gap between distributed and face-to-face communication and provide a strong sense of instructor immediacy and social presence while still maintaining a high level of flexibility.

They further add that although the rich media available through synchronous video provides immediate feedback and geographical flexibility, it does not provide flexibility in time because—just as in face-to-face instruction—it requires both instructor and student to designate a common time for instruction. In contrast, asynchronous communication lacks immediate feedback yet still provides the geographical flexibility, while adding to it the time flexibility that many students require. Through the use of an asynchronous video communication tool a blended learning course can efficiently establish a strong sense of immediacy and social presence with a minimum amount of face-to-face classroom instruction (see Figure 3). This allows instructors to maintain the high level of flexibility available in a distributed, asynchronous course while improving the fidelity of the communication occurring in the course (see Figure 4).

CONTEXT

Several years ago instructors teaching the educational technology courses (IPT286/287) for preservice public school instructors at Brigham Young University (BYU) began searching for solutions to instructional challenges they were facing that would simultaneously allow for increased student flexibility as well as maintain the BYU emphasis on high quality instructor-learner interaction in undergraduate courses. A blended learning approach that combined face-to-face with online learning experiences seemed like a good approach. A blended learning structure was created that required students to attend class face-to-face the first and last weeks of the semester with learning taking place online during the other twelve weeks of the semester. Students in the blended learning sections also had the option of attending face-to-face classes in a traditional section any time they wanted.

With this blended structure the flexibility requirement was achieved but instructors felt that they wanted something to help them connect

Figure 4. Dimensions of interaction in an asynchronous video based online environment

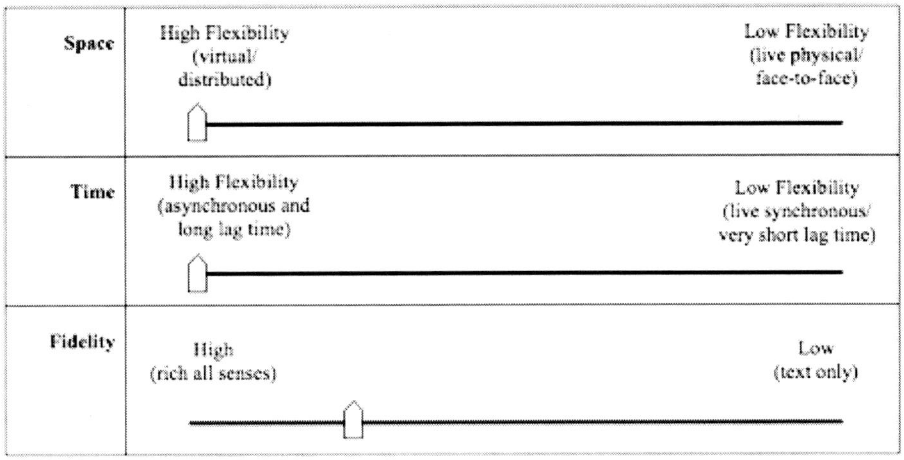

more closely with the students than they felt text-based email or discussion boards would allow. As a result instructors began exploring the use of asynchronous video as a means of communication with students during the online portions of the class. The feeling was that asynchronous video would maintain a high level of flexibility while simultaneously allowing the learner and instructor to communicate in a richer way.

Several different tools and approaches were explored, as described by Griffiths and Graham (2009a, 2009b, & 2010 in press) and Velasquez, Graham, and McCollum (2009). In this chapter we will describe three cases that highlight the different approaches we used and what we learned about how the affordances of different asynchronous video technologies impacted student and instructor perceptions of their relationships in their blended courses. Table 1 describes the three cases that we will describe in the rest of the chapter. These cases include our use of Facebook, VoiceThread, and a video blog created by BYU's Center for Teaching and Learning. Griffiths' (2010) dissertation outlines several general principles under the title Asynchronous Video Learning Model (AVLM) that were developed to help guide instructors using asynchronous video in their blended learning courses.

In our context, students who chose to participate in the blended learning sections were required to either purchase a webcam or to use a webcam located in a school computer lab for regular video-based communication during the semester. The remainder of the chapter will include a discussion of the affordances, strengths, and weaknesses of the tools we have used for sharing asynchronous video. This chapter will also share experiences and student reactions from those blended learning courses where asynchronous video was used and provide guidelines and suggestions to those who wish to incorporate asynchronous video communications into blended learning courses.

Case One: Facebook Video Messaging

One of our first explorations with the use of asynchronous video in blended courses involved the use of Facebook. We had considered using several stand-alone video messaging tools, like TokBox (http://www.tokbox.com). We decided to use Facebook because it was a tool already being used by almost all students enrolled in the IPT287 course and it also had video messaging already built right into its features (although most of the

Table 1. Three cases of a technology integration course using asynchronous video communications

Cases	Semester	Description of Video Communication
Case 1: Facebook	Fall 2008	Instructor and students shared weekly private video communication through a messaging feature within Facebook. The instructor also created weekly orientation videos that were placed on the course group page.
Case 2: VoiceThread	Fall 2009	Students commented weekly on content related topics using the online program VoiceThread. The instructor also created weekly orientation videos that were placed on the course wiki page.
Case 3: Video Blog	Winter & Fall 2009	Each student was given access to a group and an individual video blog. Students participated in several group content related discussions. A student's individual blog was used primarily to host private instructor-student conversations.

students had never used that feature of Facebook previously).

The IPT287 instructor created a Facebook group that included all class-enrolled students during the Fall 2008 semester. The instructor created weekly videos that were then posted in a public place on the Facebook group page for all students to view. The weekly video provided general feedback regarding patterns of student performance during the previous week, addressed common student questions and issues, and oriented them to current assignments. The Facebook messaging feature was used by students to record and send the instructor a weekly private video message. These weekly video messages addressed each student's perceptions of the week's assignment, reported on individual progress in completing the assignment, and raised any concerns or difficulties they were experiencing. Typically, student videos were one to three minutes in length. The instructor then replied individually with a video response to each student providing individualized feedback and encouragement (see Figure 5). Several weeks during the semester technical problems on Facebook prevented videos from being sent, and during these weeks students sent the instructor a text-based message in Facebook.

The instructor found that with a class of 40-50 students it took 2-3 hours a week to communicate with each student personally, which was approximately the amount of time he would have spent in class for a traditional face-to-face section. Students who were struggling typically sent longer video messages that required longer, more detailed feedback. Students who were performing well required less personal time but still received feedback and encouragement for the good work they were doing. In this model, students had less overall exposure (in raw minutes) to the instructor then they would have had in a face-to-face environment. However, the nature of that exposure changed to a more personal student-instructor relationship. The video communication was motivating for the instructor because it provided a feedback loop that he did not have before. He was able to see the excitement in students' faces when things were going well and the frustration when they were struggling. This enabled him to respond in a more individualized way to provide encouragement as well as more intense technical help for those who needed it most. While many students appreciated the personal attention, the instructor felt that there were a number of students in the class who didn't really want a more personal relationship with the instructor in the course. These students were predominantly efficiency oriented in their approach to their studies. These students valued the efficiency and convenience of text-based communication over the added fidelity the video provided.

Following the semester, students provided feedback regarding their perceptions of the usefulness of video messaging during the course. Students were asked to respond to the following question: "What did you value and/or dislike about communicating with the instructor using

Figure 5. Sample Facebook communication used to hold weekly instructor-student conversations

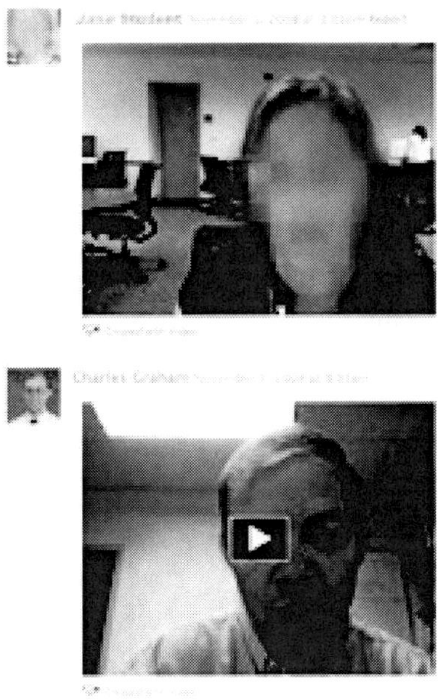

video?" Some students expressed the perception that text emails could have been adequate without the added cost of purchasing a webcam. However, the majority of students valued the regular video messaging and several student comments show the communication was successful in establishing instructor presence. These comments included:

- "I liked it a lot actually. It made the instructor seem more 'real I guess i would say."
- "I thought it was a great way to QUICKLY stay in touch and much more personal"
- "It was good to know that if I needed help, I could get it and it wasn't just emails, I was actually able to see the professor and get adequate feedback."
- "I thought it was nice that the video communication was so personalized and it made me feel like I could ask any question and it would be answered, …"
- "I valued it because he was so good at communicating. If I [had] any questions or concerns he always answered quickly."
- "It was nice to get feedback and see what the instructor thought. It also helped me know that he cared if I was having difficulties."
- "It was nice to still feel connected to an actual professor, and it allowed prompt feedback if I needed help or had a question."
- "I liked it a lot actually. It made the instructor seem more 'real' I guess i would say."

One student said "I am not used to such personal communication with a teacher and it almost makes me uncomfortable...I am not sure why I feel that way." indicating that she was receiving more personal communication from the instructor than she normally received in a more traditional face-to-face instruction. Although the weekly video communication was intended to improve instructor immediacy, one student also expressed it improved her social presence in the course, "I liked that I felt like I was part of the class and able to express my opinions and talk about any concerns or things I was learning."

Students were also asked to evaluate the use of Facebook as an academic communication tool. Students liked using a familiar tool that they were already regularly using and students who did not like it usually cited privacy concerns or wanting to keep their social life separate from their academic life. From the instructor perspective, Facebook provided quick and easy access to the students. Students seemed to get messages more quickly and respond more promptly than he experienced with regular email. The instructor really appreciated the asynchronous video aspect of the messaging because it allowed him to get to know the students by face better. Video messages also allowed him to get a sense for the excitement or frustration that a student was experiencing in the class and address that directly in the communications with the student.

Case Two: VoiceThread Video Commenting

During the Fall 2009 semester of IPT287, VoiceThread (http://voicethread.com) was used in an attempt to increase social presence and to facilitate weekly conversations among students in the blended learning section. VoiceThread is an online program designed to promote asynchronous discussions around media such as pictures and video. When creating a VoiceThread, one or multiple pictures or video clips can be uploaded and made public, thus allowing any VoiceThread member to comment, or they can be kept private so only invited members have the ability to respond. VoiceThread allows several different types of comments, including video, audio, and text. As a way to lower anxiety, comments can be previewed prior to posting on the VoiceThread and can also be deleted after they have been posted. Similarly, the creator of the VoiceThread has the ability to moderate all comments made on the VoiceThread. As comments are made, they are identified by a small profile picture and placed around the VoiceThread in descending sequential order (see Figure 6). Viewers can then click on selected videos to watch or simply press play and watch all the comments in the order they were given. A constraint of VoiceThread is that it does not show the thread of the discussion.

The first two authors of the chapter co-taught the course. After the first face-to-face meeting of the semester, students followed a weekly online agenda. Most weeks, a brief video was created by the instructor to introduce the class to the week's activities and orient them to parts of the unit that they should pay particular attention to. An important part of each week was the students' participation in the VoiceThread discussion. On the first day of the blended learning course students were introduced to VoiceThread and organized into one of six VoiceThread groups containing six to nine students. During the 14 week semester each group was asked to respond to eight VoiceThreads. (Students were not required to participate in VoiceThread discussions during their off campus practicum experience because the face-to-face section was not required to attend class.) The instructor uploaded an image to each VoiceThread containing the discussion topic. Most VoiceThreads also included a video comment from the instructor providing the students with additional instructions on the discussion topic. Most topics focused on student perceptions and the possible applications of technology tools learned in class. VoiceThreads were then embedded into a class wiki and all students were required to record and post video responses using a webcam.

The instructor enjoyed listening to students' thoughts and he found himself checking for new comments several times during the course of a week's conversation. The instructor was also surprised to find how quickly he was able to learn the blended learning students' names and recognize students while on campus. He was able to learn the names of the blended learning students and felt closer to the blended learning students than he did to the students in the face-to-face section who he met with each week. However, to avoid

Figure 6. Sample VoiceThread used to hold weekly conversations on content related topics

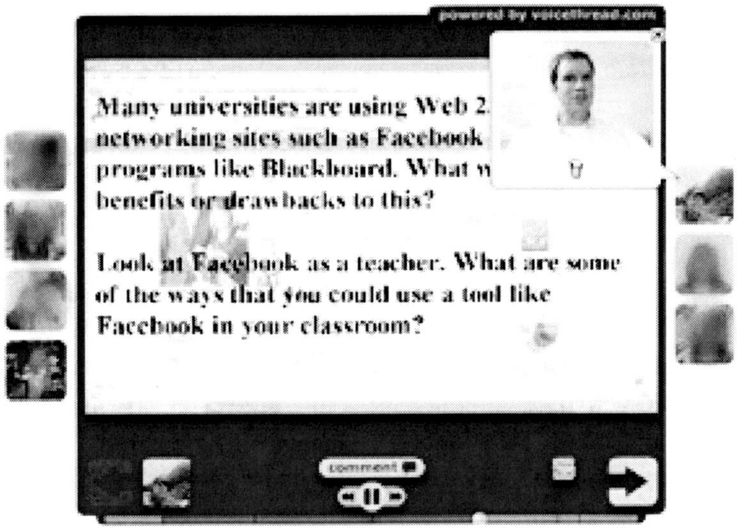

dominating the VoiceThread conversation the instructor only participated in two of the eight conversations (once to better focus the conversation topic and the other to summarize and thank students for their thoughts and comments).

The instructor also found the richness of video comments helped to better assess student understanding and feelings on class topics. Facial expressions and student tone of voice helped the instructor to recognize student frustration and confusion stemming from students' inability to see how learned technological skills could be used with young students. This allowed the instructor to adjust future VoiceThread topics to include video examples of actual technology use in early elementary grades, thus creating a better understanding of possible applications. Student facial expression and tone of voice also clearly showed when students were excited. These emotions may have been missed by the instructor in a purely text-based conversation.

One example where the media richness of video helped the instructor to identify student confusion came in the third week of instruction. The instructor wanted to help students to recognize the technology, content, and pedagogy used in a particular example of classroom instruction. He found a video on YouTube created by a school district showcasing their technology use. Although a large majority of the video showed technology use in an elementary setting, only a few showed the use of technology in the early elementary grades. That week's VoiceThread required students to view the video and in their comment cite a specific example and identify the technology, content, and pedagogy used and evaluate its effectiveness. Two students in the Early Childhood Education (ECE) group expressed concerns regarding technology use in early grades. The following is the transcript of one of the students' comments:

After watching the YouTube video I had mixed feelings on it. I think that it's a good idea for the older grades. I'm in the ECE major so I don't know how effective it would be with the younger children. I think I could [pause] You know the third graders or the second graders might have a good time with it but it's definitely I think for the older kids. But it is very beneficial in the classroom because it opens up so many more resources than a textbook does because you are able to search in all these different places in the web and the students are able to find so much more information that way. So I think that is really cool that the teacher does that with her class and they seem to really enjoy it. So I think that it is a really good idea for some classrooms and certain settings and for certain grades of course.

Although this transcript shows some level of inability on the part of the student to visualize technology use in early grades, it was the student's nonverbal cues in the video including avoiding looking into the camera and tone of voice that showed her level of discouragement and dissatisfaction with the assignment. Although the instructor did not respond directly to the student's comment, he decided to include an example of young children creating a digital storytelling project (a technology the class was currently learning) in the next week's VoceThread. The following is a transcript of her comment to that week's VoiceThread:

Ok, I really enjoyed watching the video of all the children doing the different digital storytellings and I guess I assumed that this project would be more for the older grades, maybe fourth and up. But watching this I realized that even someone in preschool could do this because all they have to do is draw the picture and have the teacher help them with the sound or speaking or whatever they are going to do.

Although the transcript indicates that the student was better able to apply her learning from the course to future teaching settings, it was the student's nonverbal cues that showed her excitement and improved satisfaction with the assignment. Unlike the previous student video comment, during this comment the student made prolonged eye contact through the webcam and smiled often. Her tone of voice also changed from the previous comment reflecting her excitement. The student's level of discouragement and excitement could have been easily missed if it weren't for the non verbal cues contained in the media richness of the video.

Following the semester, students provided feedback regarding their perceptions of the usefulness of using the video communication during the course. Using a six-point Likert scale, students were asked to respond to the following statement, "I could easily express my thoughts and feelings using VoiceThread." Of the 40 respondents, 35 responded affirmatively with six strongly agreeing, 17 agreeing, and 12 somewhat agreeing. Using the same scale, students were asked to respond to the statement, "I feel like I got to know my instructor better because of VoiceThread." Although the instructor took more of an administrative role and did not actively participate in the discussion, 22 of the 39 students responded affirmatively with two strongly agreeing, nine agreeing, and 11 somewhat agreeing. However, students perceived VoiceThread video communication as less useful in getting to know their peers. Although students reported watching an average of 2.3 peer comments each week, when asked to respond to the statement, "I feel like I got to know my peers better because of VocieThread." 22 of the 40 students responded negatively with five strongly disagreeing, eight disagreeing, and nine somewhat disagreeing (see Figure 7). One student explained, "I thought it was interesting and a good use of technology. I just don't feel like I 'got to know' people better by using it because of the content we were reporting on. It's not really 'get to know you' type content."

Students were also asked the open-ended question, "What did you value and/or dislike about using VoiceThread?" Most students showed a positive perception of the use of VoiceThread. Positive comments focused on the ease sharing thoughts and ideas and the chance to hear peer comments without having to attend class. These comments included:

Figure 7. Student responses to survey items regarding student perception of video communications using VoiceThread

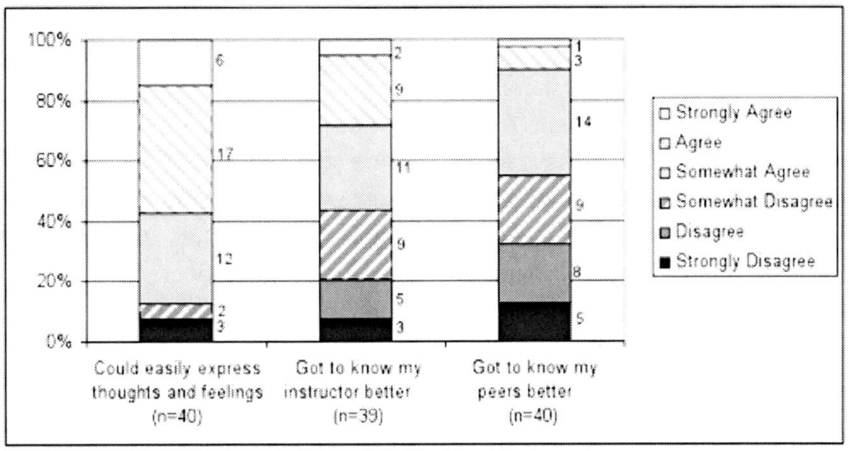

- "It was a good way to keep connected with my class, even though I did not see them on a weekly basis."
- "I liked hearing ideas from my peers and being able to do it on my own time at my own pace."
- "I thought it was pretty easy to use, and it was nice that the instructors were able to see the students actually make the comments."
- "I liked being able to put in my two cents without the pressure of being in front of the class."
- "I liked that it was easy to use and it was easy to express my thoughts rather than writing them."

Although there was evidence that students were watching their peers' video comments, the discussion was not threaded to alert students that a peer had elaborated or responded to their comment. As a result some students had the perception that no one was listening to their comments and the discussions were busy work. Others had technical problems that added to the time it took to make a comment, which seemed to lessen VoiceThread's perceived value. One student commented, "I had problems with getting the voice thread to work every week (probably my webcam). I do not like recording myself, and I feel like I would have been able to express myself better face-to-face or through text."

The following semester (Winter, 2010) the instructor continued to use VocieThread. Unlike the previous semester, the first VoiceThread gave students the opportunity to introduce themselves to their group in an attempt to strengthen students' social presence. In an attempt to improve instructor immediacy, the instructor also became an active participant in the discussion, most weeks making two comments to each group's VoiceThread to respond to student comments and thoughts. In addition each student created a personal VoiceThread where the instructor could provide students with individualized feedback. Initial observations appear to indicate that this course has a higher level of instructor immediacy and students have an improved sense of social presence as compared to the previous semester.

During Fall 2009, in addition to VoiceThread videos, the instructor recorded weekly videos that were posted as part of each week's online agenda found on the class wiki site, along with text-based instructions. The weekly video provided general feedback regarding students' performance during the previous week and oriented them to the current week's assignment. One purpose of these orientations was to give the students a sense of who the instructor was as a person. The videos were not scripted and the instructor oriented students to the week's activities much like he would have done the first five minutes of a face-to-face class. Below each media rich video the instructor included similar orientation information as text. Although viewing of the video was not required, survey responses and YouTube view counts indicated that most students chose to watch the videos. There was also evidence that the weekly video helped to increase the instructor immediacy in the course. Using a six-point Likert scale, students were asked to respond to the following statement, "I felt that the weekly orientation video helped to know my instructor better." Of the 40 respondents, 28 responded affirmatively with five strongly agreeing, 13 agreeing, and 10 somewhat agreeing.

Some students felt that the text instructions were sufficient or that the videos were too long. However, the majority saw the video orientation as a helpful addition. Students were asked to respond to the following question, "Was having the instructor do a video orientation in the weekly online agenda valuable to you? Why or why not?" Their comments included:

- "Yes. It always clarified what I needed to do and what he wanted. It also reminded me that I had a teacher there that cared and was willing to help."
- "Yes. It gave me an overview of what to expect and what to do. It also helped me to get to know my instructor better, and it reminded me he was there to help us."
- "Yes, it was nice to hear him tell us what to do instead of just reading it."
- "Yes, since he clarified the agenda more. I appreciated watching the teacher and having that as a resource."
- "Yes, because I could actually see what we were supposed to do."

Case Three: Video Blogs

Also during the Fall 2009 semester in another blended learning section of the same course, another instructor chose to use video blogs as a way to host both private and public instructor-student and student-student video communications. The video blogs were created by BYU's Center for Teaching and Learning as a design solution to improve participation and engagement in the blended section. Each student was given access to various group video blogs and one individual blog. Group blogs allowed the instructor to select various students to be in a group video discussion. Everyone in the group could then post comments to their group and see others' posts. The individual blog allowed only one student and the instructor access to postings. Students had the ability to make video, audio, and text comments on the blogs. It was required that students make video comments, but in cases when a video posting was not possible, students used the audio or text features to post their comment. As comments were made, they were placed in ascending sequential order on the page (see Figure 8). The video blogs gave the instructor the pedagogical flexibility to create small group discussions by using the group blogs, as well as maintain an individual relationship with each student in the course through the individual blog. Students were able to post multiple comments on a single forum allowing for extended peer-to-peer conversations. However, as a new online tool, the video blogs did not have all the affordances the instructor wanted. For instance, students could not preview comments before posting them, and once they were posted, students could not remove them. In addition, the video blog did not show the thread of the discussion. Instead, each post appeared as a new post and not a reply to a post.

In order to create better social presence, the first assignment was a group forum where the

Figure 8. Sample video blog used to hold small group discussions on content related topics

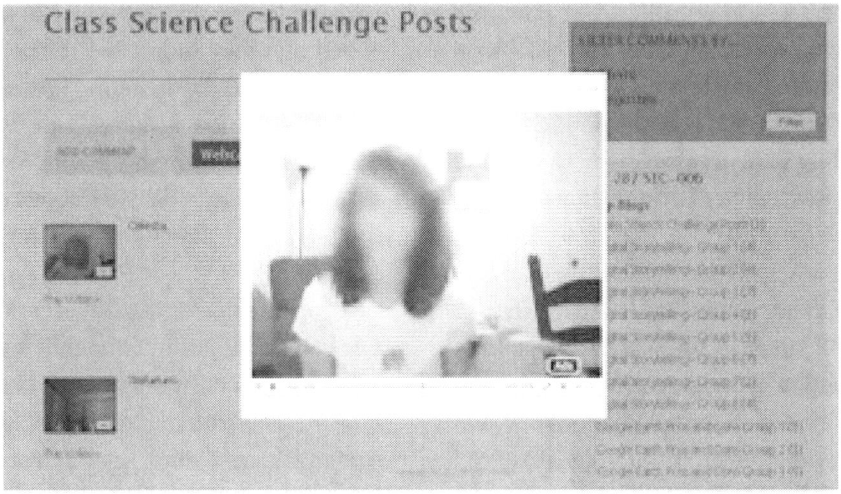

instructor and each student posted a video introducing themselves to the class. The videos were posted where all students had the ability to view them. In their videos it was common for students to use humor, facial expressions such as smiling, and comments regarding loved ones, such as boyfriends, spouses, friends, and family. In an attempt to improve instructor immediacy and to create a sense of closeness, the instructor also responded to each of the student comments by posting a video on the student's private video blog. The instructor started each response video by referring to the student by name and then giving encouragement and/or citing similarities between the instructor's and student's background. The following are some of the students' comments regarding this assignment:

- "I really liked this one because it was a fun ice breaker for the class and I loved getting the video response from the teacher. I thought it was a great way to start the class."
- "Because I was getting to know my classmates in an online setting, still I was getting to know them personally."
- "I enjoyed watching others' posts and getting to know the personalities of some of the people in the class."

For the majority of subsequent posts, students were organized into eight groups, each containing around four students. Each group was then assigned a forum and was asked to share feelings and thoughts on content-related topics. One of the topics was explored via a friendly group debate. Each student was given either a pro or a con stance and then posted video comments concerning the use of Google Earth in an elementary classroom. It was common for students to interact with peers via video posts by referring to their peers by name and/or summarizing peer comments.

After this debate assignment, the instructor opted to create more creative video assignments in order to facilitate student-to-student interaction using the video blog. One of the affordances of the video blog is that students can lead group discussions alone, without the presence of the instructor. Although, the instructor was usually present in the discussions, students were encouraged after each posting to watch the postings of their colleagues. Sometimes, responding to others' posts was part of the assignment. This created a larger audience for the students in the course and provided them with multiple perspectives to consider. One example is when a student posted a pessimistic outlook on the use of technology to teach Google Earth. A number of students in the class responded to her posting providing many reasons why she should reconsider her perspective. This situation provided an opportunity for others in the class to think critically, it also helped the student by showing her that others in her same situation (not just the instructor) were open to the use of technology with this particular subject, and it reduced the instructor's workload in terms of convincing the student on the relevance of technology. A survey was used to obtain student feedback regarding their perception of the usefulness of video blogs during the course. The following are some of the students' positive comments about the video blog:

- "I liked watching other videos and it helped it feel like we were part of a class."
- "It's a cool tool and an easy way to put a face with people, not just text on the screen."
- "I thought it was really fun and a great tool to learn how to use. I had problems with it at first, but after I figured it out, I really liked it. It's fun to actually see people talking."

The following are some of their negative feedback:

- "Not a fan. It is too much of a hassle and no one wants to watch them. You gain the same thing from a normal blog."
- "Sincerely, I rather make a comment in a real classroom then in a video blogging tool. But it is an amazing tool though."

In general, many students liked listening to others' opinions on content related topics. Students valued the social nature of the video tool. However, others questioned the affordance of the tool in helping students work in groups and connect with each other. Those who did not like the tool stated that they didn't see the benefit of a video blog over a traditional blog posting because they didn't see value in interacting with others and the professor through the video medium. When asked if the use of the tool in the course improved the quality of the course, 21 out of 34 students answered yes.

The instructor found that video tools should be designed to afford student-to-student interaction along with assignments that make use of this affordance to create a community where students learn from other students and not solely from the instructor. With this in mind the video blogging tool will be undergoing an evaluation and redesign. One of the aspects of the tool that will be targeted in the analysis is its ability to help students work in groups and communicate with each other. When the tool was initially designed and developed, this criterion was not part of the design but it will be one of central focus in the second iteration of the tool.

FUTURE RESEARCH DIRECTIONS

The findings shared in this chapter were rooted in student perceptions. A logical next step in the research would be to examine the effects that asynchronous communications have on student behavior and performance in a blended learning environment. In particular, there is a need to understand how instruction that is centered around instructor-learner interaction (as opposed to primarily learner-content interaction) shapes learner dispositions. Research should also examine the use of asynchronous video communication in other blended and online learning contexts including that of K-12 education. K-12 educators are particularly interested in the role of caring and nurturing pedagogies in a learning environment (Sirotnik, 2001). It is important to investigate the effectiveness of strategies that allow instructors to develop and maintain a nurturing relationship with learners despite being separated in time and space. Different approaches to using asynchronous video may provide insightful ways to use technology to strengthen the student-instructor relationship in a blended learning environment. Researchers need to document cases that highlight practical pedagogies that effectively use the affordances of asynchronous video to facilitate and assess student learning.

Although asynchronous video may approach the level of fidelity found in a face-to-face learning environment, it is not the argument of the authors that asynchronous video communication replace all face-to-face instruction. More research is needed to identify those tasks that are more effectively performed in a face-to-face environment and those that can be effectively done online. In addition, instructors and researchers should seek to find which online tasks require human interaction around content and which can be done through learner-content interaction alone.

CONCLUSION

Instructors in a blended learning format struggle to find an effective balance between face-to-face instruction that is high in fidelity and online instruction that is high in flexibility. The three cases shared in this chapter show that asynchronous video communication can help to provide the best of both methods and offer students instruction high in fidelity and flexibility. Although the medium for sharing asynchronous video varied between three sections of the blended learning course, findings indicate that video in all sections was a useful tool to improve instructor immediacy and/or social presence with a minimum amount of face-to-face instruction and maintaining a high level of flexibility. The instructors in all three cases saw asynchronous video communications as an effective way to communicate with students. Instructors found that students' nonverbal cues alerted them to confusion and frustration that may have been missed in text based communication. The majority of students in all three cases responded positively to asynchronous video communications. Students commonly cited that they felt the video communications helped them to get know the instructor and peers better than they would have in text-based interactions.

However, some students also expressed concerns and/or a dislike of video communications. Some students expressed the perception that text communications would have been sufficient for course communication. Other student comments focused on the constraints of the communication tool chosen for the section of the course. In the course section where Facebook was used, students liked using a familiar tool that they were already regularly using and students who did not like it usually cited privacy concerns or a desire to keep their social life separate from their academic life. In the course section that used VoiceThread, many students encountered technical problems when using the unfamiliar tool, which seemed to lessen their perceived value of the video communication. VoiceThread and the video blogs lacked the affordance of threading conversations, which may have contributed to a perception that others were not viewing or responding to their comments.

REFERENCES

Christensen, L., & Menzel, K. (1998). The linear relationship between student reports of teacher immediacy behaviors and perceptions of state motivation, and of cognitive, affective, and behavioral learning. *Communication Education*, *47*(1), 82–90. doi:10.1080/03634529809379112

Christophel, D. M. (1990). The relationship among teacher immediacy behaviors, student motivation, and learning. *Communication Education*, *39*(4), 323–340. doi:10.1080/03634529009378813

Christophel, D. M., & Gorham, J. (1995). A test-retest analysis of student motivation, teacher immediacy, and perceived sources of motivation and demotivation in college classes. *Communication Education*, *44*(4), 292–306. doi:10.1080/03634529509379020

Daft, R. L., & Lengel, R. H. (1986). Organizational information requirements, media richness and structural design. *Management Science*, *32*(5), 554–571. doi:10.1287/mnsc.32.5.554

Garrison, D. R., Anderson, T., & Archer, W. (2000). Critical inquiry in a text-based environment: Computer conferencing in higher education. *The Internet and Higher Education*, *2*(2-3), 87–105. doi:10.1016/S1096-7516(00)00016-6

Gorham, J. (1988). The relationship between verbal teacher immediacy behaviors and student learning. *Communication Education*, *37*(1), 40–53. doi:10.1080/03634528809378702

Graham, C. R. (2006). Blended learning systems: Definition, current trends, and future directions. In Bonk, C. J., & Graham, C. R. (Eds.), *Handbook of blended learning: Global perspectives, local designs* (pp. 3–21). San Francisco, CA: Pfeiffer.

Graham, C. R. (2008). Blended learning models. In Khosrow-Pour, M. (Ed.), *Encyclopedia of Information Science and Technology* (*Vol. 2*, pp. 375–382). Hershey, PA: Idea Group Inc.

Graham, C. R., Allen, S., & Ure, D. (2005). Benefits and challenges of blended learning environments. In Khosrow-Pour, M. (Ed.), *Encyclopedia of Information Science and Technology* (pp. 253–259). Hershey, PA: Idea Group Inc.

Griffiths, M. (2010). *Improving the asynchronous video learning model*. Unpublished doctoral dissertation, Brigham Young University, Provo, UT.

Griffiths, M. E., & Graham, C. R. (2009a). The potential of asynchronous video in online education. *Distance Learning*, *6*(2), 13–22.

Griffiths, M. E., & Graham, C. R. (2009b). Using asynchronous video in online classes: Results from a pilot study. *Instructional Technology & Distance Education*, *6*(3), 65–76.

Griffiths, M. E., & Graham, C. R. (2010. (in press). Using asynchronous video to achieve instructor immediacy and closeness in online classes: Experiences from three cases. *International Journal on E-Learning*.

Gunter, G. A. (2007). The effects of the impact of instructional immediacy on cognition and learning in online classes. *International Journal of Social Sciences*, *2*(3), 196–202.

Ice, P., Curtis, R., Philips, P., & Wells, J. (2007). Using asynchronous audio feedback to enhance teaching presence and students' sense of community. *Journal of Asynchronous Learning Networks*, *11*(2), 3–25.

LaRose, R., & Whitten, P. (2000). Re-thinking instructional immediacy for web courses: A social cognitive exploration. *Communication Education*, *49*(4), 320–338. doi:10.1080/03634520009379221

Meheabian, A. (1969). Some referents and measures of non-verbal behavior. *Behavior Research Methods and Instrumentation*, *1*, 213–217.

Overbaugh, R. C., & Casiello, A. R. (2008). Distributed collaborative problem-based graduate-level learning: Student's perspectives on communication tool selection and efficacy. *Computers in Human Behavior*, *24*(2), 497–515. doi:10.1016/j.chb.2007.02.017

Parsad, B., & Lewis, L. (2008). *Distance education at degree-granting postsecondary institutions: 2006-2007*. Washington, D.C.: National Center for Education Statistics, Institute of Education Sciences, U.S. Department of Education. Retrieved from http://nces.ed.gov/pubs2009/2009044.pdf

Rice, R. E., Hiltz, S. R., & Spencer, D. H. (2005). Media mixes and learning networks. In Hiltz, S. R., & Goldman, R. (Eds.), *Learning together online: Research on asynchronous learning networks* (pp. 215–237). Mahwah, NJ: Lawrence Erlbaum Associates, Inc.

Rourke, L., Anderson, T., Garrison, D. R., & Archer, W. (1999). Assessing social presence in asynchronous, text-based computer conferencing. *Journal of Distance Education, 14*(2), 50–71.

Rovai, A. (2002). Building sense of community at a distance. *International Review of Research in Open and Distance Learning, 3*(1).

Sirotnik, K. (2001). *Renewing schools and teacher education: An odyssey in educational change*. Washington, DC: American Association of Colleges for Teacher Education.

Velasquez, A., Graham, C., & McCollum, K. (2009). Online social networking used to enhance face-to-face and online pre-service teacher education courses. In I. Gibson, et al. (Eds.), *Proceedings of Society for Information Technology & Teacher Education International Conference 2009*. Chesapeake, VA: AACE.

ADDITIONAL READING

Bersin, (2003). *Blended learning: What works?: An industry study of the strategy, implementation, and impact of blended learning*. Bersin & Associates.

Caspi, A., & Blau, I. (2008). Social presence in online discussion groups: Testing three conceptions and their relations to perceived learning. *Social Psychology of Education, 11*, 323–346. doi:10.1007/s11218-008-9054-2

Cookson, P. (2002). The hybridization of higher education: Cross-national perspectives. *International Review of Research in Open and Distance Learning, 2*(2).

Cottrell, D., & Robison, R. (2003). Blended learning in an accounting course. *Quarterly Review of Distance Education, 4*(3), 261–269.

Driscoll, M. (2002, March 1, 2002). Blended Learning: Let's get beyond the hype. *e-learning,* 54.

Garrison, D., Cleveland-Innes, M., & Fung, T. S. (2010). Exploring causal relationships among teaching, cognitive and social presence: Student perceptions of the community of inquiry framework. *The Internet and Higher Education, 13*(1-2), 31–36. doi:10.1016/j.iheduc.2009.10.002

Garrison, D. R., Anderson, T., & Archer, W. (2010). The first decade of the community of inquiry framework: A retrospective. *The Internet and Higher Education, 13*(1-2), 5–9. doi:10.1016/j.iheduc.2009.10.003

Garrison, D. R., & Kanuka, H. (2004). Blended learning: Uncovering its transformative potential in higher education. *The Internet and Higher Education, 7*(2), 95–105. doi:10.1016/j.iheduc.2004.02.001

Garrison, D. R., & Vaughan, N. D. (2007). *Blended learning in higher education: Framework, principles, and guidelines*. Jossey-Bass.

Graham, C. R. (2006). Blended learning systems: Definition, current trends, and future directions. In Bonk, C. J., & Graham, C. R. (Eds.), *Handbook of blended learning: Global perspectives, local designs* (pp. 3–21). San Francisco, CA: Pfeiffer Publishing.

Graham, C. R. (2008). Blended learning models. In Khosrow-Pour, M. (Ed.), *Encyclopedia of Information Science and Technology* (*Vol. 2*, pp. 375–382). Hershey, PA: Idea Group Inc.

Graham, C. R., & Allen, S. (2005). Blended learning environments. In Howard, C., Boettecher, J. V., Justice, L., Schenk, K. D., Rogers, P. L., & Berg, G. A. (Eds.), *Encyclopedia of Distance Learning* (pp. 172–179). Hershey, PA: Idea Group Inc.

Graham, C. R., & Allen, S. (2009). Designing blended learning environments. In Rogers, P. L., Berg, G. A., Boettecher, J. V., Howard, C., Justice, L., & Schenk, K. (Eds.), *Encyclopedia of Distance Learning* (*Vol. 2*, pp. 562–570). Hershey, PA: Idea Group Inc.

Graham, C. R., Allen, S., & Ure, D. (2005). Benefits and challenges of blended learning environments. In Khosrow-Pour, M. (Ed.), *Encyclopedia of Information Science and Technology* (pp. 253–259). Hershey, PA: Idea Group Inc.

Graham, C. R., & Dziuban, C. D. (2008). Core research and issues related to blended learning environments. In Spector, J. M., Merrill, M. D., van Merrienboer, J. J. G., & Driscoll, M. P. (Eds.), *Handbook of research on educational communications and technology* (*Vol. 3*, pp. 269–276). Mahwah, NJ: Lawrence Earlbaum Associates.

Graham, C. R., & Robison, R. (2007). Realizing the transformational potential of blended learning: Comparing cases of transforming blends and enhancing blends in higher education. In Picciano, A. G., & Dziuban, C. D. (Eds.), *Blended learning: Research perspectives* (pp. 83–110). Needham, MA: Sloan Consortium.

Leh, A. S. (2002). Action research on hybrid courses and their online communities. *Educational Media International*, *39*(1), 31–38. doi:10.1080/09523980210131204

Morgan, K. R. (2002). *Blended Learning: A Strategic Action Plan for a New Campus*. Seminole, FL: University of Central Florida.

Osguthorpe, R. T., & Graham, C. R. (2003). Blended learning systems: Definitions and directions. *Quarterly Review of Distance Education*, *4*(3), 227–234.

Picciano, A. G., & Dziuban, C. (Eds.). (2007). *Blended learning: Research perspectives*. Needham, MA: The Sloan Consortium.

Picciano, A. G., & Seaman, J. (2007). K–12 Online Learning: A Survey of US School District Administrators. *The Sloan Consortium. [Online]*http://www.sloan-c.org/publications/survey/K-12_06

Reay, J. (2001). Blended learning - a fusion for the future. *Knowledge Management Review*, *4*(3), 6.

Richardson, J. C., & Swan, K. (2003). Examining social presence in online courses in relation to students' perceived learning and satisfaction. *Journal of Asynchronous Learning Networks*, *7*(1), 68–88.

Rooney, J. E. (2003). Blending learning opportunities to enhance educational programming and meetings. *Association Management*, *55*(5), 26–32.

Rovai, A. (2002b). Sense of community, perceived cognitive learning, and persistence in asynchronous learning networks. *The Internet and Higher Education*, *5*(4), 319–332. doi:10.1016/S1096-7516(02)00130-6

Schutt, M., Allen, B. S., & Laumakis, M. A. (2009). The effects of instructor immediacy behaviors in online learning environments. *Quarterly Review of Distance Education*, *10*(2), 135–148.

Vaughan, N. D. (2010). A blended community of inquiry approach: Linking student engagement and course redesign. *The Internet and Higher Education*, *13*(1-2), 60–65. doi:10.1016/j.iheduc.2009.10.007

Waddoups, G., Hatch, G. L., & Butterworth, S. (2003). Blended teaching and learning in a first-year composition course. *Quarterly Review of Distance Education*, *4*(3), 271–278.

Waddoups, G., & Howell, S. (2002). Bringing online learning to campus: The hybridization of teaching and learning at Brigham Young University. *International Review of Research in Open and Distance Learning*, *2*(2).

Wade, W. (1994). Introduction. In Wade, W., Hodgkinson, K., Smith, A., & Arfield, J. (Eds.), *Flexible Learning in Higher Education* (pp. 12–16). London: Kogan Page Limited.

KEY TERMS AND DEFINITIONS

Asynchronous Video: Video communication that is distributed in time and space.

Blended Learning: Any community of learning that combines face-to-face instruction with computer-mediated instruction.

Hybrid Course: A course that combines face-to-face instruction and computer-mediated instruction – same as a blended learning course.

Immediacy: Verbal and nonverbal communication/behavior that facilitates a sense of closeness with another individual.

Media Richness: The level of fidelity a tool has to convey information.

Social Presence: The ability to convey oneself as an individual with emotions, feelings, and senses of humor.

VoiceThread: An online program designed to promote asynchronous discussion around media such as pictures and video.

Chapter 4
Blended Learning Revisited:
How it Brought Engagement and Interaction into and Beyond the Classroom

Pablo Ortega Gil
University of Alicante, Spain

Francisco Arcos García
University of Alicante, Spain

ABSTRACT

The universe of blended learning started uncertainly, as all new ventures, amid overt resistance of traditionalist teachers, but boosted by the drive of a few enthusiasts that wanted to bring novel perspectives into education. Everyday practice, together with the growing services it is rendering, has turned blended learning into the mainstay of education. The authors review some of the projects they have been carrying out in later years, all of them involving the use of Learning Management Systems for different target groups. They provide details about students' response, teachers' attitudes, and parents' opinions. They also show how their model has grown richer and richer thanks to the feedback obtained from all parts. Finally, future lines of development are suggested, among which mobile learning stands out. A recently launched mobile learning project is summarized.

INTRODUCTION

Although blended learning has already become a widespread practice in many primary and secondary schools, this chapter must necessarily begin by parsing, however clear it may look at first sight, what this phrase means and its many implications. Let's first scrutinize the phrase head, *learning*: we may agree that it refers to the process of acquiring knowledge and applying it in particular contexts in order to achieve certain results. As it is understood now, learning leads to the acquisition of competencies and must be continued beyond school years, because the constant updating of one's skills

DOI: 10.4018/978-1-60960-479-0.ch004

seems to be a requisite for keeping one's job. Traditionally, learning has been carried out in a classroom where students followed their teacher's explanations and instructions. But not any more: the teacher-centered approach just depicted has given way to more dialogical approaches where students take a leading role in the process and teachers tend to act more as facilitators or coaches than as didactic instructors (Adler, 1984; Wiggins & McTighe, 2007, 2008). Now it is in this new learning environment that we must look for the origin and motivation of the modifying element in the phase, the *blended*, which makes reference to the introduction of a new ICT component in teaching to supplement and enrich the in-person lessons. This computer-mediated component is carried out through a Learning Management System (henceforth LMS) that intends to multiply the students' learning opportunities and make the experience more efficient and dynamic.

If we now stop for a moment to consider the contrast between previous classrooms, in which silence and order were demanded, and nowadays classrooms, in which teamwork and controversies are encouraged, we will discover that it somehow resembles the tension between order and disorder, often described in sociology. According to Shotter (1997, p. 165), "many social theorists in the past have suggested that the provenance of order is to be found in disorder, on the edge of chaos, in spontaneity and playfulness". There is a powerful resonance in this quote, as if suggesting that unstructured activity may be the source of creativity. How these different variables interplay is not relevant here, although the interplay of different spheres is mentioned somewhere else by Shotter (p. 121), when he says that the "human world in which we live is best thought of as a whole 'multiverse' or 'social ecology', of unique but dynamically interdependent regions and moments of human communicative activity".

This is a very suggestive idea to us because it somehow captures our conception of learning not as a single channel conveying information from one end to the other, but —using the analogy— a multiverse of interaction and opportunities. The informed reader has probably realized that, in the first instance, teaching is represented as a simplification of Jakobson's diagram of language as communication (1960), where an addresser (the teacher) sends a message (the lesson) to an addressee (the student) in a context (the classroom) using a shared code. In striking contrast to that linear, quasi-univocal scheme, the learning multiverse we envision is built around blended learning and it offers:

- **New learning environments:** the classroom is no longer the sole "floor" for learning. The LMS lets students learn at their own home, at their peers' home, at the library, in a hotel room if they are on holiday, in a hospital room if they are ill, etc. Any given space can become a learning environment provided you have a laptop.
- **More windows of opportunity for learning:** traditionally, the 9 to 5 school time has set the limits of learning opportunities for most students. However, blended learning provides students with access to learning 24 hours a day, 365 days a year.
- **Less dependence on teachers:** once the LMS is functioning, students can learn on their own with little recourse to teachers, as activities usually enclose the necessary explanations, hint buttons and answer buttons.
- **A multiplicity of relations:** once the teacher recedes into the background and becomes a facilitator of content, a multiplicity of relations naturally appears among students. Cooperation is fostered; alliances are forged and shifted according to current needs; relevant information is shared using the forum or the chat… These are dynamics that greatly encourage teamwork.
- **Students take responsibility over their own assessment:** the LMS promotes self

and co-assessment through self-checked activities and the workshop. The latter is an option that automatically sends several essays to each student, who grades his/her peers' essays according to a rubric previously developed and agreed by the group. The fact that grades are not an exclusive prerogative of the teacher, as it used to be, makes the classroom less asymmetric and gives students responsibility over their own learning.
- **Reinforces effort and provides recognition:** following Marzano's proposals (2001), we believe that blended learning is a great way to teach the importance of effort and keep track of it, because students know that the more activities they do, the higher the grade they obtain. Likewise, the LMS feedback is devised to reinforce praise and attenuate criticism.

As we will later argue, blended learning is a versatile tool with which to address all sorts of problems, to analyze their nature and to treat them with greater depth and scope than other, more traditional approaches. Blended learning taps multiple resources in order to bridge the gulf between ordinary, everyday classrooms and the 21st century skills our children should acquire. But let us not dwell longer on such general observations and let state instead our purpose in this chapter, which is actually twofold: in the first place, to give a detailed account of how blended learning has been deployed in our courses. In the second place, to make some informed guesses about the route the latter may take in the near future. The first will be dealt with under the next heading.

BLENDED LEARNING EXAMPLES ON EDUCATION

For several years now, the two authors have worked respectively as an inspector of education and a language advisor. Very often, in meetings, workshops or even in informal conversations with teachers, we are asked baffling questions which usually stick to this formula: how would you solve this problem that remains unsolved so far? The ultimate basis of all the projects explained below must be sought precisely in those generic questions. We turned them in our minds until we reached the conclusion that, in order to answer them, we must resort to a system whose backbone is blended learning. Where some may be tempted to see similar answers to similar problems, we see a complex system in which each project has its individual traits, its own structure and focus, as we hope to prove in the coming pages. The answers and projects we have been mentioning have resulted in written papers on the use of blended learning for different target student groups: struggling students (Ortega & Arcos, 2009a), truants (2009e), youths at risk (2009b), special needs students (2009d), as well as for specific purposes, such as homework (2008) and digital storytelling (2009c). All of them are reciprocally related, refer to one another, and collectively coalesce into a unified conception: we are convinced that successful teaching in this digital age demands a new paradigm in the classrooms, a set of techniques and procedures focused on the student as the main actor of his or her own learning.

In what follows, we summarize three of the projects we have carried out in recent years: first, we talk about homework; next, we move on to struggling students, and we finally tackle the problem of truancy. In all of them, blended learning is the organizing principle.

E-Homework

At the beginning of the 2007 academic year, the principal of Poeta Pla y Beltran School, a primary school in the South-Eastern Spanish city of Ibi, came to us with a problem she didn't know how to handle: parents and teachers at her school had engaged in a bitter dispute about the amount and nature of homework. Everybody knows that, at present, homework is probably the most contentious topic in schools, judging from the media attention it receives; a topic where each involved sector shows its most confrontational side. In fact, homework is now the area where the tensions of the educative system seem to be staged. Let's see in a concrete instance how most parents feel about this issue and why they are enraged by what they consider excessive homework: most of them spend now more time working and commuting than ever before; the last thing they want after an exhausting day out is to find their children waiting for them at home because they couldn't do this task or just because they need some supervision. Add then that, for reasons difficult to pinpoint, the amount of homework has soared in the last 20 years, so much so that, according to Burby (2006), "a 2004 national survey of 2,900 American children conducted by the University of Michigan found that time spent on homework is up 51 percent since 1981" (p. 1). Consider now the teachers' plights: they often complain they have to cover larger curricula than ever, are forced to deal with greater differences in learning styles, as well as with racial and ethnic differences within their classrooms.

After interviews with teachers and parents, we advised the principal that she should use blended learning to solve the conflict at her school (Ortega & Arcos, 2008): the in-person lessons would go on as usual and the computer-mediated component would be exclusively devoted to homework. But that required a previous consensus on the meaning and sense of homework, consensus for which we drafted the following guidelines:

- Homework must move along a progressive gradient, from very little to just enough.
- It is not the parents' responsibility to help their children do homework or supervise what they do. Parents must check that their children did the tasks they had to by the end of the week.
- Every homework task must be related to classroom instruction and must be self-standing; that is, understood in itself or, if necessary, must come with enclosed explanations and examples.
- Every homework task must be meaningful and relevant, instead of mechanical and tiresome. It must begin with a clear model of what is expected and must subsequently provide feedback.

Once the different stakeholders had agreed on the above guidelines, we helped the school design, establish and manage their own LMS (using Moodle) focused on e-homework. Initially we chose the fifth grade, 49 children between 10 and 11 years old, divided into two groups. As a point of departure, we suggested that all the students should be initially assessed so that homework could be customized. Note how revolutionary this was, because it meant a move from "everybody gets the same" to "everybody gets what he/she needs", a basic principle of differentiated instruction. As the LMS included a wide range of tasks, each student could have a task suited to his/her abilities, which in the end brought about major improvements in the work of students with learning difficulties. The latter were also helped by what we called 'time frame', an estimate of the time needed to complete a task based on similar activities previously tested in other schools. We all know that some children find it very difficult to work on their own because they cannot focus their attention and tend to daydream or are lost in reveries. We thought that attaching a time frame to every task would help them, as if it were a point of reference against which to measure their performance. The time frame was slack enough to accommodate the slowest students, but even so, we allowed for commentaries: if someone thought that the time frame was miscalculated, he or she could send a commentary explaining his or her own experience.

It was also essential for us to underlie the value of completed homework, shifting the emphasis from what the school used to do (punishment or coercive measures) to what we believed the school should do (recognizing effort and providing recognition after achievement). To attain this goal, we modified certain deeply rooted routines that, in our view, were counterproductive. First, instead of giving homework on a daily basis, it was given on a weekly basis; that implied greater autonomy for children, but also greater responsibility, because little work along the week may result in a very busy weekend. Second, as explained above, every task included a model to refer to, as well as a clear explanation of its purpose. Finally, as the tasks are self-check, all children could retake the exercise if they had not done well the first time. In case of doubt, the hint option provided a clue to the right answer.

Results so far have proved that the number of students who don't complete homework is much lower now (6 out of 49, a bit above 12%) than it used to be (12 out of 49, which is more than 24%). We are coming up with new ideas to reach out to the six reluctant children, although we are conscious that this may be difficult as they belong to broken or very disadvantaged families. It may also be worth mentioning that a small number of teachers showed great reluctance at the beginning of the project because, no doubt, blended learning requires a great investment of time and effort at the beginning, although it pays back gradually and, eventually, becomes a time-saver. It wouldn't be honest to say that we won the adherence of all the teachers —there are still a few who favour old-style homework—but most of them are glad they followed us and show willingness to go ahead on their own in a near future.

Struggling Students

Our second blended learning project was focused on struggling students (2009a); that is, those students who do not perform well at school as a consequence of one or more disadvantages. The project was carried out at Lloixa Secondary School, located in the Spanish city of Alicante, and it involved a cross section of 40 struggling students aged between 12 and 15. They were being given remedial instruction in small pullout groups, but this strategy was offering very poor results. Out of frustration with ineffective measures, the principal asked for help in organizing an LMS especially devised for struggling students. To assess the real impact of blended learning for target groups, we proposed carrying out a survey along the following lines: the original cross-section group would be divided into two subgroups made up of twenty randomly-chosen students each. Subgroup A would work with our LMS for six months, whereas subgroup B would receive remedial instruction as described above. After the six-month period, progress of both subgroups would be gauged and compared according to a pre-established template. It was agreed that, if successful, the same approach would be extended to all struggling students in subsequent years.

But before we go any further, we must explain the principles behind our LMS in order to understand the different choices we made. We devised tasks to be meaningful, contextualized and related to everyday tasks. We also paid special attention to the development of key competencies; those that will help students succeed in their own lives. If a student attains the key competencies at school, his/her possibilities of success in later life are greatly increased. This is often referred to as transfer, which is very important for all students—and more so for those who don't perform well at school. Transfer ensures that things learned at school can be used beyond school walls in later years. This concept raises key questions, but here we merely need to emphasize that it was taken into account when designing the tasks. Even more fundamental in this design were some principles of differentiated instruction, as enumerated by Wormelli (2006): treating academic struggle as strength, providing opportunities for self-definition and creative expression, allowing multiple pathways to achieve success, and giving formative feedback.

Let's give some specific examples of how our LMS gave expression to the just-mentioned principles:

Treating academic struggle as strength: Struggling students need to try once and again to attain a goal. Consequently, the tasks in our LMS can be retaken, which allows students to learn from their mistakes and keep working until they are satisfied with the grade obtained in the task. To ease the process, every task includes the hint option, which can be used to overcome those moments where one cannot go further. If clicked, the hint button will give a clue to the answer. On the other hand, the solution of a problem sometimes depends on cooperation. The LMS allow students to work cooperatively through the discussion forum, where questions can be asked and opinions shared. Finally, if needed, students can also send a question to their teachers using the e-mail option. It may be interesting to point out here that the average answer time for teachers along the six-period project was 14 hours. An answer in 14 hours from your teacher is, no doubt, faster than waiting for the next class, which is often two days away. In the end, treating academic struggle as strength teaches students that difficulties demand the best of us and that, when faced with a problem, we try by ourselves, we ask for help, we try again, but we never give in.

Providing opportunities for self-definition and creative expression: Struggling students have, in general, low self-confidence and self-esteem. We asked ourselves how we could boost and reinforce these human dimensions. Maybe if struggling students were given the opportunity of telling others about their passions and interests, they may feel more confident. That's why we incorporated digital storytelling into our LMS. There are several authoring tools for digital storytelling: all of them combine images, music and voice to tell a story. Soon we discovered that the students' stories were disparate, with little or nothing in common. So we devised a rubric to streamline their stories. Once finished, the stories were uploaded to the LMS and, through the workshop activity, the system automatically sent two or three stories to each student so that they could grade them according to the just-mentioned rubric. Apart from providing opportunities for self-expression and reinforcing self-confidence, digital storytelling had an unexpected advantage: it transformed a task they hated (writing essays) into a favorite, a container where they could pack the music they loved, the images they had taken and the stories they wanted to tell.

Allowing multiple pathways to achieve success: When one works with struggling student, one soon discovers that they show some reluctance, when not overt resistance, to the beaten track, an image by which we refer to the mainstream instruction in which they have been lagging behind others for years. For that reason, our LMS lets students customize their own learning routes thanks to its adaptive dimension. How is this carried out? All tasks have an index of difficulty and are connected to related tasks higher or lower in the difficulty scale. Thus, learning becomes a process of discovery, in which students can freely move up and down the scale, although there is greater recognition in going up than in going down. In summary, to attain a general goal, students can choose multiple routes: it is assumed that they choose the one that best suits their interests and skills.

Giving formative feedback: Every LMS provides constant feedback intended to help students along the learning process. Following the recommendations of Vovides, we included stop and think triggers to encourage students (Vovides et al., 2007, p. 71) "to interact with the e-learning course content. These triggers can be implemented as 'feedback loops' to help learners toggle and adapt their cognitive strategies as they learn new content". Feedback loops send students to tasks we believe may reinforce their learning and, in the last instance, help them move up to high-complexity tasks. They also encourage students to share responsibility for their own learning, as they are forced to make decisions on their route to learning.

Let us now share some of the data obtained at the end of the six-month period. The information in the templates proved that students in subgroup A had learned faster and deeper than those in subgroup B. Keep in mind that subgroup A worked with the LMS and subgroup B worked in pullout groups. According to the teachers in charge of the project, the first subgroup was more involved, more cooperative and more motivated than the second one. They also agreed that establishing an LMS for all struggling students was a "must" for subsequent years because, although it had initially been time consuming, it had eventually become a highly rewarding initiative. The nature and depth of the contrast between the two groups can be quickly inferred from the following diagram, which uses bars to show the performance of each group in the subsequent units of the course.

LEVELS IN ACTIVITY INVOLVEMENT AND RESULTS

It can clearly be seen from the diagram above that Group A boosted right from Unit 4 onwards, and progressed steadily to reach figures nearing excellent levels. Conversely, Group B continued the same dull attitude, which suggests lack of involvement and enthusiasm. Results in tests were very similar: 88% of the students in Group A passed and some of them with good marks whereas only 40% of Group B managed to succeed. In consequence, the school decided to offer the LMS to all struggling students the next year. (Figure 1)

We also got positive feedback from the students, many of whom said that they had loved personalising their learning route and had found that some of the tasks were really challenging and engaging, in contrast to remedial lessons. Digital storytelling was undoubtedly their favourite: not only did they tell a story but then they also had their peers' response, which greatly encouraged their self-esteem.

The Use of Blended Learning to Keep Truants in the Classroom

Unauthorized absence from school or truancy is arguably one of the most serious problems in many Western countries, although few—if any—offer reliable information. According to the British press, (Shepherd, 2008) "the government calcu-

Figure 1. Results from test and homework completion

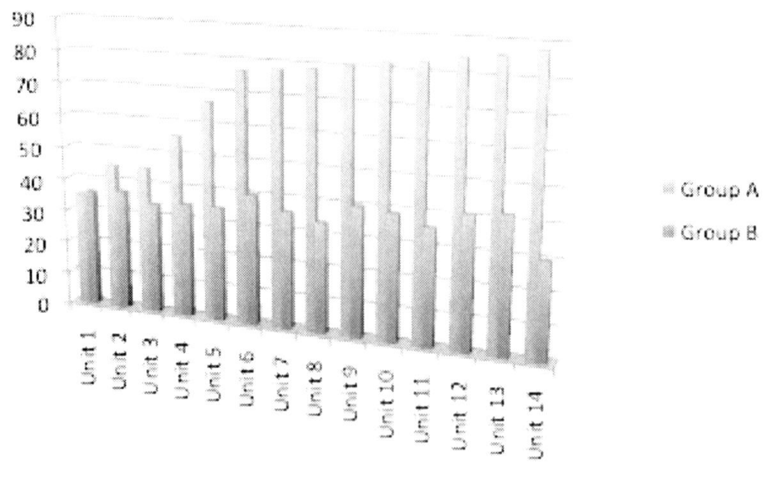

lates absence and truancy rates by the number of half-days of school missed. In the autumn term of 2008 and the spring term of this year [2009], pupils in state primary and secondary schools missed 1.03% of possible half-days without a teacher's permission." This is a rather opaque statement, although the same article states truancy is on the rise. Some months earlier, the BBC (18 June 2009) gave more precise information: the absence rate for primary and secondary schools rose from 6.26% in autumn 2007 to 6.42% last autumn. In Spain, truancy figures are often at the centre of a very hot controversy, with critics estimating them over 10% and government officials reducing it to between 4% and 5%.

The attempt is made again and again to make socio-economic conditions the exclusive explanation of truancy. And the truth is that students from certain social groups (mainly from immigrant or disadvantaged families) tend to become truants, sometimes at a very early age, for a wide variety of reasons among which Reid (2008) stressed the following: disaffection, lack of vocational courses, learning difficulties, self-fulfilling prophecies, low self-concepts, some parental collusion, and what he calls disenfranchisement (now that schools are being assessed and in some countries even rated, low achievers are not desirable for schools). What intrigues us about this problem, which we have tried to recapitulate in brief, is not that some students become truants but that, after being traced, found and asked to return to school, they rarely stay there more than a couple of months. This is what in our opinion weakens the socioeconomic explanation, the fact that schools find nothing that is appealing to these students, because it is not only that certain students are marked out from their very entrance into the education system, but also that some schools show little or no interest in keeping them inside.

There is no point in denying that efforts are made to fight against truancy, and that those efforts come from all quarters: local, regional and national authorities propose and implement new expensive programs every year to reduce truancy, but they seem to reap little or no success. Said in a nutshell, these programs intend to find truants and bring them back into the classroom. But, once back, they are offered exactly the same kind of teaching which in the first place originated their truancy: passive lessons which are far above their current academic competence. In our view, this recurrent practice is essentially wrong because it doesn't go to the root of the problem: the system must adapt itself to truants, and not the other way round. To break the vicious circle of truants relapsing into truancy after several weeks, we must reward them with proper incentives. For instance, more interactive formulas must be put into practice; and blended learning is probably the most optimized tool today.

When we were asked for advice (2009e) by the education department in the city of Alicante, where truancy was apparently rampant (close to ten per cent) on the two previous academic years—2006-2007 and 2007-2008—our answer was blended learning. At that point, we immediately thought that we needed to create a buffer period, a segment of several months that would allow truants to progressively accommodate to the school routine. Obviously, that could not be done without altering the average schedule, which for the rest of secondary students takes from 30 to 32 lessons a week. Let's refer to truants brought back into the system as 'interim truants' while they are along the buffer period. We suggested a 25-lesson week for interim truants, during which they would share some lessons of a practical nature with their age group (say music, sports, technology, arts, etc.) and would work on the hard-core subjects (Math, Spanish, History, Science, etc.) through an LMS in a small pullout group. The balance we sought to strike involves an effort to keep truants in classroom and the need to teach them useful things with a value beyond school walls. To that end, we believe that an LMS (in our case, Moodle) can encompass both the aims teachers pursue and the motivation truant students need to keep coming to school. With that purpose in mind, we devised tasks that were less boring, more engaging, more motivating, and often more demanding than traditional tasks, to which interim truants showed extreme reluctance. But we didn't stop there; we wanted the tasks to have a strong bias towards transfer so that whatever interim truants may learn could be useful to them beyond school walls in later years. And thanks to the adaptive nature of every LMS, we managed to customize the learning program of every interim truant according to his or her specific needs.

The result of this project will be better understood if we provide some figures: initially, the small pullout group was made up of 15 interim truants aged between 14 and 16. Although they had been originally in different schools across the city, we thought that concentrating them in one single school for the buffer period was a good option because of several reasons: it was easier to find funding for one school than for three or four; and, secondly, we chose the school with the higher number of teachers who volunteered to work with interim truants. Along the buffer period, which lasted four months, only two out of the 15 students reverted to truancy. Both teachers and interim truants praised the LMS and expressed their desire to keep working with it in the future. No such good news ensued after the end of the buffer period, when each of the 13 remaining interim truants was sent back to their original schools and to the normal 32-lesson schedule. Four of them left after two weeks, three more after a month, and of the other six, only three stayed in school until the end of the academic year. This uninviting fact takes us to a dilemma: shall we offer truants a modified curriculum to keep them in the classrooms? Or shall we keep losing students to truancy because of a curriculum which some of them cannot possibly or are not willing to follow?

FURTHER STEPS: FROM BLENDED TO MOBILE LEARNING

From its commencement, blended learning has always been fueled by the energy of a very challenging goal, which was to build up a new teaching paradigm based not only on the exploration of new teaching possibilities, but most especially on the search for the learner's interaction combined with the focus on transfer. It may probably be well said that one of the most outstanding features of blending learning is technological innovation, which is bringing improvements to this field at an ever-increasing pace.

From our own perspective, and after having been decidedly promoting blended learning for some years, the emergence of mobile learning is challenging us to keep moving ahead. Last year, we decided to implement m-learning in several English Language courses we teach at the University of Alicante, aimed at improving pronunciation and general language skills. Our students were all used to working with an LMS, but to go into this new project, they were asked to install the Mobile Learning Engine (henceforth MLE) client on their mobile phones or PDAs (henceforth mobile devices). The MLE grants them access to some of the learning activities and resources in our LMS from a mobile device. Keep in mind that we do not want to reinvent blended learning, but to supplement the present LMS with new possibilities and greater interactivity. This will undoubtedly benefit our students by providing immediate feedback and new ways of learning. Just before we go any further, let us assure that, for any student familiar with an LMS, MLE is quite user-friendly: when you open the MLE, the appearance is almost identical to the LMS, although not all the options are at the moment available, some simply because they are not well suited for this medium (i.e. units of learning made up of many different activities). Eventually, more and more possibilities will become available through the students' mobile devices. At the moment, the following ones are active:

A message-delivery system that provides a layout of every face-to-face lesson and links each item in the lesson with an activity in the LMS. It is a fact that some university students cannot come regularly to in-person lessons for many reasons, most frequent among which are work and courses abroad. For these, as well as for those temporarily ill, this message-delivery system was a suitable measure: it gave them a record of all the topics reviewed in class and it encouraged them to keep up in their LMS commitments, instead of lagging behind and leaving everything for the end of the term.

Free logging to the University Wi-Fi. Internet access from a mobile device is not free: you have to pay for the service to a company. Therefore, using a MLE for learning may result in unexpected expenses for students. However, within the premises of the University of Alicante, students can log in to the University Wi-Fi, a service that is completely free. We encourage our students to make use of this service to prevent them from incurring in any unnecessary expenses. Alternatively, you can access the Internet via Bluetooth4 or Wi-Fi5, provided that your device supports any of them. In this case it is possible to run the MLE client without actually having a SIM card in the device, using it as a plain data terminal without the ability to make device calls or write text messages.

Distant training in phonology. The use of IPA symbols to make phonological transcriptions is probably one of the hardest tasks for students of English, but it eventually turns out into a fruitful accomplishment. In training our students to improve their IPA skills, we use the Flashcard Trainer and the Virtual Keyboard. The Flashcard Trainer offers the student a card with a front and a rear view. On the front they find the phonological transcription of an English word, and the point of the exercise is that they have to predict the spelling they will find on the rear. They make their guess before turning the card, and the result is recorded. Likewise, every day we send the spelling of a word to our students and they are required to send back the phonological transcription using the virtual keyboard. To provide this activity with an added value, we tell our students in advance that some of the words they transcribe over the semester will be included in the written exam.

Digital storytelling through their mobile devices. We already explained above why we chose storytelling and how we exploit this activity. In this particular case, after students have created their own stories and uploaded them to the LMS, the "workshop" activity automatically delivers as many files as the teacher/instructor has programmed, to each student for revision and grading. This is a highly structured process which sticks to the following steps: the student needs first to open the workshop activity, where he/she can read a storytelling model provided by us, attached to which he/she finds a rubric. The rubric offers directions on how to create a story and on how to value each of its traits. Ours is shown in Table 1.

Following the rubric, the student grades the model storytelling. Then, he/she writes the script of his/her story in a pop-up box and attaches his/her own digital storytelling. This is a sort of podcasting: the system then delivers the story to other students' mobile devices so that they have a chance of watching the stories wherever they are and whenever they please. Every student may receive an average of three stories, which have to be marked the same way as the lecturer's model. In the end, everyone gets a mark that is a composite of the marks given to him or her by several of their peers and by the lecturer, who has access to all the stories.

So far, the use of MLE has fulfilled our expectations. Among other things, both the text messaging system and mobile storytelling are greatly attuned to the students' way of communicating among themselves. Then, the use of rubrics for assessment guarantees objectivity as everybody knows beforehand what is expected and on which

Table 1. Stories are graded and created in accordance with this rubric

CATEGORY	4	3	2	1
Point of View - Purpose	Establishes a purpose early on and maintains a clear focus throughout.	Establishes a purpose early on and maintains focus for most of the presentation.	There are a few lapses in focus, but the purpose is fairly clear.	It is difficult to figure out the purpose of the presentation.
Voice - Consistency	Voice quality is clear and consistently audible throughout the presentation.	Voice quality is clear and consistently audible throughout the majority (85-95%) of the presentation.	Voice quality is clear and consistently audible through some (70-84%)of the presentation.	Voice quality needs more attention.
Voice - Pacing	The pace (rhythm and voice punctuation) fits the story line and helps the audience really "get into" the story.	Occasionally speaks too fast or too slowly for the story line. The pacing (rhythm and voice punctuation) is relatively engaging for the audience.	Tries to use pacing (rhythm and voice punctuation), but it is often noticeable that the pacing does not fit the story line. Audience is not consistently engaged.	No attempt to match the pace of the storytelling to the story line or the audience.
Soundtrack - Emotion	Music stirs a rich emotional response that matches the story line well.	Music stirs a rich emotional response that somewhat matches the story line.	Music is ok, and not distracting, but it does not add much to the story.	Music is distracting, inappropriate, OR was not used.
Images	Images create a distinct atmosphere or tone that matches different parts of the story. The images may communicate symbolism and/or metaphors.	Images create an atmosphere or tone that matches some parts of the story. The images may communicate symbolism and/or metaphors.	An attempt was made to use images to create an atmosphere/tone but it needed more work. Image choice is logical.	Little or no attempt to use images to create an appropriate atmosphere/tone.
Content	All content is in the students' own words and is accurate.	Almost all content is in the students' own words and is accurate.	At least half of the content is in the students' own words and is accurate.	Less than half of the content is in the students' own words and/or is accurate.
Clarity and Neatness	Storyboard is easy to read and all elements are so clearly written, labelled, or drawn that another student could create the presentation if necessary.	Storyboard is easy to read and most elements are clearly written, labelled, or drawn. Another person might be able to create the presentation after asking one or two questions.	Storyboard is hard to read with rough drawings and labels. It would be hard for another person to create this presentation without asking lots of questions.	Storyboard is hard to read and one cannot tell what goes where. It would be impossible for another person to create this presentation without asking lots of questions.
Spelling & Grammar	No spelling or grammatical mistakes on a storyboard with lots of text.	No spelling or grammatical mistakes on a storyboard with little text.	One spelling or grammatical error on the storyboard	Several spelling and/or grammatical errors on the storyboard.

continued on following page

Table 1.continued

CATEGORY	4	3	2	1
Cooperation	Worked cooperatively with partner all the time with no need for adult intervention.	Worked cooperatively with partner most of time but had a few problems that the team resolved themselves.	Worked cooperatively with partner most of the time, but had one problem that required adult intervention.	Worked cooperatively with partners some of the time, but had several problems that required adult intervention.
Required Elements	Storyboard included all required elements as well as a few additional elements.	Storyboard included all required elements and one additional element.	Storyboard included all required elements.	One or more required elements was missing from the storyboard.

aspects attention will be focused. We often remind our students that the emphasis must be placed on the correct use of the language rather than on other aesthetic aspects. The rubric also promotes co-assessment, which gives students responsibility over their peers' grades and promotes reflection on the learning process. To some, it may be surprising to discover that, above all, students value this new sense of freedom MLE provides, where the public and private spheres of their lives merge and allow for learning to be done in unexpected ways.

CONCLUSION

The universe of blended learning started uncertainly, as all new ventures, amid overt resistance of traditionalist teachers, but boosted by the drive of a few enthusiasts that wanted to bring novel perspectives into education. All along this chapter, we have furnished many possible applications of blended learning with a view to hint at its future promise; we have also tried to prove that it is one —among several— way of evading the pitfalls into which traditional classroom practice is ever lapsing, most importantly lack of motivation for students, compliancy to teacher-dictated rules, no due attention to diversity, etc. As Prensky claimed in one of his articles (2001, p. 1) "our students have changed radically. Today's students are no longer the people our educational system was designed to teach." And yet we could provide many different examples of how traditional practices are perpetuated in young teachers, simply because many of them tend to imitate other more experienced teachers, often without questioning whether those practices are still effective. In striking contrast to that unmediated imitation, Harrison and Killion (2008) list and elucidate ten roles of teacher leaders. We quote them here because, in our opinion, they connect naturally with blended learning: resource provider, instructional specialist, curriculum specialist, classroom supporter, learning facilitator, mentor, school leader, data coach, catalyst for change, and learner. These roles draw a sharp distinction between the old style teaching and teachers using state-of-the-art technology, all of whom must strive to transform their students into active learners. That transformation brings about clear consequences (Zmuda, 2008): learning becomes messy and noisy as a consequence of teamwork, scores favors thinking over repeating, students get constant and constructive feedback, and they are given time to think things out by themselves. We could not have imagined a better summary of what students find in blended learning. In the same measure in which the LMS widens the field of learning and increases the gamut of activities, opening the classroom to technology, its users undergo a progressive transformation from passive into active learners.

It may be very fitting to end this chapter sharing with the readers the many lessons we have learned from our different projects. With time, we have managed to streamline our LMSs, but it goes without saying that this was not 'success at first try', but the result of constant tinkering and toggling with the LMS. Here are some examples which may be instructive to others because they reflect the slow and stepwise transformation of weak points into strong points:

Layout: It comes almost naturally to quickly upload to your LMS all the tasks that have even the slightest intersection with the topic you are dealing with. After all, it takes time to think and develop a new task, so when you find a finished one in your computer, your first temptation is to make use of it. Resist the temptation or, else, you will soon realize that your LMS has become a hodgepodge where even you have trouble in ascertaining some ordering principle. This is counterproductive, as students are usually on their own when working with the LMS and the last thing you want is an intimidating layout that scares them away. Imagine a book index, and try to build your course so that anyone, even a guest, can easily find his/her way around.

Relevance: As a consequence of what we have just stated, imposing a logical order in your LMS will certainly imply removing many tasks. You will be surprised to discover that you had no definite criteria to choose the tasks, or —at best— that the criteria was non-strict. Keep in mind that the greater the relevance of the task, the easier it is for your students to learn from it.

Differentiated instruction: Once you have fine-tuned the relevance question, don't forget to scaffold each task into three or four levels of difficulty so that your LMS caters for diversity. This can be easily done by adding or deleting complex structures. If the task was created with an authoring tool such as Hot Potatoes, go to the options menu and select

Configure output: This will allow you to modify the exercise appearance or to shuffle the order of questions and answers. Blended learning is especially efficient in dealing with differentiated instruction so don't underuse this advantage.

Evaluation: If we had to pinpoint which element has best contributed to improve our LMSs, we would go without any hesitation for the students' opinion. From the very beginning, we kept an open forum where they voiced their opinions. When they said that an exercise was not working or seemed irrelevant, we immediately acted upon. If they said that assessment was unfair, too strict, or disproportional to the effort the task demanded, we immediately acted upon. Their introspections have always been the major source of improvement for the LMS as it has helped us in quickly identifying its weak and strong points.

Align the LMS for success: As you may infer from the previous point, an LMS is not the work of one day. For instance, you don't create an LMS during a summer holiday and then live on the initial effort all the year long. The LMS demands constant adjustment if you want to align it for success.

The foregoing considerations have shown how blended learning can be applied to different purposes, all of them obviously interwoven, and how each of these applications make their individual contribution to a more interactive and creative learning process. Along the later years, blended learning has gradually waxed great and has overpowered a lot of resistance from traditional teaching. The years ahead will certainly see even more astonishing accomplishments from blended learning.

REFERENCES

Adler, M. (1984). *The Paideia program: An educational syllabus*. New York, NY: MacMillan.

Arcos, F., Amilburu, A., & Ortega, P. (2008). *The language blend*. INTED2008. International Technology, Education and Development Conference, (pp. 1-10).

Black, S. (1996). The truth about homework. *The American School Board Journal, 183*(10), 48–51.

Burby, L. (2006, September 17). The great homework debate. *Newsday*.

Harrison, C., & Killion, J. (2008). Ten roles for teacher leaders. *Educational Leadership, 65*(1), 74–77.

Jakobson, R. (1960). Concluding statements: Linguistics and poetics. In Sebeok, T. A. (Ed.), *Style in language*. Cambridge, MA: MIT Press.

Marzano, R. J., Pickering, D. J., & Pollock, J. E. (2001). *Classroom instruction that works*. Alexandria, VA: Association for Supervision and Curriculum Development.

Ortega, P., & Arcos, F. (2008). *How e-homework can solve the homework debate in primary schools*. ENMA2008. International Conference on Engineering and Mathematics. pp. 5-10. Bilbao, Spain: Kopiak.

Ortega, P., & Arcos, F. (2009a). *How can Moodle help struggling students?* EDULEARN2009. International Conference on Education and New Learning Technologies, (pp. 2337-2340).

Ortega, P., & Arcos, F. (2009b). *Blended learning: An efficient response to some of the problems raised by youths at risk*. INTED2009. International Technology, Education and Development Conference, (pp. 637-642).

Ortega, P., & Arcos, F. (2009c). *CLIL enhanced through digital storytelling*. ENMA2009. International Conference on Engineering and Mathematics. (pp. 228-231). Bilbao, Spain: Kopiak.

Ortega, P., & Arcos, F. (2009d). *Moodle applied within a special needs classroom*. IASE 2009, 11th Biennial Conference. (pp. 204-207).

Ortega, P., & Arcos, F. (2009e). Zeroing in on truancy: The use of blended learning to keep truants in the classroom. *IATED, 2009*, 288–291.

Prensky, M. (2001). Digital natives, digital immigrants. *On the Horizon, 9*(5). NCB University Press.

Prensky, M. (2008). Turning on the lights. *Educational Leadership, 65*(6), 40–45.

Reid, K. (2008). The causes of non-attendance: An empirical study. *Educational Review, 60*(4), 345–357. doi:10.1080/00131910802393381

Resnick, M. (2002). Rethinking learning in the digital age. In Kirkman, G. (Ed.), *The global Information Technology report: Readiness for the networked world*. Oxford University Press.

Shepherd, J. (2009, October 20). Truancy rates on the rise. *The Guardian*.

Shotter, J. (1993). *Conversational realities: Constructing life through language*. London, UK: Sage.

Tsou, W., Wang, W., & Tzeng, Y. (2006). Applying a multimedia storytelling website in foreign language learning. *Computers & Education, 47*, 17–28. doi:10.1016/j.compedu.2004.08.013

Vovides, Y., Sanchez-Alonso, S., Mitropoulou, V., & Nickmans, G. (2007). The use of e-learning course management systems to support learning strategies and to improve self-regulated learning. *Educational Research Review, 2*, 64–74. doi:10.1016/j.edurev.2007.02.004

Wiggins, G., & McTighe, J. (2007). *Schooling by design*. Alexandria, VA: ASCD.

Wiggins, G., & McTighe, J. (2008). Put understanding first. *Educational Leadership, 65*(8), 36–41.

Wormelli, R. (2006). Differentiating for tweens. *Educational Leadership, 63*(7), 14–19.

ADDITIONAL READING

Andrade, H., & Du, Y. (2005). Student perspectives on rubric-referenced assessment. *Practical Assessment Research & Evaluation, 10*(3), 1–11.

Arcos, F., & Ortega, P. (2009). Adaptive Blended Learning: A literature of assets. In Lazinica, A., & Calafate, C. (Eds.), *Technology, Education and Development. Vokovar: In-Teh* (pp. 247–264).

Aveling, N. (2001). 'Where Do You Come from?': critical storytelling as a teaching strategy within the context of teacher education. *Discourse: studies in the cultural politics of education*, 22, 1, 35-48.

Masie, E. (2002). Blended Learning: The Magic Is in the Mix. In *A. Rossett, The ASTD E-Learning Handbook* (pp. 60–65). New York: McGraw-Hill.

Mink, L. O. (1978). Narrative form as a cognitive instrument. In Canary, R. H., & Kozicki, H. (Eds.), *The Writing of History: Literary Form and Historical Understanding*. Wisconsin: University of Wisconsin Press.

Simkins, M. (2000). 'Developing and Implementing a Rubric for Assessing Student Multimedia Projects'. Presented at the Annual Meeting of the American Educational Research Association, *Creating Knowledge in the 21st Century: Insights From Multiple Perspectives*. April. New Orleans, Louisiana.

Singh, H. (2003), Building Effective Blended Learning Programs. November - December *Issue of Educational Technology*, Volume 43, Number 6, Pages 51-54.

Thorne, K. (2003). *Blended Learning: How To Integrate Online and Traditional Learning*. London: Kogan Page Limited.

Valiathan, P. (2002). "Blended Learning Models." Learning Circuits. www.learningcircuits.org/2002/aug2002/valiathan.html

William, H. R. (2007). *Moodle Teaching Techniques*. Birmingham: Packt Publishing.

Zhang, D., J. Zhao, L. Zhou and J. Numamaker. (2004). Can e-learning replace classroom learning? *Communication of the ACM, 47*(5), 75–78, 2006.

KEY TERMS AND DEFINITIONS

Blended Learning: A mixture or blend of face-to-face lessons and distance learning, the latter most usually through a LMS.

Digital Storytelling: A new way of telling stories through a combination of music, images and voice.

E-Homework: Homework given through a LMS, and which consequently is available 24/7. The homework tasks can be done when the students feels more creative or enthusiastic.

Leaning Management System (LMS): A system that allows teachers to run online courses.

Mobile Learning: Learning which can be achieved anywhere, provided the location has internet access, often through mobile devices.

Modular Object-Oriented Dynamic Learning Environment(MOODLE): One among the many possible LMSs.

Struggling Students: Students who do not perform well at school as a consequence of one or more disadvantages.

Truants: Students who do not come to school because of a variety of reasons: disaffection, lack of vocational courses, learning difficulties, self-fulfilling prophecies, low self-concepts, some parental collusion, etc.

Section 2
Practising Blended Learning

Chapter 5
Blended Learning Examples in Education and Chemistry

Robert Hogan
University of the South Pacific, Fiji

ABSTRACT

The blended revolution that has empowered students in developing nations is just now spreading to developing countries. With improved Internet access, students in these regions now have opportunities to experience blended and mobile learning, creating new markets in Asia, Africa, and the Pacific for universities that offer blended programs. Unlike the e-learning revolution of the 90s that was dominated by for-profit institutions, public universities will be major competitors for international students wishing to earn foreign degrees. The Asian Development Bank report (2008) emphasizes that it is essential for economic development to provide increased numbers of skilled workers. Blended and mobile learning can assist countries with increased educational access and online providers opportunities to reach new international markets. Another emerging market for blended and mobile learning in developing countries is the untrained teacher. Until recently, adequate Internet access was not available to some regions most needing increased educational access. Now, the technology is falling into place to support blended and mobile learning. This chapter discusses two international blended and mobile learning courses—an undergraduate chemistry course and a graduate education course for teachers in online learning—being delivered to developing countries in the Pacific. The chapter focuses on instructional design, cultural considerations, technical issues, and initial findings.

INTRODUCTION

Technology has fueled the distance-learning evolution from correspondence courses, to radio and TV, to videoconferencing, to online, and now to blended and mobile learning. With each advance, the quality of distance learning has improved. Correspondence courses, televised courses, and radio delivery, once popular, increasingly are giv-

DOI: 10.4018/978-1-60960-479-0.ch005

ing way to online delivery. In the 1990s, online learning epitomized *distance learning*. With recent advance in educational technology, the level of interaction between students and the instructor in online courses now approaches that available to students in face-to-face classes. Progressing from email exchanges and web posting, today's online students can expect close interaction with instructors and classmates, prompt feedback, and a variety of online student services. Recent online advances have added audio and video communication, blogs, wiki's, and mobile access to the online mix. Whereas early distance learning distanced the instructor and student, blended learning and mobile learning can provide a level of teacher/student interaction approaching face-to-face learning. When students at a distance can see and talk with their instructors and classmates throughout the week, the *distance* in distance learning may disappear. For the new learner, large lecture classes may be the new distance learning.

The growth of online learning is the educational phenomenon of the twenty first century. According to Picciano and Seaman (2007), three million university students, and more than one million K-12 students were taking online courses in 2007—a 47 percent increase in just two years. Nevertheless, according to Adams (2008), some universities and businesses continue to prefer traditional degrees because online learning lacks face-to-face training and mentoring. Wang (2009) noted a similar resistance in the academic community to introduce online chemistry because it is recognized that personal interaction and laboratory activities are essential parts of the chemistry experience. With the marrying of online and face-to-face classes, blended learning can address this issue.

This chapter discusses two blended and mobile learning courses. The first, *Foundations Chemistry I*, is a freshman inorganic chemistry course. The second, *Online Methods of Instruction*, is a graduate education course for teachers. Both courses are available in the Cook Islands, Kiribati, the Marshall Islands, Nauru, Niue, Samoa, Solomon Islands, Tokelau, Tuvalu, Tonga, Tuvalu, and Vanuatu. The education course also crosses the Equator, being taught throughout Micronesia.

The courses, which are approximately 80% online, incorporate a course management system (CMS), simulations, wikis, blogs, Skype, REACT, Nicenet, Facebook, You Tube, and Twitter. The face-to-face components consist of laboratories for the chemistry course, and training seminars for the education course. The instructional design for both courses is based upon the work of B.F. Skinner (operant conditioning) and Malcolm Knowles (1984). As such, the courses include weekly assessment and feedback, discussions, individual activities, and team projects. The instructional approach, which adapts many of the successful methods championed by the University of Phoenix, is designed to reduce stress, develop time management skills, and promote student engagement—all important factors in promoting student success and reducing attrition. The technology and instructional methods are described in the following sections.

Both courses were designed for low-bandwidth environments because several regional countries continue to have limited bandwidth and many students have slow home Internet connections. The chapter concludes with a discussion of future directions in blended and mobile learning.

DEFINITIONS OF BLENDED AND MOBILE LEARNING

The term *blended learning* in this chapter refers to courses delivered with a mix of online and face-to-face sessions. Approximately 80% of the two courses described in this chapter were delivered online. This proportion best met the needs of the students for ease of access and the university for cost of delivery. The term *online*, which is used interchangeably with *eLearning*, refers to a highly interactive, *student-centered learning*, method that uses both synchronous and asynchronous learning to actively engage students, allowing them to take more responsibility for their learning. The teaching style employs problem-based discussions, individual activities, and team projects that empower students to set personal learning goals (Pedersen & Liu, 2003).

Mobile learning in this chapter refers to use of a variety of wireless devices as instructional tools. These devices include laptops with WiFi, MP3 players, IPods, USB drives, personal digital assistants (PDAs), eBook readers, and smart phones. In the two courses, IPods, and PDAs were not used because they are not currently available in the region. eBook readers are available but eBooks can only be downloaded online. Wireless access is not yet available.

BACKGROUND

A Matter of Timing

When the first online courses appeared 20 years ago, universities envisioned students would flock to enroll from home, from corporations, and from all corners of the globe. That did not happen. Instead, it was the on-campus students who wanted online courses because such courses were convenient and reduced the time to graduate. So, why were the visionaries wrong? The answer is they were not. According to Gladwell (2008), the time was not right. It would be another 20 years before the technology, the students, the universities, and the world economy were ready. Now is the time. The technology has matured, students are computer savvy, universities have changed, and the new global economy demands increased numbers of skilled workers.

At this particular point in time, the technology-driven global economy has created three blended-learning markets: *survivor students*, *evolving employees*, and *global graduates*. The *survivor students* represent the significant number of additional citizens countries must train as skilled workers to enable business and industry to compete in the international market place. The second, blended-market is the *evolutionary employee*, who must continuously up skill to be eligible for career advancement. The third blended learning opportunity is the international student market, which is comprised of students who seek to emigrate to countries with better career opportunities. These *global graduates* place greater value on a foreign degree that will be more marketable. In the past, the international student market was limited to those who could afford to study abroad. Blended learning enables students to study in foreign universities without leaving home. Blended learning also benefits the university since it costs the same to teach a student in Bombay or the Bronx.

Benefits

As the for-profit universities have demonstrated, institutions can afford to invest more in the development of blended learning courses compared to face-to-face, because there is a better return on investment due to the larger market size. The *design once, teach many times* principle enables providers to spend more on course design, assured they will recover the investment in just a few semesters. The benefit for the student is a well designed course. Another benefit of blended learning can be shorter semesters. Since students typically work on a blended course three to five days per week, the courses can shorter. As a result, students can take more courses in less time and graduate sooner. Another student benefit is smaller class size, which can be used to personalize and customize course delivery to the individual needs of students, which is a particular concern of this university in educating students in developing countries. Through the use of educational technology, it may be possible to significantly improve distance student's success in science courses. Akcay (2006) reported that students using simulations, computer programs, and media actually scored higher on the tests and also reported more positive attitudes toward chemistry. Bayrak (2008) found similar results for physics students.

Using part-time online instructors is another benefit of blended learning, especially for universities in emerging nations where there is a shortage of qualified teachers. Even if a university had the funding to hire full-time teachers, there would not be a sufficient number of qualified applicants willing to relocate. However, recruiting online teachers is a different matter. As the baby boomers reach retirement age, they teach on remote islands from the comfort of their back porch, pool, or favorite restaurant. The students benefit from access to highly qualified instructors; the university benefits from reduced teaching costs and exceptionally qualified faculty; and the retirement-aged instructor benefits by share his expertise and experience in a global classroom.

DISTANCE LEARNING ISSUES IN DEVELOPING COUNTRIES

Traditional Delivery

In the South Pacific, distance is a barrier. The countries served by this regional university cover an area one third of the Earth's surface. The only solution for many regions was to establish small local campuses served by a regional university. In such an environment, it is a challenge to provide adequate educational resources. Courses can only be offered sporadically when faculty is available to travel throughout the region. As a result, despite having a regional campus for over 40 years, half the secondary teachers in the Marshall Islands are still untrained. Even if such island countries can establish a strong local university, it will not be able to adequately serve the needs of outer islands with small populations. The reality is that with rising fuel costs and faltering economies traditional methods of course delivery will not adequately serve the countries.

Correspondence Courses

Unlike the United States and Canada where affordable Internet access has been available for nearly two decades, many developing countries have continued to rely on correspondence courses to serve students at a distance. At the University of the South Pacific, a regional university serving 12 member nations, correspondence courses have been the principle distance learning modality. In the past videoconferencing was tried, but it was found to be too expensive, unreliable, and limited. Online learning was not an option because of limited technology.

In the last five years, Internet access significantly improved throughout the region. However, faculty and programs have been slow to adapt, continuing to rely on correspondence courses, which have been the preferred approach for more than 40 years.

In a 2008 study, Hogan surveyed students taking correspondence courses in eight island nations served by the university. He identified several significant pedagogical issues. One student concern was that correspondence course materials often did not arrive until the sixth week of the course. A second student concern was lack of feedback on assignments. Student reported that often the feedback did not arrive until after the final examination. As shown in Figure 1, these problems are due to the time that it takes to ship materials. Students reported that it often took a minimum of 5-6 weeks to get feedback on an assignment.

A third student concern with the correspondence courses was lack of communication with teachers. Of the students surveyed, 53% said they wanted contact with instructors. Students reported almost no contact with their instructors in science, mathematics, and foundations courses, but students in computer-science and law courses were very satisfied, saying that their instructors supplemented the print materials with online instructor access, class discussions, and the prompt feedback. Another student concern was equal

Figure 1. Typical six-week shipping time for feedback in correspondence courses

access to educational resources. Unlike on-campus students who had had weekly face-to-face classes with the instructor and tutorial sessions, correspondence-course students did not have weekly classes, and tutorials were subject to the budget and tutor availability.

The study also found that students taking courses at a distance had lower pass rates compared to on-campus students. Table 1 shows the five-year comparison in pass rates for selected courses delivered in traditional and print modes. As the table shows, students taking courses by correspondence are disadvantaged compared to on-campus students.

Technology

The good news is that technology has arrived. Due to the global economic turmoil, emerging nations are convinced they must improve Internet and educational access to compete in the world market. In the 2008 study, Hogan verified that university campuses in Tonga, Samoa, the Marshall Islands, Fiji, and the Cook Islands already had sufficient Internet connectivity to make e-Learning viable. By 2010, Nauru, Tuvalu, Micronesia, and Vanuatu had joined the list of countries capable of supporting online learning.

Table 1. Comparison of student success in traditional and print courses at a Pacific Island Regional University

Course	Pass Rate/EFTE[1]	
	Face-to-face	Print
Intro to Accounting	*72.6%* 159.4	*63.7%* 191.5
Intro to Language Studies	*78.0%* 25.6	*70.4%* 60.8
Math for Social Science	*67.6%* 382.4	*48.4%* 263.3
Intro to Psychology	*79.0%* 41.8	*61.1%* 85.3
4-course comparison	***70.1%*** 609.1	***57.3%*** 600.8

[1]EFTE (Equivalent full time enrollment)

The bad news is that although Internet access is available in major towns and university campuses, many rural areas and outer islands still lack connectivity and even electricity. Nevertheless, even that is changing as mobile telephone companies have added Internet access. While Internet monthly charges are still high, costs have begun to drop. In Fiji, for example, charges to Internet service providers dropped by 40% in 2010. With continuing reductions in price and cheaper laptops, more people will be able to afford home access. As prices fall and access increases, the market for blended and mobile learning will continue to increase.

Culture

One concern raised by faculty about online learning is culture. Critics argue that in cultures that place a high value on respect for authority, discussion is considered disrespectful. A related problem is that local teachers often prefer teacher-centered learning that places the instructor in the role of *master*, and students are accustomed to just wanting to know what to study for on tests. Transforming students and teachers from a culture of lecture to a student-centered approach that fosters critical thinking will be a challenge. The following are typical quotes from Pacific Island students:

Should we teach students to question? "No." They don't like being placed in critical situations where they can't answer questions. It challenges their standing. Their predecessors did not allow inquiry. That's how it has been done."—Roshila

Contradicting comments during discussions are considered as arguments and disrespect towards elders and/or male members of the community. .. men as the decision makers and women as the followers, often resulting in complete male dominance during classroom discussions and presentations.—Mosese

Although faculty and students with no experience in blended learning express cultural concerns about blended learning, students who have taken online courses do not agree. Compared to a lecture hall, an online classroom may free students to express themselves. Preliminary studies by Bostick and Wu (2005) and Meyer (2006) suggest that the use of online discussions may actually reduce gender issues, especially with discussions of controversial topics. Nevertheless, it is important for online providers to be sensitive to the cultures. It is also good business because the fastest growing markets are in Eastern cultures (Edmundson, 2007). As Gaskell (2008) and Robbins 2004 observe, teaching across international borders can involve nor only cost and quality concerns, but also cultural issues.

Another cultural issue is motivation. Students may place higher priorities on socialization, family, and work ahead of education. The instructional approach in these blended courses is to make the online class so personal and engaging that students want to attend. The environment encourages students to interact and develop new friendships. In this way, relationships with team members and the instructor reinforce commitment to learning. As a former student, a math teacher at the College of Micronesia wrote:

I never got around to withdrawing from class. By then I was too busy monitoring the discussions, providing feedbacks, reading articles, doing my assigned weekly "team leader" thing, researching online university, writing the team paper.... I had taken a bite of the "forbidden" fruit of "on-line" learning and swallowed the hook, sinker, line, and the whole works.—Yen Ti

The premise is that blended learning and mobile learning can remove the isolation students experience in lecture and correspondence courses.

It is hoped that the supportive online classroom environment will motivate students and promote success.

Blended Learning Issues

Blended learning offers many advantages for students, but online providers also need to address areas of concern shown in Table 2.

Language skills are an important issue that can be a barrier to online learning. For some students in developing countries, English is their second, third, or even fourth language. In Vanuatu, for example, there are three official languages–English, French, and Bislama, but there are 113 indigenous languages that are still actively spoken. Accordingly, teaching materials must be written at the appropriate level to accommodate the language diversity (Hussin, 2007, Rutherford and Kerr, 2008).

Mobile Learning Issues

According to Corbel and Valdez-Corbel (2007), there are two issues that determine whether individuals are ready to use mobile learning in education. The first is accessibility to mobile learning technology. In the South Pacific, much of the technology is still too expensive or not yet available. For example, IPods and e-book readers are not supported by the local technology. Blackberry is, but the monthly charge is beyond the reach of students and teachers. On the other hand, laptops with Wi-Fi, MP3 players, and mobile phones readily are available and increasingly affordable. In the freshman chemistry class, the majority of students did not have laptops or Internet access at home, but nearly all students in the graduate course had laptops and home Internet; about half had laptops with Wi-Fi. In other emerging regions, mobile learning is already an option. According to Aderinoy et al. (2007), Traxler, (2007), Mapuva, (2009), and Fozdar and Kumar (2006), mobile has great promise in Africa and India.

The second issue is experience with mobile learning activities such as downloading and listening to podcasts, audio books, eBooks, and streaming movies. Other activities include texting, instant messaging, portable storage devices, taking photos with mobile phones, and playing interactive online games. Based on these criteria, 90% of the students and 60% of the teachers at the University of Texas at Brownville were ready for mobile learning. At the present time, the percentages in the Pacific region are closer to 25% of the students and 5% of the faculty.

For universities planning to deliver courses by blended and mobile learning, it is important to assess student readiness. However, the situation is rapidly improving as telecoms and Internet service providers recognize new business opportunities in the mobile technology market. In the wink of an eye, students jumped from mobile phones, to texting, to photos. The rest of mobile learning will soon follow.

Table 2. Pedagogical and administrative benefits of blended learning

Student Benefits	Student Issues
Access to education Analytical skills Cultural awareness Interaction with facilitator and peers Motivation Success and satisfaction	Analysis skills Computer skills Internet/computer access Language skills Time management skills Writing and typing skills

STUDENT-CENTERED PEDAGOGY

Student-centered instruction was introduced into the United States in the early 1900s under the umbrella of constructivism, which was popularized by the work of John Dewey and Russian psychologist Lev Vygotsky. Nevertheless, prior to 1957, science education remained primarily teacher-centered, focusing on filling students with information. That changed with the Russian launch of Sputnik I in 1957. Following that event, Congress quadrupled funding for the National Science Foundation and initiated an educational revolution that resulted in a new science curriculum and innovative pedagogical approaches designed to increase both student aptitude and interest in science and mathematics. Over the next 20 years, the US introduced a series of innovative curricula and teaching approaches such as Biology Sciences Curriculum Study (BSCS Biology), Chemical Education Material Study (CHEM Study), and Physical Science Study Committee (PSSC Physics) that led to resurgence in science interest and achievement. These approaches were accompanied by increased use of student-centered problem-solving methods, inquiry, peer tutoring, and team learning. All of which were incorporated to improve achievement, analysis, and student satisfaction. I recall a chance meeting with a Japanese educator in 1984. He explained he was in Washington studying American teaching methods that could be adapted to improve the creative and problem-solving skills of Japanese science students. He explained that while their students were strong in the subjects, they often had difficulty applying the principles to solving problems and new applications.

Twenty-five years later, teaching students how to think remains a critical issue. In this program, online teachers actively involve students in the learning process, serving as facilitators who guide students rather disseminating facts. The teaching approach gives students more responsibility for discussions and team leadership. With students attending from more than 20 countries, the pedagogy is designed to relate the subject matter to the students' personal experiences and to include activities that apply the principles to regional problems. The approach is for students to learn by doing. The aim is to teach students to learn to apply information to investigate problems that apply to their lives, rather than emphasizing the acquisition of facts.

The blended chemistry and graduate education courses were developed within a student-centered framework. The activities were created to promote critical thinking, analysis, and application. The various social interactions were designed to engage students and to promote respect for culture, ethnicity, and gender. The following describe the course elements.

Blogs

Although the course management system (CMS) had the capability to create team forums, the authors wanted to create a more open learning environment that encouraged students to venture beyond the safety of the CMS. An unanticipated outcome was that some students took the opportunity to design visually attractive sites, demonstrating both creative and media skills.

Discussion Questions

A key element of the course is the use of weekly discussion questions that challenge students to apply the subject principles to practical real-life situations. The aim of the questions is to have students relate the subject to their lives. Critical thinking and analysis, not the right answer, are the aims. The following are examples of chemistry discussion questions for a non-major introductory course.

Moon Water. Recently NASA crashed a vehicle into the moon in search of water. If they find water, will it be different than Earth water. *Fiji Water* is a great commercial success. Do you think there would be a market for *Moon Water?*

Boyles Law at the beach. You drive with friends along a sandy beach where your car gets stuck, but you remember chemistry and let air out of the tires. It works and you drive off the beach. What did you know that saved the day and the car?

Becoming extinct. *Do* you think an animal that cannot see using visible light is at a disadvantage and might even become extinct? Justify your answer.

Properties of water! In the previous DQs, you applied chemistry. Now you will take the next step – *predicting*. Each team is to decide the impact on the Earth's environment, if water was a gas at room temperature.

Assessments

In the online chemistry course, the tests and final examination are face to face. The rationale was to ensure a valid comparison of student achievement across modes. In the graduate education course, the midterm examination is online. In both courses, the additional assessments are individual activities, team projects, and weekly participation.

Facilitation

The role of the instructor is to facilitate or guide. The facilitator establishes a classroom environment that allows students to engage and be responsible for their learning through active participation. All of the course activities are arranged to engage students, motivate them, and encourage them to become critical thinkers.

Feedback (Weekly)

The feedback philosophy, based upon the work of B.F. Skinner, is to use variable interval, positive reinforcement on discussions, activities, assignments, and exams. The facilitators and tutors respond to student questions within 24 hours. Students receive *weekly feedback* on participation and assignment within six days, and all assignments are graded and returned within the same period.

The purpose of weekly grading and feedback is to reduce student stress. By making the assignments and feedback more frequent, students are encouraged to develop better time management skills. In this way, student attrition is reduced. The personalized feedback and positive reinforcement also help to reduce students' sense of isolation. In this way, the feedback is used to reinforce the desired behaviors, build motivation, and help students succeed.

Globalized Learning

In developing Pacific countries, students have not had the Internet immersion common to western cultures. Many university students do not have personal email addresses and are hard pressed to name their favorite web sites. Similarly many faculties are new to online learning and feel most comfortable with a textbook and nestled securely within the confines of their CMS.

For this reason, both online courses—chemistry and online learning—were designed to make the world the classroom by integrating the Internet. At first, chemistry students were leery of interacting, but it took no time before students were popping online at all hours of the night, writing to the instructors and tutors, saying" Hi, I see you are online. How are you tonight?" Similarly, the graduate students had to adjust to blogs, Tweets, and Skype, but once they did the genie was out of the bottle. By midcourse, it was common for the instructor to engage in simultaneous chats with students throughout the evening. Another change noted in both the undergraduate and graduate students was a new tendency to search online sources to support the students' case in the discussion questions. In this way, the scientific method was transformed from a term to memorize into a method that students used to analysis.

Individual Activities

The individual activities were designed to reinforce learning through practice, analysis, and application. For example, chemistry students first viewed a Monty Python video in which villagers had to use the scientific method to determine if they have caught a witch (http://www.youtube.com/watch?v=GUQUqV0_PTc&feature=related). Then the chemistry students were given a series of exercises where they had to apply the scientific method to solve problems. Other activities included online sites to assist with chemical computations, simulated laboratory exercises, and skill developers. In the education course, students research Internet sites to create curriculum that infuses technology in their teaching. Students also had an online practicum in which they demonstrate the various facilitator skills.

Peer Learning

The homework problems were designed as formative assessments to help students prepare for the examinations. As such, learning teams were encouraged to work together in mastering the problems. For students isolated in low-population regions, this was a great advantage, giving students in the blended course 24/7 peer assistance.

Quiz Review

Previous quizzes and a final examination were transformed into online, self-paced reviews that students used to prepare for tests.

Skype

All students set up Skype accounts at the start of the course and were shown how to call, video call, conference call, chat, and conference chat. The ease of access to classmates, facilitators, and tutors was a new experience—one that has been observed to breakdown cultural and gender inhibitions.

Team Activities

The first team activity is to develop a learning team charter that specifies team expectations, individual responsibilities, and procedures to resolve disputes. The contract in created using a wiki that enables students to work collaboratively to shape the document. Later in the course, team members will evaluate their team members on the major project. The primary team project for the education course is a research paper that includes individual and team components. For the chemistry course, the major team project is a series of international debates between classes in several countries. These debates are run as a series of videoconferences using REACT. All may view the live debates. Throughout the semester, there are smaller team activities designed to encourage analysis, team building, and presentation skills. Students get individual grades for all team activities.

Tutors

For most students, tutorial assistance previously consisted of a one-hour, face-to-face session where the tutors solved problems on a white board, which may explain why so few students attended the tutorial sessions. In contrast, the students in the online chemistry course had access to tutorial help 24/7. When a student posted a question, the tutor responded within 24 hours, usually less. The tutor also held two hours of synchronous online sessions per week. Like the facilitator, the tutor's role was transformed from teacher to facilitator. No longer the *giver of answers*, the tutor guided students. In the graduate education course, tutors were replaced with mentors who were recent graduates of the course. Each mentor was assigned to a team throughout the course, which resulted in the formation of strong bonds.

Twitter Weekly Summary

In the chemistry course, it was decided to have students post 200-word weekly summaries that were counted as part of their participation grade. In the graduate course, Twitter was used for this purpose. The students learned to write succinct summaries that were sent to all members of the class. Twitter was new to most and the first Tweets were a challenge. Then the students got comfortable and began asking why all courses did not use Tweets. The Twitter was used to provide even faster feedback and in a summative way so that the instructor and students were able to get a quick snapshot of the week. The feedback was instrumental in assessing the quality of the various activities.

Both the chemistry and education courses used the same pedagogy with the exception of the blogs and Tweets. These were reserved for the education course because the first-year students needed to spend more time learning how to navigate the CMS and develop computer skills. The two courses are described in detail in the following sections.

FOUNDATIONS CHEMISTRY

Course Description

This course, *CHF02 Foundations Chemistry 1,* is the introductory course in the undergraduate chemistry major. Previously delivered face-to-face on the main campus and by correspondence course throughout the region, the chemistry course was transformed for blended delivery in 2010. Similar to the findings of Akcay (2006), it was recognized that the success rate of students in print-based chemistry was much lower than in face-to-face classes. The aim of the blended approach is to remedy the weaknesses in the print delivery.

In support of this aim, class size is limited to 15 students to ensure they received the individual attention and support needed to develop time management, computer, and online skills. Another consideration in developing this course was the lack of science resources available in the regional countries. For this reason, the blended course incorporates Internet resources, which not only address the resource issue, but also teaches students to use the Internet as a library. By introducing to the students to Internet resources, a village student in the mountains of Fiji (Figure 2a) has the same online access to information as a student studying in New York (Figure 2b).

The course activities are set up to encourage students to become adept at using the Internet as a research and problem-solving tool. One example of this process is the individual activity that asks students, *If scientists drilled a hole through the centre of the Earth to China, would you jump in?* The question catches students' fancy. The physicist types worry about temperature, pressure, and exit velocity. The humanity students are more concerned with how long the trip will take and can they bring along enough food. One student worried about her hair and makeup! Overnight the students have the Net

Figure 2. Internet is the great educational equalizer, providing anytime anywhere access to educational resources

(a) (b)

humming. The exercise not only gives students great experience searching the Internet, it also makes learning fun. A young woman summed it up by writing, "I'll take the 42-minute ride—The China shopping bargains are worth the risk." Figure 3 shows a typical online week.

Weekly Activities

As shown in Table 3, the blended course e is highly interactive. Students must participate online four days per week; the instructor participates five days and responds to all student questions within 24 hours. The *Discussion Questions (DQs)* encourage students to develop online communication skills, apply chemistry to solve real-life problems, and to think critically. The *Tutor HelpDesk* forum links students with a tutor who responds to their questions within 24 hours. The tutor works with students to help them understand the problems. The tutor is not an online answer machine or an avatar that writes solutions on a whiteboard. Besides helping students to problem solve, the *HelpDesk* reduces student isolation and therefore fear and stress. Reducing the sense of isolation is an aim of all the course activities. The activities serve to link students with their classmates, teammates, and the instructor.

The *individual activities* reinforce chemistry principles in the readings. For example, while

Figure 3. Week 3 blended course activities

Table 3. Blended course features

Daily	Weekly	Other
• Student-instructor, student-student, and student-team contact • Questions forum • Discussion Questions • Tutor HelpDesk	• Individual/team activities • Chats, student-teacher calls • Student Feedback • Tutorial • Weekly Summary	• Biweekly labs[1] • Tests [1] • Practice tests[2] • Peer Evaluations

[1]administered face to face [2]available on the web site

learning about the gas laws, students use an online simulation shown in Figure 4 that demonstrates the effects of changing temperature, pressure, volume, and amount of gas.

The *team activities* enable the students to engage in more complex activities and to develop teaming skills. Students learn to work in groups, to meet deadlines, and to deal with conflict in a team setting. To help students learn to work in teams, their first team activity is to develop a contract in which team members agree on what they will contribute and how the team will respond if a member fails to perform. The contract is completed in the team forum on a wiki.

The major team activity in this chemistry course is an *international debate* between student teams in the member countries. Debate topics always link chemistry with a significant environmental issue such as:

"Does chemical pollution contribute to climate change and rising seal level that threatens South Pacific islands like Kiribati and Tuvalu?"

The debate activity develops research, writing, communication, analytical, and presentation skills. As the project develops, students discover that their teammates possess different skills and interests.

Figure 4. Individual student activity: Boyle's Law

Boyles Law: Pressure and Volume

Go to http://cheminfo.chem.ou.edu/~mra/CCLI2004/GLHeNeAr.htm, where you will see simulation to understand Boyles Law. Once you do, you will never forget it.

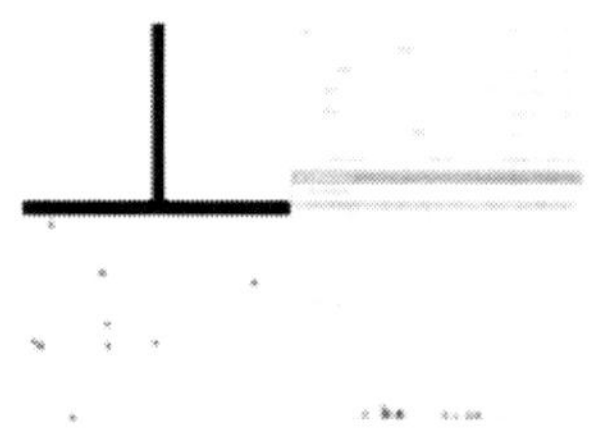

How Pressure changes Volume

1. Press reset
2. Click the circle to the left of volume
3. Change the pressure as shown and record the Volume

Pressure (atm)	Volume (L)
1	
2	
4	

Challenge

1. Have you taken some plastic bubble wrapping and popped the bubbles? If so, can you now explain what you changed to make it pop?

2. Often when a plane is coming down to land, babies will begin to cry. Can you use Boyles law to guess why?

3. The gas law (PV = cT) predicts how P, V, and T interact. Can you guess how the pressure in a tire will change on a hot day? How will the volume of a balloonif you put it in the refrigerator?

Some students prefer to research, others to create PowerPoint slides, and still others to debate. The teams learn how to use theses skills. The team debates are organized like baseball "Playoffs." The teams compete and the winners move to the next round. The two winning teams then face off in the Sevens debate. (Sevens is the rugby equivalent of the World Series.) All the debates are broadcast live to all the campuses using the REACT software. The students ended up working harder than they had imagined, and they loved it. In the process, they learn chemistry, research, and presentation, communication, and social skills.

Chats are fundamental to the course. The instructor, tutor, and all students set up Skype accounts so that it is easy to communicate synchronously. Students find the ability to have a quick chat extremely valuable. In the Pacific, where students are taught to respect and honor teachers, which is inherited from the British tradition, the *chats* help students to be more open and willing to engage in discussions with the instructor. Each week the instructors will switch from *chat* to a Skype voice call. The personal contacts forms bonds with students that lead to better retention and student satisfaction. An unanticipated outcome of this approach is that students maintain the connections after the end of class. Often when working in the evening, the instructor will received a Skype chat message from a former student just to say "Hi."

The *Student Feedback* consists of a personal email to students summarizing their participation, contributions to the discussion questions, and their results on assignments submitted that week. The feedback serves as a positive reinforcement, but it clearly explains any weaknesses and suggests how to improve. The feedback motivates students, gives them direction, and lets them know how they are doing and what they can do to improve. This is an enormous benefit compared to a correspondence or typical lecture course. In every end-of-course survey, students comment that the feedback sustained them to complete the course. In educational jargon, the feedback serves as a formative and summative assessment, and as a positive reinforcer. In layman's terms, the feedback tells the students that the facilitator recognizes their efforts.

The culmination activity each week is the *Weekly Summary*. The activity teaches students to polish and focus their writing and it provides useful information for the facilitator.

Face-to-Face Classes

In this blended program, students meet with the instructor at the start of the course and again a mid-semester. In addition, all students take biweekly face-to-face laboratories, followed by videoconference debriefings.

Principles of Blended Learning for Teachers

Course Description

The course, *ED403 Principles of Blended Learning for Teachers,* is a graduate education course in the Masters in Education (MEd) program. The aim of the course is develop online teaching skills. Course topics include online pedagogy, educational resources, assessment, and course management. A typical week of the course is shown in Figure 5.

At the start of the course, participants assume the roles of online students—engaging in discussion questions, individual assignments, and team formation. Throughout the weeks students study the literature on issues, pedagogy, and culture. Students observe and reflect on techniques used to organize, manage, and assess online learning.

The major individual assignment is to complete an in-depth study an online university. The research includes entry requirements, tuition, student services, curriculum, employer acceptance, pedagogy, policies, and marketing. Later in the course these individual research efforts become a starting point for team research on trends in online teaching.

Figure 5. ED403 principles of distance learning schedule

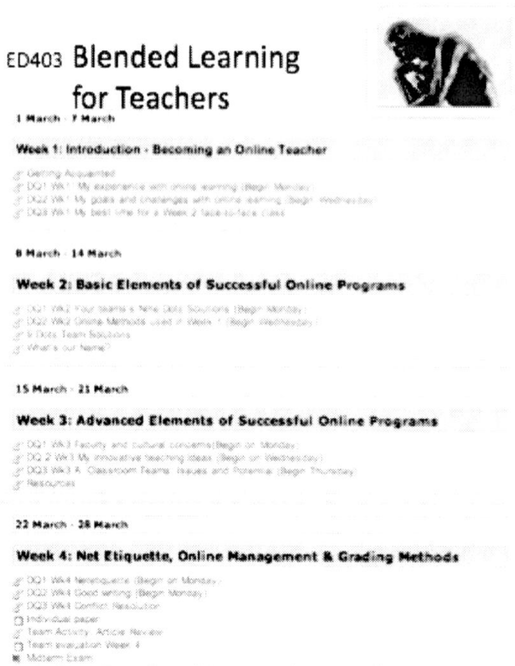

In mid-semester, the roles reverse with students becoming facilitators. During the practicum, the students take over leading discussions, providing feedback, issuing grades and dealing with a series of unanticipated scenarios such as inappropriate students interactions, cultural clashes, refusal to participate in team activities, and direct challenges the facilitator. These scenarios are designed to have no simple answer, forcing students to ask themselves *What now facilitator?* Students report these scenarios as a highlight of the course.

Instructional Variations

There are several instructional differences between the online chemistry and education courses. The first is the level of reliance on the CMS. In the chemistry course, many first-year science students have limited computer skills (Lim, 2006), and benefit from having most activities completed on the website. This approach builds confidence, as students become comfortable in a safe, virtual classroom. In the education course, the aim is to wean students off the CMS so that students begin to develop their online independence. For this reason, the graduate students build their own team forums on Blogger (www.blogspot.com).

A second difference is the greater use of mobile learning in the education course. The majority of the class has laptops with WiFi and mobile phones. Students Tweet, Skype, chat, blog, and Facebook throughout the week. Students also use Yahoo Messenger, Google Talk, or any other software they choose to investigate.

Weekly Activities

The weekly activities are very similar to those used in chemistry. The performance standards are shown in Table 4.

In the first week, students meet online, get acquainted, and join their learning teams. The

Table 4. Instructor and student performance requirements

	Facilitator	Student
Participation	• 5 days per week • Offline no more than 24 hours • Notify class prior to absence	4 days per week
Manage discussions	5 days/week	4 days per week
Discussion questions	5 days/week	4 days per week
Weekly feedback	By Wednesday in next week	By last day of current week
Student questions	Respond within 24 hours	Respond within 24 hours
Return Assignments	Within 7 days	Within 7 days

teams build their team charters on a wiki and come up with their unique team name. Each week the students are graded on their level of activity and the quality of their participation in the discussion questions. Students receive personal feedback and grades each week.

A central point of each week's discussion questions are journal articles on online learning. Topics include faculty, student, and institutional concerns, workload, compensation, technical support, student services, and quality of teaching and learning. In each case, the research serves as the starting point. Then students reflect on their teaching and vigorous discussions ensue. The net result is that students develop a clear understanding of the strengths and weaknesses of blended and mobile learning and issues they will encounter in their teaching setting.

Face-to-Face Classes

The course begins with an in-person class in which students at a distance participate by videoconference. During the session, Skype is demonstrated and student learns how to set up their accounts. During the first class, the syllabus is reviewed and the technical questions are addressed. Following the meeting, students begin using Skype and the CMS.

The second face-to-face meeting is in Week 5. By this time the students are so immersed in their online communications that they have become friends. The second class is almost a party, as they discuss aspects of their research papers and the upcoming practica.

The third meeting is in Week 9 is the celebratory meeting where student teams present and discuss the results of their research, describe plans for their online teaching, and raise issues they may face as their courses go online. By the time the meeting ends, students are experiencing the mourning phase of team building. They realize the online friendships they made and feel a sense of loss that the course is ending. Soon they find these online friendships will not end with the course.

FUTURE DIRECTIONS

Universities used to see themselves as *ivory towers* of learning, immune from the everyday concerns of business and politics. Were that ever the case, today higher education faces budgets and competition—the realities faced by business and families. The for-profit universities were the first assault on the old educational ways. Recognizing the changing needs of students, these institutions aggressively developed products to capture the new market. The traditional universities are now aggressively competing, but it took time. Davis and Badkin (1994) point out that most organizations resist change, unless they are faced with a catastrophe. Today, competition and the global economy have *ivory towers* looking increasingly like *Wal-Mart Universities* that must offer quality products at competitive prices.

Now, the market has again changed. The new technology-based global economy requires greater numbers of skilled workers (Morris, 2008; Idling & Skouge, 2002), and the market is no longer local. With the advent of blended and mobile learning, tomorrow's market is national and international. Already the trend toward charging local tuition for all students taking courses by blended learning is growing. For foreign students, local tuition rates will be an attractive selling point, and the reality is that it does not cost the university more to offer blended courses to the international market.

In the United States, the marketing wars are already in progress. As for the Pacific, it is the new Frontier. Already settlers are arriving and staking claims. However, unlike the American Frontier, the rush for gold is global.

Just as the pioneers needed more than a horse and gun to tame the frontier, so too universities must have the tools to enter the blended and mobile learning market. Quality teaching is not about the technology. It is about the teaching. Yes, technological infrastructure is required, but it does not ensure quality teaching and learning. The pedagogical expectations must be clearly defined so that teaching standards are uniform. Specifically, blended providers will need policies for teacher participation, grading, and feedback to students. Teachers will need to be trained, mentored, and evaluated to ensure they have the appropriate online teaching skills. Then the teachers will need refresher training in student-centered learning, assessment, critical thinking, learning teams, course management, and other online techniques.

In additional to technology and teaching, vision is another ingredient for success. Students have demonstrated they are willing to pay for easy access and convenience. Students want shorter semesters, courses offered every semester, smaller classes, online access to university services. Managers with vision will need to be flexible about class size, teacher work load, and student services. For example, it may be that online courses are more effective with smaller classes. If this is the case, then providers that offer smaller classes can market the pedagogical advantages. This is where vision and adaptability are needed. It was the entrepreneurial approach of the for-profits that enabled them to identify markets and quickly develop new products that met the market needs. One last ingredient is assessment. To be successful, universities must assess their blended programs and continuously demonstrate that graduates have the same or better skills than traditional students.

In summary, the ingredients for success in blended and mobile learning are technology, student support, management, vision, and teaching. Some universities, especially in developing countries, lack these ingredients. For them it is better to unhitch their wagon and stay home, or partner with another online.

Twenty years ago traditional universities scoffed at online learning, leaving it to community colleges and for-profit institutions. Will history repeat itself with blended and mobile learning in the international market? Universities that understand this opportunity and can deliver will flourish. Universities that fail to adapt will find a new *Monster under the bed* (Davis and Batkin, 1994).

Before moving to the chapter conclusions, let me relate an unexpected online event that occurred in the graduate education course. This event has implications for future directions in global education. The story began one night with several emails from students reporting that their team blogs had suddenly become inaccessible. Seeing this as an opportunity for a problem-based-learning exercise, the teams were asked to identify the cause of the problem and suggest possible solutions. It took two class two days to discover the cause. It seems the military dictatorship had blocked access to the blogs into Fiji. The class proposed four possible solutions:

1. Use a web program such as UnblockandSurf to bypass the block to the blog
2. Call the dictator to ask for an exemption
3. Move the team forums back on the CMS
4. Find another external team host

Several students who were government workers voted against the first solution, fearing they could lose their jobs. The instructor voted against the second, fearing the loss of his work permit. Quite unexpectedly, the entire class voted against the third solution to move the team forums back to the CMS, saying they preferred the privacy and independence of the blogs. The class agreed to move the team forums to another online classroom on the Web (www.Nicenet.org). Within 30 minutes, the bypass software was used to move the files and the teams were back online.

The lesson from this blocking experience is the possibility that blended courses in the international arena will experience similar attempts to block the free exchange of information. Therefore, online programs will need to plan accordingly.

CONCLUSION

The two blended courses—online chemistry and teacher training—were successfully delivered in low-bandwidth, technologically limited regions of the Pacific. The courses, delivered to Fiji, Vanuatu, Micronesia, Tonga, the Marshall Islands, and the Solomon Islands did encounter some technological and administrative problems. The administrative problems involved contacting students. Both undergraduates and graduate students experienced problems with the student email system, which tended to become clogged with spam. The instructors addressed the problem by having students switch to private email accounts. When the undergraduate students were asked for their email accounts, it was learned that most did not have personal email accounts. This information suggested that that these students would benefit from additional training to assist them with online learning. The instructors recommended that the university make available workshops in basic typing, effective writing, and time management.

The technological problems were Internet speed at the Vanuatu campus and too few computers in the Solomon Island computer laboratories. Both issues were addressed, although it took half a semester. There were no computer issues in the graduate course because those students had their own wireless laptops and home/work computers.

Even with these problems, the students rated the blended courses highly and asked for more blended classes. Students were especially positive about the student-centered teaching approach of the facilitators and tutors, the highly interactive classroom environment, and the activities. Students reported that they preferred the online tutorials to classroom sessions.

Following the first experimental, blended chemistry course, the department made it permanent. The department now plans to develop the follow-up chemistry course and mathematics in blended mode. The department gave two reasons for this decision: The positive student response and that the blended format will greatly increase student access. Although there is not yet sufficient data, it is hoped that students will be more successful taking courses in blended mode compared to print courses. What made this decision so dramatic was the fact that prior to the blended chemistry course, no courses in that department had ever used a CMS. It took just one semester to demonstrate that blended learning value of blended learning.

In both the undergraduate chemistry and the graduate education courses, issues of gender, ethnicity, and attitude toward authority were not evident. Some graduate students surveyed said they expected these to be issues, but were not. One reason for this outcome may be that warm online classroom environments promoted open discussion. In fact, the female students seemed to most benefit. Several commented they had never felt so free to express themselves. However, this is a preliminary finding. More research is needed to confirm this observation. The initial findings suggest that cultural issues may be less important in blended courses compared to traditional classes.

There were three lessons learned in these courses. First, Internet access in the Pacific is adequate to support blended learning. Second, computer and network issues encountered are easily corrected. In fact, they already have been. Third, the primary challenge to student success is time management, which must be addressed for students to be successful in blended learning.

REFERENCES

Ackay, H., Durmaz, A., Tuysuz, C., & Feyzioglu, B. (2006). Effects of computer based learning on students' attitudes and achievements towards analytical chemistry. *The Turkish Online Journal of Educational Technology*, *5*(6), 44–48.

Adams, J. (2008). Understanding the factors limiting the acceptability of online courses and degrees. *International Journal on ELearning*, *7*(4), 573-587. (Document ID: 1580113111).

Aderinoye, R. A., Ojokheta, K. O., & Olojede, A. A. (2007). Integrating mobile learning into nomadic education programmes in Nigeria: Issues and perspectives. *The International Review of Research in Open and Distance Learning*, *8*(2). Retrieved May 5, 2010, from http://www.irrodl.org/index.php/irrodl/article/view/347

Ariadurai, S., & Manohantha, R. (2008). Reasons for student discontinuation in engineering degree courses offered at a distance. *The Turkish Online Journal of Educational Technology*, *9*(3), 74–86.

Asian Development Bank. (2008). *Education and skills: Strategies for accelerated development in Asia and the Pacific*. (pp. 1-134). ISBN: 978-971-561-702-4. Retrieved on April 15, 2010 from http://www.adb.org/Documents/Studies/Education-Skills-Strategies-Development/

Ayo, C. K., Akinyemi, I. O., Adebiyi, A. A., & Ekong, U. O. (2006). The prospects of e-commerce implementation in Nigeria. *Turkish Online Journal of Distance Education*, *8*(4), 125–134.

Badat, S. (2005). South Africa: Distance higher education policies for access, social equity, quality, and social and economic responsiveness in a context of the diversity of provision. *Distance Education*, *26*(2), 183–204. doi:10.1080/01587910500168843

Bayrak, C. (2008). Effects of computer simulations programs on university students' achievements in physics. *Turkish Online Journal of Distance Education*, *9*(4), 53–62.

Blumenstyk, G. (2003). Companies' graduate programs challenge colleges of education. For-profit institutions find a new market: School teachers. *The Chronicle of Higher Education*, *50*(2), A30.

Bostock, S., & Wu, L. (2005). Gender in student online discussions. *Innovations in Education and Teaching International*, *42*(1), 73–85. .doi:10.1080/14703290500048978

Cercone, K. (2008). Characteristics of adult learners with implications for online learning design. *AACE Journal*, *16*(2), 137–159.

Cook, R., Ley, K., Crawford, C., & Warner, A. (2009). Motivators and inhibitors for university faculty in distance and e-learning. *British Journal of Educational Technology*, *40*(1), 149–163. .doi:10.1111/j.1467-8535.2008.00845.x

Corbel, J. R., & Valdez-Corbel, M. E. (2007). Are you ready for mobile learning? Frequent use of mobile devices does not mean that students or instructors are ready for mobile learning and teaching. *Educause Quarterly*, *30*(2), 51-58.Retrieved on June 13, 2010 from http://net.educause.edu/ir/library/pdf/eqm0726.pdf

Davis, S. M., & Batkin, J. W. (1994). *The monster under the bed: How business is mastering the opportunity for knowledge for profit*. New York, NY: Simon & Shuster.

DeFleur, M., & Adams, J. (2004). Acceptability of online bachelor's degrees as criteria for admission to graduate programs. *Journal of Computing in Higher Education*, *16*(1), 150–161. doi:10.1007/BF02960287

Edmundson, A. (2007). Using level 1 e-learning to support socio-economic development. *Educational Media International*, *44*(2), 99–111. .doi:10.1080/09523980701295109

Fozdar, B. I., & Kumar, L. S. (2006). Teaching chemistry at Indira Gandhi National Open University. *Turkish Online Journal of Distance Education*, *7*(2), 80-89. ISSN 1302-6488

Gaskell, A. (2007). Open and distance learning on the move: Mobile learning, crossing borders, rethinking roles. *Open Learning*, *22*(3), 197–200. doi:.doi:10.1080/02680510701619778

Gladwell, M. (2008). *Outliers: The story of success*. New York, NY: Penguin Press. ISSN.

Hogan, R. (2009). Attitudes of indigenous peoples toward distance learning in the South Pacific: An empirical study. In G. Siemens & C. Fulford (Eds.), *Proceedings of World Conference on Educational Multimedia, Hypermedia and Telecommunications 2009* (pp. 1064-1072). Chesapeake, VA: AACE. Retrieved from http://www.editlib.org/p/31621

Hogan, R. (2009). Societal issues, legal standards, & international realities universities face in the distance-learning market. In Song, H. (Ed.), *Distance learning technology, current instruction, and the future of education: Applications of today, practices of tomorrow* (pp. 284–301). Hershey, PA: IGI Global.

Insung, J. (2009). The emergence of for-profit e-learning providers in Asia. *TechTrends: Linking Research & Practice to Improve Learning*, *53*(2), 18–21. doi:.doi:10.1007/s11528-009-0262-1

Knowles, M. (1984). *Androgogy in action*. San Francisco, CA: Jossey-Bass.

Lim, K. F. (2006). Use of spreadsheet simulations in university chemistry education. *Journal of Computer Chemistry, Japan*, *5*(3), 139–146. doi:10.2477/jccj.5.139

Mapuva, J. (2009). Confronting challenges to e-learning in higher education institutions. *International Journal of Education and Development using Information and Communication Technology*, *5*(3), J1-J14. (Document ID: 1881793981).

Meyer, K. (2006). When topics are controversial: Is it better to discuss them face-to-face or online? *Innovative Higher Education*, *31*(3), 175–186. .doi:10.1007/s10755-006-9019-3

Morris, D. (2008). Economies of scale and scope in e-learning. *Studies in Higher Education*, *33*(3), 331–343. .doi:10.1080/03075070802066164

Pedersen, S., & Liu, M. (2003). Teachers' beliefs about issues in the implementation of a student-centered learning environment. *Educational Technology, Research and Development*, *51*(2), 57-76. (Document ID: 358280011).

Picciano, A., & Seaman, J. (2007). *K-12 online learning: A survey of U.S. district administrators*. The Sloan Consortium. Retrieved on April 15, 2010 from http://www.sloan-c.org/ publications/survey/pdf/K-12_Online_Learning.pdf

Rao, K. (2007). Distance learning in Micronesia: Participants' experiences in a virtual classroom using synchronous technologies. *Innovate*, *4*(1), 1-6. Retrieved on February 1, 2010 from http://www.innovateonline.info/index.php?view=article@id=437

Rockwell, K., Schauer, J., Fritz, S., & Marx, D. (1999). Incentives and obstacles influencing higher education faculty and administrators to teach via distance. *Online Journal of Distance Learning Administration, 2*(4), 1-8. Retrieved December 26, 2008, from http://www.westga.edu/~distance/ojdla/winter24/rockwell24.html

Thompson, W. R. (2009). *Overcoming doubts about online learning*. Southern Region Education Board, Southern Region Education Board. Retrieved on April 15, 2010, from http://publications.sreb.org/2009/09T02_Overcoming_Doubts.pdf

Traxler, J. (2007). Defining, discussing, and evaluating mobile learning: The moving finger writes and having writ. *International Review of Research in Open and Distance Learning, 8*(1). Retrieved on April 29, 2010, from www.irrodl.org/index.php/irrodl/article/ view/346/875

Wang, L. (2009). Learning chemistry online. *Chemical and Engineering News, 87*(36), 97–99. doi:10.1021/cen-v087n036.p097

Wolcott, L., & Betts, K. S. (1999). What's in it for me? Incentives for faculty participation in distance education. *Journal of Distance Education, 14*(2), 34-39. Retrieved December 25, 2008, from http://cade.athabascau.ca/vol14.2/Wolcott_et_al.html

ADDITIONAL READING

Adams, J. (2008). Understanding the factors limiting the acceptability of online courses and degrees. *International Journal on E-Learning. 7*(4), 573-587. Retrieved on May 13, 2010 from http://www.editlib.org/p/24314.

Adams, J., & DeFleur, M. H. (2006). The acceptability of online degrees as a credential for obtaining professional employment. *Communication Education, 55*(1), 32-45. Retrieved on June 16, 2010 from Academic Search Premiere.

Aderinoye, R. A., Ojokheta, K. O., & Olojede, A. A. (2007) Integrating mobile learning into nomadic education programmes in Nigeria: Issues and perspectives. *The International Review of Research in Open and Distance Learning, 8*(2). ISSN: 1492-3831.

Allen, I. E., & Seaman, J. (2007) Online nation: Five years growth in online learning. Report sponsored by the Alfred P. Sloan Foundation. Retrieved on December 2, 2008 http://www.sloanconsortium.org/publications/survey/pdf/online_nation.pdf.

Ash, K. (2010, March). Full speed ahead in higher ed:Mobile learning is gaining momentum in higher education at a much faster pace than in K-12, making it a sort of laboratory for best practices. *Education Week, 29*(26), 30-31. Retrieved May 19, 2010, from Research Library. (Document ID: 2030552611).

Badat, S. (2005). South Africa: Distance higher education policies for access, social equity, quality, and social and economic responsiveness in a context of the diversity of provision. *Distance Education, 26*(2), 183–204. doi:10.1080/01587910500168843

Boitshwarelo, B. (2009). Exploring blended learning for science teacher professional development in an African context. *International Review of Research in Open and Distance Learning, 10*(4), 1-19. Retrieved from ERIC Database on March 15, 2010.

Bonk, C. J., & Zhang, K. (2006). Introducing the R2D2 model: Online learning for the diverse learners of this world. *Distance Education, 27*(2), 249–264. doi:10.1080/01587910600789670

Brown. T. H. (2005). Towards a model for m-learning in Africa. *International Journal on ELearning, 4*(3), 299-315. Retrieved November 25, 2010, from Research Library. (Document ID: 867322561).

Bruner, J. (2007). Factors motivating and inhibiting faculty in offering their courses via distance education, *Online Journal of Distance Learning Administration, 10*(2), 1-18. Retrieved on August 24, 2009 from http://www.westga.edu/~distance/ojdla/summer102/bruner102.htm.

Calandra, B., Barron, A. E., & Thompson-Sellers, I. (2008). Audio use in E-Learning: What, why, when, and how? *International Journal on E-Learning, 7*(4), 589–601. Retrieved from http://www.editlib.org/p/24297.

Connolly, M., Jones, C., & Jones, N. (2007). New approaches, new vision: capturing teacher experiences in a brave new online world. *Open Learning, 22*(1), 43–56. doi:10.1080/02680510601100150

Copley, J.. (2007). Audio and video podcasts of lectures for campus-based students: production and evaluation of student use. *Innovations in Education and Teaching International, 44*(4), 387-399. Retrieved June 19, 2010, from Research Library. (Document ID: 1379908171).

Corbel, J. R., & Valdez-Corbel, M. E. (2007). Are you ready for mobile learning? Frequent use of mobile devices does not mean that students or instructors are ready for mobile learning and teaching. *Educause Quarterly, 30*(2), 51-58. Retrieved on June 13, 2010 from http://net.educause.edu/ir/library/pdf/eqm0726.pdf.

Davis, H. C., & Fill, K. (2007). Embedding blended learning in a university's teaching culture: Experiences and reflections. *British Journal of Educational Technology, 38*(5), 817–828. .doi:10.1111/j.1467-8535.2007.00756.x

DeFleur, M., & Adams, J. (2004). Acceptability of online bachelor's degrees as criteria for admission to graduate programs. *Journal of Computing in Higher Education, 16*(1), 150–161. doi:10.1007/BF02960287

Donoghue, F. (2008). *The last professors: The corporate university and the fate of the humanities*. NY: Fordham University Press.

Donovan, M. S., & Bransford, J. D. (Eds.). (2005). *How students learn: Science in the classroom.* Committee on How People Learn. National Academies Press. Retrieved on May15, 2010 from http://www.nap.edu/catalog/11102.html.

Dunlap, J. C., & Lowenthal, P. R. (2009). Tweeting the night away: Using Twitter to enhance social presence. *Journal of Information Systems Education, 20*(2), 129–135.

Ellis, R. A., Jarkey, N., Mahony, M. J., Peat, M., & Sheely, S. (2007). Managing quality improvement of eLearning in a large, campus-based university. *Quality Assurance in Education: An International Perspective, 15*(1), 9–23. doi:10.1108/09684880710723007

Gallien, T., & Oomen-Early, J. (2008). Personalized versus collective instructor feedback in the online courseroom: Does type of feedback affect student satisfaction, academic performance and perceived connectedness with the instructor? *International Journal on E-Learning, 7*(3), 463–476.

Germain-Rutherford, A., & Kerr, B. (2008). An inclusive approach to online learning environments: models and resources. *Turkish Online Journal of Distance Education, 9*(2), 64–85.

Gulati, S. (2008). Technology-enhanced learning in developing nations: A review. *International Review of Research in Open and Distance Learning, 9*(1), 1–16.

Gupta-Bhowon, M., Jhaumeer-Laulloo, S., & Wah, H. L., & Ramasami, P. (Eds.) (2009). *Chemistry education in the ICT age.* Springer, DOI: 10.1007/978-1-4020-9732-4.

Heine, H. C. & Emesiochi, M. A. (2007). Preparing and licensing high quality teachers in Pacific region jurisdictions. *Issues & Answers.* Pacific Resources for Education and Learning (PREL). Retrievied on June 3, 2010 from ERIC Database.

Henderson, L. (2007). Theorizing a multiple cultures instruct!ional design model for e-learning and e-teaching. In Edmundson, A. (Ed.), *Globalized e-learning cultural challenges* (pp. 130–153). Hershey, PA: Information Science Publishing.

Herbst, M. (2008, November). The high barriers facing foreign workers. *Business Week Online*. Retrieved March 24, 2009, from Academic Search Premier database.

Keane, M. (2008). Science education and worldview. *Cultural Studies of Science Education*, *3*(3), 587–621. doi:10.1007/s11422-007-9086-5

Kyong-Jee, K., Bonk, C. J., & Teng, Y. (2009). The present state and future trends of blended learning in workplace learning settings across five countries. *Asia Pacific Education Review*, *10*, 299–308. .doi:10.1007/s12564-009-9031-2

Larson, D. (2009). Comparing student performance: Online versus blended versus face-to-face. *Journal of Asynchronous Learning Networks*, *13*(1), 31–42.

Lau, R., Ip, R., Chan, M., Kwok, R., Wong, S., So, J., & Wong, E. (2010). Podcasting: An Internet-based social technology for blended learning. *IEEE Internet Computing, 14*(3), 33-41. Retrieved June 2, 2010, from ProQuest Computing. (Document ID: 2016290971).

Lefoe, G. E., & Hedberg, J. G. (2006). Blending on and off campus: A tale of two cities. In Bonk, C., & Graham, C. (Eds.), *Handbook of blended learnring environment: Global perspectives, local designs*. San Francisco: Pfeifer.

Lockhart, M., & Goodwin, I. (2007). Transforming how courses are delivered: A model for teaching faculty how to design effective distance education courses using constructivist theory. *Journal of Faculty Development*, *21*(2), 73–79.

Luschei, T. F., Dimyati, S., & Padmo, D. (2008). Maintaining e[3]-Learning while transitioning to online instruction: The case of the Open University of Indonesia. *Distance Education*, *29*(2), 165–174. doi:10.1080/01587910802154962

Maguad, B. (2007). Identifying the needs of customers in higher education. [from Academic Search Premier.]. *Education*, *127*(3), 332–343. Retrieved March 24, 2009.

Marsh, C., & Hogan, R. (2005). Distance education the Pacific way. *The International Journal of Learning*, *12*, 3–7.

McCarthy, M., & Murphy, E. (2010). Blended learning: beyond initial uses to helping to solve real-world academic problems. *Journal of College Teaching and Learning, 7*(5), 67-70. Retrieved June 15, 2010, from ABI/INFORM Global. (Document ID: 2039337331).

McGuire, J. M. (2007). Why has the critical thinking movement not come to Korea? *Asia Pacific Education Review*, *8*(2), 224–232. doi:10.1007/BF03029258

Means, B., Toyama, Y., Murphy, R., Bakia, M., & Jones, K. (2009). Evaluation of evidence-based practices in online learning: A meta-analysis and review of online learning studies. *U.S. Department of Education.* Retrieved on February 3, 2010 from www.ed.gov/about/offices/list/opepd/ppss/reports.html.

Meyer, K. (2006). When topics are controversial: Is it better to discuss them face-to-face or online? *Innovative Higher Education*, *31*(3), 175–186. .doi:10.1007/s10755-006-9019-3

Mortera-Gutierrez, F. (2006). Faculty best practices using blended learning in e-learning and face-to-face instruction. *International Journal on E-Learning*, *5*(3), 313–337.

Narayan, G. (2007). Addressing the digital divide: E-governance and M-governance in a hub and spoke model. *The Electronic Journal on Information Systems in Developing Countries*, *31*(1), 1–14.

Paterson, A. (2005). Changing the 'landscape' of learning: The future of blended learning provision in newly merged South African higher education institutions. *International Journal of Education and Development using Information and Communication Technology, 1*(2), 25-41. Retrieved June 17, 2010, from ProQuest Education Journals. (Document ID: 1059133091).

Rennie, F., & Mason, R. (2007). The development of distributed learning techniques in Bhutan and Nepal. *International Review of Research in Open and Distance Learning*, *8*(1), 1–11.

Rutherford, A. G., & Kerr, B. (2008). An inclusive approach to online learning environments: models and resources. *Turkish Online Journal of Distance Education*, *9*(2), 64–85.

Sife, A. S., Lwogoa, E. T., & Sanga, C. (2007). New technologies for teaching and learning: Challenges for higher learning institutions in developing countries. *International Journal of Education and Development using ICT. 3*(2), 57-67.

Smith, T. (2005). Fifty-One Competencies for Online Instruction. *The Journal of Educators Online*, *2*(2), 1–18.

Starkman, N. (2007). eLearning: Going the distance. *T.H.E. Journal*, *34*(2), 18–24.

Sulcic, V., & Lesjak, D. (2009). E-learning and study effectiveness. [from ABI/INFORM Global.]. *Journal of Computer Information Systems*, *49*(3), 40–47. Retrieved April 19, 2010.

Tallent-Runnels, M., Thomas, J., Lan, W., Cooper, S., Ahern, T., & Shaw, S. (2006). Teaching courses online: A review of the research. *Review of Educational Research*, *76*(1), 93–135. doi:10.3102/00346543076001093

Tang, M., & Byrne, R. (2007). Regular versus online versus blended: A qualitative description of the advantages of the electronic modes and a quantitative evaluation. *International Journal on E-Learning*, *6*(2), 257–266.

Thang, S. M. (2005). Comparing approaches to studying of Malaysian distance learners and on-campus learners: Implications to distance education. *Turkish Online Journal of Distance Education*, *6*(2), 70–86.

Tomei, L. A. (2006).The Impact of Online Teaching on Faculty Load: Computing the Ideal Class Size for Online Courses. *Journal of Technology and Teacher Education, v14* n3 p531-541 Jul 2006.

van Rosmalen, P., Sloep, P., Kester, L., Brouns, F., de Croock, M., Pannekeet, K., & Koper, R. A. (2008). Learner support model based on peer tutor selection. *Journal of Computer Assisted Learning*, *24*(1), 74–86. doi:10.1111/j.1365-2729.2007.00245.x

Vaughan, N. (2007). Perspectives on blended learning in higher education. *International Journal on ELearning, 6*(1), 81-94. Retrieved June 17, 2010, from Research Library. (Document ID: 1214866641).

Wagner, E.. (2008). Realizing the promises of mobile learning. *Journal of Computing in Higher Education, 20*(2), 4-14. Retrieved April 18, 2010, from ProQuest Computing. (Document ID: 1898109221).

Wang, L. (2009). Learning chemistry online. *Chemical & Engineering News, 87*(36), 97-99. Retrieved on February 12, 2010 from Academic Search Premier database.

Wang, M. (2007). Designing online courses that effectively engage learners from diverse cultural backgrounds. *British Journal of Educational Technology, 38*(2), 294–311. doi:10.1111/j.1467-8535.2006.00626.x

Wang, M., Shen, R., Novak, D., & Pan, X. (2009). The impact of mobile learning on students' learning behaviours and performance: Report from a large blended classroom. *British Journal of Educational Technology, 40*(4), 673–695. .doi:10.1111/j.1467-8535.2008.00846.x

Wright, C., Dhanarajan, G., & Reju, S. (2009). Recurring issues encountered by distance educators in developing and emerging nations. *The International Review of Research in Open and Distance Learning [Online] 10*(1). 1-25. Retrieved on June 19, 2010 from http://www.irrodl.org/index.php/irrodl/article/view/608/1181.

Wuensch, K., Aziz, S., Ozan, E., Kishore, M., & Tabrizi, M. H. N. (2008). Pedagogical Characteristics of Online and Face-to-Face Classes. *International Journal on E-Learning*, 7(3), 523–532. Retrieved from http://www.editlib.org/p/24201.

KEY TERMS AND DEFINITIONS

Blended Learning: A combination of two learning modes: distance learning and traditional classroom-based environments. Distance learning may include a variety of formats such as online (eLearning), chats, audio conferencing, podcasting, print, and self-paced. The percentage of each mode will vary, depending upon the course program goals.

Correspondence Courses: Refer to a learning approach that is primarily self-directed, text-based learning.

Culture: As related to blended learning describes the attitudes and behaviors characteristic of a particular social group toward education. Culture impacts members' attitudes and acceptance of various instructional approaches such as discussions, self-paced learning, group work, and lecture.

Developing Nation or Third World Country*:* Refers to nations that struggle to implement learning innovations such as blended learning due to poverty: culture, and limited educational and technical infrastructures.

Facilitation: A teaching approach that empowers students to take an active role in their learning through the use of student-centered learning. In support of this approach, the instructor guides using a Socratic questioning approach. Common facilitative teaching methods include discussions, individual activities, positive reinforcement, frequent feedback, and group activities.

Mobile Learning: Refers to use of the use wireless devices to make online learning even more *anytime anyplace*. Devices include laptops, MP3 players, IPods, personal digital assistants (PDAs), eBook readers, and smart phones.

Online Learning or eLearning: Refers to education via the Internet. Online learning can be synchronous, highly interactive, or self paced. Online learning can include traditional classroom sessions and virtually any other delivery method. What distinguishes online learning from blended, print, and face-to-face is the proportion of time, typically 80% or more, in online learning.

Student-Centered Learning: Places the student at the center of the learning circle. Rather than acting as a knowledge expert, the teacher encourages students to acquire the information, relate it to their experiences and through discussion and reflection learn to analyze and apply the information to real world applications.

Chapter 6
Blended and Mobile Learning: Experiences from a New Zealand Faculty of Law

Sue Tappenden
University of Waikato, New Zealand

ABSTRACT

In New Zealand, law schools are constrained as to what they can do to incorporate blended or mobile learning into the core programme. There are two major factors to take into consideration when designing any course: a conservative profession, and the cultural needs of Maori students. This chapter will focus on the author's personal experiences of the practical applications of blended and mobile learning within the Law Faculty and will discuss student expectations of technologically aided teaching practices.

INTRODUCTION

I returned to New Zealand in 2001 having taught law in an English University for the previous ten years. I joined Te Piringa - the Faculty of Law at the University of Waikato, with every intention of promoting eLearning at Waikato. At that time our Learning Management System (LMS), Classforum, was being developed in-house and I embraced every opportunity to introduce its use to my colleagues, some of whom were very suspicious and reluctant. During that time those of us who were willing to try radical new ways of offering university papers expended our energies in finding ways of utilising the new technologies to disseminate information and assist student engagement. Now, nearly ten years on, even colleagues who were previously averse to using the basic LMS have seen the necessity of exploring technologically assisted teaching, having discovered that students bring a complex digital environment with them into the university and their expectations about connectivity are high. Having established computer labs across the campus for student use over the past ten years, the University continues to provide funds to cover the costs of meeting the

DOI: 10.4018/978-1-60960-479-0.ch006

need for new infrastructure, for example providing wi fi hot spots and provisions for using laptops and hand-held devices in lecture theatres. However in the Faculty of Law we are very mindful of our stakeholders. In particular we are subject to the rules and limitations placed on us by the council for Legal Education (CLE). Most of our students will go on to be members of the legal profession which is for the most part a very conservative body that casts doubt on the validity on degree components offered in anything but the traditional way. We are also bound by the Treaty of Waitangi to ensure that the Maori students receive a legal education that is culturally appropriate.

I am very conscious of the strictures that are imposed by the requirement to adhere to CLE requirements as well as the cultural differences of Maori students. I am devising ways of best utilizing new technologies within those restrictions to the extent that I have begun to wonder whether our students are actually learning better than they were before. In trying to meet the demands of the stakeholders at the same time as keeping up with students' expectations of connectivity there is a danger that neither group will be properly served. In this chapter I will describe my experiences of trying to reconcile the demands of constructivist teaching practice with the constraints imposed by a conservative professional body and the specific cultural needs of our indigenous population.

BACKGROUND

According to the Tertiary Education Strategy, published by the Hon. Michael Cullen in 2007, the challenges in university education in New Zealand remain the same as they always were – to provide a broad and inclusive system that provides access to quality, relevant tertiary education for all. The emergent international agenda for higher education policy, anchored in globalization demands the development of knowledge economies and learning societies. The transition to a global knowledge economy is dependent on the creation and application of new knowledge and consequently this has placed greater demands on higher education (Weber, 2010). This means finding ways of creating learning environments that promote active learning and critical thinking. By engaging in collaborative learning, students take part in knowledge creation.

By placing the student at the centre of the experience, utilizing all the educational strategies that we have available, including technologically assisted techniques, we can engage the student using a cognitive approach to learning. Individuals develop their own ways of utilizing their existing knowledge to solve problems that are meaningful to the anticipated learning outcomes while remaining comfortably supported. The student is able to move through the stages of Bloom's Taxonomy of the Cognitive Domain from knowledge to comprehension, having had time and opportunity to ensure a firm knowledge basis, in a format that is guided by the lecturer but not constrained by the limitations of the lecture theatre. From there the student can proceed to the next stage in the Taxonomy which is application, by engaging in problem solving tasks with the minimum of direction.

There may be a dichotomy between students' expectations that they will be taught everything they need to know and lecturers' suppositions that their role is promote independent learning. As lecturers we are encouraged to facilitate students' learning in an environment in which each student is responsible for his or her own learning. There are also new challenges to face. There is a need for understanding new literacies, as staff as well as some students, have to become competent in ways of disseminating and receiving digital information. Some mature students are very uncomfortable with the idea that they must learn new skills to access parts of the curriculum. A survey was commissioned by the NZ Ministry of Education and released on Education Counts in 2009 identifying student needs, orientations and aspirations. The sample size was 1811 from seventeen NZ tertiary institutions including six universities and five polytechnics. It showed that traditional modes of teaching (lectures, tutorials and printed study materials) were preferred above online materials but some differences in age were apparent. Whereas 40% of students under 23 years old preferred online learning modes, 31% of students aged between 24 and 41 preferred eLearning modes, dropping to 27.7% of students aged over 42. This is a significant statistic for the Waikato Law Faculty as more than 35% of the student body consists of 'non-traditional' students. Students from the millennial generation (born after 1982) showed preferences for learning by listening, using visuals and working collaboratively whereas they were not so successful as the older students in intrinsic motivation, independent learning and goal focus.

There are also significant differences in the social and economic barriers that students face. In a report compiled by Professor Stephen May which studied learning foundations for Maori, many students surveyed lacked support and had children to care for. This was particularly true of Maori students who also reported that they resist mLearning for fear that they will have to pay for an advanced mobile phone or other hand-held device. One of the founding principles of the Waikato Law Faculty is to make legal education accessible to Maori who generally are more likely to fall into the lower socio-economic groups than Pakeha (people of European descent).

LEARNING ENVIRONMENT AT WAIKATO

At Waikato the primary use made of computer technology is in the administration of papers, download of assignments and to ensure that audio and visual recordings of lectures can be available to be watched on i-pods, computers or even mobile phones either as the lectures are being delivered or at the very least soon afterwards.

However merely attending or downloading a lecture does not develop higher order thinking skills. Student engagement is necessary to ensure analysis and critical thinking and students learn well when they spend time and energy devoting their resources to activities designed to enhance their learning. The concept of engagement differs among students and any student's ability to engage in an effective way may be influenced by extraneous issues arising out of social, emotional or cultural issues. For example Maori values and protocols are highly valued by Maori students and are seen as central to the success of programmes (May, 2009). These include *Te noho hei whanau* – a deliberate act of teamwork; *Te noho rumaki* - protocols and customs; *Kanohi kit e kanohi* - meaning face to face, implying frankness; *Te manaakitanga* – fostering relationships and *Te whakapono* – trust. The presence of these factors in a programme of study will influence the Maori learner's likelihood of success. Understanding how a student learns, acquires new information and retains previous information should guide our choice of methods of teaching. For Maori, deliberate acts of teaching and learning in a safe and supportive environment gains results. Traditional Maori teaching takes place in groups representing the family unit or *whanau*, where everyone helps one another without the element of competition that the *pakeha* students are more accustomed to. It has been described as functioning as a whole as in a *waka*, or canoe. If learning is to take place outside the classroom it may be possible to create an on-line *whanau* where the interconnections between the participants can be preserved.

As educators the advent of mLearning offers an opportunity for us to re-examine our teaching practices and strive to cultivate a learning environment in which all students can readily engage with the information presented. If used well technology can help create an information rich environment but to be successful educators all aspects of our students' learning environment should be considered when designing the curriculum.

M-learning can augment other learning modes without replacing them. For example there are several levels of content delivery. Mobile phones can carry alerts to students, for example about room changes, reminders about assignment hand-in dates etc. Interactive messaging is possible using mobile phone technology making it possible for a lecturer to send students an interactive quiz that can be completed wherever and whenever the student chooses. Those who have net-book or smart-phone capability can access reference materials and most mobile phones these days allow for media-based course content to be distributed, both video and audio. By utilizing digital technology with which students are familiar the aim is to increase student engagement with course content. This may be particularly helpful when students are preparing for examinations. Whereas students may show reluctance to sit in the university library and attempt to write answers to old examination questions, they may be motivated to participate in practice questions when they are available on their mobile digital device and available wherever the student wishes to be. However, these are not higher order thinking skills and using the technology in these ways will not ensure that students achieve skills in critical thinking or analysis.

The m-learner can work at an individual pace, and is given the opportunity to formulate questions related to the topic or to engage in independent research of the topic. When we design e-learning courses we are very much aware of the need to accommodate individual rates of progress yet this is easily forgotten when designing face to face courses, when the focus is on the whole class and not the individual. It is no wonder that some students get lost along the way if we forget at the outset just how specific each of their needs are and that they are not just part of an amorphous crowd. This is equally true of Maori students who share the same culture but who bring complex and diverse experiences to the course. However, programmes of education are most successful for Maori when they are built on the foundations of Maori culture and identity.

There have been some encouraging results in secondary schools in some of the lower socio-economic areas of Auckland where students' willingness to participate in learning has increased by making course content available via their mobile phones. This does not develop higher order thinking skills. The university's role is to promote the students' ability to become independent learners. To so this we must be aware of every stage of a student's development towards becoming critical thinkers. At this advanced level of study we must aim to enhance students' cognitive abilities. If we choose methods of teaching that aid cognition we are more likely to be effective educators. Mere use of hand-held electronic devices does not aid cognition. Passing information from the short-term memory to the long-term memory store is the precursor to being able to manipulate and analyze the information. Understanding the information processing skills of students enhances the ability to design programmes of study that are likely to lead to high levels of thinking and learning skills being reached. If learning is to occur then we must ensure that new information is processed in a way so that it can be retained in the long-term memory, and from there can be processed. Once that has happened the student can begin to interpret the information, apply principles to complete a problem based on prior learning, hypothesize, and finally engage in critical or analytical thinking.

In New Zealand it has been recognized that students are most effective learners when the environment recognizes their spiritual and emotional needs. (May, S. 2009) For Maori this means having active support in an environment based on trust and a sense of belonging. This means that social and cultural constructs surround students' learning to the extent that they are an integral part of the learning and should be taken into account in the design of courses. In the broader context, culture shapes the minds of individuals and informs them in their conceptions of themselves. Within Freire's approach (1970) to education the process of learning was an integral part of understanding how the world operates both socially and culturally. Ultimately this analysis provided a starting point for people to take action in an attempt to change the world and create social processes that were more just. Subjecting students to an environment that is not conducive to their learning because it does not take account of their needs may lead to a position where the student becomes disaffected and does not learn effectively.

A Waikato University professor, Russell Bishop, was instrumental in introducing the programme called Te Kotahitanga starting in 12 schools in 2001. The aim was to change the culture of learning through generating increased interaction by teachers in the classroom. The key element in this project was to make the teacher become a guide rather than a voice at the front of the classroom. The project has now expanded to 49 schools and about 46,000 students are involved, of whom around 20,000 are Maori. In Te Awamutu College before the implementation of Te Kotahitanga, students were failing to perform despite their possessing the potential for success. The change in approach developed an environment wherein the students felt able to succeed and committed to their studies. It was achieved by changing the teachers' approach to teaching in order to address problems at three different levels, individual, small level and, when students were ready, at the whole class level. The results have been very promising. The achievement level of the students in the schools involved in external examinations has risen dramatically. This is especially true of Maori students whose attainment level in one school rose from 18.8% to 63.9%. It is my understanding that when we devise methods for utilizing digital technology or teaching online we are still addressing those same three levels of student/teacher interaction from individual to whole class. Students have different needs according to their age, ethnicity, disabilities, and stage of life but the one thing they all have in common is their legitimate expectation that the university will provide for an environment that enables the fulfillment of their learning potential.

TEACHING NZ LAW STUDENTS

My own area of expertise is property law and as a teacher of law I expect my students to acquire cognitive skills and ethical principles, become independent researchers, to be efficient and effective problem solvers and to commit to memory large amounts of information. As well as professional skills students need to learn transferable skills to take to the workplace, and lifelong learning skills to equip them for the future. Never before has the university population been so diverse. However, Jerome S. Bruner (1966) tells us that the human being is a natural learner but educators often fail "to enlist the natural energies that sustain spontaneous learning" (Bruner, 1966, p. 127). Tapping into our students' "natural energies" may promote deep learning. John Dewey (1938) considered that the teacher's role is to provide the right kind of experience through which the learner may acquire knowledge and understanding. So perhaps the utilization of mLearning is simply an extension of the kinds of experiences we can offer to assist the learner to achieve that understanding.

Turning to another well-known author on the theory of learning, Malcolm Knowles (1990) emphasizes the significance of the climate for learning, in which the teacher manages the learning experience and the learners are active participants in every stage of the learning process. We take appropriate steps to ensure that our learners are active participants. However, the main stratagem for teaching in New Zealand law schools continues to be the lecture followed by a tutorial in some form or other coupled with required reading. There is a certain romanticism attached to the traditional university teaching format and the Dearing Report (1997) referred to it in terms of instilling: "vitality, originality and excitement". The stance of the CLE in resisting mLearning in law schools reflects this attitude. The reality experienced by students may be entirely different in classes of more than 200 participants in lectures that last two hours, some of which may be given by lecturers who refuse to wear microphones or use teaching aids beyond a printed hand-out and whose presentation of the material is sometimes more likely to induce sleep than excitement.

This is not to say that lectures have no place at all, but, by reexamining the role of the lecture in the overall experience that we are offering our students, we should be able to create the proper student-centred environment for all our learners to become self-motivated and active participants in the process. In the lecture environment the effective lecturer will act as educator and agent of change, who presents stimuli to the learner; but it is the learner who must then actively engage in the process that effects the change and results in learning. The emphasis must move from the instructional phase to the creation of self-motivated student who takes a high degree of responsibility for his or her own progress. Regardless of whether the teaching is conducted face to face or by means of mLearning, the focus is on how to enable learners to find, identify, manipulate and evaluate existing knowledge, integrate this knowledge, solve problems and finally communicate what they have learned to others. The Maori way of approaching this transitional phase is to practice 'scaffolding'. This is where the instructor stays with the learner and gradually reduces support as the learner gains in confidence and the ability to act alone. However this may be seen as a preference for classroom teaching since it is implicit that the student will be physically proximate to the one maintaining the scaffold.

As I have explained, in the Faculty of Law where I teach we are required by our professional body to deliver our core subjects via face-face lectures and tutorials. However in the optional subjects we have more freedom. One of the best ways I have found to use mLearning to enhance the value of what I am teaching is to encourage students to create the content of a paper for themselves. The topic was insolvency and creditors' remedies. Lectures were delivered in the lecture theatre and also podcast so students could have unlimited access. When I spoke about what I was proposing to do many of my colleagues worried that if the lectures were available as recordings no one would come. However Professor Marc Loudon of Medicinal chemistry at Purdue University says, "If a podcast can capture everything you do in class, you deserve to have nobody coming." (Louden, M., 2005). As a higher level paper the students had to engage in original research. The students decided collectively that they would study the failure of several finance companies whose investors had sustained heavy losses while the directors of these companies retained their wealth through the device of the Family Trust. Once an asset was in the trust it was very difficult for the creditor to gain access to the money owed. The students acted collectively in small groups to collate information about their chosen company storing the information electronically. Between them they created an information commons which was openly available and gave permission for the information to be used by future classes. The next task was to research the different areas of law that may give some redress to the creditor, for example Equity, Company law and Crimes. Having found the law they were asked to apply the law to the cases they were researching in order to come to a conclusion as to which area of law would be most likely to help the creditors. All of this was effected with no instruction from me, although I was there to give advice when needed. Students exchanged information by downloading it to central computers from where it could be downloaded to their iPods. These could be supplied by the Faculty of Law to anyone who needed one for the paper. The participation level of the students was extremely high and the pass rate was 100%. However where students are self-selecting, as on optional papers, it is possible that the pass rate would in any case have been high.

The most exciting aspect of this paper for me was the opportunity for students to produce content. I was able to draw on the theory of cognitive flexibility, as expounded by Spiro et al (Spiro, R., Feltovich P., Jacobsen, M., & Coulson, R., 1991). Cognitive flexibility means the ability to spontaneously restructure one's knowledge in adaptive response to changing situational demands. This seems to fit the ideal approach to legal education. The theory is concerned with the transfer of knowledge and skills beyond their initial learning situation. The knowledge sources should be highly interconnected rather than compartmentalized, which suited this paper exactly where the students had to use their prior knowledge of Criminal law, Equity and Company law and apply this knowledge to novel situations in the context of the insolvency of this particular group of companies. The teaching was case-based and emphasized knowledge construction, not the transmission of information. If students needed to communicate as a group or with me at times when we could not meet, we used Skype with video to discuss questions and issues that had been raised during the process of research.

Some years ago I was tasked with devising distance learning papers for a new Diploma the Law Faculty wanted to present. I wanted to organize the material in the same way that I would for a classroom-based learner, independently taking responsibility for his/her own learning as a self-determining agent. However I found that taking this approach limited the scope of the learner at distance. For example my campus-based students rely very much on the materials I prepare for them, whereas the distance students were more ready to be guided towards exploring the internet and acquiring information for themselves. It was soon apparent that those who participated in mLearning were willing to go beyond the confines of the information presented via the LMS. The difference lay in my approach to the students. The ones in the classroom relied on me to guide them to the 'right' passages to read whereas the m-Learners were able to research the most useful information for themselves.

COURSE DESIGN TO DEVELOP INDEPENDENT LEARNERS

The difference between this approach to learning and student expectations of being passive recipients, whether in the traditional lecture mode or by way of m-learning techniques, goes a long way to explain the gap which is sometimes perceived in the university environment, between what the lecturer taught and what the students learnt, or failed to learn. The lecturer is aiming his or her teaching towards an audience that he or she thinks are self-motivated learners, whereas the students themselves are passively exerting pressure on the educator to adopt a didactic stance. If students are remote from the teacher they have to be more independent. When I develop papers for distance learning I place great emphasis on course design to ensure the student becomes actively engaged with the work and to make sure there is adequate support for students if they are unsure about how to proceed. I have come to realize that I need to take the same approach to campus delivered courses to make sure every student becomes as independent and actively engaged as possible.

However inspiring a lecture may be or however carefully a tutorial problem has been constructed, or however cleverly the information has been captured on a digital device, the learner who is not actively engaged in the process simply will not learn from the activity. Carl Rogers (1969) said that we cannot teach another person directly; we can only facilitate his learning. To be a facilitator of learning instead of a teacher requires a shift in focus away from dependency on the teacher and instruction to an environment of contextual, active, self-directive and reflective learning. This has proven difficult to achieve in traditional law schools. M-learning technology may help in this by delivering the material in a way that encourages interaction and which is already familiar to the majority of students.

It is true to say that the didactic, instructional approach to teaching is very useful when the learners have no, or limited, prior experience of the subject matter, and seems to be preferred by most students (Jeffrey, L.M., Atkins, C., Laurs, A., & Mann, S., 2006). However the aim of tertiary education is not merely transmitting large bodies of knowledge but of developing independent knowledge workers who are able to think for themselves, taking more responsibility for their own learning, becoming critical thinkers and life-long learners.

In a typical Law School, after the information on a topic has been disseminated there is a period in which the student is expected to do further research, engage in reflective study and prepare for the tutorial, in which problems based on the law being studied will be discussed. In theory the tutorial is intended provide the small group stage of cognition, giving students a safe learning environment in which they can enjoy the support of their peers. However with pressure of numbers on a reduced teaching staff these basic tenets of good teaching are being forgotten. Instead of six to a tutorial, which I was used to twenty years ago my small groups are usually limited to twenty five, if I am lucky. The inception of asynchronous discussion groups via learning platforms such as Moodle greatly enhanced my students' ability to work in small groups. As long as each person engages in the discussion for the required number of times, it is possible for each person to learn at his or her own speed. By using the technologies mLearning I can improve the experience of campus-based students. By introducing a blended learning environment the asynchronous discussions can be used as preparatory tools for the traditional tutorial. Using m-learning techniques it will be even easier to facilitate leaning at different speeds and is as close as we can come to personalized learning. The tutorial can take place when and where the student pleases and can be fitted around work or other commitments. Using a PC or a mobile phone a group of students can access the tutorial questions, submit answers via text or email and finally access the correct answers. The exercise may be set up to make sure students cannot access the answers until he or she has made attempts at finding the answer. However it is difficult for a tutor to engage directly with each student as, with 200 in a class individual answers are not possible. The tutor might only be contacted when the student perceives that there is a problem with their level of understanding. Without the constant presence of the tutor the students' assessment of his/her progress is purely subjective and may be faulty.

Tutorial work constitutes a group activity which is beneficial to students, more so than engagement in individual exercises, because each member of the group has to interact with the material and each other in order to effectively participate in the problem solving. The group activity may be face to face or conducted online; the important difference is the presence of a facilitator, either in real time or asynchronously. The tutorial efficacy of a good, well structured lecture that will assist students with the cognitive tasks of processing information and retention of knowledge in the memory. Retention of information and schemes for processing and analyzing data in the memory is the first step towards deep learning and the ability to recall from the memory ideas and principles in the approximate form in which they are learned is the first stage of Bloom's Taxonomy of the cognitive Domain, known as knowledge. However I also believe that students must be made ready to respond to the experience if they are to gain the maximum from it. Students must feel valued as individuals and protected as part of a group. Being in a large group, yet remaining unconnected to most of the others can present a threatening situation which can only be detrimental to the learner. Good relationships among students and between students and teachers enhance students' performance. This includes including caring for them as culturally-located individuals, caring for their performance and using a wide range of interactions to ensure the learning process endures.

If we accept that events in the classroom or lecture theatre (Instructional Events) have a relationship with learning processes then we can see that the absence of these instructional events leads to disruption of the learning process. For example if the instructional event is the stimulation of recall of prior learning this enables the learning process of retrieval of the previously learned material into the working memory where it can be linked with new material. Because of the link the new material will be more easily stored in the student's memory. If the instructional events do not occur the student is at a disadvantage brought about by the lecturer's failure to understand the student's cognitive processes. In the same way a teacher's lack of understanding of the students' need to feel valued and capable of success may have the same inhibiting effect.

INFORMATION PROCESS AND ANALYSIS: METHODS FOR SUCCESSFUL LEARNING

We offer information to our students in many different forms. Whichever form we use, that information will be retained in the short-term store and passed to the long-term store by organization and repetition. However, we know from experience that repetition, or rote-rehearsal, is effective in the short term but does not lead to learning in its sense of leading to relatively permanent change in the thinking of the individual, whereas organization leads to storage in the long-term memory, from where it can be recalled later. This has enormous implications for teachers because, if repetition and rehearsal are not sufficient to produce a lasting effect, information must be presented in such a way that it can be incorporated into the memory structure. An example of this from law teaching would be when students are instructed in the methods used for case analysis. We try to establish a structured approach to the task by practice until a 'scheme' is set up in students' minds to enable them to follow a specific pattern. In this way, concepts, principles, rules etc are stored in the long-term memory to form strategies for similar problem solving and for future learning. This is true whether the student is on campus or on line, or using a mobile digital device.

As professional educators we seek to ensure that our students have the best possible environment in which to study successfully. The didactic method of live lectures at the outset of a topic can offer a sense of cohesion to the larger group and ensures that the course's learning outcomes are fully understood. The use of a simple podcast or DVD can give a student unlimited access to the spoken lecture and may be combined with a PowerPoint slide show, to allow for repetition of difficult or improperly understood areas. One very interesting aspect of the research undertaken by Atkinson and Shiffrin (1968) and expanded by Baddeley (2003) is the revelation that audio, visual or linguistic data are stored and accessed in a similar way. That is to say that there is no advantage to the students understanding of the information if it is received as written or spoken words, as aural or visual inputs. The key to successful deep learning is by associating the information with pre-existing knowledge or strategies. To me this is the key to using the technology usually associated with eLearning or mLearning to better serve my students who come to the university. It doesn't matter whether the students receive the information in front of me or from miles away, it's the way I present and structure the material that is important.

The most successful learners interact with multiple representations of content and cognitively develop interconnected networks, or 'knowledge structures'. Successful processing of information depends on how big, how elaborate and how well organized these structures are, and how strong the connections within the structures are. The key to these knowledge structures is that the more connections and interconnections there are, and the stronger they are, the easier it is to assimilate new information and the easier it is to retrieve and use prior knowledge for problem solving.

Successful learning activities are those where multiple representations of content are provided. This may be coupled with the teaching of cognitive strategies. The concept of cognitive strategies are guiding procedures that students can utilise to help them complete less structured tasks or higher level operations such as comprehending what they are reading. This sort of procedural aid can be offered by a mLearning based exercise very easily as and is similar to the support structures or scaffolding which is a well developed technique in Maori teaching. It is a process that offers support while the student bridges the gap between current abilities and the required standard. As the student increases in skill, the scaffolds can be faded out. This does not mean that the content is oversimplified but that is it approached in a methodical way. A simple and common example is to provide procedural prompts to assist in questioning the text asking "who" "when" "why" "how" "what". This is one way in which the needs of Maori students may be satisfied using mLearning techniques.

It is important to acknowledge that the mobile source of information and interaction is much more attractive to many of today's students as an initial point of reference than printed text. It is the source to which students are accustomed to turning, as opposed to the reference book. We may disapprove of this generally because of a notion that words on the screen are only skimmed whereas deeper understanding is attained through reading from printed text. While I have been assured that the current generation have brains that are wired differently enabling them to deal with information off a screen more readily, it is true that if a lot of text is to be studied it is usually printed off the screen. We can exploit this tendency by integrating texts into our technologically assisted work by posing questions electronically that can only be answered by detailed reference to the text. The advantage to posing the question electronically and not face to face is that the student, having entered the answer, can be directed back to the text if the answer is wrong.

This kind of work with the text is especially important with regard to preparation for tutorials. On line tutorials can work well, but like face-to-face sessions, they are undeniably subject to the difficulties of all group dynamics and must be controlled carefully from the outset. It takes a skillful and tactful tutor to facilitate a face-to-face meeting and allow everyone to participate and even then less experienced or weaker students may continue to be reluctant to offer answers in an atmosphere that is less than supportive. The Pakeha model tends to encourage competition which makes the Maori students even more reluctant to speak up. So struggling students fail to ask the tutor the questions they want to, for fear of being seen as less able. The anonymity of the on line group, in so far as the presence is not physical, overcomes a lot of this fear. Tutorials also rely for their success on the students' preparation. Students are often ill-prepared for face-to-face classes and come to the session hoping to glean the answers from the tutor or other students. Tutorials on line or via mobile digital devices avoid these problems also because the student is not expected to contribute until ready, within certain time frames. This flexibility is of great benefit to weaker students.

Proponents of traditional face-to-face teaching construe the benefit as being interactive and offer an opportunity for communication. It is at this stage that we should see students proceed to the next levels in Bloom's Taxonomy, of analysis and synthesis. Students have the opportunity to examine and analyse hypotheses, assumptions and statements; to go on to produce original ideas and to integrate them in the development of new hypotheses. This perceived communicative interactive element of tutorials is often cited as the reason for disapproval of law teaching by way of any form of mobile or distance learning. It is very rare in today's LLB classes that groups have as few as 10 members and groups of 20 or even 30 are not uncommon. A session where a tutor has an average of 1 or 2 minutes per student is not truly interactive and communication is reduced, thus reducing the effectiveness of the environment for students to move towards engaging in analysis or synthesis. Interactivity is not solely student/tutor interaction because it is just as important for students to interact with each other.

CONSTRUCTIVIST THEORY AND MAORI LEARNING

Facilitative methods of teaching are more likely to give students the opportunity to be active learners and to participate in their own learning rather than being passive recipients of the teacher's model of the subject. Being active learners means they are more likely to process the information gathered into long-term memory and achieve deep learning. Malcolm Knowles (Knowles 1990) expands upon the guidelines for a facilitator of learning provided by Carl Rogers (Rogers, 1969). These include setting a mood of trust in which individuals can be allowed freedom in order to create a climate for learning. This was put into practice in Te Awamutu College as part of Te Kotahitanga. Resources for learning should include every conceivable method by which their students can be assisted in their learning and the inclusion of technologically assisted learning techniques will ensure a comprehensive learning environment, using resources that the students are familiar with and confident in using. There is no proven need for any group that is studying the same topic to be proximate in space, nor even in time. The learner works best if it is at his or her own pace. If there are language difficulties he or she has time to become accustomed to the terms being used. For shy students or those who are unsure of themselves the opportunity to participate using mobile technology tends towards a more worthwhile experience and lead to greater participation, which in turn leads to greater understanding.

While much can be achieved by a learner working independently, the Maori attitude to education is quite different. Maori adopt an holistic approach to teaching where the importance of working together as a group is centrally placed. This is not a new idea to western pedagogy. Vygotsky's theory (Vygotsky, L.S., 1986) suggests that students learn well by being guided by explanation, demonstration, and participation and those who are taught in this way can attain higher levels of thinking if they are guided by more capable persons. This conception is better known as The Zone of Proximal Development (ZPD). The ZPD is the gap between what is known and what is not known. It is the difference between what students can accomplish independently and what they can achieve in conjunction or in collaboration with another, person, more competent in the area to be studied. The Zone is created in the course of interaction. Our aim is for students to achieve higher levels of knowing. The ability to attain higher levels of knowing is facilitated by interaction with tutors, lecturers and more advanced students. Through increased involvement, students are able to extend themselves to higher levels of cognition. If the desired outcome of tertiary education is to promote the ability to think critically and independently, then a constructivist approach to teaching may be the way forward.

Providing a constructivist learning environment means that teachers and students share knowledge and responsibility for the students' learning. The constructivist theory of learning most closely represents Maori traditional values. This responsibility for learning passes to the student gradually. The teacher adopts a new role of guide or facilitator for students who operate in small groups to solve problems using a wide variety of resources. In this environment learners are encouraged to actively engage in their own development. Instead of being dependent on the lecturer, the student becomes independent, self-directed, taking more responsibility for, and at the centre of, his or her own learning. The constraints that are imposed on law teaching in New Zealand have little to do with teaching theory but much to do with a conservative profession which is reluctant to adjust to new learning techniques. Just as the oral tradition of the ancient Greeks or Romans gave way to a print based educational environment so we hope, in the future, to be able to embrace an environment where we utilise every available resource that will enhance the cognitive development of our students. M-learning represents just a sample of available resources and should be embraced in the pursuit of giving students the opportunity to learn better.

REFERENCES

Atkinson, R. C., & Shiffrin, R. M. (1968). Human memory: A proposed system and its control processes. In Spence, K. W., & Spence, J. T. (Eds.), *The psychology of learning and motivation* (*Vol. 2*, pp. 89–195). New York, NY: Academic Press.

Baddeley, A. (2003). Working memory: Looking back and looking forward. *Nature Reviews. Neuroscience*, *4*, 829–839. doi:10.1038/nrn1201

Bruner, J. A. (1966). *Towards a theory of instruction*. Cambridge, MA: Harvard University Press.

Dewey, J. (1938). *Experience and education*. New York, NY: Macmillan.

Duderstadt, J. J. (2000). *A university for the 21st century*. Ann Arbor, MI: Michigan University Press.

Freire, P. (1970). *Pedagogy of the oppressed.*

Jeffrey, L. M., Atkins, C., Laurs, A., & Mann, S. (2006). *E-learner profiles: Identifying trends and diversity in student needs, orientations and aspirations*. Education counts, New Zealand.

Knowles, M. (1990). *The adult learner: A neglected species* (4th ed.). Houston, TX: Gulf.

May, S. (2009). *Hangaia te matapuna o te mohio: Learning foundations for Maori adults*. New Zealand: Education Counts.

Rogers, C. (1969). *Freedom to learn*. Columbus, OH: Merrill.

Vygotsky, L. S. (1986). *Language and thought*. Cambridge, MA: MIT Press.

Weber, L. E. (2010). *University research for innovation*. Paris, France: Economica.

ADDITIONAL READING

Andrews, R., & Haythornthwaite, C. (2007). *The Sage handbook of e-learning research*. Los Angeles, CA: Sage Publications.

Beetham, H. (2007). *Rethinking pedagogy for a digital age: Designing and delivering e-learning*. New York: Routledge.

Bishop, R., & Glynn, T. (1999). *Culture counts: Changing power relations in education*. Palmerston North, New Zealand: Dunmore Press.

Bishop, R., & Graham, S. (1997). *Implementing Treaty of Waitani goals in tertiary institutions: a case study.* Wellington, NZ: Syndicate of Educational Developments of NZ Universities.

Bonk, C. J. (2009). *The world is open: How Web technology is revolutionizing education*. San Francisco, CA: Jossey-Bass.

Brown, T. H. (2005). Towards a model for m-Learning in Africa. *International Journal on E-Learning*, *4*(3), 299–315.

Burridge, R. (2002). *Effective learning & teaching in law*. London: Kogan Page.

Coiro, J. (2008). *Handbook of research on new literacies*. New York: Lawrence Erlbaum Associates.

Duderstadt, J. J. (2000). *A University for the 21st Century*. Ann Arbor, MI: Michigan University Press.

Keegan, D. (2003). The future of learning: From eLearning to mLearning. http//www.fernuni-hagen.ae/ziff.

Kumar, D. (2006). *Education for the 21st Century: Impact of ICT and digital resources*. New York: Springer. doi:10.1007/978-0-387-34731-8

Kwan, R. (2008). *Enhancing learning through technology: research on emerging technologies and pedagogies*. Singapore, Hackensack/NJ: World Scientific.

Lankshear. C., & Krobel, M. (2006) *New Literacies: Everyday Practices & Classroom Learning.* Maidenhead, Berkshire: Open University Press.

Littlejohn, A., & Pegler, C. (2007). *Preparing for blended e-learning*. New York: Routledge.

Lytras, M. D. (2008). *Technology enhanced learning: best practices*. Hershey, Pa: IGI Publishing.

MacDonald, J. (2006). *Blended learning and online tutoring: a good practice guide. Burlington, VT*. Aldershot: Hants.

Paliwala, A. (1991). *Information technology in legal education: a resource book*. Coventry, England: University of Warwick.

Rosenberg, M. J. (2006). *Beyond e-learning: Approaches and technologies to enhance organizational knowledge, learning and performance*. San Francisco, CA: Pfeiffer.

Webber, B. (1996). *He paepae korero: Research perspectives in Maori education*. Wellington, New Zealand: New Zealand Council for Educational Research.

Wheeler, S. (2009). *Connected minds, emerging cultures: Cybercultures in online learning*. Charlotte, NC: Information Age Publishing.

KEY TERMS AND DEFINITIONS

Auckland: Largest city of New Zealand.

Blended Learning: Traditional learning techniques are used alongside electronic technology.

CLE: Council for legal Education in NZ, a professional body.

Cognitive Flexibility: Spontaneous restructuring of knowledge as adaptive response to changing situational demands.

Connectivity: Availability of technology allowing flexible learning.

Didactic: Teaching by instruction from the front of the class.

Maori: Indigenous population of New Zealand.

Mature Students: Over 20 years.

Mobile Learning: Learning takes place wherever the student is using mobile communication devices.

New Literacies: Competence in digital technologies.

Pakeha: European, Caucasian non-Maori.

Skype: Video phone available via computer technology.

Stakeholders: Those who have an interest in Te Piringa, including the law profession and professional bodies.

Te Awamutu: A North Island country town in NZ.

Te Kotahitanga: Holistic method of teaching where the students are centred in their own cultural environment.

Te Piringa: The Maori name for the Faculty of Law, Waikato University.

Treaty of Waitangi: A founding document from 1840 stating the balance of power between Maori and colonial government.

Tutorial: Small learning group which meets regularly.

Whanau: Extended family of Maori.

Chapter 7
Towards Alleviating the Post-Apartheid Education Crisis in South Africa

Pragashni Padayachee
Nelson Mandela Metropolitan University, South Africa

Ansie Harding
University of Pretoria, South Africa

ABSTRACT

Post-apartheid South Africa is witnessing an education crisis of significant proportions. The new outcomes-based education system has failed to deliver, and universities are suffering the consequences of under-preparation of learners for tertiary studies. The educator corps is lacking, and it has become common practice for universities to deploy augmented programmes in mathematics for secondary school learners in the surrounding area. This chapter describes a particular model of blended learning, devised for the Incubator School Project (ISP), an initiative of the Nelson Mandela Metropolitan University (NMMU) in the Eastern Cape of South Africa. The defining feature of this blended model is that it incorporates DVD technology, which offers an affordable and accessible option for the particular group of learners. DVD technology was used as an ingredient in this blended learning approach since it is easily available to the majority of learners and to the schools they attend. This chapter describes the particular blended model and reports both qualitatively and quantitatively on its success: qualitatively, based firstly on a questionnaire completed by learners and secondly on interviews of educators; quantitatively, based thirdly on learner performance before and after the intervention and fourthly on a single school case study where the mathematics performance of the learners who participated in the ISP is compared to those who did not participate in the ISP. Finally, the scope of blending of this model is evaluated by means of a radar chart, adapted from an existing radar measure. The findings of the study suggest that the use of DVD technology in the blended learning approach impacted favourably on the mathematics learning and enhanced the mathematics performance of these learners.

DOI: 10.4018/978-1-60960-479-0.ch007

INTRODUCTION

Hailing the end of the apartheid era in South Africa in 1994, the new dispensation brought expectations of entering an era of equal opportunities for all citizens. Education had previously been contentious as favouring the privileged communities of South Africa and the political change brought a vision of equity. It was also felt that many of the learners in the current school system did not develop the required problem solving skills and the ability for critical reasoning in the learning process (Department of Education, 2000). The perception was that learners sat listening to the educator, passively taking notes and not actively participating in the learning process. A new education system became a priority and in 1997 the then minister of education, Sibusiso Bengu, announced the implementation of a new education system which was to follow an outcomes-based education (OBE) approach, to be implemented for the first time in 1998. Bengu (1997) suggested that OBE

> *... aims at equipping learners with the knowledge, competencies and orientations needed for success after they leave school .... Its guiding vision is that of thinking, competent future citizens ... the new curriculum will integrate education and training incorporating a view of learning which rejects a rigid division between academic and applied knowledge and skills ... and foster learning which encompasses a culture of human rights, multilingualism and multi-culturalism. (p. 1)*

OBE was implemented to address the imbalance in education and the changing demands of the society. In addition, the shift away from a teacher-centred approach to a learner-centred approach, advocated by OBE, was a selling point of the new system. The vision of the new education system was to integrate education and training in a life long process of learning. OBE provided learners with more mobility between the different fields of study and occupations (Graven, 2002). The OBE system brought about many changes, not only a change in approach but also changes in curriculum.

The new education system required all learners to do mathematics up to Grade 12. Learners interested in tertiary studies were advised to do Mathematics whereas others are required to do Mathematics Literacy. Prior to OBE, learners could choose among Higher Grade Mathematics and Standard Grade Mathematics or neither. Although there are similarities between Mathematics in the OBE system and the former Higher Grade Mathematics, Mathematics Literacy bears no resemblance to the former Standard Grade Mathematics. Mathematics Literacy aims at providing learners with mathematical skills that will equip learners for life in general.

The transition from one education system to another was a serious step to take. In South Africa, the transition created great concern especially because it happened shortly after the 1994 election, which gave the transition to the new approach and curriculum a political colour. Furthermore, the OBE system was criticised because it had already failed in a number of other countries, since it is a system that requires many resources (well-trained teachers in particular) in a country where education resources were already under pressure. Jansen (1998) predicted that it would be widening instead of narrowing the gap between rich and poor learners.

Sixteen years after the demise of apartheid, it is generally accepted that many of the misgivings were justified and that there is a national education crisis in South Africa, bigger than ever before, especially with regard to teaching and learning of mathematics (Mail & Guardian, 2007; Nicolson, 2009). The concern has been raised at the tertiary level that students are not meeting the expectations of preparedness met by their predecessors (Engelbrecht & Harding, 2008). The change of curriculum has created many challenges for learners, teachers and universities and instead of improving the situation has worsened it (Daniels, 2009). As a result fewer learners have the necessary skills for successfully completing mathematics and science based courses at university (Reddy, van der Berg, Lebani & Berkowitz, 2006). With regard to this crisis it seems that the previously disadvantaged communities are still the most affected post-apartheid (Ocampo, 2004).

In their submission to the Council of Educator Ministers, the Mathematics Education Community (2000) highlighted the under-preparedness and inadequacies of mathematics school teachers. Teachers in many South African schools, especially in the fields of mathematics and science are often under-qualified (Simkins, Rule, & Beinstein, 2007). This crisis is further intensified because there are large numbers of mathematics teachers leaving the country or entering into industry (Mphala & Tshishonge, 2008). South African schools are struggling to fill 62,000 vacant posts in an effort to close the maths and science teacher gap (News24, 2008; Ngosana, 2009). The level of mathematics teaching needs to be upgraded at schools attended by the vast majority of the population (Umalusi, 2008).

The situation as described above certainly motivates a need for intervention in the teaching and learning of mathematics. A phenomenon that is becoming more and more prevalent is that universities initiate outreach programmes for learners in their surrounding area, especially in science and mathematics. In so doing, learners become more prepared and motivated for university studies, thus strengthening the cohort of educators and scientists. This chapter describes such an intervention, aimed at preparing a group of learners for entering university and increasing the science and mathematics cohort of teachers. The objective of this chapter is to describe a particular blended model used in an intervention programme, how it was implemented and what was the success of the implementation of the blended model.

BACKGROUND

The South African Minister of Education, Naledi Pandor, in her address to the media after the 2007 Grade 12 results were released, stated that the South African goverrment and its partners should find ways to put effective measures in place so that better results could be achieved at all school levels in future (Pandor, 2007).

The Mathematics Incubator School Project

A need for intervention was identified by the Govan Mbeki Mathematics Development Unit (GMMDU) situated in the Mathematics and Applied Mathematics Department of the Nelson Mandela Metropolitan University (NMMU) in Port Elizabeth. Port Elizabeth, in the Eastern Cape of South Africa, is an area that is particularly affected by the education crisis. There was a critical lack of resources at schools attended by the majority of learners (Mathematics Education Community, 2000). One of the projects of the GMMDU was the Mathematics Incubator School Project (ISP) that was initiated in 2004. The aim of the ISP was to address the serious shortage of suitably qualified secondary school mathematics educators and the shortage of students from Eastern Cape schools entering into higher education in the fields of science, mathematics and technology.

The question was how to structure such an intervention programme in order to best augment school instruction and aid learners in their learning of mathematics. The decision was taken to have regular Saturday morning sessions, attended by learners who were selected on grounds of their interest in mathematics and science. Staff members involved with the ISP conducted the presentation of material and facilitation of learning. Initially, from 2004 to 2006, the presentation developed from traditional classroom instruction to PowerPoint slides, both of which left learners with little to study at home. In 2006 it was decided to go the technology route, specifically involving DVD technology. One of the more prominent reasons for implementing DVD technology is of particular interest. It is not common for families in townships and rural areas to have a computer or, in addition, internet access in households. Intervention via the internet to alleviate the education crisis was therefore not an option. Television, however, plays an important role in township and rural life and it is quite common for households to have a television set as well as a DVD player. Television sets and DVD players are relatively inexpensive compared to computers and internet. DVD technology therefore offers a way of addressing the education crisis by means of "relatively accessible and affordable technologies" (Nieuwoudt, Nieuwoudt & Monteith, 2007, p. 29).

In 2007, a series of 20 DVDs was created and implemented in the teaching and learning of mathematics. The fixed mathematics content of the DVD ensured that mathematical concepts could not be watered down or misrepresented during presentations. This was particularly helpful to learners during the 2007 teacher strike that impacted on the mathematics learning of many of the learners.

Upon reflection, it was decided that technology alone was not effective in the teaching and learning of mathematics and a decision was taken to use this technology within a blended learning environment. Graham (2006) defines *blended learning* as a combination of face-to-face instruction and computer-mediated instruction. In the context of this study we broaden the concept of computer-mediated instruction to include DVD technology.

As further motivation for employing technology within a blended environment we note that as technology becomes more advanced and easily accessible, there is a shift from the traditional teacher-centred classroom instruction to a more learner-centred approach to teaching and learning (Cohen, Grady & Springer, 2007). The traditional teacher-centred approach is inappropriate to outcomes-based education with its central focus on learner-centeredness (Badenhorst & de Beer, 2004).

The GMMDU intervention is not the only of its kind. Other interventions in response to the crisis in the teaching and learning of mathematics in South Africa are documented in literature. Interventions that specifically target the learner include the Maths and Science Academy in Mossel Bay (PetroSA's Maths, Science Academy, 2008), the Schools of Excellence Project (Zenex Foundation, 2007), and the national Dinaledi schools (Department of Education, 2002) whose aim it is to improve maths and science education in South Africa. There are also interventions where the aim is to improve the skills of the teacher such as the Ergo program (AngloGold Ashanti, 2009). None of these secondary school mathematics interventions, however, make use of DVD technology in the teaching and learning of mathematics within a blended learning approach.

THE BLENDED LEARNING APPROACH

It has become increasingly evident that the use of computer technologies could facilitate and enhance learning (Gibbins, Hadibi, Urbaczewski & Vivian, 2007) and thus form a valuable ingredient in a blended learning composition. However, many researchers were quick to point out that technology alone was not effective (Garrison & Vaughan, 2008; Luca, 2006; Singh, 2003). This idea was supported by Singh and Reed (2001) who cited research from Stanford University and the University of Tennessee which suggested that blended learning was better than either traditional methods or the use of technology alone. Furthermore, Singh and Reed (2001) suggested that in order to develop an efficient and effective blended learning model, consideration should be given to the achievement of the learning outcomes when using the "right technology" to match the learning styles of the learner. Therefore, blended learning involves the use of an appropriate mix of delivery techniques and technologies to enrich the learning experience and to achieve the outcomes of this learning (Maguire & Zhang, 2006).

To enhance the learning process, there needs to be a blending of different modes of delivery. Graham (2006) described blended learning as a mix of the best of two worlds: on the one hand a traditional face-to-face learning environment and on the other hand, a distributed learning environment which involves the use of computer technology. Graham also emphasised the central role of computer-based technologies in blended learning and so a blended model is an integrated strategy used to enhance teaching and learning. Pratt (2005) said that the challenge is to blend resources and activities that have the potential to enhance learning.

There are many possibilities that constitute a blended learning approach and the particular blend needs careful consideration. Graham (2006) said that a more effective pedagogy was one of the results of a blended learning approach since blended learning aims to create an environment that allows a shift to more learner-centeredness. The challenge was to blend the right resources and activities to optimally enhance the learning experience.

Osguthorpe and Graham (2003) detailed six reasons why instructors and designers of learning programmes chose blended learning: pedagogical richness, access to knowledge, social interaction, personal agency, cost effectiveness and ease of revision. The blended learning approach could consist of a number of possibilities, including "formal and informal, technology and people based, independent and convivial, directive and discovery orientated" (Rossett, Douglis & Frazee, 2003). Garrison and Vaughan (2008) said that "blended learning offers the opportunity for all students to be cognitively engaged and feel that they are learning individually by participating in, and contributing to, a community of inquiry" (p. 29).

Singh and Reed (2001) highlighted the following as key ingredients of a blended programme: (a) cognisance of the level of knowledge that the learners bring to the program, the different and shared learning styles of the learners, their motivation level and their ability to access technology, (b) content analysis to determine the selection of appropriate delivery modes, (c) financial implications of delivery need to be considered, and (d) structure to support the use of technology needs to be considered.

The ingredients of a blended programme as highlighted by Singh and Reed (2001) were considered in the design of the 2007 ISP. Learners' level of mathematics knowledge was based on their Grade 11 mathematics results. However, learners attended different secondary schools and did not write a uniform mathematics examination. It became clear after the 2007 ISP implementation that a pre-test should be administered in order to determine the mathematics knowledge of learners. Content analysis was done and it was decided to divide the content into 20 sizable units, to be discussed later. The financial considerations of such a programme are quite formidable but fortunately the GMMDU was able to attract external funding from the business sector and therefore tuition and transport were free of charge for learners. The infrastructure for such a programme comprises the physical facilities as well as human resources. NMMU provided the facilities, available on a Saturday morning. Four lecturers who acted as facilitators and a number of student tutors were selected for the ISP because of their interest in the project. Although they were financially compensated, dedication, altruism and a desire to provide better education in the country were necessary attributes.

STRUCTURE OF THE ISP PROGRAMME

A total of 184 Grade 12 mathematics learners from local schools in the Nelson Mandela Metropole were selected to participate in the 2007 ISP. These were all learners doing Mathematics and not Mathematics Literacy as a subject. The learners were selected on the basis of their Grade 11 mathematics marks and their interest in pursuing studies in Science, Engineering, Technology and Mathematics and Science education. These learners were mostly second-language English speakers with one of a variety of African languages as a mother tongue. Learners were split into four groups.

Learners attended a series of five-hour sessions on Saturdays, during which two DVDs of one hour each were presented to learners using a DVD player connected to a data projector. After each session learners engaged with tutorials problems. This was an interactive session with discussions and assistance from facilitators as well as from student tutors.

Each DVD covering a particular concept in the Grade 12 mathematics syllabus was designed for viewing in short sessions. This allowed for facilitator discussion, tutor interaction and peer interaction and also for working on assigned tutorial problems in between sections during contact sessions. Once the learning outcomes were completed for a particular section the DVD presentation was resumed again and so the cycle continued to the end of the DVD. Learners were given hard copies of all the tutorials as well as solutions to the tutorial problems. In addition each learner was given a personal copy of the DVD to view at his/her own pace at home. Learners were given the opportunity for self-assessment at home via quizzes on the DVD and were then formally assessed on the concepts covered on the DVD on their return the following Saturday.

The blended model under discussion therefore combines self-paced learning with instructor or facilitator support to develop specific knowledge and skills. In particular formal live face-to-face activities (facilitator-led), informal live face-to-face activities (mentoring by tutors and collaborative learning with peers) and the self-paced learning (DVDs) were used in all ISP deliveries (Rossett, Douglis & Frazee, 2003).

Table 1 represents the list of blends that were used in the ISP deliveries:

THE LEARNING CYCLE

The learning cycle that was followed in the ISP is a variation on the well-documented 5E learning

Table 1. Blending components used in the ISP deliveries

Facilitation	**Two mathematics lecturers and one high school teacher took the roles of facilitators during these deliveries**
DVD Viewing	Two DVDs were presented per Saturday session
Discussions	Centred around issues raised by learners, tutors and/or facilitators
Tutorials	Learners worked on problems based on the concepts covered, assisted by two senior mathematics students
Weekly Tests	Based on the concepts covered on the previous week
Self Study	Take home DVDs and additional exercises
Hard copies of lessons, tutorials and solutions	Printed copies of the lessons as well as the tutorials and their solutions were handed out to each learner.
Hard copies of tests with solutions	Printed copies of all test and test solutions were given to each learner.
Assessment	Self-assessment, assessment via the DVD and paper assessment on Saturdays

cycle, a research-supported method for education (Edutech Wiki, 2010). This learning cycle promotes student inquiry and exploration as a process for learning and proposes that learning something new, or understanding something familiar in greater depth, involves making sense of both our prior experience and first-hand knowledge gained from new explorations. The 5E cycle divides learning experiences into five stages and each stage builds upon the previous as students construct new understanding and develop new skills. The five phases in the cycle are as follows:

- *Engage*: Learners' interest is captured and the topic is established, connections are made to past and present learning experiences.
- *Explore*: Learners construct knowledge on the topic, they begin to formulate their understanding of the basic concepts.
- *Explain*: The facilitator leads a discussion to refine the students' understanding, more abstract concepts not easily explored in earlier activities are introduced and explained.
- *Extend*: Learners apply their newfound knowledge to a different situation by engaging in problems, exploring additional relationships.
- *Evaluate*: The instructor continually observes students' learning to monitor their progress using questioning techniques and discussions, more formal evaluation can be conducted.

The 5E learning cycle was adapted to accommodate the blended learning model of the ISP. The normal 5E cycle was adapted to include a smaller cycle that signifies the activities taking place when learners go home after a Saturday morning session. The learning cycle is really a learning spiral, starting at the Engage phase and winding ever upwards as learning takes place. The upward spiral symbolises an increase in knowledge as new topics are mastered. Diagrammatically the learning cycle is as follows, starting at the top: (See Figure 1).

In the ISP presentation, the *Engage* phase is a face-to-face introduction to the topic during the Saturday morning sessions. Learners' interest is triggered and appropriate pre-knowledge is recalled. This leads to the *Explore* phase when the DVD on a particular topic is presented and the learner's knowledge is extended. Watching the DVD presentation is interspersed and followed by the *Explain* phase when the facilitator leads discussion and clarifies issues. The learning cycle moves into the *Extend* phase when learners engage with tutorial problems. Before formal evaluation happens, learners go home equipped with the DVD and more exercises to do at home. Therefore, learners go through another, smaller learning cycle consisting again of the *Explore* phase when they re-watch the particular topics on DVD and the *Extend* phase when they do more exercises in order to prepare for the *Evaluation* phase that occurs when they return the following Saturday. It is important to note that the different phases do not stand in isolation but intermingle based upon the needs of the learner.

Figure 1. Learning cycle used in the ISP

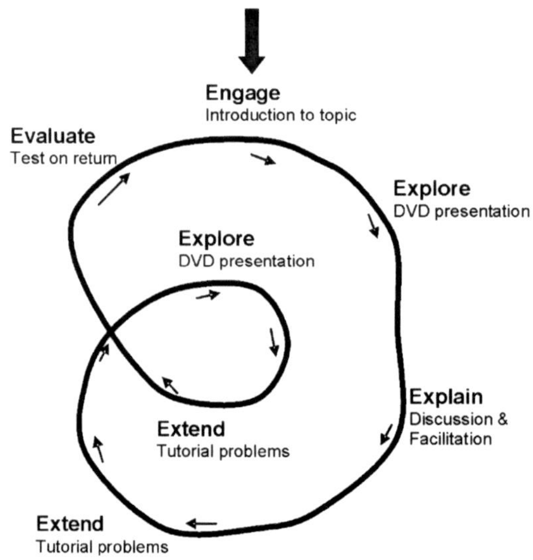

INSTRUCTIONAL DESIGN OF THE DVDs

Each DVD covered one particular topic in the syllabus. The topic was then divided into micro-lessons. For example, one DVD was on Basic Algebra, consisting of the first micro-lesson on Factorization and the second micro-lesson on Algebraic Fractions.

Each micro-lesson of a DVD topic started with an introduction and definitions of the concepts. This was followed by fully explained examples pertaining to the particular concept. The intention was to give learners an understanding of the thought processes involved in solving a problem and to help learners who would have no idea where to begin (Aminifar, Porter, Caladine, & Nelson, 2007). The micro-lesson ended with tutorials problems to be attempted by the learner that were intended to give learners a way to assess their understanding of the micro-lesson. Finally, a set of comprehensive solutions was handed out that could be viewed after learners had attempted the tutorial problems. This approach ensured that immediate feedback was available to any learner who had struggled with the tutorial problems.

Table 2 identifies the content topics covered in the 2007 Mathematics DVD series.

Animated PowerPoint slides with voice narration formed the basis of the DVDs and were developed to explain each mathematical concept. These slides were then recorded in a studio by a member of the GMMDU team, normally a lecturer in the Department of Mathematics and Applied Mathematics at NMMU. Recordings involved using a tablet PC and presenting the PowerPoint slides with explanations. In addition other software packages such as Autograph were used to illustrate sections requiring graph drawing. A second academic staff member of the GMMDU evaluated the recordings to ensure that the DVDs were free of mathematical errors. Re-recording of an erroneous slide took place immediately if required. Thereafter the DVDs were edited by a technical media specialist to produce master DVDs with a menu driven system.

ACTION RESEARCH AS METHODOLOGY

The described ISP was monitored closely so that the outcomes of this process could be researched. For this purpose we followed a process of action research (McNiff, 2008), which runs through five phases: (a) planning and designing the intervention, (b) implementing the intervention, (c)

Table 2. Topics covered in the set of DVDs

DVD Topics	
DVD 1: Basic Algebra	DVD 2: Remainder and Factor Theorem
DVD 3: Quadratic equations, nature of roots	DVD 4: Solving non-linear inequalities
DVD 5: Basic Graphs	DVD 6: Applications of Graphs
DVD 7: Indices, Logarithms and Surds	DVD 8: Absolute Value and Linear Inequalities
DVD 9: Analytical Geometry I	DVD 10: Analytical Geometry II
DVD 11: Introduction to Differential Calculus	DVD 12: Applications of Differential Calculus
DVD 13 Solving Exponential and Logarithmic equations	DVD 14: Trigonometric: Compound Angles
DVD 15: Trigonometric Equations	DVD 16: Trigonometric Graphs
DVD 17: Geometry: Proportion	DVD 18: Geometry: Similarity
DVD 19: Arithmetic Sequences and Series	DVD 20: Geometric Sequences and Series

evaluating the intervention, (d) reflecting on the evaluation, (e) implementing the changes and (f) beginning another cycle.

Action research provides an important link between research and teaching, particularly when the research is actively conducted with the aim of influencing teaching and learning and challenging ways of incorporating technology into the curriculum (Manchester, Ralph & Shipova, 2005). Action research was an appropriate design in the research study in order to reflect on the processes that were followed and to refine the ISP before a next cycle of implementation.

The first of the five two phases – planning and designing, and implementation – have been described above. We next focus on the third phase in the action research cycle, the evaluation of the ISP intervention and in so doing concentrating on factors that contributed to a supportive and encouraging learning environment. In particular, the focus was on the experiences of the learners and the impact of the blended learning approach on the mathematical ability of the learners. Finally, the fourth phase, reflecting on the evaluation, will be discussed and a description will be given as to how the fifth phase of implementing the changes was deployed.

EVALUATION OF THE BLENDED MODEL

In the evaluation phase, we analysed and interpreted the implemented programme from five perspectives: (a) learners' experiences, (b) facilitator observations, (c) performance analysis, (d) case study analysis, and (e) scope of blending.

Learners' Experiences

At the end of the 2007 program, learners completed a questionnaire aimed at evaluating the teaching and learning approach they had experienced in the program. The questionnaire contained open-ended questions and provided rich descriptive data with regard to the factors that provided a supportive and encouraging learning environment. According to Denscombe (2007), "the process of analysis involves the search for things that lie behind the surface content of the data - core elements that explain what the thing is and how it works" (p. 247). After collecting the data we tabulated the data and searched for recurrent themes or issues. We then identified themes and grouped these together in order for categories to emerge. These categories were then related to the elements of the ISP blended learning program. Two levels of coding were used: In the first level coding descriptive tagging was completed and in the second level coding categories were established.

Based upon the analysis and the synthesis of the data collected from learners' questionnaires the following themes emerged:

New Experience. More than half of the learners felt that the approach was refreshing and a different way of learning mathematics. Many learners said that they found this way of learning enjoyable and exciting. A few learners said that the DVD was different from a textbook since there was a "voice" explaining the concepts.

DVD as a resource. Learners were positive in general about the DVDs as a resource. Learners felt that the concepts were presented well and that explanations of the mathematical concepts were done well. The DVDs were particularly useful to them in sections that required visual representation (graph drawing) and in the topic of calculus since it was "not done well" at school. Many learners said that they found mathematics easy to understand because of the many examples and illustrations on the DVDs. A few learners said that they found it easier to concentrate as opposed to having someone standing in front explaining what to do while others found it difficult to concentrate using the DVD approach. One learner said that it was easy to "move your concentration elsewhere" unless you had a lecturer to intervene with discussion or explanations.

Many learners said that the DVD approach gave more insight than school attendance provided and that they found it helpful for understanding concepts to do a section on a DVD during a Saturday session before it was done at school. Learners also used the DVD to "test and check" their understanding of a particular concept. They found that the DVD series was a good resource to consult when faced with homework or in preparation for a test or examinations. Many learners said that the DVDs allowed them to learn at their own pace and to watch a section "over again" until they understood the concepts. It was encouraging that many learners reported on watching the DVDs at home and revising together with the resource material. This approach helped to enhance their understanding and supports the effectiveness of the additional small learning cycle as shown in Figure 1.

Constructive criticism came from learners as they felt that some of the DVDs did not illustrate every step of a mathematical problem and that this lead to confusion. They asked for more detail and more examples on the DVDs.

The Blended Learning Environment. Most of the learners agreed that the DVD was a useful resource and also expressed appreciation for the blended environment within which this was embedded. They appreciated facilitators and tutors providing explanations and discussions while pausing the DVD. They needed the facilitators' explanations to bridge gaps where the DVD skipped steps or they had problems in understanding. According to learners, the tutors, facilitators and discussions with other learners helped them view mathematical concepts from multiple angles.

Learners felt that their English proficiency improved as a result of the blended learning approach. Only one learner suggested providing the DVDs in his mother tongue, an issue that is always contentious as there are eleven official languages in South Africa of which English is *lingua franca*. Learners said that they liked the way the ISP presentations blended the tutorials, DVDs and discussions and that this made it easier for them to concentrate for longer periods.

The point made by almost all learners was the ease with which learners could view the DVD and replay and pause whenever they wanted to. A few learners also said that their teacher used these DVDs at their schools to teach certain topics such as calculus. Some learners formed study groups and watched the DVDs in their study groups over weekends. The blended learning approach using DVDs presented a new way of learning mathematics for the learners and most of them were positive that the method benefited their understanding of the subject. The approach allowed them the freedom to access a variety of different resources, allowed them to work at their own pace and allowed them to revise at home.

Some learners noted, however, that at first they needed to adjust to this new learning environment but once they had adjusted they could see the advantages of being exposed to different modes of delivery. The majority of the learners agreed that this blended environment of teaching and learning mathematics fostered a deeper understanding of the subject for them. The most important point raised by learners was the fact that DVDs alone were not sufficient to ensure success. They believed the DVDs together with facilitators' and tutors' explanations and discussion coupled with the hard copy resources were the best blended approach for learning mathematics.

Facilitator Observation

It was important to obtain feedback from the facilitators, all experienced university lecturers. For this purpose data were also collected in the form of weekly reports by the four facilitators during 2007.

The facilitators' observations of learners' experiences of the blended learning environment were positive and encouraging. All the facilitators felt that the learners' confidence improved as a result of this approach. One facilitator noted that as the project progressed, communication and engagement between the facilitators and learners, between tutors and learners and amongst learners themselves improved. Another facilitator said that the level of mathematics questions posed by the learners improved with time. Although learners experienced the DVD technology as strange at first, all the facilitators agreed that the interaction within the blended learning environment was lively and fruitful.

According to yet another facilitator the "DVD was a powerful resource allowing learners to work at their own pace and review solutions and procedures until they understood the concept". All four facilitators said that they believed that DVDs should be used in conjunction with other face-to-face methods of teaching and learning, thus creating a stimulating blended environment. They believed that, used in isolation, the DVDs would not prove to be such a successful resource in the teaching and learning of mathematics.

Performance analysis: The learners' final Grade 11 mathematics results were compared with their final Grade 12 mathematics results to determine if an improvement in mathematical performance had occurred as a result of this blended learning intervention.

As a measure of success for the blended model the Grade 11 and Grade 12 mathematics marks of the 184 ISP learners were compared. It should be noted at the onset that this is not an ideal comparison as the Grade 11 examination is a local exam for which papers are drawn up at individual schools whereas the Grade 12 examination is a national examination where more stringent quality measures apply. The mean, standard deviation and median are given in Table 3.

There is a statistically significant improvement between the mean scores, although no practical significance is noted. This is confirmed by the *t*-test ($t = 2.35$, $d.f. = 183$, $p = .020$, $d = 0.17$). The distribution of marks, shown in Figure 2, is of interest as there is a clear shift to the right in marks from Grade 11 to Grade 12 but also an observed stronger tail.

The distribution for Grade 11 marks peaks with the majority of scores between 40 and 59 whereas the distribution for Grade 12 is more evenly spread. The Kolmogrov-Smirnov Test (K-S

Table 3. Grade 11 and grade 12 percentages for mathematics courses

	Grade 11	Grade 12
Mean (%)	48.41	51.36
Standard deviation	9.997	18.21
Median (%)	48.0	50.0

Figure 2. Distribution of grades 11 and 12 marks

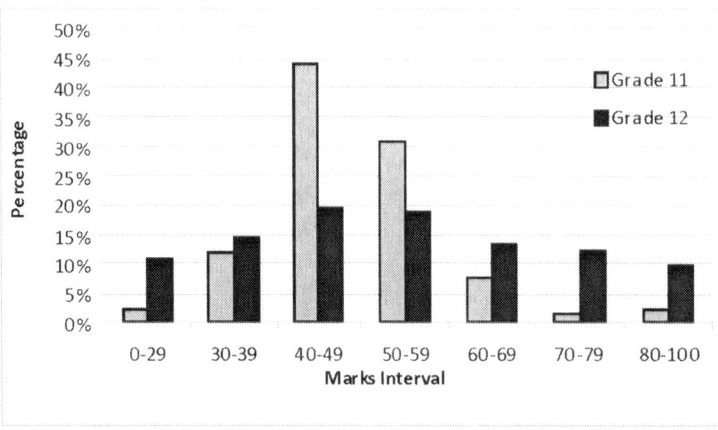

D = 0.245, $p < .01$) confirms a significant difference in distribution.

It is pleasing to note that in the higher intervals from 60 upwards there is clearly an improvement of marks from Grade 11 to Grade 12. In the categories 70+ there is an increase from Grade 11 to Grade 12 from 4% to 22%. Unfortunately there also are more learners who performed badly in Grade 12 compared to Grade 11. In fact, there is an increase in the category 0-39 from 14% in Grade 11 to 26% in Grade 12.

The relationship between the categories of marks for Grade 11 and Grade 12 is depicted in Table 4.

No learners from the 0-39 category in Grade 11 moved to the 70+ category in Grade 12 and similarly none of the learners in the category 70+ in Grade 11 moved to the 0-39 category in Grade 12. It is noteworthy that 25% of the learners in the 40-49 category in Grade 11 moved to the 70+ category in Grade 12.

It became clear from the quantitative data that not all learners responded to this particular blended learning approach. This is not a surprising finding, however unfortunate. Within a blended environment learners need to take ownership and responsibility and this was sadly not always the case. The DVDs are intended for follow-up study at home that cannot be enforced. The fact that a percentage of learners performed worse in the Grade 12 exam can also by no means be attributed to the blended approach of the ISP. The Grade 12 paper, as mentioned before could have been more difficult which makes the improvement of the higher performers even more impressive.

Case Study Investigation

A case study of a single school of 20 learners, six of whom were ISP participants and 14 were non-ISP participants, was performed. A school in a rural area neighbouring Port Elizabeth was used as a case study in order to compare performance between learners from the same school who participated in the ISP with those who did not. Only 19 of the learners' marks were used because of one absenteeism. Six of these learners participated in the 2007 ISP. Their 2007 final Grade 12 mathematics marks are compared with their 2006 learners' Grade 11 end of year mathematics marks (see Table 5).

Results of the learners who were on the ISP improved remarkably whilst those learners not on the ISP generally presented lower Grade 12

Table 4. Contingency table: grade 11 and grade 12 marks

	Grade 12							
Grade 11	**0-39**		**40 – 69**		**70+**		**Total**	
0 - 39	18	69%	8	31%	0	0%	26	100%
40 - 69	29	19%	85	56%	37	25%	151	100%
70+	0	0%	3	43%	4	57%	7	100%
Totals	47	26%	96	52%	41	22%	184	100%

Table 5. Grade 11 and grade 12 end of year marks for mathematics

	ISP Participants							Non ISP Participants													
Learners	1	2	3	4	5	6		7	8	9	10	11	12	13	14	15	16	17	18	19	20
2006	46	47	46	51	52	40		28	34	35	44	37	32	47	39	42	37	44	42	43	39
2007	80	60	60	60	70	70		10	10	10	40	10	10	40	10	42	10	10	40	40	A

Table 6. Average marks for ISP participants and non-ISP participants for 2006 and 2007

	2006	2007
ISP participants	7.0	66.7
Non-ISP participants	38.8	21.7

final results. It should be noted that the learners who took part in the ISP showed more interest in mathematics and science and are not surprisingly better performers. The results are summarised in Table 6.

To verify that the difference was statistically significant a Mann-Whitney U Test ($z = 3.38$, $p = 0.001$, $d = 3.20$) was conducted. A Cohen's d test was conducted for practical significance. It was found that the difference in means was of high practical significance ($d > 0.8$) which reflects a large difference.

Scope of Blending

We adapted a method of analysis developed by Harding, Engelbrecht, Lazenby and le Roux (2006) to assess the scope of blending of this blended model.

This radar chart measure offers a visual presentation that shows at one glance what the scope and extent of blending of a model is and to indicate the associated strengths and weaknesses. The Harding radar chart measure applies to a blend between face-to-face and online instruction, specifically web-based instruction. We adapted and generalised the measure to apply to a blend of face-to-face instruction and instruction via computer based technology that is not necessarily web-based. Six radials are identified, each with a question to quantify the measure:

Dynamics and Access: What is the frequency of use of computer technology necessary for success in the course?
1: Once per term
2: Once per month
3: Once per week
4: Two or three times a week
5: Daily

Assessment: How much of the assessment is done via computer technology?
1: Little
2: Almost half of it
3: More than half of it
4: Most of it
5: All of it

Communication: How much of the communication happens via computer technology?
1: Little
2: Almost half of it
3: More than half of it
4: Most of it
5: All of it

Content: How much of the content is available via computer technology?
1 for each component - study content, problems, tutorials, course information, course administration, with a maximum score of 5.

Richness: How many enriching components does the computer technology based part of the course have?
1 for each component such as computer algebra system, graphics, Java applets, slide presentations, video and sound clips; in effect more than text communication with a maximum score of 5.

Independence: How independent is success in the course from face-to-face contact?
1: Fully contact lecture and tutorial driven; technology and add-on
2: Contact lectures but computer technology based tutorials or assessment
3: Limited regular contact
4: Sporadic contact
5: No face-to-face contact

The ISP blended model scores as follows:

- Dynamics and Access: Score: 4. Learners view the DVDs on Saturdays and need to view it at least once at home during the week, in total two to three times per week.
- Assessment: Score: 2. Self-assessment at home is done by means of the technology, other assessment is disjoint of technology. Problems can be accessed on the DVDs.
- Communication: Score: 1. Communication is one-way while the DVD is presented and two-way communication only happens face-to-face.
- Content: Score: 4. All the content is given on the DVDs and is only supplemented face-to-face if the need arises.
- Richness: Score :4. In addition to voice-over presentations, animations are given, graphics are presented as well as step-by-step exposition.
- Independence: Score: 3. There is limited regular face-to-face contact between educators and learners.

The radar chart is given in Figure 3.

The area of the radial diagram gives an indication of the extent of blending of face-to-face contact and computer technology - the larger the area, the greater the technology component and the smaller the area the greater the face-to-face component. A convex shape, partially filling the chart area points to a well-blended course. The first three radials – dynamics, assessment, and communication – could be grouped under the heading *interaction.* The second three radials – content, richness, and independence could be grouped under the heading *material.*

The ISP blended model offers a fair blend between face-to-face learning and computer technology-based learning although it is not well-balanced around the centre. The model is deficient with respect to interaction, especially with respect to communication and to a lesser extent assessment. The low score in communication is the cause for the diagram to be concave. The model is well-balanced with respect to material and offers a good blend between face-to-face delivery and computer-based technology.

Reflecting on the Evaluation

We now move to the fourth phase of the action research cycle and reflect on the evaluation of the blended learning model.

Figure 3. Radar chart for ISP blended model

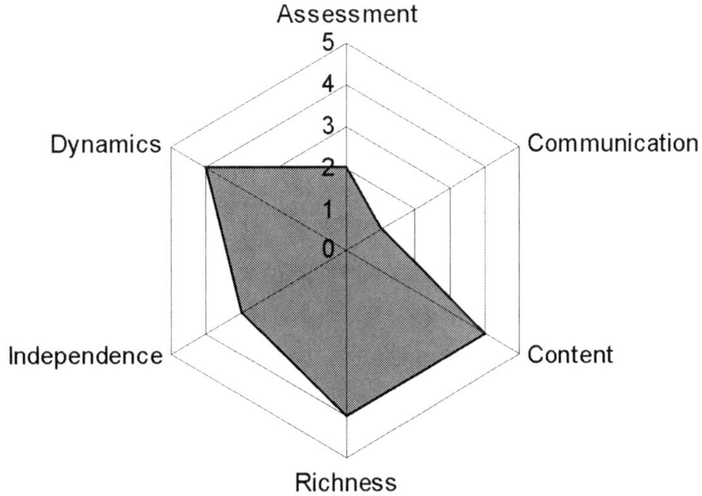

Qualitative results indicated that both learners' and teachers' experiences were largely positive with concerns identified that offer opportunity for improvement. Learners valued the blended environment of learning and expressed appreciation for the different components. The face-to-face discussions extended learners' concentration whereas the DVDs provided opportunity for repeated watching. Most learners attributed their better understanding of the mathematical concepts to the DVD approach that was used in conjunction with the other traditional modes of delivery.

An important finding is that learners spontaneously formed study groups for repeated watching of the DVDs over weekends. This practice should be encouraged. The radar chart measure pointed to too little communication via computer technology. Perhaps study groups can address this problem in the sense that communication will happen between students around the computer technology.

It is significant that the facilitators reported positively on the blended learning model and observed increased confidence and communication amongst learners. The value of blended learning was again emphasized.

Quantitative results indicate that there was a statistically significant difference when comparing the mean scores for learners' Grade 11 and Grade 12 results, although not of practical value. According to Calldo and du Plooy (2008) students who passed mathematics declined from 7.2% in 2006 to 6.9% in 2007 (as a percentage of the total number of Grade 12 learners). In the face of these declining results for mathematics in the 2007 Grade 12 examination (Pandor, 2007), our results seem to suggest that the DVD approach of blended learning could have in some way contributed to the improvement in mathematics results that was noted amongst many of the ISP learners, especially for the better learners. It is disappointing that a large group of the borderline learners did not seem to benefit from this blended learning approach. This finding is reason for concern as these are the learners that should be targeted and the reason for this disappointing deterioration has to be investigated.

The final phase in the action research cycle is that of implementing changes before a new cycle begins. For the blended model changes are implemented annually, based on feedback from both learners and teachers. DVDs are revised and streamlined and concerns expressed by students are addressed such that some example problems show too few steps. The presentation during Saturday morning sessions are also adapted along suggestions from facilitators and learners alike.

FUTURE RESEARCH DIRECTIONS

Harding, Kaczynski and Wood (2005) suggest that in order to be successful in using blended learning one has to not only implement learning reforms but it is important to evaluate these reforms and in so doing provide learners with the best possible outcomes. The ISP saw the implementation of DVD technology for the first time in 2007 and this research aimed to evaluate its value to the teaching and learning of mathematics. In order to provide learners with the best possible outcomes, "it is important that we continue to identify successful approaches of blended learning at institutional, program, course and activity levels that can be adapted to work in contexts" (Graham, 2004). The DVD blended learning approach still requires further development and refinement especially with regard to the skills of facilitators within such a blended learning environment and the development of materials. This and other issues will be looked at in future research initiatives.

Although the DVDs were intended for the usage of ISP learners it appeared that some of the teachers also made use of these in a classroom environment. Following the change to an outcomes-based education system many teachers found themselves under-prepared for the new challenge. The new education system exacerbated the problem of an already under-qualified teacher corps. It would be of interest to investigate the possible usage of the DVDs within either a classroom situation or by teachers themselves.

CONCLUSION

This chapter set out to describe a blended learning model devised with the purpose of contributing in alleviating the crisis in secondary school mathematics in post-apartheid South Africa. This blended model's defining feature is that it incorporates DVD technology that offers an affordable and accessible option for the particular group of learners. From the study it is clear that this blended approach not only offers a workable teaching approach but that there are definite advantages to this approach. One of the advantages of using DVD technology within a blended approach is the accessibility of the subject content and presentation outside the classroom to a community that does not have internet access in general.

The fact that the DVD technology is easily accessible and affordable supports a case that the DVD approach could also help to address the shortage of adequately qualified teachers and the lack of teaching resources at previously disadvantaged schools in South Africa. Solving the education crisis in South Africa is an enormous challenge and needs to be addressed at governmental level. Yet by offering workable local solutions the crisis is indeed alleviated and enables individual learners to secure a future and realise their dreams. The blended model described here is the initiative of one tertiary institution, driven by people who conducted the program on top of an already full schedule. The target group of learners was a small local group and contributes in a small way to alleviating the post-apartheid South African education crisis. Although such efforts are valiant it is important that government should take note of such workable solutions and introduce these on a country-wide level.

REFERENCES

Aminifar, E., Porter, A., Caladine, R., & Nelson, M. I. (2007). Creating mathematical learning resources-combining audio and visual components. *Australian and New Zealand Industrial and Applied Mathematical Journal*, *47*, C934–C955.

Anglogold, A. (2004) *Report to society*. Retrieved August 2009, from http://www.anglogoldashanti.co.za/subwebs/InformationForInvestors/Report-ToSoceity04/values b us principles/community/c cs sa 7 9.htm

Badenhorst, J. J. C., & de Beer, K. J. (2004). Blended learning at the Central University of Technology, Free State. *Emerge 2004 Proceedings*. (pp. 1-11) Retrieved February 2010, from http://emerge2004.net/connect/site/UploadWSC/emerge2004/file20/emerge2004article.doc

Bengu, S. M. E. (1997). *Foreword in Curriculum 2005: Lifelong learning for the 21st century*. Pretoria, South Africa: Department of Education.

Calldo, F., & du Plooy, T. (2008). *Researcher's solidarity. Eskom: Skills Facts*. Retrieved 20 October, 2009, from http://www.solidariteitinstituut.co.za/docs/skills_fact.pdf

Cohen, M. L., Grady, M., & Springer, S. (2007). Centering on learning at Penn. *Talk About Teaching and Learning - Almanac, 50*(9). Retrieved December, 2009, from http://www.upenn.edu/almanac/v50/n09/teaching.html

Daniels, G. (2007). SA – maths = crisis. *Mail and Guardian Online*. Accessed March 16, 2008, from http://www.mg.co.za/articlePage.aspx.articleid=300522&area=/ the_teacher/teacher_features

Denscombe, M. (2007). *The good research guide for small-scale social research projects. New York, NY: McGraw-Hill Education Department of Education. (2000). Instructional leadership. School management teams*. Pretoria, South Africa: Department of Education.

Department of Education. (2002). *Report on some of the key programmes of the department of education presented at the parliamentary media briefing on 15 August 2002*. Retrieved August 2008, from http://www.search.gov.za/info/previewDocument.jsp?dk=%2Fdata%2Fstatic%2Finfo%2Fspeeches%2F2002%2F02081610461001.htm%40Gov&q=%3Cphrase%3E+(project+management)&t=Asmal%3A+Parliamentary+Media+Briefing+(Education+progress+report)%2C+August+2002

Edutech Wiki. (2010). *5e learning cycle*. Retrieved February 2010, from http://edutechwiki.unige.ch/en/5e_Learning_cycle

Engelbrecht, J., & Harding, A. (2008). The impact of the transition to outcomes-based teaching on university preparedness in mathematics in South Africa. *Mathematics Education Research Journal*, *20*(2), 57–70.

Garrison, D. R., & Vaughan, N. D. (2008). *Blended learning in higher education: Framework, principles, and guidelines*. San Francisco, CA: Jossey-Bass.

Gibbins, M. L., Hadibi, R., Urbaczewski, A., & Vivian, C. (2007). Technology-enhanced learning in blended learning environments: A report on standard practices. *Communications of the Association for Information Systems*, *20*(46), 741–759.

Graham, C. R. (2006). Blended learning systems: Definition, current trends, and future directions. In Bonk, C. J., & Graham, C. R. (Eds.), *Handbook of blended learning: Global perspectives, local designs* (pp. 3–21). San Francisco, CA: Pfeiffer.

Graven, M. (2002). Coping with new mathematics teacher roles in a contradictory context of curriculum change. *The Mathematics Educator*, *12*(2), 21–27.

Harding, A., Engelbrecht, J., Lazenby, K., & le Roux, I. (2006). Blended learning in undergraduate mathematics at the University of Pretoria. In Bonk, C. J., & Graham, C. R. (Eds.), *Handbook of blended learning: Global perspectives, local designs* (pp. 400–418). San Francisco, CA: Pfeiffer.

Harding, A., Kaczynski, D., & Wood, L. (2005). Evaluation of blended learning: Analysis of qualitative data. *Uniserve Science Blended Learning Symposium Proceedings* (pp. 56-62). University of Sydney, Australia.

Jansen, J. D. (1998). Curriculum reform in South Africa: A critical analysis of outcomes-based education. *Cambridge Journal of Education*, *28*(3), 321–331. doi:10.1080/0305764980280305

Luca, J. (2006). Using blended learning to enhance teaching and learning. In D. Tolhurst & S. Mann (Eds.), *Proceedings of the 8th Australian Conference on Computing Education* (pp. 3-4). Hobart, Australia.

Maguire, C., & Zhang, J. (2006). *Effective blended learning for development.* Workshop on Designing and Delivering Blended Distance Learning Programs through GDLN. World Bank Tokyo Development Learning Center and DGHE Indonesia, Jakarta.

Mail & Guardian online. (2009). *Mantashe: Education struggles with apartheid legacy*. Retrieved February 2010, from http://www.mg.co.za/article/2009-10-08-mantashe-education-struggles-with-apartheid-legacy.

Manchester, H., Ralph, S., & Shipova, O. (2005). The teacher's role in using WebCT as a communication tool with postgraduate students. *The International Journal of Learning*, *12*(4), 101–107.

Mathematics Education Community. (2000). *Submission to the Council of Education Ministers* (CEM). Retrieved February 2010, from http://academic.sun.ac.za/mathed/AMESA/NGO.htm

McNiff, J. (2008). *Planning, designing and doing action research.* Retrieved June 2010, from http://www.actionresearch.net/writings/jack/jmplanar.pdf

Mphala, D., & Tshishonge, N. (2008). Khanya project. *Innovation insights 10, Case study 2.* Public Services Innovation CPSI. Retrieved February 2010, from http://www.cpsi.co.za/documents/Innovation%20Insight/Insight%2010,%20march%202008.pdf

Ngosana, C. (2008). *SA needs teachers*. Retrieved December 2009, from http://www.news24.com/Content/SouthAfrica/News/1059/6920a322b4e44e9ba7ff6e68f209b623/01-06-2008-02-30/SA_needs_teachers

Nicholson, Z. (2009). Matric maths crisis looms. *Weekend Argus.* Retrieved February 2010, from http://www.iol.co.za/index.php?set_id=1&click_id=13&art_id=vn20090726064117725C376939&singlepage=1

Nieuwoudt, S., Nieuwoudt, H., & Monteith, J. (2007). Influence of a video class system on learners' study and learning strategies band their achievement in mathematics. *African Journal of Research in Mathematics. Science and Technology Education, 11*(1), 29–35.

Ocampo, M. L. (2004). *A brief history of educational inequality from apartheid to the present.* Seminar paper from Global Perspectives on Human Language: The South African Context. Retrieved November 2009, from http://www.stanford.edu/~jbaugh/saw/Lizet_Education_Inequity.html

Osguthorpe, R. T., & Graham, C. R. (2003). Blended learning environments: Definitions and directions. *The Quarterly Review of Distance Education, 4*(3), 227–233.

Pandor, N. (2007). *Statement by Naledi Pandor MP, Minister of Education, on the release of the 2007 senior certificate examination results.* Sol Plaatje, Pretoria. Retrieved July 2008, from: http://www.gov.za

Petro, S. A's Maths, Science Academy. (2008). *South Africa information.* Retrieved February 2010 from: http://www.southafrica.info/business/economy/development/petrosa-291008.htm

Pratt, D. D. (2005) Communication skills online three years down the line: Reflecting on design principles in blended learning. *Proceedings of 7th Annual Conference on World Wide Web Applications.* Cape Technikon, Cape Town, 29-31 August 2005. Retrieved June 2008, from http://www.uj.ac.za/www2005/documents/Pratt,%20DD.pdf

Reddy, V., Van der Berg, S., Lebani, L., & Berkowitz, R. (2006). A trend analysis of matric maths performance. In Reddy, V. (Ed.), *Marking matric: Colloquium proceedings* (pp. 139–160). Cape Town, South Africa: HSRC Press.

Rosset, A., Douglis, F., & Frazee, R. V. (2003). Strategies for building blended learning. *Learning Circuits.* Retrieved December 2008, from http://www.learningcircuits.org/2003/jul2003/rossett.htm

Simkins, C., Rule, S., & Beinstein, A. (2007). *Doubling for growth. Addressing the maths and science challenge in South Africa's schools: A report for Centre for Development and Enterprise.*

Singh, H. (2003). Building effective blended learning programs. *Educational Technology, 43*(6), 51–54.

Singh, H., & Reed, C. (2001). *A White Paper: Achieving success with blended learning.* ASTD State of the Industry Report, American Society for Training and Development, March 2001.

Umalusi (2008). Improving the quality of teaching: Making a difference in public schooling. Retrieved October 2009, from http://www.umalusi.org.za/ur/publications/20080910Improvingthequalityofteaching.pdf

Zenex Foundation. (2007). *The Zenex Foundation's ten-year strategy 2006-2015*. Retrieved August 2009, from http://www.zenexfoundation.org.za/strategy.php

ADDITIONAL READING

Acharya, C. (2003). Outcome-based education (OBE): A new paradigm for learning. *CDT Link*, *7*(3), 8–9.

Alexander, S., & Boud, D. (2001). Learners still learn from experience when online. In Stephenson, J. (Ed.), *Teaching and learning online: pedagogies for new technologies*. London: Kogan Page.

Bersin, J. (2003). What works in blended learning. *Learning Circuits*. Retrieved October 26, 2008 from http://www.learningcircuits.org/2003/jul2003/bersin.htm

Bonk, C. J., Kim, K. J., & Zeng, T. (2005). Future Directions of Blended Learning in Higher Education and Workplace Learning Settings. In Bonk, C. J., & Graham, C. R. (Eds.), *Handbook of blended learning: Global Perspectives, local designs*. San Francisco: Pfeiffer.

Bouslama, F., Lansari, A., Al-Rawi, A., & Abonamah, A. A. (2003). A novel outcome-based educational model and its effect on student learning, curriculum development, and assessment. *Journal of Information Technology Education*, *2*, 203–214.

Braimoh, D., & Osiki, J. O. (2008). The impact of technology on accessibility and pedagogy: the right to education in Sub-Saharan Africa. *Asian Journal of Distance Education*, *6*(1), 53–62.

Brodie, K. (2006). Teaching mathematics for equity: learner contributions and lesson structure. *African Journal for Research in Mathematics. Science and Technology*, *10*(1), 13–24.

Creswell, J. W. (2003). *Research design: qualitative, quantitative, and mixed methods approaches* (2nd ed.). London: Sage Publications.

Driscoll, M. (1998). *Web-based training: Using technology to design adult learning experiences*. San Francisco: Jossey-Bass.

Driscoll, M. (2002). Blended learning: let's go beyond the hype. *E-learning*, 54.

Garrison, D. R. & Anderson, T. (2005). *E-Learning in the 21st Century: A Framework for Research and Practice*. London: Routledge Farmer .

Graham, C. R. (2004). Blended Learning Systems. In Bonk, C. J., & Graham, C. R. (Eds.), *Handbook of blended learning: Global perspectives, local designs*. San Francisco: Pfeiffer.

Kerres, M., & De Witt, C. (2003). A Didactical Framework for the Design of Blended Learning Arrangements. *Journal of Educational Media*, *28*(2-3), 101–113.

McNiff, J., & Whitehead, J. (2002). *Action Research: Principles and Practice* (2nd ed.). New York, London: Routledge Farmer.

Northedge, A. (2003). Rethinking teaching in the context of diversity. *Teaching in Higher Education*, *8*(1), 17–32. doi:10.1080/1356251032000052302

Oliver, R. (1999). Exploring strategies for online teaching and learning. *Distance Education*, *20*(2), 240–254. doi:10.1080/0158791990200205

Parkinson, D., Greene, W., Kim, Y., & Marioni, J. (2003). Emerging themes of student satisfaction in a traditional course and a blended distance course. *TechTrends*, *47*(4), 22–28. doi:10.1007/BF02763508

Rogan, J. M. (2004). Out of the frying pan ...?: Case studies of the implementation of Curriculum 2005 in some science classrooms. *African Journal of Research in Mathematics. Science and Technology Education*, *8*(2), 165–179.

Rovai, A. P., & Jordan, H. (2004). Blended Learning and Sense of Community: A Comparative Analysis with Traditional and Fully Online Graduate Courses. *International Review of Research in Open and Distance Learning*, *5*(2), 1–17.

Rynearson, K., & Kerr, M. S. (2005, Fall). Teaching Statistics online in a blended learning Environment. *Journal of Computing in Higher Education*, *17*(1), 71–94. doi:10.1007/BF02960227

Smith, P. L., & Ragan, T. J. (2005). *Instructional Design* (3rd ed.). Hoboken, NJ: Wiley.

Valiathan, P. (2002). Blended learning models. *Learning Circuits*. Retrieved October 26, 2005 from http://www.learningcircuits.org/2002/aug2002/valiathan.html

Verspoor, A. (1989). *Pathways to change. Improving the quality of education in developing countries*. Washington: The World Bank.

Whitehead, J., & Mc Niff, J. (2006). *Action Research Living Theory*. London: Sage.

Zuber-Skerritt. (2002). A model for designing action learning and action research programs. *The Learning Organization*, *9*(4), 143–149. doi:10.1108/09696470210428868

KEY TERMS AND DEFINITIONS

Apartheid: A previous political dispensation in South Africa that advocated race discrimination.

Blended Learning: A combination of face-to-face instruction with computer-mediated instruction, including DVD technology.

Incubator Schools Project: An initiative of the Nelson Mandela Metropolitan University aimed at increasing the level of mathematics in schools around Port Elizabeth.

Outcomes-Based Education: A learner-centered education system that aims to provide learners with more mobility between the different fields of study and occupations.

Scope of Blending: The extent to which various components of the learning model are blended with respect to face-to-face and computer mediated instruction.

Chapter 8
The Role of Blended Learning in 21st Century Medical Education: Current Trends and Future Directions

Geoffrey W. Payne
University of Northern British Columbia, Canada

ABSTRACT

The teaching of medical students is of paramount importance for society as the goal is to have well-educated and competent physicians that can help address the healthcare issues facing today's society. The pedagogical influences that drive medical education have seen many advances in the past 30 years, but one that is seen as a leader for the future is the use of blended learning. This chapter will highlight that blended learning in medicine allows learners to be flexible in their education, as they are not constrained by time or distance as they move towards developing core competencies needed for their chosen discipline. One of the key drivers of this momentum in medicine is technology, and blended learning is one of the leading pedagogical influences in medical education for the future.

INTRODUCTION

The global debate of healthcare access and social detriments of health in the 21st century continue to coalesce our thoughts around the paramount question how we are teaching the future physicians of the day who are an integral part of the team that delivers healthcare to us as a society. Given the challenges that society faces with the rapidly aging population and increase in chronic diseases such as obesity, diabetes and hypertension, are we delivering healthcare education in manner that allows them to be both educated and competent in order to combat the health problems of global society? This might be considered a grandiose question when thinking of the latest

DOI: 10.4018/978-1-60960-479-0.ch008

pedagogical methods used in medical education today but this is where we need to begin in order to assess the role of new methods of educational delivery for medical training and determine if they are indeed the most appropriate for the task at hand. The education of medical students in the 21st century should not come without some reflective thought and in thinking back over the past 100 years in medical education, this reflection has not occurred since the first definitive report by Abraham Flexner in 1910 on the landscape of teaching methods used in medical schools at the turn of the century. That report culminated with a harsh and systematic review of the state of medical education of the day and provided clear guidelines that evoked broad sweeping changes that have since governed medical education for past 100 years and has shaped the direction of how medical students should be taught and by what methods.

Flexner's principles have influenced medical education for the past century but it has truly been in the past 30 years that we have witnessed tremendous growth in medical education teaching practices. According to Harden (2000), we can think of this growth in two fundamental ways. Harden argues:

We can look at the changes taking place in medical education as a journey where the future is a continuing evolution of what has happened in the past three decades or so-an evolutionary approach. Alternatively, we may visualize a more dramatic journey to a different world where there are fundamental changes in medical education, some of which we have difficulty envisaging at this point at the beginning of the 21st century- a revolutionary approach. (p. 435)

I would suggest that today's teaching of future physicians resonates with the latter of Harden's comments and this is a result of a what can be considered a "perfect storm" in medical education that combines the rapidly advancing technology being developed, the changes in the medical student as a learner and the context in which the learning occurs. The confluence of these circumstances will allow a fundamental cultural shift in teaching the next generation of physicians. This cultural or paradigm shift in medical education pedagogy can be put under the umbrella of moving teaching practices towards a blended learning approach.

In the recent *Futures of Medical Education in Canada Report* (2010) delivered by the Association of Faculties of Medicine of Canada (AFMC) one of the key recommendations was to diversify learning contexts in which physicians must provide continuing medical care in a wide range of institutional and community settings. To achieve this, the learning experiences throughout the MD education program must include a variety of settings ranging from small rural communities to complex tertiary care settings. To enable this mandate, current medical schools must modify current MD curricula and adapt and improve the use of technology (i.e., blended learning). This suggestion aligns with an earlier report of the American Association of Medical Colleges (AAMC) (2007) institute for improving medical education in which it was concluded that medical educators must continue to increasingly use technology to supplement the delivery of learning resources. These two reports and the highlighted recommendations suggest new teaching modalities are required to teach the future physicians and in my opinion the blended learning approach is the ideal method to meet the developing needs of teaching these students.

The focus of this present book is blended learning and this addresses more than just new frontiers in medical education pedagogy but is also at the forefront of many disciplines such as chemistry, nursing, business, and education among others. The scope of this chapter is not to provide a plethora of examples of blended learning or e-learning in medicine but rather to highlight how medical education has evolved to capitalize on blended learning opportunities and its potential to improve the future training of physicians. As stated, this may be the time whereby such a change could harness the unprecedented advances that have taken place in technology to allow new models of medical education to be developed (Horton, 2001). We must ensure that the use of blended learning produces benefits associated with its use. We must also address limitations of this approach and remain cognizant of these limitations to maximize the benefit of this approach to both the learner and the educator in a profession that is driven by "competency" and "outcome measures".

The goal of medical education is to facilitate expertise or mastery of one's chosen discipline and to do so requires extensive practice to achieve this mastery of performance. The four steps to this are repetition of a skill, rigorous assessment of that performance, feedback pertinent to the skill practiced and improved performance (Ericisson, 2001). As we will see in this later in this chapter that it may be useful to use a blended learning approach to deliver on these four pillars of medical education and combat the many challenges facing medical educators including increasing student numbers in medical schools, changes in medical practice and globalization. The response to this by the current medical schools has been to expand the learning environments to rural and small communities and this may require the latest charge of distributed medical education. This meets the current mandate by the governing bodies that regulate and provide accreditation to medical schools in North America and worldwide.

BLENDED LEARNING IN MEDICINE

To begin the discussion of the role of blended learning in medical education models and impact on any medical curriculum we must first define what is it that we mean or would include as blended learning in medical school curricula. Given the method by which medicine is taught and the premise of its curricula, the definition may vary with other definitions in other disciplines discussed in this book. In medicine today most blended learning is also described as e-learning as the two appear almost interchangeably in the literature. Therefore, when we use *blended learning* in context of teaching medical students and for the purposes of discussion in this chapter the definition of blended learning that will be used is any learning that integrates the traditional face-to-face didactic one-way or transmission teaching modality to a model of interactive engagement where the learner has the opportunity to "blend" traditional teaching models with some form of supplementary learning that provides necessary feedback to ensure competency or outcomes are achieved. In this blended environment the student has a self-directed learning objective, competency or outcome in which they rely on technology to review that is supplemented with an educator or instructor providing necessary feedback. More-importantly as we will see when discussing the future of medical education and training the key will lie in the mobility of the blended learning activities as the landscape of what constitutes a medical school is changing and also the associated ideology.

Opportunities for Blended Learning in Medical Education

When we think of the opportunities that are available for blended learning to occur in medical education we first have to establish what the curricular landscape is prior to this discussion. This is vital to see the limitless potential of blended learning opportunities in medical education. The degree in Doctor of Medicine (MD), and subsequent profession of a practicing physician, is a complex spiral curriculum that provides continuous learning opportunities long after graduation. The basic premise is a system of set core competencies and associated knowledge base that one must be able to demonstrate mastery of prior to attaining their MD degree. This period of undergraduate education, albeit in a professional program, in which student usually already has a previous undergraduate university degree, takes four years to complete. Within those four years there is a division between the pre-clinical years in which the student takes foundational courses in anatomy, physiology, biochemistry, genetics, microbiology, histology, pathology and pathophysiology among others. These courses are usually lecture based delivery in which the number of lectures in a given week in variable given the medical school. There are also foundational pre-clinical courses in which the student begins to build the framework of history taking, communication skills and basic clinical skills. Following the pre-clinical years begin the clinical years which there is an intense third year of the MD program where the student builds upon the foundational core knowledge and basic competencies and begins to add the fundamental core competencies of the 10 major disciplines of medicine which are surgery, anesthesia, pediatrics, internal medicine, obstetrics, psychiatry, ophthalmology, emergency medicine, dermatology and orthopedics. These discipline specific curricula are delivered with a combination of lectures and clinical work where the purpose is again to build the foundational core competencies. At the end of intense third year of training the student spends the final year of the MD program engaging in more discipline specific training usually in blocks of three-four weeks where they begin to focus on disciplines that will shape there future career direction. The teaching modality during this period is very clinical that is emphasized on the student learning the desired competencies of the discipline and assessed by current physicians in the specific discipline. At the end of this period the student graduates and obtains the degree of MD. This does not end their medical training as to become an independent practicing physician the recent graduate must now enter the residency years (post-graduate) that can take anywhere from two years for the specialty of Family Medicine or five years for the remainder of the core disciplines such as surgery or psychiatry. During these residency years the learner continues to engage in activities that are specific to the core disciplines of their chosen discipline and evaluated by educators to assess their knowledge and level of skill in their chosen discipline.

In describing this intense complex training where as stated the profession of medicine is built upon the mandate of core competencies, practice and mastery following many feedback sessions with educators, I hope it is apparent that there exist endless opportunities for the learner to use blended learning techniques. Briefly, the learner could adapt the traditional face-face-face learning of the competencies and revisit the material through a variety of modalities such as e-learning and apply the acquired new knowledge to receive feedback on whether the learning has occurred and further, what the learner needs to work towards to achieve the desired objective. Within this chapter we will discuss specific examples of this but the goal of this section is to begin to address the complexity of medical education and training and highlight the potential for blended learning to help the learner during the course of their long educational path. At the end of residency there is not end to the learning as one of the cornerstones of being a physician is continuing professional development (CPD) and continuing medical education (CME).

As the title of this section suggests "Opportunities for Blended Learning in Medicine" for the historical view of the delivery of this curriculum has been on the emphasis on traditional lecture based and face-to-face delivery for the learner. For example there has been a shift towards more integrated and multi-disciplinary curricula (Association for the Faculties of Medicine of Canada, 2010; General Medical Council, 1993; Harden et al., 1984; Harden, 2000b) to problem- and task-based learning, (Barrows & Tamblyn, 1980; Davis & Harden, 1999; Harden, 1996), to student centered learning, (Harden, 2000, Harden, 2001), which as we will discuss is fundamental to the success of latest blended learning approach, to the development of core curricula with special discipline specific modules (Harden & Davis, 1995) to community-based education (Snadden, 2009) and outcome-based education (Harden, 1999). These are only some of the shifts in medical curriculum but what this "outside the box" thinking is doing is beginning to change the landscape of how medical students are taught and that it is ok to change in order to maximize learning. What is also allowed was a softening the traditional views of medical curriculum and teaching that would allow medical schools to begin to capitalize on the booming educational technology that was quickly becoming available and utilize it for medical education. Furthermore, as we will see in subsequent sections allow medical schools to utilize this technology to deliver the next wave in medical education; distributed or distance medical education.

History of E-Learning in Medicine

Now that the landscape of the MD program curriculum has been outlined and the potential use of blended learning to achieve success for the learner has been discussed let us now be reflective in what has been the used previously to shape where we may go in the future based on continuing shifts in medical training and medical school ideology. Blended learning or e-learning has now been used in some components at all levels of medical training from undergraduate through to post-graduate and beyond into continuing professional development. I am not stating that medical schools are complete with reshaping curriculum to use blended learning and technology as we will see latter but we must look at how it has been used to date and where it needs to go.

The use of blended learning can help to meet any curriculum gaps and there is no doubt that if delivered appropriately, can be effective and enrich the learning experience for the student while at the same time allowing the educator to take on a more productive role Harden (2008). It has been suggested that blended learning and e-learning can contribute to the learning outcomes such as critical thinking, self reflection, multiculturalism, team work and intra-professionalism, which are vital to the success in educating future physicians (Harden, 2008). What is also abundantly apparent is that in the old traditional methodology of face-to-face teaching that these learning outcomes would be unrealistic to attain (Hughes et al., 2008).

In a systematic review in 2004 conducted by Lau and Bates to address the role of e-learning in undergraduate medical education, terminology was critical. As stated in the opening sections of this chapter the words blended learning and e-learning are sometimes viewed interchangeably and this review is solid effort to address was actually being delivered from a e-learning perspective. We can retroactively apply our definition to determine if the learning that occurred within these medical school's curriculum was indeed blended learning. Take into account as well that this is all at the undergraduate level and not at the post-graduate level and beyond but irrespective a good starting point.

What Lau and Bates achieved was a search of the literature using the key words of e-learning, undergraduate medical education, distance, and Internet covering the years of 1997-2002. There was also a subsequent search using the key words of video-conferencing, medical and education. Overall, 193 articles were reviewed and within the context of e-learning, they evaluated curriculum on the basis of technology, type of learner, subject area and learning activity. To highlight some of the major findings within this review were that under the discussion of technology that the types reported included Web-based platforms, Internet connectivity tools, streaming video, interactive CDs, videoconference and specialized software but what was more striking that over 95% of the curriculum delivery reported that it was an asynchronous delivery of the curriculum through online content to enhance self-learning by students or to supplement traditional classroom/lab sessions by instructors (i.e., potentially blended learning). In regard to type of learning it was shown that e-learning was being used in both the pre-clinical and clinical years of undergraduate medical training but predominantly in the pre-clinical and there was no area of study that predominates in the use of teaching via an e-learning method. Overall, most of the e-learning curriculum delivery that was reported was focused on the deployment of interactive content to enhance individualized learning. Although favorable comments were made by students regarding the use of e-learning delivery during their studies there needs to be further evaluation needed to have been conducted to validate success of outcomes and competencies achieved by the students. From here we need to ascertain what is the rationale for the use of blended learning in future of medical education as a step beyond these e-learning activities and further validated for success of the modality.

WHY USE BLENDED LEARNING IN MEDICINE?

As we have outlined in the previous sections there is a potential in the current medical curriculum and changing medical school ideology to use blended learning opportunities to teach its learners but this decision to embark on such direction in medical education that will ultimately change how we train future physicians and must be rooted in a rationale that is sound. One should never undertake such a curricula change just because it is there so to speak. In the context of medical education and medical training of all learners in medicine from undergraduate to postgraduate years there is potentially four pillars of which to provide the rationale and framework to use aspects of blended learning in the medical curriculum. In a recent discussion on blended learning, Graham outlines the reasons of "why blend?" in the context of overall educational delivery. Graham states that there are many reasons to blend over traditional face-to-face methods which include first and foremost (1) pedagogical richness, (2) access to knowledge, (3) social interaction, (4) personal agency, (5) cost effectiveness and (6) ease of revision (Graham, 2004). For the discussion of why should medical schools use blended learning in their curriculum I believe the focus should be on five key reasons of which that is pedagogical richness, access to knowledge and flexibility, cost effectiveness, the 21st century learner and finally mobility. As we will see later in the discussion of the future of medical education, these five reasons are soundly grounded in facilitating the most robust and effective medical school curriculum as we move forward in medicine and medical training. This section will discuss each of these reasons for using blended learning separately as it pertains directly to medical education except for the rationale of mobility, which we will discuss later in the section on the future of medical education.

Pedagogical Richness

The roadmap to obtaining a MD degree and subsequent post-graduate residency training journey is extremely complicated, diverse and heavily weighted on acquiring core competencies and delivering outcomes that are specific to an individual's choice of career discipline. There is no doubt that in the medical education literature that transmissive one-way learning is teacher-focused rather than student-focused and this can be problematic because this type of learning is not interactive. In a discipline such as medicine where practice and feedback are essential for learning one would suggest that interactive learning would allow the learner to continually revisit core knowledge topics and practice them in a clinical setting while receiving feedback from the educator of what has been cemented and what needs more practice. For example, one use of a blended learning approach to something as rudimentary as the understanding of basic hospital skills for second year medical students. One would think that skill would be easily taught but what we do know that most students entering their first "clinical exposure" in hospital settings have great difficulty in bridging the gap between a typical lecture-based curricular model to now dealing with live patients and using such skills as communication in their first forays in history taking.

In a recent study from McGill University in Canada as part of their second year introduction to the medical practice course that is designed to prepare medical students for the clerkship years, which as you may recall in the third year of the undergraduate MD program, they noticed that students have difficulty with this transition and utilization of basic skills as history taking, data collection, completing hospital forms, writing progress notes and other procedural aspects of working in a hospital setting is difficult and forgotten easily (Bass et al., 1997; Duque et al., 2006). Despite the traditional preparatory course that was delivered in a face-to-face manner whereby the professors of the medical school would provide was an orientation to clinical life both students and educators felt that they were underprepared for this critical transition and required core competency.

To address this major gap in the student-learning trajectory the thought was to combine traditional lectures with use of interactive software and web-based technology to simulate the clinical setting of that of third year clerkships. The course began with a series of two-one hour lectures showing a clinical case scenario using video and more importantly the students were able to interact with a hospital forms that were pertinent to the case and required to be completed in a normal situation. The second part of this course was a second interactive case that utilized a web-based case construct software that reproduced a "patient" interview online. Following the completion of this patient interview the students completed the course by summarizing the information and completing an online form. The learning activity was completed when feedback was given back to the students by the educators describing the merits and areas to improve on in their tasks.

The outcome of this endeavour into a blended learning approach that it highlighted that blending the educational material with both lecture and web-based exercises was an effective way to teach basic hospital skills. The students could improve their data collection skills with immediate feedback, students could improve their performance during their early clerkship rotations through the use of this activity and finally the educators felt that student performance improved significantly using this blended learning approach.

Now, this type of learning was basic but does fit with the premise of medical school profession and ideology that in order to proficient as a physicians these core competencies must be acquired and in a way to allow progression to the next level. The next question is could blended learning be used for more complex clinical situations?

In another recent study a group from the University of Glasgow addressed the fundamental problem to what is the best method to teach acute care management to undergraduate medical students just prior to graduation (Shah et al., 2007). In particular this area has been poorly taught in the past (Smith et al., 2007) and given its importance, as a core competency, new methods should be adopted. What this group constructed was a virtual learning environment (VLE) to complement the clinical teaching that was already being taught to the students. Within the VLE there was a collection of clinical cases that resembled real-life medical scenarios including the common cardiovascular and respiratory emergencies so often seen by physicians. There was also a collection of pertinent resources for the students to use when working through the specific cases. The cases begin with history taking and clinical examination, which is similar to what would be supplied when a real patient presented at the hospital. The student is meant then to order tests and decide a course of investigation for the patient with subsequent follow-up until final diagnosis is confirmed. Attached to each case is a series of multiple-choice questions that the students are meant to answer. On completion of all the questions the student submitted their answers for marking and received feedback of both the correct and incorrect answers and information about why. Remember, these virtual cases are being conducted at the same time that students continue to take the traditional clinical course teaching with the teaching physicians. The benefit to this mode of blended learning is the VLE provided an excellent resource to exam revision and students could take the tutorials multiple times as needed. This type of learning allowed the individual students to work on areas that were deficient to them in their clinical reasoning and work on mastery of core competencies prior to graduation. From an educator perspective it allows for rapid curriculum shifts to highlight areas that were not well taught to all students and overall improvement of the curriculum so in the end a more complete a robust model of education is presented to the students.

In these two examples we can see quite clearly that the use of blended learning demonstrated a pedagogical rationale that is well grounded in not just providing an optional learning opportunity or experience to the medical students but it decisively allowed for students to practice and attain core knowledge and competency vital for their career. Prior to this option or new modality in teaching this type of learning would not have been possible or that students were continuing to underachieve. Thus, using these two examples it highlights that the use of blended learning provided a pedagogical richness to the medical curriculum that was well received by both student and educator. It also allowed self-identification of the student that more practice is required which is key in a competency driven profession.

Access to Knowledge and Flexibility

It is clear from the above examples that the availability of knowledge and the flexibility as to when and where to access the knowledge is conducted has been shifted from the teacher/educator to that of the student. This is a fundamental key to success in a blended learning delivery model as in traditional learning face-to face model, either be it in a lecture hall or and the bedside in hospital, the learning would take place at the discretion of the teacher. For example the "the lecture on heart disease will take place at 11:00 tomorrow morning"; what this implies is that at this time only will the information be delivered. There would likely be a handout of the lecture and the associated textbook but it assumes that every student will acquire the knowledge at the same level and rate from this one lecture. What an blended learning approach has shown in the teaching of acute care management example from the University of Glasgow is that with increase access and flexibility the student has the ability to assess knowledge level, revisit information, re-test and apply knowledge in a real situation. This level of learning and feedback is powerful as a learning modality. I will not discuss the benefit of this further as it is apparently clear that increased access and flexibility to the knowledge is beneficial and using a blended learning approach in this new found access begins to shift the ownership of learning more equally between educator and learner. The fundamental benefit is it allows medical students to be more confident in their abilities as future physicians given to the ability to revisit and re-test acquired knowledge independent of an educator and set time ensures to the medical educators that the vital information delivered to the student was received and acquired and more importantly sustainable which is integral in the high stakes field of healthcare and being a physician.

Cost-Effectiveness

In terms of cost-effectiveness by using a blended learning that utilizes technology in its approach it begins to remove the burden teaching from the educator and allows learning to occur almost anywhere (i.e. removes the physicality of learning medium). Lets consider this from a medical perspective and in particular the clinical years that are from year three of the undergraduate MD program and beyond in their training. The bulk of the training during these years requires teaching by already active physicians who are of course busy delivering healthcare to their patients and further requires the student to go to where these "educators" are for all of their learning. By using a blended learning approach there would be less time needed to be actively engaging in face-to-face learning as the students would have the ability to revisit material in the "virtual" capacity. By virtual this could include everything from web-based platforms to interactive CDs among others. Furthermore, if the student was not able to get to the location of the lecture then he/she could review the material virtually and then engage the educator at a more opportune time for the both. One of the other interesting aspects from a cost effective perspective is if you think back again to the roadmap of complexity of medical training and all of disciplines that fall under the umbrella of medicine from pediatrics to surgery then the use of blended learning would allow information from these experts available to more distant sites that need not have the student physically engage with them on such a regular basis. Additionally, through the use of the technology enabled blended learning approach allows the student and expert to engage at times more appropriate them and less regularly as students can "practice" on their own time and experts could provide feedback on their own time from anywhere (think of the acute management model above). This is an intriguing thought as we discuss the future of medical education the next section. There is no doubt that blended learning is more cost-effective and given the high cost to train a medical student or build a new medical school that is a useful method of teaching that as we can see has merits for success of the learner and progression to physician.

21st Century Medical Student

I think this statement says a lot in is the intangible qualities observed in today's medical student that will facilitate the success blended learning approaches to the future of medical education. What I mean in this statement is the today's medical students are well versed in technology in almost every aspect of their daily lives. Most medical students spend vast amounts of time looking at resources online as UpToDate (a clinical resource that is web-based) or the fact that most of their textbooks are online now. Students carry PDAs or the Apple ITouch's that have "applications" for medical students such a digital histology images, anatomy tools, clinical skills, clinical algorithms tips, virtual surgery among countless others. Due in part to the busy schedules of medical students today and the differing abilities that they enter medical school with that they want the ability to access information whenever and wherever they see fit (Twenge, 2009) to continue to build upon their core knowledge and improve. More importantly, and like no other generation of medical student before them, the ability to learn and master skills through a virtual medium allows them to be successful using a technology enabled blended learning approach. This type of student fits the key requirement of the blended learning approach that promotes a cultural shift in medical education from the teacher-expert primary education location focus to a student-learner distance focus. Therefore, I believe that that today's medical student is the most apt to facilitate the sustainability and success of a blended learning medical education curriculum.

FUTURE OF MEDICAL EDUCATION AND ROLE OF A BLENDED LEARNING CURRICULUM

As we have been reflective in the context of medical education and the training of learners with regard to the use of blended learning modalities it is now time to shape the future of medical education and more importantly does blended learning play an integral role in its future. As I have stated that we are at a perfect storm in medical education's future with the increase in numbers of students, the type of student (21st century learner) and push to increase the scope of training to more rural and community based locations I believe the two "buzz" words leading the future of medical education that will be tied together by the use blended learning modalities of teaching are Distance and Simulation of which we will discuss separately.

Distance Education

The recommendations from the Future of Medical Education in Canada report outline the need to train students in more rural and community based locations but the rationale also behind such a recommendation is the landscape of where people leave in Canada and for that matter worldwide as seen by similar reports from the medical schools located in the United States and Australia. The need for more rural physicians has never been more apparent than in the past 25 years but to address this concern medical schools have debated the best course of action. However, in the past 5 years in particular within Canada there has been a push to direct the historical ideology of medical schools of big city/one medical center to more regional medical campuses that are at a significant distance from the main campus. Thus the creation of smaller satellite campuses that have more affinity for rural and small community based areas. By training physicians in these regions it will increase the likelihood that upon graduation these students will ultimately stay and practice in these regions (Snadden & Bates, 2005; Worley et al., 2006). The early data is that this mandate will be successful. Now, not a topic for this discussion in this chapter, but what is important is the teaching methodology that will allow for successful training of these students in these areas. I hope at this stage that blended learning jumps to conscious mind as the best solution for this way of training medical students based on what has been outlined earlier. To supplement the learning of the medical students in these more rural or small communities is a series of interactive technology enabled blended learning modules and platforms combined with state of the art video conferencing technology to allow interaction of the student in these areas with educators from the larger center. The medical student will still has the ability to learn all of core competencies required for completion of medical school and will do so with using this combination of technology enabled blended learning. Furthermore, allowing learning to occur when it most suitable and thus continue to drive medical education to a more student-centered approach. If you remember from the 5 pillars of success for utilization of blended learning in medical education outlined earlier, mobility was the final one of these pillars for medical education and blended learning and subscribes to this distance or distributed ideology in the most complete sense and without this pillar the future of medical education would be hampered as will healthcare delivery.

Simulation

One of the most perfect examples of blended learning in medical education and that has such potential in the distance model setting of medical education is the use of simulation. This is not say that this should not be used in big centers and main campuses as it should but this is a great way for medical students in rural areas and communities to apply their theoretical knowledge in a situation that provides constant feedback from the simulator and educator. Simulation can be used to practice all disciplines in medicine and a robust method to practice patient care away from the bedside. The rationale is that the students have the ability to develop a baseline level of competency prior to working with patients and thus has outstanding pedagogical advantages due to the immediate feedback and ability to practice techniques in multiple disciplines at flexible times. Surveys have shown that patients are more willing to have students perform procedures on them after they have undergone education via simulation (Graber et al., 2005). From a faculty or educator perspective the implementation of simulation would be very cost-effective from both time constraints placed on them and would allow them to be engaged in other things than teaching and finally the cost to run a program in most disciplines would be reduced with simulation (Okuda, 2008). Overall, when using simulation it subscribes to the five pillars of why one would use a blended learning model and fundamentally for the learner it allows for repetitive practice, integration of multiple disciplines, increased difficulty to adjust to the individual learner, capture clinical variations, a controlled and safe environment for the learner, measurable and relevant outcomes and finally has been validated (Okuda et al., 2009). The one piece of information not discussed is simulation can be done anywhere, which increases it mobility application in distance medical education platform that the future of medical training is heading.

CURRENT LIMITATIONS

Within the context of medical education and the use of blended learning in both current and future the picture has been painted as favorable for its use throughout this chapter. Although this section is entitled "limitations" it could be couched as things we should think about prior to using it. The three major things to think about in my opinion are faculty development, assessment of the individual learner and moving beyond small pilot projects.

In regard to faculty development, it should be ensured that the upper administration of medical schools has the expertise to design and implement well executed curriculum with emphasis on blended learning. It is far too often that the faculty development of the educators on how and why blended learning modalities should be used has not occurred with the resultant effect being a less than rewarding experience for the students of the program. This is not an easy task given the complexity of medical curriculum and diverse nature of the educators but one that it is vital for its success. Since the focus of blended learning does put the emphasis more on the learner and allowing the learner to actively control ones education there has to be a considerable focus of medical schools and its educators to track feedback of individual students given the potential for students to be at different levels given what success they are having with a given blended learning program. For example, if we think back to the example from University of Glasgow when the students are going through acute clinical care modules to improve clinical reasoning, there has to be a due diligence on the part of the educator that each student attains the same level of expertise or more importantly, students in difficulty are monitored and helped to attain the core competency required for a given discipline. Remember the ultimate goal of medical education despite the teaching modality is deliberate practice of techniques to achieve a given competency. The final thing to consider when discussing the implementation of blended learning in medical education is to guard against collection of pilot projects within a given curriculum. What is typical at this stage of development of blended learning in medical education are small pilot projects run by individuals who are keen or able to run a blended learning aspect of a curriculum. To be successful now I think the appropriate course of action is a complete overhaul the medical education ideology within a given school to such the direction of blended learning is promoted. Medical school curriculum is taught by 100s, if not 1000s, of educators across multiple disciplines and many years of training (undergraduate to post-graduate). Therefore, in order to be truly successful one must implement from the top down to fully engage everyone not just the few with clear objectives how all parts of the curriculum can be blended to improve the educational pedagogy and outcomes by students and beyond in their career.

CONCLUSION

In conclusion, blended learning offers the future of medical education an ability to complement the face-to-face lectures with a variety of technology enabled options to supplement the medical students learning. What it has been demonstrated in this chapter and quite well in the context of such modalities as simulation is that blended learning is a viable, successful and mobile method of teaching that parallels with the current mandate of medical schools to increase diversity of environment for its students to more rural and community based teaching, increase more physicians by delivering distance medical education and increase the use of technology and the 21st medical student in a perfect model to use this learning to be successful.

REFERENCES

AAMC Institute for Improving Medical Education. (2007). *Effective use of educational technology in medical education* (p. 3). Washington, DC: Association of American Medical Colleges.

Association of Faculties of Medicine of Canada. (2010). *Future of medical education in Canada*. AFMC.

Barrows, H. S., & Tambyln, R. M. (1980). *Problem-based learning: An approach to medical education*. New York, NY: Springer.

Bass, E. B., Fortin, A. H., Morrison, G., Wills, S., Mumford, L. M., & Goroll, A. H. (1997). National survey of clerkship directors in internal medicine on the competencies that should be addressed in Medicine core clerkship. *The American Journal of Medicine*, *102*, 564–571. doi:10.1016/S0002-9343(97)00054-5

Carbonaro, M., King, S., Taylor, E., Satzinger, F., Snart, F., & Drummond, J. (2008). Integration of e-learning technologies in an intraprofessional health science course. *Medical Teacher*, *30*, 25–33. doi:10.1080/01421590701753450

Davis, M. H., & Harden, R. M. (1999). AMEE medical education guide no 15: Problem-based learning, a practical guide. *Medical Teacher*, *21*(2), 130–140. doi:10.1080/01421599979743

Duque, G., Roberts, A., Hui, J., Posel, N., Fleiszer, D., & Chui, Q. (2006). From the facts to the screen: A blended model of teaching basic hospital skills to 2nd year medical students. *Medical Teacher*, *28*(8), 729–733. doi:10.1080/01421590601032450

General Medical Council. (1993). *Tomorrow's doctors: Recommendation on undergraduate medical education*. London, UK: General Medical Council.

Graber, M. A. (2005). Does stimulation training for medical students change patient opinions and attitudes towards medical student procedures in the emergency department. *Academic Emergency Medicine*, *12*, 635–639. doi:10.1111/j.1553-2712.2005.tb00920.x

Graham, C. R. (2004). *Blended learning systems*. San Francisco, CA: Wiley Press.

Harden, R. M. (2000). Evolution or revolution and the future of medical education: Replacing the oak tree. *Medical Teacher*, *22*(5), 435–442. doi:10.1080/01421590050110669

Harden, R. M. (2000). The integration ladder: A tool for curriculum planning and evaluation. *Medical Education*, *34*, 551–557. doi:10.1046/j.1365-2923.2000.00697.x

Harden, R. M. (2000). Independent learning. In Dent, J. A., & Harden, R. M. (Eds.), *A practical guide for medical teachers* (pp. 147–157). Edinburgh, UK: Churchill Livingstone.

Harden, R. M. (2001). AMEE guide no 21: Curriculum mapping: A tool for transparent and authentic teaching and learning. *Medical Teacher*, *23*(2), 123–137. doi:10.1080/01421590120036547

Harden, R. M., Crosby, J. R., & Davis, M. H. (1999). AMEE guide no. 14: Outcome-based education: Part-1-an introduction to outcome-based education. *Medical Teacher*, *21*(1), 7–14. doi:10.1080/01421599979969

Harden, R. M., & Davis, M. H. (1995). AMEE medical education guide no 5: The core curriculum with options or special study modules. *Medical Teacher*, *17*(2), 125–148. doi:10.3109/01421599509008301

Harden, R. M., & Hart, I. R. (2002). An international virtual medical school (IVIMEDS): The future for medical education. *Medical Teacher*.

Harden, R. M., Laidlaw, J. M., Ker, J. S., & Mitchell, H. E. (1996). AMEE medical education booklet no 7, part 1: Task-based learning: An educational strategy for undergraduate, post-graduate and continuing medical education. *Medical Teacher*, *18*, 7–13. doi:10.3109/01421599609040254

Harden, R. M., Snowden, S., & Dunn, W. R. (1984). ASME medical education booklet no 18: Some educational strategies in curriculum development: The SPICES model. *Medical Education*, *18*, 284–297. doi:10.1111/j.1365-2923.1984.tb01024.x

Horton, W. (2001). *Leading e-learning*. Alexandria, VA: ASTD.

Hughes, C., Toohey, S., & Velan, G. (2008). eMED teamwork: A self moderating system to gather peer feedback for developing and assessing teamwork skills. *Medical Teacher*, *30*, 5–9. doi:10.1080/01421590701758632

Lau, F., & Bates, J. (2004). A review of e-learning practices for undergraduate medical education. *Journal of Medical Systems*, *28*(1), 71–87. doi:10.1023/B:JOMS.0000021522.30587.ff

Okuda, Y. (2009). The utility of simulation in medical education: What is the evidence? *The Mount Sinai Journal of Medicine, New York*, *76*, 330–343. doi:10.1002/msj.20127

Okuda, Y., & Quinones, J. (2008). The use of simulation in the education of emergency care providers for cardiac emergencies. *International Journal of Medicine*, *1*, 73–77.

Shah, I. M., Walters, M. R., & McKillop, J. H. (2007). Acute medicine teaching in undergraduate medical curriculum: A blended learning approach. *Emergency Medicine Journal*, *28*, 354–357.

Smith, C. M., Perkins, C. D., & Bullock, I. (2007). Undergraduate training in the care of the acutely ill patient: A literature review. *Intensive Care Medicine*, *33*, 901–907. doi:10.1007/s00134-007-0564-8

Snadden, D. (2009). From medicine's margins-why all the interest in rural and remote education? *Medical Teacher*, *11*, 967–968. doi:10.3109/01421590903307857

Snadden, D., & Bates, J. (2005). Expanding undergraduate medical education in British Columbia: A distributed campus model. *Canadian Medical Association Journal*, *173*(6), 589–590. doi:10.1503/cmaj.050439

Twenge, J. M. (2009). Generational changes and their impact in the classroom: Teaching generation me. *Medical Education*, *43*, 398–405. doi:10.1111/j.1365-2923.2009.03310.x

Worley, P., Prideaux, D., Strasser, R., Magarey, A., & March, R. (2006). Empirical evidence for symbolic medical education: A comparative analysis of the community and tertiary-based programmes. *Medical Education, 40*(2), 109–116. doi:10.1111/j.1365-2929.2005.02366.x

ADDITIONAL READING

Bridge, P. D., Jackson, M., & Robinson, L. (2009). The effectiveness of streaming video on medical student learning: A case study. *Med Educ Online, 14*(11), 1–5.

Choules, A. P. (2007). The use of e-learning in medical education: a review of the current situation. *Postgraduate Medical Journal, 83*(978), 212–216. doi:10.1136/pgmj.2006.054189

Cook, D. A., & Dupras, D. M. (2004). A practical guide to developing effective web-based learning. *Journal of General Internal Medicine, 19*(6), 698–707. doi:10.1111/j.1525-1497.2004.30029.x

Ellaway, R., & Masters, K. (2008). AMEE Guide 32: e-Learning in medical education Part 1: Learning, teaching and assessment. *Medical Teacher, 30*(5), 455–473. doi:10.1080/01421590802108331

Ellaway, R. H., Dewhurst, D., & Cumming, A. (2003). Managing and supporting medical education with a virtual learning environment: the Edinburgh Electronic Medical Curriculum. *Medical Teacher, 25*(4), 372–380. doi:10.1080/0142159031000136789

Ellaway, R. H., Kneebone, R., Lachapelle, K., & Topps, D. (2009). Practica continua: Connecting and combining simulation modalities for integrated teaching, learning and assessment. *Medical Teacher, 31*(8), 725–731. doi:10.1080/01421590903124716

Gray, K., & Tobin, J. (2010). Introducing an online community into a clinical education setting: a pilot study of student and staff engagement and outcomes using blended learning. *BMC Medical Education, 26*(10), 6. doi:10.1186/1472-6920-10-6

Hansen, M.M. (2008). Versatile, immersive, creative and dynamic virtual 3-D healthcare learning environments: A review of the literature. *J Med Internet Res, 10(3)* (online).

Harden, R. M. (2005). A new vision for distance learning and continuing medical education. *The Journal of Continuing Education in the Health Professions*, (1): 43–51. doi:10.1002/chp.8

Horstmann, M., Renninger, M., Hennenlotter, J., Horstmann, C.C., & Stenzl A. (2009). Blended E-learning in a Web-based virtual hospital: a useful tool for undergraduate education in urology. *Educ Health, (2),* 269.

Lehmann, R., Bosse, H. M., & Huwendiek, S. (2010). Blended learning using virtual patients and skills laboratory training. *Medical Education, 44*(5), 521–522. doi:10.1111/j.1365-2923.2010.03653.x

Lewin, L. O., Singh, M., Bateman, B. L., & Glover, P. B. (2009). Improving education in primary care: development of an online curriculum using the blended learning model. *BMC Medical Education, 10*(9), 33–40. doi:10.1186/1472-6920-9-33

Masic, I., Pandza, H., Kulasin, I., Masic, Z., & Valjevac, S. (2009). Tele-education as method of medical education. *Medicinski Arhiv, 63*(6), 350–353.

Masters, K., & Ellaway, R. H. (2008). e-Learning in medical education Guide 32 Part 2: Technology, management and design. *Medical Teacher, 30*(5), 474–489. doi:10.1080/01421590802108349

Patricio, M., & Harden, R. M. (2010). The Bologna Process - A global vision for the future of medical education. *Medical Teacher*, *32*(4), 305–315. doi:10.3109/01421591003656123

Ruiz, J. G., Mintzer, M. J., & Leipzig, R. M. (2006). The impact of E-learning in medical education. *Academic Medicine*, *81*(3), 207–212. doi:10.1097/00001888-200603000-00002

Sajeva, M. (2006). E-learning: Web-based education. *Current Opinion in Anaesthesiology*, *19*(6), 645–649. doi:10.1097/ACO.0b013e328010bec8

Wong, G., Greenhalgh, T., & Pawson, R. (2010). Internet-based medical education: A realist review of what works, for whom and in what circumstances. *BMC Medical Education*, *2*, 10–12.

Woollard, B. (2010). Many birds with one stone: opportunities in distributed education. *Medical Education*, *44*(3), 222–224. doi:10.1111/j.1365-2923.2009.03609.x

KEY TERMS AND DEFINITIONS

Clinical Undergraduate: This period of study is the final two years of the Medical Doctorate Program.

Continuing Professional Development (CPD): As a practicing physician it is required that they complete continuing education following completion of residency training to maintain a license to practice.

Pre-Clinical Undergraduate: This period of study is the first two years of the four year Medical Doctorate Program.

Residency: This is post-graduate training following the completion of the MD program. This period can be form 2 years to 7 years depending on the discipline.

Section 3
Extending Blended Learning

Chapter 9
Fundamental Design Elements of Pervasive Games for Blended Learning

David Metcalf
University of Central Florida, USA

Clarissa Graffeo
University of Central Florida, USA

Luke Read
University of Central Florida, USA

ABSTRACT

Though not widely researched or implemented in the field of blended learning, pervasive game frameworks in the alternate and augmented reality game genres are highly relevant to education, particularly in curricula seeking to use blended principles. Key characteristics of alternate and augmented reality games are identified, along with specific game examples, and their applicability to various learning theories including situated learning, guided experiential learning, and integrated thematic instruction. Several learning projects using these frameworks conducted by the Mixed Emerging Technology Integration Lab are described, and the Moving Knowledge Engine delivery system and game engine for pervasive blended learning solutions is outlined. The chapter concludes by discussing future possibilities for implementing pervasive games in blended learning programs to achieve deep, complex learning and high student engagement.

INTRODUCTION

New approaches to learning are emerging almost as fast as new technologies to serve and deliver them. Frameworks for meeting learning and performance objectives must be fast and flexible enough to accommodate both the speed of change and the breadth of new models. The level of complexity entailed, as a designer, to make something simple and well tuned to the learning needs of a particular audience requires the integration of multiple disciplines and tool sets. Meeting the learner's needs

DOI: 10.4018/978-1-60960-479-0.ch009

within the context of their role is a key tenet of situated learning and often vital for professional education, where blended learning practices are frequently deployed. The opportunity to use location and other contextual elements to meet learning and performance outcomes can be seen in the disciplines of augmented reality, alternate reality games, mobile learning games, and other location-based learning initiatives.

Research and implementation in the field of blended learning has primarily focused on the domain of eLearning, perhaps combined with traditional classroom instruction, but the intersection of blended learning with games research and design has been minimal. In this chapter we will discuss the significance to blended learning in one specific subset of digital gaming, the field of technologically enabled pervasive games, with a focus on technologically enabled solutions in the alternate reality game (ARG) and augmented reality game genres. This chapter will highlight several models and examples and provide case-based information on several approaches that have proven effective. Details of past examples and the theoretical underpinnings will also be presented, along with future research directions and recommendations.

We will begin by providing brief background information on the field of pervasive gaming in general, as well as some foundational research on the use of games for learning. In the following section, we will describe alternate and augmented reality games in more detail, identifying their key design features, how they are pervasive, and briefly describe several notable examples of each type. As much work in pervasive gaming is outside the education space, we have provided both general examples to further describe the general history and frameworks of these games, but also follow up with more examples specifically from the learning space.

Following these sections, we will discuss several of the projects our Mixed Emerging Technology Integration Lab has implemented using conceptual frameworks from alternate and augmented reality gaming. Project descriptions are followed by a discussion of our Moving Knowledge engine that provides technical capability for automated and learner-triggered content delivery across platforms and formats, which can be deployed for direct learning content as well as narrative scaffolding for complex training game frameworks.

The chapter will close with a discussion of how these design and technology solution frameworks fit into the overall concept of blended learning, and may illuminate potential for expanding and transforming existing content into new educational techniques, along with augmenting curricula and programs with discrete game exercises. We discuss how these pervasive game frameworks enable blended learning programs across platforms, formats, and learning theories, and ways to leverage simple and inexpensive techniques and technologies to accomplish these solutions.

BACKGROUND

Pervasive Games

Pervasive games are a broad and often contested category. We define them here as games structured to cross temporal, location, and medium boundaries, "pervading" multiple types and spaces of play; this identifies pervasive gaming according to its foundational thought processes and blended design approaches, as well as their social components (Montola, 2005; Stenros, Montola, & Mäyrä, 2007) rather than defining them strictly according to certain types of delivery technologies (Nieuwdorp, 2005; Walther, 2005). Pervasive games exist on a continuum of digital and physical, with some games focused almost entirely on players moving in and interacting with physical locations as in *The Go Game* while others, including some alternate reality games like *Majestic,* may exist entirely online. Play spaces crossed or mixed through pervasive games may be blending digital/virtual interaction with physical; involving multiple different types of delivery technologies, particularly tools or technologies not commonly associated with game play; or blurring the "magic circle" or boundary between play experiences and daily life through augmented reality or immersive narrative and design conventions common to alternate reality games.

Though this definition of pervasive gaming is quite broad, we restrict ourselves here to alternate and augmented reality games as we feel their general structure, as well as their current use in educational pilots and research projects, are particularly suited to blended learning practices. ARG frameworks involve a much stronger focus on narrative than many other pervasive game formats, and demonstrate techniques for relying primarily or entirely on common digital solutions that may be easily accessible to eLearning and mLearning programs. Augmented reality offers a range of narrative integration, and may be attractive for learning programs where situated integration to physical environments will prove beneficial, as well as for less heavily localized mLearning programs. Both also strongly integrate collaborative processes, a current and growing focus in education and training programs, while still allowing flexibility for individualization.

Games for Learning

Though the use of games for education has a shorter research history than pure simulation, a growing community of researchers is exploring both off the shelf and custom game solutions for learning. Research and commentary on games for learning has focused on two primary aspects. First is the potential for games as a more powerful method for knowledge acquisition and retention due to their complex, interactive structures, built in knowledge and skills progression, superior assessment possibilities through logging and scoring, and ability to create situated learning experiences (S. Chen & Michael, 2006; de Freitas, 2006; Gee, 2004; Jenkins, 2002; Prensky, 2000). The second is, even if games are equivalent for learning to traditional methods, that games are inherently more motivating than traditional instruction because of their ability to absorb learners, creating a state of Flow (J. Chen, 2007; Csikszentmihalyi, 1991).

Empirical evidence for learning in games has been somewhat mixed, varying between games demonstrating equivalent learning gains and significantly higher gains for games over traditional methods, though motivation and enjoyment among students using games have demonstrated more consistently positive results (Hays, 2005; Randel, Morris, C. D. Wetzel, & Whitehill, 1992; J. J. Vogel et al., 2006). Alternate and augmented reality games have also demonstrated promising educational and motivational gains for various subject areas and skill sets, which we will return to in the next sections.

Assessment of these results are complex, however, due to a significant amount of variation in the quality of study design and the particular game solutions examined (Egenfeldt-Nielsen, 2005; Hays, 2005). Some research involves qualitative observation of learning behaviors exhibited during engagement with standard entertainment games, suggesting possible transfer to learning disciplines (Gee, 2004; McGonigal, 2007; Steinkuehler, 2004). Many studies involving educational games assess student reactions and performance to determine whether they are at an acceptable level, but do not always include a control group to assess how performance compares to traditional instructional methods such as lecture (Connolly et al., 2008; Facer et al., 2004; Moseley, 2008; Squire & Jan, 2007; Squire, 2004), providing evidence that games may be effective tools for learning but may be best used as a supplemental exercise rather than an alternative to traditional instruction. Some studies have demonstrated strong performance of games when compared against control groups using only traditional instruction (Blunt, 2007; Gremmen & Potters, 1997; J. J. Vogel et al., 2006).

Of course, further studies and research reviews indicate that, as one might expect, while games demonstrate strong potential for learning and motivation, not all games are necessarily equally useful for all individuals. The quality of game design can vary greatly, which may contribute to some lackluster results, especially as much of the instructional game field has been dominated by "edutainment" games often created by developers with little to no instructional background (Egenfeldt-Nielsen, 2005). Additionally, some studies have demonstrated variable results, within the same groups and with one or more game programs, suggesting mitigating factors including existing student knowledge or test score history (Fraas, 1982), the subject area being taught (Randel et al., 1992), the degree of alignment between core learning objectives and the game environment or tasks (Hays, 2005; Ke, 2008), and adaptive facilitation provided by the program or instructor to assist with mental connections and learning transfer (Dunleavy, Dede, & Mitchell, 2009; Leutner, 1993; Squire, 2004). This has led to a focus in ongoing research toward identifying the elements of games that facilitate learning, and design techniques to enable creation of effective learning games.

ALTERNATE AND AUGMENTED REALITY GAME FRAMEWORKS

Alternate Reality Games

In terms of pervasive games' effort to expand gaming outside of specific technology delivery methods or locations, alternate reality games (ARGs) were created with the intent to blur the boundaries between players' everyday lives and their engagement with a game. This idea was accomplished with two methods: storytelling devices and technology solutions. Sean Stewart, one of the lead developers and writers on a foundational ARG—the promotional game for the film *A.I.*—describes the key elements of ARGs as being fragmented narrative, the narrative not being bound by medium or platform, a collective audience, and interactive participation by the audience that can affect how the storyline progresses (Stewart, 2006). ARG developers used role playing and narrative through character and fictional world artifacts paired with a lack of overt discussion of the meta game or developers to heighten suspension of disbelief. Players speak directly to characters (played by members of the development team or hired actors), websites are set up for companies in the narrative, etc. Further realism and boundary erosion was accomplished not only by using a variety of delivery methods but by relying predominantly on standard methods of communication and interaction such as email, websites, and online video. In this way, alternate reality games can be seen as entering the pervasive game space not only from standard gaming practices, but via framing devices and narrative techniques from other media, as well as general trends toward media convergence.

The storytelling methods developed for ARGs were very similar to literary and cinema traditions such as the epistolary novel or the faux documentary. Epistolary novels framed fictional narratives as collections of supposedly real documents, usually letters but occasionally news reports or academic papers as well. They increased the sense of realism in fictional works but also involved the reader much more directly by giving them a sense of participation or closer relationship with the characters through presenting artifacts of their lives and allowing the writer/editor and reader to bring "primary and seemingly chaotic yet authentic material" into narrative sequence (Koepke, 1990). Fictional movies have used similar techniques and framed the tale as documentary footage, either for parody in the case of *This is Spinal Tap*, or for heightened sense of realism in the case of *The Blair Witch Project* or *Cannibal Holocaust*.

As epistolary fiction used common communication and information techniques of the day including letter writing and newspapers, ARGs use common modern digital formats including email, blogs, websites, or even Flash applications. The nature of these formats, however, enable additional techniques such as interactivity, dispersed narrative rather than all items presented as an ordered collection, and branching capabilities as explored in hypertext fiction. This can also be viewed in the context of media convergence, a key force in the way people get and relate to information and media. The process of media convergence is the continuing trend in which media becomes spread across a multitude of platforms and audiences become ever more active, following media across those platforms, seeking out information and making connections between dispersed content, interpret media collectively, and demanding more control over and interaction with media. Consumers build a "personal mythology from bits and fragments of information" while taking advantage of access through various formats and interactions with others to compensate for the proliferation of media overwhelming the capacity of individuals to retain all necessary information (Jenkins, 2006) just as players of ARGs assemble the game narrative from planted artifacts and interactions with performed characters, and participate as a collective to solve huge challenges.

In addition to the general origin and concepts of ARGs, the frameworks of actual games will be instructive to connecting these games to learning practices and blended learning in particular. Below, we discuss several examples of both commercial non-educational ARGs as well as some initial pilot projects in using ARGs to teach.

General ARG Examples

ARGs originated in, and continue to be primarily created for, the entertainment and advertising markets. Though these games are not directly designed to educate on any specific subjects, their frameworks remain instructive in the application of these games to blended learning, and have demonstrated the ability to spur collaboration, completion of complex projects, and teach new concepts and skills to players. One of the primary early ARGs, I Love Bees—created as marketing and an extension of the Xbox video game Halo 2—established not only many of the core elements of ARGs but also demonstrated ways to mix digital interactions with live events and unexpected delivery formats. The game delivered narrative detail and interactive puzzles through web sites, blog posts, audio and video files, custom programming code, and even traditional radio-drama style recordings accessed via standard public pay phones. Players were tasked with collaborating in an enormous team to methodically investigate and assemble the game narrative from scattered fragments, decode GPS data, learn an original programming language developed for the game, organize live demonstrations and gatherings, and create and maintain a knowledge base for the game; players not only had to learn and synthesize new information and skills, but rapidly organize their efforts, giving many a crash course in collective intelligence and rigorous problem solving processes (McGonigal, 2005, 2007; Stewart, 2006). Another entertainment game, Perplex City, augmented these techniques with the incorporation of physical artifacts like collectible puzzle cards marketed to players ("Puzzle Cards," 2007) and even tasked players with collaboratively authoring an entire book, *Tales from the Third Planet*, to be published both in our reality and the game's fictional alternate dimension through self-publisher Lulu.com (http://www.lulu.com/content/225745).

ARG frameworks have traditionally been created for large groups of players, entailing challenges and skill requirements far too difficult and diverse for players to handle alone. As these types of games are gaining greater mainstream popularity as promotional tools, and also in organizations or for learning purposes that may necessitate smaller scales and reusability, more developers are experimenting with concentrated and single-player experiences. One example is

Freefall, a promotion for the film *Eagle Eye*, which is only 10 minutes long and uses a single web site and calls to a user's cell phone (http://eagleeyefreefall.com/).

Educational ARGs

The use of ARGs for educational purposes is still in the very early stages, but several institutions have begun designing and using these frameworks for learning and collective intelligence. Games have been developed and launched to meet specific course learning objectives, as well as for general skills education, social awareness, future forecasting, and encouraging exercise and better health choices. This section describes several notable projects, grouped together by the general information or practices they foster.

Future Forecasting and Social Innovation Games

Pervasive and ubiquitous games researcher and developer Jane McGonigal is working at Institute for the Future to create ARGs centered on player-generated content for crisis awareness, collective intelligence for future forecasting, and spurring innovation and activism. World Without Oil, an awareness and future forecasting game for possible global oil shortages, and Superstruct, a similar project incorporating multiple classes of global threat: food shortages, disease epidemics, power struggles over energy, skyrocketing crime rates and organizational destabilization, and massive refugee populations, tasked players with writing their own stories in these situations, brainstorming potential solutions, and sharing them through blogs, websites, and video reports (McGonigal, 2009; Waite, 2007). These games have surpassed initial participation and activity expectations, and follow-up with players over a year afterward has indicated ongoing changes in players' daily behaviors, as well as outreach on the core issues to non-players (McGonigal, 2010a). A 2010 game for the World Bank Institute, EVOKE, is planned to educate and empower young people about collaboration, social activism and ingenuity, and will earn educational certifications for players who complete all challenges (McGonigal, 2010b).

Curriculum-Based Games

A few educators and research organizations have begun implementing ARGs both within and as supplement to existing curricula. Some efforts have been targeted to K-12 education, but most projects have been conducted at the University level, likely due to greater resources, more current online courses being conducted, and a greater need for teaching higher-order and complex tasks.

The ARGuing project pursues development, implementation and research on ARG frameworks to augment foreign language instruction. Students are tasked with helping to build a virtual Tower of Babel—in this case a collaboratively authored wiki site—by solving puzzles, completing assignments and quests, and participating in discussions with teachers and fellow students using email, podcasts, blogs, video clips, and other Web 2.0 tools (Connolly et al., 2008). The project is conducted both during class time and in students' free time at home, and is intended as a supplement to basic language instruction for increased motivation, engagement, and additional practice opportunities. Initial pilot results have shown favorable student responses and indicated engagement comparable to entertainment games (Hainey et al., 2009).

ARGs often require players to engage in large amounts of research, hunting for minute details and snippets of information. It's no surprise, then, that several of the educational projects have been geared toward teaching and developing research skills either for libraries (discussed in another section) or for history courses like the University of Leicester's Great History Conundrum. Over the course of four weeks 200 students participated in a mystery game featuring regular puzzle and task updates requiring the use of both online and offline resources and covering a range of course topics. Students solved a total of 3,301 puzzles (avg. per student = 17) and posted 4,387 forum messages (avg. per student = 23); the majority of participating students passed the course, with high student engagement (Moseley, 2008).

Student Orientation Games

New students at college have a number of concerns and needs apart from course curricula. A few projects have used ARG frameworks to assist new students with campus orientation, socialization into the college community, and even healthy habits for students.

The Alternate Reality Games for Orientation, Socialisation and Induction (ARGOSI) project at Manchester Metropolitan University and University of Bolton developed the ViolaQuest ARG spanning the first eight weeks of a semester, intended to help students develop information literacy skills, learn their way around campus and the surrounding town, and meet new people. Students follow the story of a fictional MMU student who finds a letter hinting at a secret society and a hidden machine in the area. In addition to general orientation and social outcomes, subplots were included for specific learning outcomes related to digital literacy and information fluency (Whitton, 2008).

The University of Brighton implemented a similar project with studentquest 2006 or "Who is Herring Hale?" The game extended for the entire term, delivering a different clue or task per week, usually involving around 30 minutes of activity to complete. Rather than general orientation information, all clues and tasks were specifically crafted to introduce and familiarize students with specific support or information services at the University. Participation and completion rates were not very high, but generally in line with optional programs. Feedback from students who completed the game indicated a much improved level of information retention about campus support services (Piatt, 2009).

Many new college students need education on fitness and healthy habits, as they may be experiencing a number of lifestyle changes that affect diet and exercise routines. The Skeleton Chase ARG was developed at Indiana University and tested with students enrolled in a Foundations of Fitness and Wellness course. Web-based technology and media were combined with physical challenges in the area, with a continuing goal for all teams to reach 50,000 steps per member per week. Over half of participants met the weekly goal at least four times, with a significant difference in steps per week and change in daily activity over the control group (Johnston, Massey, & Sheldon, 2009).

Augmented Reality Games

Augmented reality, sometimes also called mixed reality, is a technique for merging or overlapping the real and virtual worlds. Physical objects and surroundings are augmented with interactive data or 3D models through a number of available technologies, such as head-mounted displays, handheld devices, or direct projection onto physical objects (Azuma, 1997; Milgram & Kishino, 1994). For the purposes of this chapter, we primarily focus on handheld devices and location-based interactive data rather than wearable displays and computers, augmented toys or touch table displays, or direct projection onto physical objects, due to device commonality and ease of use both for students and developers.

Unlike pervasive gaming in general and much of alternate reality gaming, augmented reality stems from efforts in ubiquitous computing and virtual reality and is heavily dependent on mobile computing and advanced display devices, which, until recently with the popularity of smart phones, have not been standard tools. For this reason, narrative is not as central to augmented reality as compared to alternate reality gaming, though naturally it is quite simple to deliver narrative while using augmented reality techniques. Contextual data and interactivity is the key component of augmented reality, which offers its own relevance and benefits to learning.

In the remainder of this section, we will provide several examples of common augmented reality projects. Since the object of this chapter is for regular learning implementation, we place the majority of our focus on mobile device-enabled, non-immersive techniques. We offer several general commercial examples as well as learning projects to give an idea of the overall framework as well as its educational applications.

General AR Examples

Though augmented reality has a somewhat more established presence in educational research than ARGs, many examples that can outline general trends and capabilities are in the commercial sector, particularly on increasingly popular smart phone platforms such as iPhone and Google's Android operating system. The availability of handheld devices with integrated cameras, GPS location tracking, and reasonable processing power is finally beginning to bring augmented reality to greater public attention, where wearable devices like backpack computers and helmet or goggle head-mounted displays are not yet viable for the common market.

A majority of augmented reality applications gaining popularity on smart phones are reference or performance support tools that work by overlaying textual and graphic data onto real world surroundings either live through the camera or after taking a photograph. This information can guide users around unfamiliar locations or provide contextual information. The mappr software from acrossair uses GPS data and local transportation maps to guide users to local subway stations and show route maps. Other applications provide more general contextual data: Wikitude will overlay information culled from Wikipedia, while the Layar program allows developers to reference and include many data sets—for example, marking locations in your area where money from the American Recovery and Reinvestment Act of 2009 was allocated.

The intersection of augmented reality and pervasive gaming began with projects like AR-Quake, a wearable backpack PC and head-mounted display configuration that enabled users to play a modified version of the Quake first person shooter video game viewed as an overlay on their real surroundings (Piekarski & Thomas, 2002), and Human Pac-Man, which used wearable GPS, inertia trackers, and Bluetooth enabled devices to match a human playing as Pac-Man in the streets with online users chasing him or her as ghosts (Cheok et al., 2003). Several other high profile game implementations were conducted by Blast Theory, using GPS to integrate people in real environments with users online and in virtual worlds for games of tag or scavenger hunts, like Can You See Me Now and Uncle Roy All Around You (Benford et al., 2006, 2004).

As in the performance support space, however, greater strides and commercial popularity are happening through handheld mobile devices using similar camera plus data overlay techniques as discussed above. Several ghost hunting games have been created, allowing the player to see images of ghosts overlaid onto their surroundings, including Ghostwire for the DSi handheld gaming platform, Augmented Reality Ghost Hunter, and Zero Ghost for the iPhone. Use of 3D 'popup' augmented reality are emerging as well, such as a simple interactive baseball avatar on Topps baseball cards, or Georgia Tech's ARhrrrr augmented reality zombie shooter, which allows a fixed city environment to be viewed through a handheld computer on top of a paper map and then populated with zombies—and even allowing players to use Skittles as bombs.

Educational AR

The heavier dependence on devices for augmented reality, particularly larger and more expensive wearable technology in its earlier phases, has made wide implementation in education problematic, but a number of researchers have conducted pilot projects and studies. These have primarily involved the use of handheld devices, either PDAs or cell phones, though a few have used wearable technology. This section discusses several key examples of augmented reality games on handhelds or using wearable technologies.

General Higher-Order Skills Learning

The MIT Media Lab has conducted several pilots of augmented reality games using handheld PocketPC devices. In Environmental Detectives, run both on MIT campus with college students and modified for use with high school students at other locations, players use handheld computers with GPS to assess potential chemical spill threats in the area. While role playing as environmental engineers, players must navigate and synthesize primary and secondary data, then develop specific recommendations based on all information—a common task for environmental engineering students, and one that is often difficult to train. As teams explore the physical location, they use the handheld computers to access media and data for their position or perform tasks like interviewing virtual characters or collecting virtual groundwater samples to be analyzed for chemical traces. Students using the handheld augmented reality version, as opposed to other trials with virtual world interfaces, demonstrated distinct decision-making influenced by the on-the-ground view of the campus, though pilots in locations new to student teams were somewhat less successful due to lower familiarity with or connection to the area. A similar MIT pilot, Outbreak @ the Institute, used a bird flu outbreak framing story and implemented a greater reliance on a limited inventory of digital objects such as face masks, testing equipment, or medication. The project showed similar positive student engagement, challenge, and changes to complex thought processes as Environmental Detectives (Klopfer, 2008).

Alien Contact, another GPS-enabled handheld PC game, uses similar techniques to teach math, language arts, and scientific literacy to junior high and high school students. Students work in teams consisting of four roles, each of which gains access to different information and media during the course of investigations, prompting students to compile and synthesize within their team. Challenges completed by students involve using everyday objects to measure physical artifacts and analyze their ratios or proportions, read graphs, or conduct group discussions and presentations. Many low-performing students participating in the pilot demonstrated strong engagement, focus, and capability (Dunleavy et al., 2009).

Specific Content Instruction

In addition to teaching students about work processes or higher order thinking and reasoning processes, augmented reality games can be used to demonstrate how outside processes or natural systems function. Futurelab's Savannah project used Pocket PCs to teach middle school students about African wildlife by having them role play as a pride of lions. Through the device, still images and audio files describe the current surroundings at the student's location, as well as periodic updates on the individual's condition—whether he or she is overheated, hungry, etc. Play in the field was combined with group reflection after each session in a collaboration space referred to as the Den. Through the game process, children organically discovered and implemented pack behavior principles exhibited by real lion prides (Facer et al., 2004).

Some educational projects have implemented augmented reality using 3D graphics as well, both through handhelds and wearable head mounted displays. TimeWarp outfitted players with a special AR jacket, a PDA, headphones, and a display visor, through which they could perceive 3D virtual characters and information overlaid onto their surroundings. Players explore the city and virtually travel through time to different eras, while tasked to solve challenges related to the area and history (Broll et al., 2008). Though not specifically intended to teach players particular information or processes, the 'Ere be Dragons augmented reality game seeks to raise player awareness of their own body and health by encouraging physical activity, similar to the objectives of the Skeleton Chase ARG example discussed previously. In this game, players are given not only a handheld computer but also a wearable heart monitor that registers their heart rate and transmits that data to the game. As the player walks through real areas, the game progressively grows virtual plant life over the surroundings based on heart rate—too low and nothing successfully grows, but too much exertion and the area becomes overgrown and forbidding, so players are encouraged to remain at an optimal level (Davis et al., 2006).

METIL PROJECT EXAMPLES

This section details several pervasive educational games conducted by our Mixed Emerging Technology Integration Lab at the University of Central Florida's Institute for Simulation and Training. A range of implementations are presented, including varied use of location-based game play, different levels of redundant delivery modalities, a range of narrative implementations, and different degrees of curriculum focus.

Google Foundations of Leadership and Teamwork (FLT)

Google developed the FLT program to teach upcoming leaders within Google's work force both the core Google company values and how to effectively bring together and use the talents of everyone on your team. Rather than developing a centralized course on a LMS system, Google decided to make the FLT course available to all employees through learning content accessible on their existing suite of tools. The concept of using Google tools for a scaffolded, distributed curriculum was termed G-Learning or Google Learning. The idea took shape in the form of a collection of instructional assets gathered from the Google network, such as videos from YouTube, Google Sites with weekly exercises, Google Groups postings, and more. There were two primary challenges in constructing the FLT course: structure, or how to unify distributed materials into a robust and convenient curriculum; and scope, as the course needed to be built in 3 months and would be used to train hundreds of individuals. By leaving the resources in their original location and format, and utilizing the capabilities of the Moving Knowledge Engine to bridge the gaps between learning exercises and provide scaffolding information, Google was able to build an extensive learning course in a fraction of the time it would normally take.

The FLT curriculum is broken out into weeks, each with an assigned set of activities. Each week Google starts with a video conference call to review learning materials for the current week. From there, a scheduled e-mail is delivered to the students informing them of their next activity. When the student completes the activity they are given a keyword to send back to the Moving Knowledge Engine, which triggers their next activity. This progress continues until all weekly materials are finished. In the background, the Moving Knowledge Engine tracks all incoming messages and charts out the progress of each and every student. Reports can then be generated to inform the course facilitators which individuals are struggling and which ones are successfully completing the course materials. These reports quickly became a vital part of the success of the program, giving the facilitators more control over the class and allowing them to quickly communicate with those who needed additional support.

In Google's case, the Moving Knowledge Engine communicated with the users primarily through the use of automated e-mails, but maintains the ability for content delivery via voice, SMS and web data. Additional formats and media were implemented into the curriculum through links delivered in the e-mail messages.

In contrast to the ARG examples discussed previously, Google FLT did not contain a large narrative component. While the main focus was on creating a map to guide users within the cloud, narrative could be easily added to the automated delivery to create story and character scaffolding for the learning process. In similar development cases, such as for eLearning refresher modules, curriculum e-mails were written as dialog between the user and a character, and messages followed an overall story. Though automated e-mail delivery and parsing through the Moving Knowledge Engine allows less flexibility and personalization than the live character interaction common in ARGs, it serves to bridge the gap between pure curriculum deliver as shown in Google FLT and ARG implementations, while also enabling single-player interaction and reusable content (a major factor in learning projects).

DreamCorp ARG

The DreamCorp ARG is more firmly grounded in ARG frameworks, and was run as a demonstration for Elliot Maise's Learning 2008 conference. The DreamCorp ARG provided an introduction to cross-media training and ARG frameworks for corporate education and employee onboarding. Though run as an extra event at the conference and not specifically intended to accomplish particular learning objectives, factual content and learning points on real professional issues were incorporated to give a stronger sense of immersion and display potentials for learning to the audience. Players selected one of three tracks: Compliance, Leadership, or Flexible Workforce. They then took on the role of employees at the fictional company DreamCorp, including wearing a button identifying them as a DreamCorp employee to enable players to locate one another and collaborate during the conference. Each day of the conference, we provided a new challenge and supporting materials such as company newsletters which provided clues and tips about their tasks. Clues were hidden throughout the conference, largely using printed materials, to help complete the job they were given, and at the end of each exercise players would e-mail their progress and solutions to a live representative who replied with assistance and confirmation whether their answers were correct or not. Although to a lesser extent, SMS delivery was also used during the conference to trigger the same experience through automated responses. In some cases, employees were tasked with using the conference wiki and physical white boards at the conference to collaborate on and submit certain challenges. Upon finishing a chosen track, players were able to complete the remaining two tracks if they desired.

The blended experience of e-mail, SMS, and the real world made the experience very successful in the conference setting. While the majority of players participated through e-mail, possibly due to the fact that laptops were set up throughout the conference to allow consistent internet connectivity, there were a few players who were excited by the option to participate through text messaging. When asked about their text messaging experience, they felt it was just as effective as e-mail, even taking in to account SMS character limitations. The flexibility allowed them to continue participating even during conference sessions, which gave them more time to participate than just the normal hallway interaction.

In contrast to e-mail or SMS only options, portions of the DreamCorp game were directly offered through multiple avenues and media formats: printed materials (e.g. pamphlets and newsletters), e-mails, text messages, in-person interaction with METIL team members acting as DreamCorp employees, and a bonus task offered in Second Life. This distributed tasking, as well as the immersive component of the DreamCorp company and players' role as employees, helped drive the content more towards the game end of the spectrum than a pure learning solution.

mLearn 2009 Experience

MLearn, an internationally recognized mobile learning conference, was held in Orlando, FL and hosted by the University of Central Florida in 2009. Each year, for one evening the attendees are invited to an offsite special event. UCF Institute for Simulation and Training's METIL lab was charged with coordinating the event, held in Universal's CityWalk. Since CityWalk is heavy on Florida flavor, we designed a pervasive scavenger hunt and trivia game with a theme highlighting Florida culture. The game was not associated with a specific curriculum, but many of the questions and trivia points related to famous individuals, landmarks, or cultural items from Florida, allowing the players to learn about the location for the conference. Early on the decision was made to focus on content delivery for the ARG through mobile phones since CityWalk lacked reliable wireless internet access and the conference attendees most likely would not have any other means of interaction at their disposal. To mitigate possible high roaming charges or lack of workable service for foreign attendees, as well as to encourage socialization within the group, players were asked to work in teams to complete the game.

The development process began with a brainstorm at the location where the ARG would take place, where we took hundreds of pictures used to storyboard the story and challenge progression. The narrative centered on Jimmy Buffet, a well known Florida musician who owns the restaurant Margaritaville, located in Universal CityWalk. Story and gameplay development began as a rough outline document highlighting possible interactions and information points for the players around CityWalk. For immersion and role playing, players were to serve as Buffet's body guards, attempting to track him down across the venues of CityWalk after he initially gives them the slip and begins wandering to visit with friends, drink, and generally have a good time.

Once enough clues were selected and given narrative flavor, all relevant information and response messages for the game were entered into the Moving Knowledge Engine for delivery to the players' mobile phones. Two formal tests were conducted on location to make sure that the story elements flowed smoothly and were easy to follow. This turned out to be an extremely important step, which uncovered a few flaws in the initial design, mostly dealing with how players might send in the keywords associated with the clues.

The ARG ran successfully as part of the mLearn 2009 conference activities. To incentivize the players, prizes in the form of Universal Dollars (fake currency that can be used to purchase items or refreshments while on Universal property) were awarded to the first, second, and third teams to finish, and also handed out by development team members at check point locations throughout the ARG. Multiple teams finished successfully, and most of the players interviewed after the event shared positive feedback. The consensus was that the clues were generally easy to find and made sense to the players within the narrative of the game. Players were also thrilled with the Universal Dollars as a prize, since they could be used throughout CityWalk. This got the players involved and also spurred players to have fun at the various entertainment venues around CityWalk both during and after their participation in the game.

While the ARG was overall a success, there were a few lessons to be learned from some of the difficulties that arose. Due to the volume of text message traffic hitting the cell networks, many of the players experienced significant lag time in receiving text message responses to their answers to clues. This broke up the flow of the game somewhat, in addition to causing some frustration. By breaking up the continuous flow that the game was designed to have, players were not able to complete as many clues in the time originally set aside. This forced us to adjust the completion point of the ARG to roughly 70%

of the way through the original plan, so players could finish in a reasonable amount of time. A few simple solutions could rectify this problem in the future, such as: staggering when teams start to avoid a surge in traffic, designing the game play to take lag into account by getting players involved at the various clue locations while waiting for responses, or incorporating alternate forms of interaction beyond SMS. Perhaps use of more tightly location-based techniques, including the use of augmented reality and ARG development apps, would also work well, though this would limit participation to users with smart phones.

No matter how much planning or testing is done, pervasive games involve real people and therefore can change course at any moment. If there was one lesson we could learn from the mLearn game and our other projects, it is to expect the unexpected. Technology is not without failure, and it is a good idea to always have a script on hand for the live actors, or even redundant technology systems or formats, to help the game continue successfully. The ARG also showed that it is important to have backup plans and multiple seamless end points in case the game takes longer than the time allotted.

MOVING KNOWLEDGE ENGINE DESIGN AND CAPABILITIES

In order to accomplish blended learning solutions capable of implementing pervasive game solutions, we developed the Moving Knowledge Engine, an interactive content scheduling and delivery system. A number of our projects and interests relate to mobile learning, which introduces some challenges, namely that there is a huge variety in mobile devices and not everyone learns the same way based on their personal learning style or current situation. The Moving Knowledge Engine attempts to solve these problems by enabling content delivery through multiple modalities: text messaging, e-mail, interactive voice response (IVR), and web sites. Being able to seamlessly bridge the gap between smart phones, standard mobile phones, and computers allows the learning content to reach a vastly larger audience. This flexibility proves very useful in the mobile learning domain, allowing freedom of access to information on even the simplest of devices.

Development of the Moving Knowledge Engine

The Moving Knowledge Engine is built to accommodate a number of potential user groups. Initial development was for implementation of My Sports Pulse, a math and science game for middle school students. The system was designed to allow the game administrators to create scenarios containing any number of multiple choice and discrete answer questions chained in sequence. Scenarios were scheduled for delivery on specific dates and times for all students in particular classes. Students answered questions and competed for points to obtain a top leader board ranking and various prizes. Participation in the game was possible through mobile phones or online through the web portal. During one test study, IVR was used to deliver the questions through a voice message system.

During phase 2 of the My Sports Pulse Challenge, Moving Knowledge added keyword functionality, enabling students to activate new sports scenarios on demand. Instead of a controlled group where each scenario was delivered to all the students in a classroom at the same time, the students received notices when a new keyword was made available. Multiple scenarios were often available simultaneously, allowing students to select which scenarios they wished to complete, or in what order to tackle all available questions.

The engine worked well for this straightforward quiz game, but it needed to be more engaging and capable of dynamically adjusting based on user input. To achieve the capability for more complex interactions and facilitation of alternate reality game style frameworks, we developed the Event Keyword system. The functionality of the Event Keyword was initially designed as a replacement for the simple Scenario Keyword. Each delivery or interaction with a user was considered an event. Events could be triggered immediately by a user submitting a keyword, delayed on a timer following a keyword submission, immediately following a completed scenario (to allow for scenario chains), or scheduled for delivery directly by system administrators. This enabled combinations of push delivery, where specific content could be delivered to individual users or whole groups, along with pull delivery, where users could activate content on their own schedule. The Event Manager, which managed all keywords, allowed for modifying the default system responses to correct or incorrect answers, as well as assigning each scenario to an attribute for event grouping.

Eventually, the Event Manager evolved into a game engine with the addition of the Event State Tracking Machine, as the system was developed from the ground up to track user interactions through a chain of events. Each keyword was given a state, and setting the state to "triggered" would unlock new keywords based on previous user input. This would enable branching content, as well as deliver of pure narrative or scaffolding information. Figure 1 below demonstrates the current delivery and interaction flow using the Event State Tracking Machine, Event Manager, and Event Keywords. Simply by removing the system assumption of trivia questions from the equation, Moving Knowledge and METIL were able to turn a basic question delivery system into a game engine capable of delivering narrative driven learning materials across a number of mobile platforms.

Benefits of the Moving Knowledge Framework

By enabling content delivery through multiple formats, Moving Knowledge provides the flexibility to fit users' situational needs, as well giving them the ability to choose the format they prefer. For example, while driving voice content works better because it allows the driver to listen with their mobile device on a hands free setting and keep their attention on the road. If a person is in a noisy crowd, such as in a restaurant or taking a ride on a subway, voice becomes more difficult to understand and text delivery works better. Some people also prefer one format over the other, or learn more effectively through certain methods, so giving them a choice allows them to use their

Figure 1. Delivery framework for the moving knowledge engine

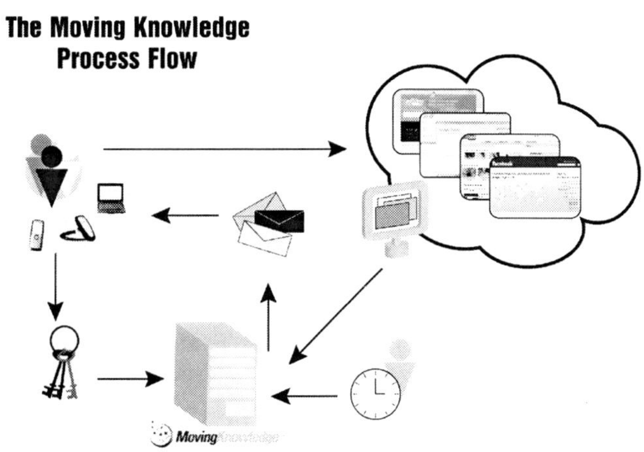

time and devices more efficiently and feel more comfortable interfacing with the software.

One specific example of physical limitations surrounding mobile learning can be found in the state of California, where law makers have banned the use of hand held devices while driving unless using a hands free system. With the average American commute exceeding 45 minutes, what if we could take back this time and put it to use for learning? Through options for voice delivery, the Moving Knowledge engine gives users the flexibility to recapture this time. Simultaneously, the ability to mirror content across different formats allows users to almost seamlessly switch between them as their situation or preference demands; for example when some material becomes too complex for voice or a user wishes to reference it later, they can request for the system to forward that information to them through SMS or e-mail. Imagine getting back up to 90 minutes per day of lost productivity. Over the course of a year that is a potential return of 375 hours of time that could be put towards learning. That's enough time to complete several college level courses, all in time that is normally considered wasted.

E-mail has been a major delivery method of interest for Google and other organizations using the Moving Knowledge Engine due to its wide daily use, the ability to deliver more comprehensive information or rich formatting through e-mails as opposed to SMS messages, and the ease of crossover between desktop and mobile interaction—users with data access on phones can check e-mail remotely if desired, but users without mobile data access or who simply prefer use of a computer can use their standard PC or laptop.

On the other hand, teens tend to prefer text messaging over e-mail. This could be in part due to the increasing number of cell phones among teens, or that they don't regularly use email as much as most professionals. In our study on the My Sports Pulse game, we found that 71% of teens liked text message delivery of information on cell phones—more than double the number that liked receiving information via the internet, which was the next most popular choice (Metcalf, Milrad, Cheek, Raasch, & Hamilton, 2008). The target audience for this study was 76 students from 5 schools in Kansas City, Missouri, and Orlando, FL. This gives a strong indication that text messaging is a viable means of distributing learning materials among teens. Text messaging is also a valuable content delivery strategy for the developing world, as standard mobile phone subscriptions far outstrip internet access, particularly broadband, worldwide (Teltscher, 2009). While there are limitations to the amount of information possible to send through text message, many recent phones also have internet capability, and a hyperlink or phone number could take the user to the full content.

RELEVANCE TO BLENDED LEARNING

Pervasive game frameworks, particular ARGs and augmented reality games, provide a powerful method for learning, particularly blended learning curricula. Considering blended learning as the process of merging various educational styles and processes, including delivery methods and learning theories (Driscoll & Carliner, 2005; Graham, 2005; Bielawski & Metcalf, 2002), the design of these games demonstrates a compelling way to deliver educational content, accomplish many learning theories traditionally difficult to manage in existing classroom and online learning, and scaffold information both within the game and from elsewhere while providing an interesting and motivating experience to learners. Pervasive game frameworks, particularly within the types presented in this chapter, are compatible with and extend current blended learning techniques that span a range of face-to-face with online learning. Augmented reality solutions on handheld devices can be integrated with or replace components for face-to-face instructor-led training (ILT) and electronic performance support techniques, while alternate reality game frameworks can be implemented across virtual ILT (both synchronous and asynchronous), self-directed virtual, and knowledge management-based techniques (Bielawski & Metcalf, 2002).

Pervasive game frameworks, when designed and deployed appropriately in relation to the learning content and well integrated into a blended learning environment, can enable the instructor to meet several goals identified as central to blended learning, including pedagogical richness, personal agency for learners, a range of access options for relevant knowledge, and in some cases ease of revision (Osguthorpe & Graham, 2003). They can provide pedagogical richness through providing a situated and constructive view of the learning content and enabling the use of various perspectives (such as through allowing multiple student roles). Since pervasive games, like other simulation and game frameworks, facilitate interaction with practical and theoretical systems as part of knowledge attainment and enactment and can support player choice and branching pathways, this can increase students' sense of personal agency in their learning. Alternate Reality Game models in particular frequently leverage multiple sources of information across several formats (e.g. video, hypertext, and printed materials), and through triggered and scheduled messaging delivery via the Moving Knowledge Engine we have smoothly integrated multiple, distributed learning aids and reference materials for students. Ease of revision can be problematic in some pervasive frameworks. Advanced augmented reality applications may sometimes require advanced media creation or programming skills, making updates difficult for instructors, but development tools such as the Moving Knowledge Engine, MIT's AR development package ("MITAR Software Download", n.d.), or the in-development ARIS editor for iPhone from the University of Wisconsin ("ARIS Mobile Media Learning Games", 2008) can enable simplified development and updates by instructors.

Due to the range of options available to game and curriculum developers for pervasive game frameworks, they are compatible with several common blended learning models. Both program flow and core-and-spoke models can be supported (Bersin, 2004). Device-dependent, and especially location-based, augmented reality games may be more suited to heavily instructor supervised use during face-to-face portions of a course; Alternate Reality Game frameworks, on the other hand, that frequently use common online tools for discovery and assembly of distributed information, may be suited to core-and-spoke designs. These same characteristics and design opportunities can also make pervasive frameworks appropriate for skill-driven, attitude-driven, and competency-driven models (Valiathan, 2002). These frameworks are also highly relevant to technology concerns in many learning programs, both face to face and online programs as well as organizations implementing mobile learning as part of their blended learning solution.

The use of ARG and augmented reality design techniques can enable instructors and curriculum designers to incorporate a number of powerful yet complex learning theories by designing core or supplemental interactive challenges. More importantly, the ability to smoothly incorporate multiple media and information sources, require students to perform information gathering and synthesis, build in student collaboration and content creation, and use narrative to scaffold these elements together enables not only the use of modern learning theories individually, but to employ multiple learning theories as demanded by the learning objectives, the students' preference, or the instructional environment. Thus, as these frameworks allow instructors and developers to "mash up" or mix real and virtual, and move between different content formats, so they also enable the creation of learning theory mashups

Figure 2. Potential mapping of learning objectives to both learning theories and delivery modalities. Branches and redundancy can be included as necessary.

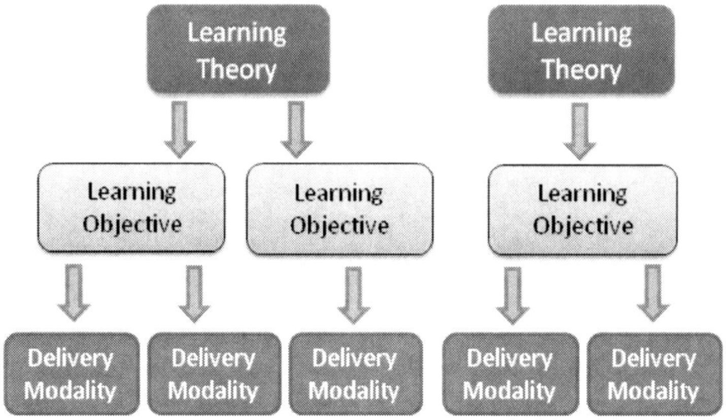

by mapping particular course items or modules to one or more learning theories that will best suit that material (see Figure 2).

There are a number of powerful learning theories that ARG and augmented reality design concepts match well with, and that may become easier to implement for some learning programs by using these game frameworks. For example, long-term processes such as heredity and evolution may be best illustrated to students using "hands on" methods, but doing so traditionally would be far too time consuming and expensive to be feasible; a pervasive game solution, however, can allow the student to view the processes involved and actively experiment much more conveniently. These concepts can also be illustrated with standard computer or console games, but pervasive frameworks allow some additional features such as location awareness.

Situated learning (Lave & Wenger, 1991) is thought to hold especially strong ties with gaming, as the process of students acclimating themselves to the game, along with the information presented therein, and the way gaming continuously stacks and expands the use of gradually obtained knowledge and skills within particular meaningful contexts, requires and engenders strong situational awareness (Gee, 2004; Van Eck, 2006). The addition of real locations enabled by ARGs and augmented reality, rather than purely virtual environments, in combination with role play and contextual performance in game tasks further supports situated learning processes.

Use of narrative within single session games, or overarching narratives in large games spanning multiple challenges and even subject areas, can provide avenues for leveraging the integrated thematic instruction technique. Story and characters become the glue holding together distributed pieces of information and separate tasks; learners use this to help organize and synthesize the materials while participating in exploration of the information space and potentially the physical space. Several of the key points for implementing ITI sound very familiar when viewed next to the ARG or augmented reality game design scheme: employing cooperative grouping, designing inquiry-based learning experiences, connecting to local surroundings, and using technology effectively (Kovalic, 1993). Both instructors supervising interaction with the games, as well as the characters or supplemental information in the games, combined with the interactive exercises core to these games also correspond well to the use of guided experiential learning (Clark & Feldon, 2008).

In most cases, ARGs and augmented reality games are cooperative exercises. This use of group participation, particularly when combined with assignment of roles (as in games like Outbreak @ the Institute or Mad City Mystery), the inability of single players to accomplish all tasks due to the variety of skills required, and the requirement to search out, combine, and synthesize distributed information fit perfectly with implementations of jigsaw learning (Aronson & Patnoe, 1997) and other types of guided, cooperative learning (Brown & Palincsar, 1989). The process of players working together to discover and assemble this information, challenge completion, and acting out roles, but also the meta-processes that players develop to track and maintain their already acquired knowledge (e.g. creating and updating wiki sites logging all events and key data from ARGs), also indicate strong potential for using constructivist and discovery learning theories (Bruner, 1967, 1990; Vygotsky, 1978).

Technologically speaking, augmented reality is currently highly applicable to mobile learning programs, but can be somewhat more difficult to develop and run, and also tends toward more device limitations and dependence. For learning areas or tasks that are highly location sensitive, however, augmented reality provides vital contextual integration with that environment. Where general programs are concerned, ARG techniques will likely demonstrate more promise due to their reliance on standard technologies. Not only does this lower development difficulty and costs, especially when compared to the development of video games requiring advanced programming and 3D modeling, but it can hold additional power for situated and contextual learning as students perform key tasks using the tools and technologies they are likely to use every day when deploying these skills.

THE ROAD FORWARD

Alternate reality games hold great potential for blended learning applications. These flexible game frameworks, which can provide a compelling experience using many different experiential learning elements and techniques, are well suited to the distributed resources and flexible, lower-cost development model needed to promote deep learning quickly and efficiently in the context of the student's daily practices. The ability to quickly layer on new learning theories, information sources, or technologies to meet learning objectives and outcomes can lead to rapid, educationally sound learning experiences. The ability to factor in various roles and learning contexts can allow greater personalization and situated learning. Most importantly, the ARG frameworks, whether personal or team-based, can accommodate the distributed nature of information found both in the physical environment, with geographically specific information, and in the rapidly expanding virtual space of the internet, internal organizational databases, and various performance support tools. Accommodating distributed information may also mean that emerging technologies to better handle these distributed content bases must also be rapidly integrated, which ARG frameworks natively support—the development question becomes not how to fit learning objectives into rigidly defined digital game frameworks, but starting from the information and learning objectives, what technology or format solution is the best choice?

Layering information and making it available in multiple formats as part of the story arc or trail of activities means more opportunities to personalize learning and achieve ubiquitous contextual learning by providing the right solution for the user's current context. An example of this layering may be access to the same information via a text message link, text within an e-mail, or embedded in a podcast that can be reviewed online, downloaded to a mobile device, or reviewed over the standard audio channel of a cell phone. Trends in emerging technology like voice-based search can add another layer of interactive simulation and mixed reality that use everyday objects around us. Even more advanced forms of artificial intelligence and natural language processing will further enhance the social and human emulation component of complex, sophisticated alternate reality experiences. While it will take some time to replace a dedicated game master or puppeteer, and the sense of reality and responsiveness of interaction with a real person may never be fully equaled by automated systems, some elements of automation or semi-automation, with links back to a live game master, are already possible through solutions like the Moving Knowledge Engine and can produce nearly seamless interactive experiences with programmed interactions for simple information, or frequently asked questions answered by an agent with a natural handoff to an instructor, subject matter expert, or other member of the ARG team for a truly intelligent response.

Location-based technologies and visual search tools will also add new elements of scale and interactivity styles to rich experiences like museum tours, visual scavenger hunts, or geospatial experiences—for example, touring a new area and experiencing a virtual overlay of historical objects that allow the user to experience of past time frames. Best of all, for learners to gain convenient access to some context of the information domain they're exploring, new forms of constructivism and action learning will be possible that are easily invoked from a user-centered locus of control that engages the curiosity of the learner. For instance, a point-based system for identifying and capturing the most objects within a certain area, and exploring those for additional challenges and reporting back on the results could evoke a young learner's curiosity, further motivate them to explore for new knowledge in a semi-structured way, and promote a love for learning based on innate curiosity about the world around them. Tempered with access to an expert or coach, the principles of guided experiential learning and other methods that enable digital coaching and personalized learning using a variety of learning theories and models to achieve deep learning and performance outcomes will be possible.

REFERENCES

ARIS. (2008). *About ARIS. ARIS – Mobile learning experiences*. Retrieved from http://arisgames.org/

Aronson, E., & Patnoe, S. (1997). *The jigsaw classroom: Building cooperation in the classroom* (2nd ed.). New York, NY: Longman.

Azuma, R. (1997). A survey of augmented reality. *Presence (Cambridge, Mass.)*, *6*(4), 355–385.

Benford, S., Crabtree, A., Flintham, M., Drozd, A., Anastasi, R., & Paxton, M. (2006). Can you see me now? *ACM Transactions on Computer-Human Interaction*, *13*(1), 100–133. doi:10.1145/1143518.1143522

Benford, S., Flintham, M., Drozd, A., Anastasi, R., Rowland, D., & Tandavanitj, N. … Adams, M. (2004). Uncle Roy all around you: Implicating the city in a location-based performance. In *Proceedings of Advanced Computer Entertainment 2004*, Singapore. ACM Press.

Bersin, J. (2004). *The blended learning book: Best practices, proven methodologies, and lessons learned*. Hoboken, NJ: John Wiley and Sons.

Bielawski, L., & Metcalf, D. (2002). *Blended e-learning: Integrating knowledge, performance support, and online learning* (2nd ed.). Amherst, MA: HRD Press, Inc.

Blunt, R. (2007). *Do serious games work? Results from three recent studies*. Presented at the The Interservice/Industry Training, Simulation & Education Conference (I/ITSEC), Orlando, FL.

Broll, W., Lindt, I., Herbst, I., Ohlenburg, J., Braun, A., & Wetzel, R. (2008). Toward next-gen mobile AR games. *Computer Graphics and Applications, IEEE, 28*(4), 40–48. doi:10.1109/MCG.2008.85

Brown, A. L., & Palincsar, A. (1989). Guided, cooperative learning and individual knowledge acquisition. In *Knowing, learning, and instruction: essays in honor of Robert Glaser, Psychology of Education and Instruction Series* (pp. 393–452). Hillsdale, NJ: Erlbaum.

Bruner, J. (1990). *Acts of meaning: Four lectures on mind and culture*. Cambridge, MA: Harvard University Press.

Bruner, J. S. (1967). *On knowing: Essays for the left hand*. Cambridge, MA: Harvard University Press.

Chen, J. (2007). Flow in games (and everything else). *Communications of the ACM, 50*(4), 31–34. doi:10.1145/1232743.1232769

Chen, S., & Michael, D. (2006). Proof of learning: Assessment in serious games. *Gamasutra: The Art & Business of Making Games*. Retrieved March 28, 2008, from http://www.gamasutra.com/view/feature/2433/proof_of_learning_assessment_in_.php

Cheok, A. D., Fong, S. W., Goh, K. H., Yang, X., Liu, W., & Farzbiz, F. (2003). *Human Pacman: A sensing-based mobile entertainment system with ubiquitous computing and tangible interaction* (pp. 106–117). Redwood City, CA: ACM.

Clark, R., & Feldon, D. (2008). *GEL, adaptable expertise and transfer of training.*

Connolly, T., Stansfield, M., Josephson, J., Lázaro, N., Rubio, G., & Ortiz, C. R. …Tsvetkova, N. (2008). Using alternate reality games to support language learning. In *Proceedings of the Seventh IASTED International Conference on Web-Based Education*. Innsbruck, Austria: ACTA Press.

Csikszentmihalyi, M. (1991). *Flow: The psychology of optimal experience*. New York, NY: Harper Perennial.

Davis, S., Moar, M., Jacobs, R., Watkins, M., Riddoch, C., & Cooke, K. (2006). Ere be dragons: Heartfelt gaming. *Digital Creativity, 17*(3), 157–162. doi:10.1080/14626260600882430

de Freitas, S. I. (2006). Using games and simulations for supporting learning. *Learning, Media and Technology, 31*(4), 343–358. doi:10.1080/17439880601021967

Driscoll, M., & Carliner, S. (2005). *Advanced Web-based training strategies: Unlocking instructionally sound online learning*. San Francisco, CA: Pfeiffer Publishing.

Dunleavy, M., Dede, C., & Mitchell, R. (2009). Affordances and limitations of immersive participatory augmented reality simulations for teaching and learning. *Journal of Science Education and Technology, 18*(1), 7–22. doi:10.1007/s10956-008-9119-1

Egenfeldt-Nielsen, S. (2005). *Beyond edutainment: Exploring the educational potential of computer games*. IT University of Copenhagen, Department of Innovation.

Facer, K., Joiner, R., Stanton, D., Reid, J., Hull, R., & Kirk, D. (2004). Savannah: Mobile gaming and learning? *Journal of Computer Assisted Learning, 20*, 399–409. doi:10.1111/j.1365-2729.2004.00105.x

Fraas, J. W. (1982). The influence of student characteristics on the effectiveness of simulations in the principles course. *The Journal of Economic Education, 13*(1), 56–61. doi:10.2307/1182871

Gee, J. (2004). *Situated language and learning: A critique of traditional schooling*. New York, NY: Routledge.

Graham, C. (2005). Blended learning systems: Definition, current trends, and future directions. In Bonk, C. J., & Graham, C. (Eds.), *Handbook of blended learning: Global perspectives, local designs*. San Francisco, CA: Pfeiffer Publishing.

Gremmen, H., & Potters, J. (1997). Assessing the efficacy of gaming in economic education. *The Journal of Economic Education, 28*(4), 291–303.

Hainey, T., Connolly, T., Stansfield, M., Boyle, L., Josephson, J., & O'Donovan, A. …Ortiz, C. R. (2009). Arguing for multilingual motivation in Web 2.0: An evaluation of a large-scale European pilot. In *Proceedings of ECGBL 2009 The 3rd European Conference on Games Based Learning* (pp. 110-119). Graz, Austria.

Hays, R. T. (2005). *The effectiveness of instructional games: A literature review and discussion*. (Technical Report No. 2005-004). Naval Air Warfare Center Training Systems Division. Retrieved from http://stinet.dtic.mil/oai/oai?&verb=getRecord&metadataPrefix=html&identifier=ADA441935

Jenkins, H. (2002, March 29). Game theory. *Technology Review*. Retrieved February 11, 2010, from http://www.technologyreview.com/energy/12784/

Jenkins, H. (2006). *Convergence culture*. NYU Press.

Johnston, J., Massey, A., & Sheldon, L. (2009). *Using alternate reality games to influence physical activity in the college population*. Presented at the Games for Health Conference 2009, Boston, MA.

Ke, F. (2008). A case study of computer gaming for math: Engaged learning from gameplay? *Computers & Education, 51*(4), 1609–1620. doi:10.1016/j.compedu.2008.03.003

Klopfer, E. (2008). *Augmented learning: Research and design of mobile educational games*. Boston, MA: The MIT Press.

Koepke, W. (1990). Epistolary fiction and its impact on readers: Reality and illusion. In Burwick, F., & Pape, W. (Eds.), *Aesthetic illusion: Theoretical and historical approaches*. Berlin, Germany: Walter de Gruyter.

Kovalic, S. (1993). *ITI: The model: Integrated thematic instruction*. Books for Educators.

Lave, J., & Wenger, E. (1991). *Situated learning: Legitimate peripheral participation* (1st ed.). Cambridge, UK: Cambridge University Press.

Leutner, D. (1993). Guided discovery learning with computer-based simulation games: Effects of adaptive and non-adaptive instructional support. *Learning and Instruction, 3*(2), 113–132. doi:10.1016/0959-4752(93)90011-N

Massachusetts Institute of Technology. (n.d.). *MITAR software download. Scheller Teacher Educational Program: Augmented reality games*. Retrieved from http://education.mit.edu/drupal/MITARSoftware

McGonigal, J. (2005). *Alternate reality learning*. Presented at the Creative Design Panel, E3 Education Arcade, Los Angeles, CA. Retrieved from http://avantgame.com/McGonigal_ILOVEBEES_education%20arcade_May%202005.pdf

McGonigal, J. (2007). Why I love bees: A case study in collective intelligence gaming. In *The ecology of games: Connecting youth, games, and learning* (pp. 199–227). The John D. and Catherine T. MacArthur Foundation Series on Digital Media and Learning.

McGonigal, J. (2009). *Superstruct: How to invent the future by playing a game*. Presented at the ETech 2009, San Jose, CA. Retrieved from http://assets.en.oreilly.com/1/event/20/Superstruct_%20How%20to%20Invent%20the%20Future%20by%20Playing%20a%20Game%20Presentation.ppt

McGonigal, J. (2010a). *TED 2010: Reality is broken. Game designers must fix it.* Retrieved from http://www.wired.com/epicenter/2010/02/jane-mcgonigal/

McGonigal, J. (2010b). *Fixing the world with online games.* Retrieved from http://www.cnn.com/video/?/video/tech/2010/02/15/jane.mcgonigal.ted2010.cnn

Metcalf, D., Milrad, M., Cheek, D., Raasch, S., & Hamilton, A. (2008). My sports pulse: Increasing student interest in STEM disciplines through sports themes, games and mobile technologies. In *Proceedings of the Fifth IEEE International Conference on Wireless, Mobile, and Ubiquitous Technology in Education* (pp. 23-30). IEEE Computer Society.

Milgram, P., & Kishino, F. (1994). A taxonomy of mixed reality visual displays. *IEICE Transactions on Information and Systems*, *77*(12), 1321–1329.

Montola, M. (2005). Exploring the edge of the magic circle: Defining pervasive games. In *Proceedings of the 2005 Digital Arts and Culture* (pp. 1--3). Copenhagen, Denmark: IT University. Retrieved from http://citeseerx.ist.psu.edu/viewdoc/summary?doi=10.1.1.125.8421

Moseley, A. (2008). *Great history conundrum: An alternative reality for research skills teaching.* Presented at the ARGs in Charity and Education Conference, London, England.

Nieuwdorp, E. (2005). The pervasive interface: Tracing the magic circle. In *Proceedings of DiGRA Conference*. Vancouver, Canada: Changing Views - Worlds in Play.

Osguthorpe, R. T., & Graham, C. R. (2003). Blended learning environments. *Quarterly Review of Distance Education*, *4*(3), 227–233.

Piatt, K. (2009, May 11). Studentquest 2006. Who is Herring Hale? *Katie Piatt.* Retrieved February 23, 2010, from http://katiepiatt.blogspot.com/2009/05/studentquest-2006-aka-who-is-herring.html

Piekarski, W., & Thomas, B. (2002). ARQuake: The outdoor augmented reality gaming system. *Communications of the ACM*, *45*(1), 36–38. doi:10.1145/502269.502291

Prensky, M. (2000). *Digital game-based learning* (1st ed.). Columbus, OH: McGraw-Hill.

PuzzleCards. (2007). *Perplex City wiki.* Retrieved February 22, 2010, from http://perplexcitywiki.com/wiki/Puzzle_Cards

Randel, J. M., Morris, B. A., Wetzel, C. D., & Whitehill, B. V. (1992). The effectiveness of games for educational purposes: A review of recent research. *Simulation & Gaming*, *23*(3), 261–276. doi:10.1177/1046878192233001

Squire, K., & Jan, M. (2007). Mad City Mystery: Developing scientific argumentation skills with a place-based augmented reality game on handheld computers. *Journal of Science Education and Technology*, *16*(1), 5–29. doi:10.1007/s10956-006-9037-z

Squire, K. D. (2004). *Replaying history: Learning world history through playing Civilization 3.* Indiana University. Retrieved from http://portal.acm.org/citation.cfm?id=1087093

Steinkuehler, C. A. (2004). Learning in massively multiplayer online games. In *Proceedings of the 6th International Conference on Learning Sciences* (pp. 521-528). Santa Monica, CA: International Society of the Learning Sciences.

Stenros, J., Montola, M., & Mäyrä, F. (2007). Pervasive games in Ludic society. In *Proceedings of the 2007 Conference on Future Play* (pp. 30-37). Toronto, Canada: ACM.

Stewart, S. (2006, June 11). Alternate reality games. *seanstewart.org*. Retrieved March 18, 2008, from http://www.seanstewart.org/interactive/args/

Teltscher, S. (2009). *The world in 2009: ICT facts and figures*. Presented at the ITU Telecom World, Geneva, Switzerland. Retrieved from http://www.itu.int/ITU-D/ict/papers/2009/Press%20briefing_Telecom09.pdf

Valiathan, P. (2002). *Blended learning models*. American Society for Training and Development. Retrieved from http://www.astd.org/LC/2002/0802_valiathan.htm

Van Eck, R. (2006). Digital game-based learning: It's not just the digital natives who are restless. *EDUCAUSE Review*, *41*(2), 16–30.

Vogel, J. J., Vogel, D. S., Cannon-Bowers, J., Bowers, C. A., Muse, K., & Wright, M. (2006). Computer gaming and interactive simulations for learning: A meta-analysis. *Journal of Educational Computing Research*, *34*(3), 229–243. doi:10.2190/FLHV-K4WA-WPVQ-H0YM

Vygotsky, L. S. (1978). *Mind in society*. Cambridge, MA: Harvard University Press.

Waite, J. (2007, July 13). World without oil: The post-game press release. *ARGNet: Alternate Reality Gaming Network*. Retrieved from http://www.argn.com/2007/07/world_without_oil_the_post-game_press_release/

Walther, B. K. (2005). Atomic actions-molecular experience: Theory of pervasive gaming. *ACM Computers in Entertainment*, *3*(3), 4. doi:10.1145/1077246.1077258

Whitton, N. (2008). Alternate reality games for developing student autonomy and peer learning. In *Proceedings of Lick 2008*, Edinburgh, UK.

ADDITIONAL READING

Aldrich, C. (2003). Simulations and the learning revolution: An interview with Clark Aldrich. Retrieved from http://technologysource.org/article/simulations_and_the_learning_revolution/.

Aldrich, C. (2005). *Learning by doing: A comprehensive guide to simulations, computer games, and pedagogy in e-learning and other educational experiences*. San Francisco, CA: Pfeiffer.

Bogost, I. (2007). *Persuasive games: The expressive power of videogames*. The MIT Press.

Culver, J. (2008, December 5). *Operation: Sleeper Cell*. PowerPoint presented at the ARGs in Charity and Education Conference, London, England.

de Freitas, S., & Oliver, M. (2006). How can exploratory learning with games and simulations within the curriculum be most effectively evaluated? *Computers & Education*, *46*(3), 249–264. doi:10.1016/j.compedu.2005.11.007

Dickey, M. (2005). Engaging by design: How engagement strategies in popular computer and video games can inform instructional design. *Educational Technology Research and Development*, *53*(2), 67–83. doi:10.1007/BF02504866

Egenfeldt-Nielsen, S. (2008). Practical barriers in using educational computer games. In *Beyond Fun: serious game and media* (pp. 20–26). ETC Press.

Entertainment Software Association. (2008). *Essential facts about the computer and video game industry*. Entertainment Software Association. Retrieved from http://www.theesa.com/facts/pdfs/ESA_EF_2008.pdf

Francis, R. (2006). Towards a theory of a games based pedagogy. Presented at the JISC Innovating e-Learning: Transforming Learning Experiences, online.

Fullerton, T., Swain, C., & Hoffman, S. (2008). *Game design workshop: A playcentric approach to creating innovative games* (2nd ed.). Burlington, MA: Morgan Kaufmann Publishers.

Garris, R., Ahlers, R., & Driskell, J. E. (2002). Games, motivation, and learning: A research and practice model. *Simulation & Gaming, 33*(4), 441–467. doi:10.1177/1046878102238607

Gee, J. P. (2003). What video games have to teach us about learning and literacy. *ACM Computers in Entertainment, 1*(1).

Gee, J. P. (2007). *Good video games and good learning: Collected essays on video games, learning and literacy* (1st ed.). Peter Lang Publishing.

Ghellal, S., & Lindt, I. (2008). Interactive movie elements in a pervasive game. *Personal and Ubiquitous Computing, 12*(4), 307–315. doi:10.1007/s00779-007-0186-8

Habgood, M. P. J., Ainsworth, S. E., & Benford, S. (2005). Endogenous fantasy and learning in digital games. *Simulation & Gaming, 36*(4), 483–498. doi:10.1177/1046878105282276

Hon, A. (2001). The guide x: A tale of the A.I. trail. *cloudmakers.org*. Retrieved from http://www.cloudmakers.org/guide/

Jenkins, H. (2006). *Confronting the challenges of participatory culture: Media education for the 21st century*. Building the Field of Digital Media and Learning. MacArthur Foundation. Retrieved from http://www.projectnml.org/files/working/NMLWhitePaper.pdf

Kim, J. Y., Allen, J. P., & Lee, E. (2008). Alternate reality gaming. *Communications of the ACM, 51*(2), 36–42. doi:10.1145/1314215.1340912

Kirriemuir, J., & McFarlane, A. (2004). *Literature review in games and learning (No. 8). Futurelab Series* (p. 39). Futurelab.

Klopfer, E., Yoon, S., & Rivas, L. (2004). Comparative analysis of Palm and wearable computers for Participatory Simulations. *Journal of Computer Assisted Learning, 20*(5), 347–359. doi:10.1111/j.1365-2729.2004.00094.x

Magerkurth, C., Cheok, A. D., Mandryk, R. L., & Nilsen, T. (2005). Pervasive games: bringing computer entertainment back to the real world. *Comput. Entertain., 3*(3), 4–4. doi:10.1145/1077246.1077257

Marković, F., Petrovic, O., Kittl, C., & Edegger, B. (2007). Pervasive learning games: A comparative study. *New Review of Hypermedia and Multimedia, 13*(2), 93–116. doi:10.1080/13614560701712873

McGonigal, J. (2006). *This might be a game: Ubiquitous play and performance at the turn of the twenty-first century* (Unpublished doctoral dissertation). University of California, Berkeley. Retrieved from http://avantgame.com/McGonigal_THIS_MIGHT_BE_A_GAME_sm.pdf

Michael, D., & Chen, S. (2005). *Serious games: Games that educate, train, and inform*. Florence, KY: Cengage Learning, Inc.

(n.d.). *Alternate Reality Gaming Network (ARGNet)*. Retrieved from http://www.argn.com/

Rouse, R. (2001). *Game design: Theory and practice* (2nd ed.). Wordware Publishing, Inc.

Salen, K., & Zimmerman, E. (2003). *Rules of play: Game design fundamentals*. The MIT Press.

Salen, K., & Zimmerman, E. (2005). *The game design reader: A rules of play anthology*. The MIT Press.

Stewart, S. (n.d.). The A.I. Web Game. *seanstewart.org*. Retrieved March 18, 2008, from http://www.seanstewart.org/beast/intro/

Williams, D., Yee, N., & Caplan, S. (2008). Who plays, how much, and why? Debunking the stereotypical gamer profile. *Journal of Computer-Mediated Communication*, *13*(4), 993–1018. doi:10.1111/j.1083-6101.2008.00428.x

Wilson, K. A., Bedwell, W. L., Lazzara, E. H., Salas, E., Burke, C. S., & Estock, J. L. (2009). Relationships between game attributes and learning outcomes: Review and research proposals. *Simulation & Gaming*, *40*(2), 217–266. doi:10.1177/1046878108321866

KEY TERMS AND DEFINITIONS

Augmented Reality: The practice of adding digital information in real time to physical, real-world locations/objects, with the intent of augmenting or improving the user's perception of or interaction with those locations/objects. Digital information added can be minimal or extensive, and can incorporate text as well as graphics (both two-dimensional and three-dimensional).

Collective Intelligence: Shared knowledge and thought processes developed and implemented through collaboration and competition among many individuals. Modern communication technologies, particularly the Internet, enable and strongly encourage the development and implementation of knowledge and decision networks, and are a chief focus of much current CI research.

Epistolary Novel: A novel presented as a series of documents, traditionally letters (or recently, emails) but also including newspaper articles, organizational memos/reports, or journal entries. Online or hypertext epistolary fiction may also include video or audio recordings. For examples, see Bram Stoker's *Dracula* or Daniel Keyes' *Flowers for Algernon*.

Head-Mounted Display (HMD): A display device worn on the user's head that places small computer displays in front of one or both eyes; the unit can range from a pair of glasses or visor to a full helmet with attached display screen(s). Some displays cover the view completely (e.g. virtual reality systems) while some still allow the user to see their surroundings (e.g. augmented reality systems).

Pervasive Games: Games designed to cross or eradicate traditional play boundaries, therefore "pervading" multiple spaces. Boundaries crossed may be technological, such as a game that uses multiple pieces of hardware or software, or physical, such as a game that is played both online and in physical space.

Serious Games: Games designed primarily to accomplish a specific practical purpose, as opposed to traditional games designed primarily for entertainment. Serious games can be used for a variety of purposes, but are most commonly intended to educate players on a specific issue or persuade players to adopt a certain viewpoint or attitude.

Simulation: The imitation or replication of an object, process, or behavioral state for the purpose of research, prediction, or training. There are several types of simulation, ranging from computational models and virtual reproductions to highly complex hardware installations.

Chapter 10
A Case Study of a Blended Doctoral Program in Educational Technology

Michele Jacobsen
University of Calgary, Canada

ABSTRACT

Educational technology is a hands-on, minds-on discipline that emphasizes knowing and doing. In this field, doctoral education needs to reflect digital and communication realities in the twenty-first century. In this case study, a blended learning approach to graduate education in educational technology is explored from the perspective of the author's own classroom. The course design and blended delivery of an Advanced Concepts in Educational Technology seminar is described in detail. Active learning opportunities, using wikis, blogs, avatars and virtual worlds, learning managements systems, email, and face-to-face learning experiences engaged doctoral students in the collaborative investigation and critique of educational technology trends and research ideas. Doctoral students investigated their emerging digital lives as scholars and developed a personal cyberinfrastructure that they can continue to build, modify, and extend throughout their educational technology careers.

INTRODUCTION

Cloud based computing, the open-source and open-content movements, social networking and mobile technologies transform the ways people can work, learn, and communicate in higher education. Educational technologies both enable and require new approaches to teaching, learning and assessment that transcend hierarchical, industrial-based content delivery models that have characterized the campus experience for the past century. Delicious, Google, Blogger, Moodle, Wikipedia, YouTube, Ning, iMovie, Facebook, Twitter, iPod, iPhone, iPad, all help to map new terrain in instant, interactive, creative and collaborative knowledge building communities.

DOI: 10.4018/978-1-60960-479-0.ch010

Educational technology is focused primarily on how people learn and then making computers and networks support and extend that learning. For educators who believe delivering content and testing recall equals learning, educational technology is not a great fit. For those who see their role as designing and creating innovative and dynamic blended learning experiences and environments by putting powerful media in the hands of students, educational technology is a natural and life-giving fit (Jacobsen & Kopp, 2008). As an educational technology scholar, I have observed how computers and networks open the door to powerful new ideas and learning practices first-hand in hundreds of classrooms through my research. In this case study, I explore in-depth an example of blended graduate education in educational technology from the perspective of my blended doctoral course.

Blended learning is defined as the combination of face-to-face and online learning experiences (Williams, 2002). Face-to-face activities can support the online activities or vice versa, depending on the emphasis placed on the two options for engagement (Crichton & Childs, 2008). The goal of a blended course should be to combine the best features of in class teaching with the best features of online learning to promote active, self-directed learning opportunities for students with added flexibility (Garnham & Kaleta, 2002). Garrison and Vaughan (2008) operationally define blended learning as "the organic integration of thoughtfully selected and complementary face-to-face and online approaches and technologies" (p. 148). For the purposes of this chapter, blended learning is defined along a continuum from chiefly face-to-face, co-located learning opportunities on campus supplemented with online activities and tasks, to primarily online learning experiences supplemented with real time interaction using teleconferencing, video-conferencing and online conferencing.

RETHINKING DOCTORAL EDUCATION

In educational technology, we know that doctoral education needs to be reshaped for the twenty-first century. "New technologies are altering and accelerating the way knowledge is shared and developed. And the marketplace for scholars and scholarship is now thoroughly global" (Walker, Golde, Jones, Bueschel & Hutchings, 2008, p. 2). The growing reliance on the Internet and social networking tools for collaboration, sharing, creating and communicating knowledge in the developed world often exists in sharp and painful contrast to the paucity of meaningful and reliable access to the Internet in many developing countries and contexts (Marshall, Kinuthia & Taylor, 2009). In short, education needs educational technology leaders and researchers who understand what has gone before in order to design and develop what is needed next in a technology enabled, knowledge society.

Helping people to learn is the primary and essential purpose of any educational technology (Janusewski & Molenda, 2008). From its beginnings in educational film and radio, through the audio-visual era and then personal computing and the Internet, the field of educational technology has shaped and has been shaped by an "increased awareness of the difference between the mere retention of information for testing purposes and the acquisition of knowledge, skills and attitudes used beyond classroom walls" (Janusewski & Molenda, 2008, p. 4). As our theories about knowledge change in concert with rapid advancements in educational technology, the field needs to consider the political, social, economic and cultural implications for learners and for learning in diverse international contexts, and that requires that the field itself examines how we prepare the next generation of educational technology scholars and leaders.

The primary mission of a doctoral program is the advancement of knowledge and the preparation of quality practitioners (Shulman, Golde, Bueschel & Garabedian, 2006, p. 25). The Blended / Online Doctor of Education in Educational Technology (EdD) at the University of Calgary is a thesis-based degree intended to prepare practitioners for careers in teaching and leadership by engaging students in exploration of learning, innovation, and technology. Students are challenged to conceptualize how this triad might transform existing and future teaching and learning environments. For years, the field of education has struggled to find a balance between the *practice* of education and *research* in education, and also in designing and delivering doctoral programs that meet the needs of a diverse student population (Shulman, Golde, Bueschel & Garabedian, 2006, p. 26). Educational technology is a hands-on, minds-on discipline that emphasizes knowing and doing; therefore, doctoral programs have to provide active learning opportunities that engage students with both the cognitive and technological tools of their discipline.

As described by Shulman, et al. (2006), the education doctorate is "intended as preparation for managerial and administrative leadership in education, focuses on preparing practitioners – from principals to curriculum specialists, to teacher-educators, to evaluators – who can use existing knowledge to solve educational problems" (Shulman, Golde, Bueschel & Garabedian, 2006, p. 26). Additionally, for those who are admitted into a doctoral program in educational technology, the emphasis for research and scholarly work needs to include history and foundations of the field, major theoretical and research foundations, current research problems and issues, and going beyond the allure of the latest digital technologies and gadgets to immerse doctoral students in the breadth and depth of the entire field of educational technology.

The goal of doctoral education in educational technology has to embrace both practice and research: "students must review our field's history with an eye towards our continued development. They must examine the concepts, constructs, as well as the objects of our history in an attempt to see the development as a progression of technological invention, theoretical development, societal and ethical contradictions and issues, and one that continues into the future" (Robinson, 2009, p. 36). In order to lead innovation in blended and online learning, doctoral students need to experience and design for learning in blended and online environments as a meaningful part of their graduate experience – which means, hands-on learning experiences using the technology, hands-on, minds-on design work with the technology, and minds-on and hands-on evaluation of the appropriate and successful use of technology for learning.

With the end clearly in mind, which is to invent new forms of understanding by applying the technology as one moves the field of educational technology ahead through experimentation, implementation and evaluation, the design of formal learning experiences in a doctoral program need to include preparing doctoral students to craft a successful dissertation proposal, to successfully complete their candidacy exam, and to carry out, write up and successfully defend their dissertation research. "The denouement of the doctorate, the dissertation, is not only a piece of original research intended to set its writer apart from all who preceded her. It is also a celebration of the scores of scholars on whose shoulders any piece of individual scholarship rests" (Walker, Golde, Jones, Bueschel & Hutchings, 2008, p. xi). With their feet firmly planted in both the practice and design of innovative digital learning spaces, and in the evaluation and study of same, then our newest educational technology doctors can lead and change the world.

A BLENDED EDUCATION DOCTORATE TIMELINE

The blended educational technology doctorate in the Faculty of Education at the University of Calgary is designed as a three to four year graduate apprenticeship during which doctoral students engage in advanced graduate courses with experienced faculty members and graduate peers, experiment with and design with existing and emerging technologies, create and defend a research proposal, successfully complete candidacy exams, then conduct research and write a dissertation. Doctoral students travel to the University of Calgary for two on-campus-then-blended experiences in their first and second year during the summer months; all other courses are completed online during regular Fall and Winter semesters.

Education doctorate students participate synchronously and asynchronously in core qualitative and quantitative research seminars and a common doctoral seminar lead by a full professor using tools such as Blackboard, a learning management system, and Elluminate, a bridge that enables instructors and students to connect in real-time. Students create online portfolios using their choice of webpages, wikis, blogs and introductory discussion forums. Students participate in required discussion forums in BlackBoard to debate, exchange and building upon each other's ideas in response to inquiry questions, scholarly readings and course texts. Monthly real-time seminars hosted by the instructor bring together PhD and EdD students from across specializations to investigate how theories of knowledge, mind, being and metaphysics relate to the study of social phenomena. The doctoral seminar and research courses are designed to help doctoral students to develop the understanding needed for the selection and development of a doctoral research proposal that results in new knowledge, new research methods and/or ideas for the field.

Doctoral students in the first year seminar are challenged to understand what is meant by a sound defense of proposed and completed field research, and are provided with on-campus and online opportunities to practice such defenses for the purposes of their own future candidacy and final dissertation oral examinations. In preparation for the candidacy exam, which takes place within twenty-eight months of starting the doctoral program, the doctoral student is mentored and supported by their supervisory committee via teleconference, video-conference and documents exchanged and peer-reviewed online. The doctoral student's supervisory committee consists of the supervisor and two other professors with research expertise in areas related to the doctoral student's proposed research.

Doctoral students communicate regularly with their supervisor to craft the research proposal – this negotiation and review takes place through email, telephone and online communication. Doctoral students complete the candidacy exam process, which consists of writing a substantive academic paper related to their doctoral research in a four week period, in their home location. The candidacy paper is submitted to the committee and is followed by a 2-hour oral exam during which five professors assess the doctoral student's understanding of educational research, the field of educational technology, and the specific area of research terrain explored by the doctoral student.

Doctoral students, faculty members and external examiners can choose to travel to main campus for a face-to-face candidacy exam or take part in the candidacy exam via video-conferencing or teleconference. It is becoming unusual to have all five professors and the doctoral candidate in the same room for a candidacy exam; increasingly, one or more persons take part in the candidacy exam using communication technology. Once a doctoral student successfully completes their candidacy exam, they are expected to spend the bulk of their time on their own research in their chosen setting under the guidance of their doctoral supervisor and supervisory committee.

EDUCATION DOCTORATE IN EDUCATIONAL TECHNOLOGY

Shulman and colleagues (2006) ask the good question about the design of a doctoral program: "what kinds of exercises, simulations, investigations, writings, and approaches to the systematic observation and documentation of practice is needed to make a grounded judgment of practitioner's competence?" (Shulman, Golde, Bueschel & Garabedian, 2006, p. 29). The point here is to make educational technology practice the template for designing the doctoral experience and to use standards from the field in the design of learning experiences on campus.

In addition to the required first-year seminar and the two research courses that all doctoral students in education take, the design team for the educational technology doctorate developed four specialization courses: one advanced educational technology course that all doctoral students are required to take in their first year, and three others from which doctoral students must select two depending upon their proposed area of research. The courses are designed to engage doctoral students in advanced study of the field of Educational Technology and current research questions, issues and trends.

In this chapter, I describe in detail the design and delivery of the *Advanced Concepts in Educational Technology* seminar. Key concepts and topics included in this required course are historical and philosophical foundations of the field of educational technology, diverse research methods in the field, educational technology standards and definitions, research ethics and society, and developing one's own identify and place within the field.

A second course, titled Inquiry and Technology, engages doctoral students from across specializations in learning science theory, innovative research methods, evaluating technology enhanced teaching and learning, and issues of providing access for all learners in a digital age for learning (for example principles of universal design for learning - UDL). A third course, titled Technology Enabled Learning Environments, engages doctoral students in actively questioning and examining digital learning experiences, from teaching a studio course online to factors that promote or inhibit collaboration in a range of technology-enabled construction environments, such as the issues, affordances and considerations to do with mobile learning technologies and virtual learning environments.

The required Advanced Concepts course, and the elective Inquiry and Technology and Technology Enabled Learning Environments courses, are offered as blended face-to-face experiences with extensive online activities following the on campus component. The foundational course is often the first course of the students' program and is designed to introduce students to the EdD program, to the professors in educational technology, to their research supervisors and fellow doctoral students. Leading scholars in the field are invited to offer seminars, either in person or online. The aim is to create a scholarly community that involves both academic faculty and doctoral students in examining the foundations of the field through sharing, reviewing and critiquing present and past research and practical issues. The scholarly community is intentionally set up for participants to share their current research work, ideas and questions with others so that all members of the community become familiar with a diverse range of topics, methods and findings in the field of educational technology.

The EdD program is blended and consists of face-to-face learning experiences and online courses. Normally, students take their blended / face-to-face courses at the beginning of their first and second year of program by attending classes at the University of Calgary campus, offered over two weeks in July, followed by four weeks of online learning experiences. The on-campus experiences are important in order to acquaint students with the program philosophy and to build a strong academic community. The on-campus experiences are also important for collaborative design experiences and experimenting with online technologies, such as BlackBoard, Elluminate, Second Life, wikis, blogging, grassroots video – the primary communication and interaction tools that are vital to the doctoral students online strategy. The Fall and Winter blended learning experiences in the doctoral program are completed primarily online, and supplemented with real time interactions and learning experiences using a range of technologies.

Introducing Doctoral Students to Research in the Field

Industrial approaches to campus teaching, listening, memorizing and mass testing, are giving way to active, engaged learning opportunities made possible through educational technology. Today's digital learners are active designers and knowledge builders whose ideas can be shared with the world. As an educational technology researcher and leader, part of my practice is to help people to understand the shifting educational and instructional paradigms by illustrating and demonstrating the power of blended learning theories and technologies through teaching, speaking and building communities of practice.

For two summers, I led the Advanced Concepts in Educational Technology doctoral seminar in the Online EDD in Educational Technology in the Faculty of Education, at the University of Calgary. There is national demand for this unique, Online EDD Educational Technology, and growing international demand for this program that I had a major role in designing, developing and implementing. This year, the graduate division received more than double the expected number of applicants for the online education doctorate in educational technology for the current admissions cycle.

The required doctoral seminar was designed to provide an introduction to the historical, social and philosophical foundations of educational technology research. Current educational technology standards and ethics frameworks used by various stakeholders to define research and practice in the field were examined and discussed (Januszewski & Molenda, 2008). Through readings, discussion and sustained inquiry, and hands-on experiences using a range of digital technologies for design, communication and visual display, doctoral students explored and developed a personal understanding of current educational research methods, ethics and leadership, and current issues, questions and trends that define the field of educational technology research and teaching (Creswell, 2009; Jonassen, 2001; Jonassen, 2004; Spector, Merrill, Merrienboer, & Driscoll, 2007; Willis, 2008).

An active social learning environment in the doctoral seminar enabled me to engage directly with each doctoral student's questions and ideas, and intentionally support students' active interaction with each other. For example, a small group of doctoral students demonstrated and used augmented reality tools to explore applications and designs for learning. The professionals we attract into our online blended doctoral program in educational technology tend to share at least two characteristics: they have already established a career in a field closely related to or in educational technology and leadership, and they are distributed across North America. It is to be expected that education students differ from those in other disciplines in that most have had careers before pursuing doctoral studies, and the sequencing of doctoral work and professional work is the inverse of other fields with doctoral work coming at mid-career stage rather than at the beginning. (Shulman, Golde, Bueschel & Garabedian, 2006, p. 26).

Our students in the education doctorate in educational technology are similar to, and also different, than the recognizable community of education researchers and leaders. For example, doctoral students currently enrolled in our blended programs primarily come from across Canada and the United States, with a growing number traveling to campus from overseas. Our doctoral students currently hold a diverse range of instructional design and media development positions in higher education, or serve as department chairs or division leaders in academic departments in community colleges, vocational and technical institutes, are directors in teaching and learning centers for both on campus and online programs in higher education institutions, hold multimedia and distance education development roles in school systems or higher education, hold faculty development positions in medical, nursing and social work faculties, and so on. Doctoral students in educational technology are already adept at using a range of digital technologies in their professional roles.

Therefore, based on the depth of career experience and successful prior graduate study represented in our doctoral students, the doctoral seminars have been intentionally designed to take full advantage of the strengths and experience that each student brings, to draw upon the strengths and experience of full time academic faculty in educational technology, and to facilitate collaborative group work and active peer dialogue and debate in an intellectual community.

Developing an Understanding of the Field of Educational Technology

Several key texts formed the basis of scholarly reading, discussion and debate in daily campus seminars, online discussions in Blackboard, and individual doctoral student pathfinders (each doctoral student created an online personal web). The definition of educational technology text, by Alan Januszewski and Michael Molenda (2008) served as a foundation for understanding how the field has defined itself in the last few decades, the key research areas and ideas in each area of learning, performance, creating, using, managing, and leading technology and change, the values and ethical stances taken in the field, how technological resources and processes are conceptualized, and the multifaceted relationship between the history, standards and current definition of the field.

Doctoral students were required to read and use the three online editions of the *Handbook of Research for Educational Communications and Technology* (Jonassen, 2004; Jonassen, 2001; Spector, Merrill, Merrienboer, & Driscoll, 2007). The three editions of the Handbooks provide up-to-date summaries and syntheses of recent research foundations, strategies, technologies, models, design, development and issues pertinent to the educational uses of information and communication technologies. As part of the course, I required doctoral students to join the Association for Educational Communications and Technology (AECT). A student membership in AECT gives the doctoral students online access to several key texts, including the three editions of the Handbook, as well as a subscription to a research journal and a professional journal, and membership in a large, international community of educational technology researchers and practitioners.

Another key text that doctoral students accessed was *the Educational Media and Technology Yearbook* (Orey, McClendon & Branch, 2009; 2008). Each year, the EMT Yearbook offers several chapters by top educational technology researchers on the trends and issues in the field, chapters on library and information science, leadership profiles, information on organizations and associations in North America, and details on graduate programs in North America. The yearbook is a valuable resource for a new, current or experience scholar in the field, media and technology professionals in schools, higher education and business contexts.

Doctoral students were encouraged to begin developing their professional library of resources and texts on their road to becoming scholars in the field. In addition to the required educational technology texts, I recommended several texts that provided guidance on reading and critiquing social science research (Holosko, 2006), preparing for and writing the dissertation (Biklen & Casella, 2007; Cone & Foster, 2006), and a guide for planning dissertations and writing grant proposals (Locke, Spirduso & Silverman, 2000). Doctoral students were required to seek out and read widely in the field by accessing peer reviewed and professional journals, especially those online and open-source journals that are freely available. As part of their membership in AECT, two journals, *Educational Technology, Research and Development* and *TechTrends*, were mailed to their homes. Doctoral students were also provided with a list of educational technology peer reviewed journals they could either access online or get more information about online:

- *Canadian Journal for Learning and Technology (CJLT) [*http://www.cjlt.ca/*]*
- *Journal of Distance Education (JDE) [*http://www.jofde.ca*]*
- *Journal of Research on Technology in Education (JRTE) [*http://www.iste.org/*]*
- *Australian Journal of Educational Technology (AJET) [*http://www.ascilite.org.au/ajet/ajet.html*]*
- *American Journal of Distance Education [*http://www.ajde.com/*]*
- *British Journal of Educational Technology [*http://www.blackwellpublishing.com/journal.asp?ref=0007-1013*]*
- *Journal of the Learning Sciences [*http://www-static.cc.gatech.edu/computing/lst//jls/*]*
- *Performance Improvement Quarterly [*http://www.ispi.org/publications/piq.htm*]*
- *Performance Improvement Journal [*http://www.ispi.org/publications/pij.htm*]*
- *Journal of Educational Technology & Society [*http://www.ifets.info/*]*
- *Educational Technology [*http://www.bookstoread.com/etp/*]*
- *Journal of Workplace Learning [*http://thesius.emeraldinsight.cjm/vl=6908840/cl=35/nw=1/rpsv/jwl.htm*]*
- *Journal of Asynchronous Learning Network (JALN) [*http://www.sloan-c.org/publications/jaln/index.asp*]*
- *The International Review of Research in Open and Distance Learning (IRRODL) [*http://www.irrodl.org/index.php/irrodl*]*
- *Mindshare Learning Report [*http://www.mindsharelearning.com*]*

In addition to the Association for Educational Communications and Technology (AECT), doctoral students were encouraged to join the Canadian Association for Innovation in Education (CNIE) and the International Society for Technology in Education (ISTE). In a digital world, doctoral students need to be explicitly connected to online scholarly communities and an increasingly online and open-source research literature.

Course Design and Blended Delivery

This blended doctoral seminar combined both on-campus and online learning experiences. Doctoral students participate in an on-campus learning experience for two weeks at the University campus, and then return to their homes or home institutions to complete the remaining four weeks of the formal learning experience. Face-to-face sessions are held on campus, Monday to Friday, for three hours per day, during two weeks of the summer semester in July.

During the on-campus component of this seminar, doctoral students collaborated on the design of an educational trends wiki that they used (i) to build critical knowledge about a current technology trend, (ii) to teach their peers about current trends, and (iii) to publish a lasting multimedia resource that contributes knowledge to the field. Doctoral students also started and regularly contributed to a personal blog to make available their summaries and critiques of articles, their developing research ideas and interests, the key ideas and issues gleaned from expert presentations and discussions, and to keep track of key people and resources that they found or were given during the on-campus learning experience. Using a Second Life avatar they designed and created, doctoral students went on guided tours to several different islands as they learned about other doctoral students' research and two professors' new instructional design models and simulations.

Real time guest seminars by eight full time educational technology professors offered doctoral students the opportunity to read and critique current research, to engage with constructed learning environments and research strategies first hand, and to discuss and debate authentic and diverse educational technology research with professors who are actively conducting research in the field. My design intentionally included presentations and discussions lead by my colleagues, who are experienced and diverse educational technology faculty members, because the doctoral students need to be immersed in an active design, practice and research culture, to become familiar with a broad range of research methods and approaches, and to interact with the community of professors who will support their doctoral study and research.

At least three times during the on campus portion of the seminar, the doctoral students were asked to do a doc talk. These in-class presentations by each doctoral student about their own learning design and research ideas were previewed, questioned, and debriefed in Blackboard discussion spaces, actively discussed in real time, and available for further reflection and comment on each doctoral student's blog. Presentation slides, scholarly articles and materials from the course professor and all guest professors were archived and available in the course management system for access during the on campus and online parts of the course.

The doctoral seminar was held in a computer lab located in our Education Library so that doctoral students and the instructor had pervasive access to digital content and the Internet, as well as physical resources like books, dissertations and theses and academic journals. Doctoral students were formally connected to the instructor and peers on-line until the end of the course in August, and informally for the duration of their doctoral program through email, blogs, web sites and wikis. BlackBoard, our online learning management system, plus open-source blogs and Wikis, and campus email were used to support on-line collaboration, communication and knowledge sharing components of the course.

This advanced, blended doctoral course was designed to support individual, paired and group inquiry and scholarship, instructional design and peer review in an active intellectual community using a range of social networking tools, from blogs, wikis and virtual worlds, to more mundane tools like the learning management system. A combination of instructor / expert presentations, group discussions, group work and presentations, individual presentations, and extensive online archive of scholarly materials, as well as self-study and regular scholarly writing, supported the development of our intellectual community.

As the course instructor, and as a faculty member who supervises both masters and doctoral students, I envisioned my role as facilitating the doctoral students' introduction to the field of educational technology, to educational research and to the group of professors who are part of the educational technology specialization in the Faculty of Education. It was also important to engage doctoral students directly with social networking tools while on campus to facilitate the use of same throughout their program; hence, while on campus, doctoral students were required to start a blog, to collaborate on a wiki, and to create an avatar to explore virtual worlds and research spaces.

While doctoral students get a thorough introduction to educational research, educational history and philosophy, and a broad range of research methods in their common doctoral seminars, the next generation of educational technology scholars must be immersed in the particulars of the field in which they aim to carry out their research and scholarship, continue present leadership roles or take on new ones, and become the stewards of future generations of students, teachers, researchers, leaders and practitioners across organizational and disciplinary contexts. While on campus, doctoral students were assigned the task of starting a personal web, a pathfinder of resources and tools that they used as part of their professional library and personal scholarship, that they built and extended upon during the online portion of the course.

Educational Technology is a vibrant field of study that has undergone many changes in its 80+ year history. While the field has worked with several definitions over the years, the current definition is: "Educational technology is the study and ethical practice of facilitating learning and improving performance by creating, using and managing appropriate technological processes and resources" (Januszewski & Molenda, 2008). The field includes quantitative and qualitative research as well as other forms of disciplined inquiry such as theorizing, philosophical analysis, historical investigations, development projects, fault analyses, case studies and program evaluations.

In order to develop their own individual questions and literature reviews, ideas and plans for their doctoral research, doctoral students in educational technology need to explore current and historical issues, questions and concepts in educational technology, and keep track of their questions, explorations and solutions. Doctoral students continue to add links, resources and ideas to the personal web that they started on campus. Doctoral students need to explore research approaches, major milestones, and historical and philosophical debates in educational technology in order to locate their proposed research within this field of study.

As part of the advanced introduction to the field, doctoral students need opportunities to review the research terrain relevant to their proposed doctoral research, with particular attention to preparation for candidacy. In the context of educational research writ large, doctoral students need to examine selected major themes and issues in educational technology research and teaching. In order to develop or refine their own knowledge building and collaboration skills, doctoral students need to participate in and contribute to a collaborative, online scholarly community to publish, exchange and consider emerging ideas. Finally, doctoral students need to develop personal philosophical, ethical and pedagogical perspectives on educational technology in a preferred area of practice or study.

A large part of the learning experience in the doctoral course was cultivated via collaborations and discussions with other learners, with faculty members, and the time doctoral students spent in active individual scholarship (i.e., literature review and critique, reflection and writing, goal setting, and project planning). From the first meeting, it was impressed on doctoral students that individual and group success depended on the development of an intellectual community and on our shared commitment and responsibility for rich learning and scholarship. Doctoral students were encouraged to take personal responsibility for learning and development, as well as to recognize an ethical obligation to contribute to the learning of others by participating fully and respectfully in seminar conversations, learning activities and tasks. Each doctoral student was expected to continue to build and extend upon what was learned in the advanced educational technology course in subsequent courses, supervisory relationships and learning experiences in their doctoral program.

Learning Tasks and Assignments

Both online and on-campus, this blended doctoral seminar in educational technology focused on each individual student's research questions and ideas in the rich social context of their peer's research questions and ideas. On campus seminars were used for active scholarship, experiential learning and extensive interaction. Doctoral students engaged first hand with different educational technology professor's active research projects and investigations. Social networking tools, like blogs, wikis, Second Life, online conferencing, and rich, authentic design assignments, scaffolded the blended learning experience.

During the online portion of the course, doctoral students published in-depth research pathfinders using a variety of self-chosen online tools (from personal web pages, wikis and blogs to online video and audio), and sought feedback from their peers and two professors online. From their distributed settings, doctoral students prepared a scholarly literature review in their doctoral research area that was researched online, prepared as a doc or pdf file, and submitted electronically for peer review and ongoing revision. Beyond reading and preparation for daily seminars, and active participation in scholarly debate within / beyond seminar using Wikis, Blogs and Blackboard, doctoral students engaged in one collaborative group learning task that was completed during the on-campus learning experience.

As an extension to the on-campus learning, doctoral students completed two individual learning tasks directly related to their personal doctoral research focus and interests. In order to model a scholarly community of inquiry, each student solicited and received online feedback and advice from the course instructor and also from doctoral student peers on each learning task. Overall assessment was based on the outcomes of one group task (completed and presented on-campus), ongoing participation in an online scholarly community, and two individual learning tasks.

Collaborative Educational Technology Trend Wiki and Presentation

The primary objective of the collaborative group task was to make sense of important ideas, issues and topics related to a current educational technology (ET) trend. Through public presentation & response, doctoral students engaged their peers in inquiry, debate and discussion in order to further their own and the group's learning. The ability to synthesize, compile and make sense of current (cutting edge) and emerging (bleeding edge) information in order to help others understand an ET Trend is a key feature in the educational technology life. This collaborative group learning task gave doctoral students practice in synthesizing and crystallizing information for clients / learners / colleagues, collaboratively designing and publishing information in an online environment for learning, and in designing a discussion and / or an activity to deepen the learning of concepts.

Shortly after they met each other in the on campus seminar, doctoral students joined one of the ET Trend groups. Doctoral students were encouraged to select an educational technology trend or two they are interested in, discuss this interest with other doctoral students in the seminar, and then form a group with others who share ONE of these interests.

The Educational Technology Trends to Watch were gleaned from the Horizon Reports compiled by the New Media Consortium (Johnson, Levine, Smith & Stone, 2010). Doctoral students were invited to consider: Mobile Broadband / M-Learning, Geo-Everything, The Personal Web & Social Computing, Data Mashups, Digital Game Based Learning, Grassroots Video and Augmented Reality & Enhanced Visualization. In small collaborative teams of three to four members, doctoral students explored, researched, analyzed and discussed one of the ET Trends, with a specific focus on issues for education, teaching and learning.

Doctoral students worked to generate in-depth knowledge and understanding of ET Trend and key issues facing educational technologists. Several questions were used to guide inquiry and to structure the ET Trend WIKI: What is this ET Trend? Who is doing it? How does it work? Why is this ET Trend significant for education?

What are the potential pitfalls? Where is it going? What research has been done on this trend? What research questions should we be asking? What are the implications for teaching and learning?

Each working team was challenged to design, develop and publish an ET Trend WIKI that would be publicly available by the second week of seminar. The ET Trend Wiki was expected to encapsulate and reflect the in-depth knowledge generated by the working team and connect diverse online resources that build and expand upon the trend. During a seminar during the second week, each of presenting groups introduced and summarized their work on the ET Trend Wiki by presenting the information they had gathered and designed into a WIKI. Using some sort of discussion or learning activity, each group was able to generate a scholarly discussion about the ET Trend key issues, questions and topics synthesized by the group.

In two years, doctoral students designed and populated several indepth, multimedia, hyperlinked ET Trend Wikis that are available online and offer enduring value: Augmented Reality, Grassroots Video, Mobile Broadband, Geo-Everything, and Mobile Learning. Wikis offered an interesting blended-temporal learning opportunity in that doctoral students who started in July 2009 chose to build and extend upon the Mobile Broadband wiki created by the doctoral students in July 2008 with their Mobile Learning wiki. Using email and face-to-face communication, the July 2009 doctoral students communicated with the previous year's doctoral students to update and expand the original wiki. As a demonstration of the diverse approaches to studying an educational technology trend, the July 2009 doctoral students created a whole new Grassroots Video wiki to complement and extend upon the Grassroots Video wiki created by the July 2008 students – in both years, the doctoral students chose to use mobile devices to capture and edit grassroots video, and YouTube as their publishing and delivery mechanism.

Participation in Online Scholarly Community

Throughout the on-campus part of the course, the doctoral students were invited to post brief reflections or contributions on issues and topics using a public, personal BLOG and / or within the secure Blackboard environment (online discussion board space). The blog posts, reflections, and peer reviews were meant to be a response to a question or activity or reading posted by the instructor or seminar group. Seminar discussions continued to be supported as needed on-line until the end of the six-week course.

BLOGs are web sites where individuals post content on an ongoing basis. Doctoral students were encouraged to participate regularly by posting to their personal blog and to Blackboard discussion groups. To cultivate a community of inquiry, and to add value to the collective learning experience, doctoral students were invited to read and respond frequently to peers' blogs and to Bb discussion group threads. Several types of individual scholarly reflection were encouraged. For example, in response to each guest professor's presentation, doctoral students were invited to post a reflection that summarized at least two new ideas, methods, perspectives and findings that they had learned about on their blog. As ongoing preparation for doctoral research talks, and to reflect on one's identity, purpose and goals as a doctoral student, and invitation was extended to post individual questions, ideas and plans for one's own doctoral research on the blog. In response to assigned readings, doctoral students were asked to publish an individual response that captured key ideas, documented impressions about an assigned reading, a critique of the author's study or arguments, a focus on key issues and ideas, selected quotations plus explanation, ideas one agreed/ disagreed with, questions one was left with, the value of the reading, and so on.

As part of our inquiry, our group discuss and debated the relative merits and concerns associated with different forms of online community discourse – for example, which media / method is best for which purpose? What are Face-to-Face learning experiences good for, and what are online learning experiences good for? What are the advantages and drawbacks of using public blogs versus secure, discussion forums for scholarly debates and discussions?

Peer review and critique is built into the two individual assignments. First, doctoral students were required to critically review one peer's pathfinder and provide constructive feedback in Blackboard (secure). Second, doctoral students were required to critically review one peer's literature review and provide constructive feedback in Blackboard (secure). The rationale for peer review was to simulate the "supervisory committee" approach to providing formative assessment, scholarly guidance and mentorship to doctoral candidates in preparation for candidacy. Our intellectual community of doctoral student peers and educational technology professors were able to provide in-depth and diverse feedback of benefit to doctoral students on the "coverage" of their research pathfinder (i.e., suggest sources that are missing, point to helpful people and resources, etc.) and literature review. Individual doctoral students benefited from serving as a peer reviewer as well as from having constructive and thoughtful feedback from a professor and peer in addition to feedback from the course instructor.

Online Doctoral Research Pathfinder

As a doctoral student becomes immersed in a graduate program, s/he builds a professional library of resources and an academic community of colleagues and researchers related to their research interests. Beyond books on a shelf, or articles in a folder, an effective method for keeping track of a growing list of contacts, experts and online sources is to build and populate a personal website related to one's own doctoral research. Borrowed from the world of library and information science, a Subject Pathfinder is an online gateway that organizes resources from across the Internet, and quickly guides a user to key information and people that will best provide information related to a specific topic(s).

The Doctoral Research Pathfinder was designed to become a personal web that brings together a diverse, high quality, comprehensive set of researchers and resources related to a doctoral student's proposed research topic. The Doctoral Research Pathfinder was meant to serve as an evolving, multimedia knowledge resource based on the individual's doctoral study and scholarship. I believe that an online pathfinder is a useful digital archival method by which one map's community and research connections in a specific area of scholarly interest. The goal for doctoral students was to create a research pathfinder to document and keep track of key researchers, scholarly sources and web-based artifacts specifically related to their dissertation research interest/topic.

Doctoral students who had completed their degree, and those who were currently in the program, had completed a pathfinder in past years. New doctoral students were provided with authentic examples of Doctoral Pathfinders that had been created by other educational technology doctoral students in the program to use as examples to think with via links on the instructor's webpage. The doctoral pathfinders are all publicly accessible websites, wordpress blogs and or wikis; only one student chose to contain the pathfinder in a password-protected space.

Doctoral students were expected to create a web-based digital artifact to document, organize and keep track of key researchers, scholarly sources and online artifacts specifically related to a defined area of doctoral study. After publishing their own doctoral pathfinder, each doctoral student sent the URL for their online research pathfinder to the course instructor, another doctoral student peer, and their supervisor (i.e., educational technology professor) for review and descriptive feedback. Students were expected to incorporate the feedback received from three other individuals in a revised version of the research pathfinder submitted to the course instructor by the end of the course.

Scholarly Literature Review

Drawing on the detailed advice offered by Creswell (2009), and many other authors who provide advice on creating a scholarly literature review and designing research, each doctoral student was required to develop a major academic paper related to a potential dissertation topic. This learning task required doctoral students to examine the historical threads of research topic as it relates to current issues and pressing questions (Januszewski & Molenda, 2008; Jonassen, 2004; Jonassen, 2001; Orey, McClendon & Branch, 2009; Spector, Merrill, Merrienboer, & Driscoll, 2007).

The scholarly challenge presented to doctoral students was to look back a few decades (or even back a century) to uncover the salient ideas, early research questions and shifts in thinking that have lead to the current research NEED or KNOWLEDGE GAP as defined by the doctoral student and as reflected in the field of educational technology.

Each doctoral student conducted a major literature review in a proposed area of study that lead to research questions / hypotheses / methodology / recommendations. Students were required to clearly define a research problem that is worth studying (likely the same one for which they created the Pathfinder). Students provided a sound and logical rationale for the need to conduct new research in this area by mapping out the historical and current terrain and educational discourse in the area and by identifying gaps / opportunities. Students were expected to draw upon assigned course texts as well as peer reviewed, scholarly articles, as part of their literature review.

Given the emphasis on blended learning, each doctoral student submitted their paper to the course instructor and to one other doctoral student peer for review and feedback (much like the pathfinder). Part of the rationale for this online approach to peer review is to simulate the "supervisory committee" approach to providing formative assessment feedback, scholarly guidance and peer mentorship to doctoral candidates. Another reason that doctoral students were expected to prepare and share the literature review electronically is that many, if not most, peer reviewed scholarly journals now manage the entire peer review process online. Doctoral students sent the literature review as an attached file using email, and received a marked-up version of the literature review from their reviewers. Students were expected to incorporate the feedback from the electronic peer review process in a final paper that the student submitted, as an attached file via email, by the end of the course for evaluation and feedback from the course instructor.

CONCLUSION

This doctoral seminar was specifically designed to develop a theoretical and practical foundation for growing the type of educational technology researchers and leaders that society needs, not just for the future, but to build the future.

Educational technologists can be recognized by the stars in their eyes. They know they are sitting on the most explosive potential of the century. Theirs is the apex of innovative motivation. Whether they are fashioning learning environments, creating media, designing instruction or effecting research and theory, educational technologists have a dream - a dream that can sustain them, and those they touch, well into the next century (Beckwith, 1988, p. 3)

Doctoral students in educational technology, and many other disciplines, need to be engaged in flexible and meaningful blended and online learning experiences because there are learning to be leaders and innovators in an increasingly digital world. Campbell (2009) asks, how might colleges and universities shape curricula to support and inspire the imaginations that students need?

In this doctoral seminar, students used online wikis, blogs, avatars and virtual worlds, learning managements systems, email and face-to-face learning experiences to collaboratively investigate and critique educational technology trends and research ideas. Doctoral students created an online doctoral pathfinder to archive and publish and organize their growing personal library of resources and connections with experts in the field. In many ways, doctoral students became, in the words of Campbell (2009), personal web and system administrators for their emerging digital lives as scholars. As part of their blended learning experience, doctoral students started to develop a personal cyberinfrastructure (Campbell, 2009), one they can continue to build, modify and extend throughout their educational technology careers.

As I examine the blogs and wikis that doctoral students have created and maintained online, I have evidence that many have continued to use these online social networking tools to expand and grow their professional and practical understanding of the field using the tools that were introduced at the beginning of their doctoral program. Several students have continued to actively blog about their learning experiences in other doctoral courses throughout the year, and blog about their leadership roles in diverse organizational contexts. A few of the ET Trend wikis have been added to and expanded upon in the last year. Therefore, I am confident that the introduction of educational technology practices and theoretical perspectives in the first doctoral course has had an enduring impact on how the doctoral students are experiencing and participating in their blended program.

As we welcome the new doctoral students into our blended educational technology program this year, there are important questions that need ongoing exploration and consideration. For example, as we experience increased national and international demand for our educational technology programs, how can we be strategic in determining how to grow and sustain the online doctoral program and continue to provide rich, blended learning experiences? What is the perfect blend of online and on campus doctoral learning experiences, and how will we evaluate these designs? How and why must we design, timetable and resource our graduate programs best to meet the diverse needs of working professionals?

Our doctoral program in educational technology is one of four online education doctorates offered in our faculty. As a faculty, we need to carry out a program evaluation, and collect detailed qualitative and quantitative information on faculty development, course design and delivery, student success and satisfaction, and the technological and human infrastructure that is necessary to sustain high quality blended doctoral programs. Beyond individual courses and specializations, there is a need to document and share the key lessons learned and disseminate the new knowledge that has been created and developed about the design, development and delivery of effective blended doctoral programs in education.

REFERENCES

Beckwith, D. (1988). The future of educational technology. *Canadian Journal of Educational Communication*, *17*(1), 3–20.

Biklen, S. K., & Casella, R. (2007). *A practical guide to the qualitative dissertation*. Teachers College Press, Columbia University.

Campbell, G. (2009). Personal cyberinfrastructure. *EDUCAUSE Review*, *44*(5), 58–59. Retrieved from http://www.educause.edu/EDUCAUSE+Review/EDUCAUSEReviewMagazineVolume44/APersonalCyberinfrastructure/178431.

Cone, J. D., & Foster, S. L. (2006). *Dissertations and theses from start to finish: Psychology and related fields*. Washington, DC: American Psychological Association.

Creswell, J. D. (2009). *Research design: Qualitative, quantitative, and mixed methods approaches*. Thousand Oaks, CA: Sage Publications.

Crichton, S., & Childs, E. (2008). Looking forward-stories of practice. In S. Hirtz (Ed). *Education for a digital world.* BC Campus and Commonwealth of Learning. Retrieved from http://www.col.org/resources/crsMaterials/Pages/edDigitalWorld.aspx

Garnham, C., & Kaleta, R. (2002). Introduction to hybrid courses. *Teaching with Technology Today, 8*(6). Retrieved from http://www.uwsa.edu/ttt/articles/garnham.htm

Garrison, D. R., & Vaughan, N. (2008). *Blended learning in higher education*. San Francisco, CA: Jossey-Bass.

Holosko, M. J. (2006). *Primer for critiquing social research: A student guide*. Thomson Brooks / Cole.

Jacobsen, M., & Kopp, G. (2008). Female tenure tracks in educational technology. In Beaudin, L. (Ed.), *Hard and soft technologies: Stories of women and technology*.

Januszewski, A., & Molenda, M. (Eds.). (2008). *Educational technology: A definition with commentary*. New York, NY: Lawrence Erlbaum Associates.

Johnson, L., Levine, A., Smith, R., & Stone, S. (2010). *The 2010 horizon report*. Austin, TX: The New Media Consortium. Retrieved January 29, 2010, from http://www.nmc.org/pdf/2010-Horizon-Report.pdf

Jonassen, D. H. (Ed.). (2001). *The handbook of research for educational communications and technology* (1st ed.). Mahwah, NJ: Lawrence Erlbaum Associates.

Jonassen, D. H. (Ed.). (2004). *The handbook of research for educational communications and technology* (2nd ed.). Mahwah, NJ: Lawrence Erlbaum Associates.

Locke, L. F., Spirduso, W. W., & Silverman, S. J. (2000). *Proposals that work: A guide for planning dissertations and grant proposals*. Thousand Oaks, CA: Sage Publications.

Marshall, S., Kinutia, W., & Taylor, W. (2009). *Bridging the knowledge divide: Educational technology for development*. Charlotte, NC: Information Age Publishing, Inc.

Orey, M., McClendon, V. J., & Branch, R. M. (2008). *Educational media and technology yearbook: Vol. 33*. Libraries Unlimited: Greenwood Publishing Group.

Orey, M., McClendon, V. J., & Branch, R. M. (2009). *Educational media and technology yearbook* (*Vol. 34*). Springer.

Robinson, R. S. (2009). Using the definition in foundation building. *TechTrends*, *53*(5), 34–40. doi:10.1007/s11528-009-0322-6

Shulman, L. S., Golde, C. M., Bueschel, A. C., & Garabedian, K. J. (2006). Reclaiming education's doctorates: A critique and a proposal. *Educational Researcher*, *35*(3), 25–32. doi:10.3102/0013189X035003025

Spector, J. M., Merrill, M. D., Merrienboer, J. V., & Driscoll, M. P. (2007). *The handbook of research for educational communications and technology* (3rd ed.). Routledge/Taylor & Francis Group.

Walker, G., Golde, C. M., Jones, L., Bueschel, A., & Hutchings, P. (2008). *The formation of scholars: Rethinking doctoral education for the twenty-first century*. Stanford, CA: Carnegie Foundation for the Advancement of Teaching.

Williams, C. (2002). Learning online: A review of recent literature in a rapidly expanding field. *Journal of Further and Higher Education, 26*(3), 263–272. doi:10.1080/03098770220149620

Willis, J. (2008). *Qualitative research methods in education and education technology*. Charlotte, NC: Information Age Publishing.

ADDITIONAL READING

AACTE Committee on Innovation and Technology. (2008). *Handbook of Technological Pedagogical Content Knowledge (TPCK) for Educators*. New York: Routledge, Taylor and Francis Group.

Association for Educational Communications and Technology. (2008). Definition. In Januszewski, A., & Molenda, M. (Eds.), *Educational Technology: A definition with commentary*. New York: Lawrence Erlbaum Associates.

Garrison, D. R., & Vaughan, N. (2008). *Blended learning in higher education*. San Francisco: Jossey-Bass.

Jonassen, D. H. (Ed.). (2001). *The Handbook of Research for Educational Communications and Technology* (1st ed.). Mahwah, NJ: Lawrence Erlbaum Associates.

Jonassen, D. H. (Ed.). (2004). *The Handbook of Research for Educational Communications and Technology* (2nd ed.). Mahwah, NJ: Lawrence Erlbaum Associates.

Kamenetz, A. (2010). *Edupunks, Edupreneurs, and the Coming Transformation of Higher Education*. Vermont: Chelsea Green Publishing.

Orellana, A., Hudgins, T. L., & Simonson, M. (Eds.), *The Perfect Online Course: Best Practices for Design and Teaching*. Charlotte, NC: Information Age Publishers.

Orey, M., McClendon, V. J., & Branch, R. M. (2008). *Educational Media and Technology Yearbook: Volume 33*. Libraries Unlimited: Greenwood Publishing Group.

Orey, M., McClendon, V. J., & Branch, R. M. (2009). *Educational Media and Technology Yearbook* (*Vol. 34*). Springer.

Spector, J. M., Merrill, M. D., Merrienboer, J. V., & Driscoll, M. P. (2007). *The Handbook of Research for Educational Communications and Technology* (3rd ed.). Routledge/Taylor & Francis Group.

Walker, G., Golde, C. M., Jones, L., Bueschel, A., & Hutchings, P. (2008). *The Formation of Scholars: Rethinking Doctoral Education for the Twenty-First Century*. Stanford, CA: Carnegie Foundation for the Advancement of Teaching.

KEY TERMS AND DEFINITIONS

Blended Learning: The combination of in-person and technology-supported learning experiences along a continuum from chiefly face-to-face, co-located learning opportunities in a classroom supplemented with online activities and tasks, to primarily online learning experiences supplemented with real time interaction using any or all of teleconferencing, video-conferencing and online conferencing.

Doctor of Philosophy Degree (PhD): An advanced degree program focused on the preparation of scholars who will pursue research and teaching careers in higher education contexts.

Education Doctorate (EDD): An advanced degree program focused on the preparation of education scholars, practitioners and leaders who pursue careers in a diverse range of educational contexts and settings.

Educational Technology: "The study and ethical practice of facilitating learning and improving performance by creating, using, and managing appropriate technological processes and resources" (Januszewski & Molenda, 2008).

Chapter 11
Blended Learning in Nigeria: Determining Students' Readiness and Faculty Role in Advancing Technology in a Globalized Educational Development

Nwachukwu Prince Ololube
University of Education, Port Harcourt, Nigeria

ABSTRACT

Blended learning requirements are increasing, in part because of the population explosion and policies pertaining to the democratization of education. Yet, thousands of students and faculty remain deficient in the use of blended learning to advance technology in developing countries, especially sub-Saharan Africa. This research employed a quantitative assessment design aimed at improving best available practices, processes, and performance in terms of the blended learning offered in a university setting. A six-point Likert-type questionnaire was used to gather data. Multiple statistical procedures were employed in the subsequent analysis—percentage, mean point values, chi-square, and ANOVA. Majority of the respondents to the questionnaire agreed that the teaching of MIS to students is effective and has a positive impact on their academic achievements. This groundbreaking research presents a realistic resource for the practical application of blended learning in university education in Nigeria, as well as a comprehensive view of the benefits and problems of the applicability of blended learning.

INTRODUCTION

The global academic landscape is changing direction, from traditional face-to-face teaching and learning methods to more sophisticated and technologically-assisted methods. The introduction of Information Communication Technology (ICT) into educational settings and curriculum has significantly altered the tools and content of learning. Such blended learning has resulted in more proactive and higher quality methods of educating students.

DOI: 10.4018/978-1-60960-479-0.ch011

Blended learning is essential in allowing access to contemporary global mainstream education. As such, ICT remains an important asset in Nigeria's national and regional development (Ololube, 2011). Nigeria must thus integrate ICT into its education sectors, especially tertiary education, as this level of education is at the forefront of national and regional development, charged with the production of equipped and adept human capital. Presently Nigerian higher education institutions are not prepared for these new challenges and have been slow to respond to calls for the expansion of ICT services (Ifinido, 2005; Igwe, 2005; Iloanusi & Osuagwu, 2009).

Globally there is an increasing demand for more and better ICT competencies among students and faculty because of advances in technology and global educational development (UNESCO, 2008). The effectiveness of any educational system depends on the ICT expertise of its students and educators. In turn, the success of teachers or educators depends on how well they are prepared for their roles within a changing and challenging system.

Teachers direct and evaluate the educational progress of their students (Ololube & Egbezor, 2009) and this progress ultimately depends on the instructional strategies employed. Faculty must have specialized training and knowledge in the application of several different instructional delivery methods (which many academics call blended learning) and their methodological application to be able to cope with day-to-day pedagogical encounters with students. In this context, the notion of competence goes beyond skills to include attitudes and stamina needed to carry action (even) through difficult circumstances (Husu, 2006; Ololube, 2009).

Blended learning is the combination of online and face-to-face learning with the objective of providing the most resourceful and effective instructional experience. The blended learning concept is most often used to explain approaches that combine several different learning delivery methods. It is also used to describe learning that mixes various event-based activities, including face-to-face classrooms, e-learning, and self-paced instruction (Graham, 2005). Barriers to ICT use in Nigerian universities have been identified as including inadequate funding, limited computer/internet access, poor infrastructure, power supply shortages and in most cases complete black outs, a lack of trained faculty/personnel, and poverty, among others (Ifinedo & Ololube, 2007). Consequently, campaigning for a total shift to the technology-assisted classroom is arguably unrealistic in most Nigerian public universities (Aladejana, 2008).

RESEARCH OBJECTIVES

This text records the findings of a research study that reviewed and codified what was already known about blended learning and student academic achievement. While we recognize the insensitive academic environment in Nigeria that researchers (Ifinedo & Ololube, 2007) have posited as being responsible for slow growth rates in Nigerian education system, however, blended learning is gradually taking shape in university education in Nigeria especially in the private universities.

Internet searches confirm that very little has been written about this domain of study in Nigeria. The enthusiasm to write this chapter arises from the desire to examine students readiness and faculty role in the use of blended learning methodologies (technology-based materials and face-to-face sessions) to present educational content. It also arises from a desire to assess students' readiness and faculty role in employing blended learning as a way of attaining teaching and learning effectiveness and, finally, a desire to determine success so far in terms of student academic achievements.

To address the above objectives, twenty one research hypotheses were formulated. The hypothesis statements are presented as follows:

there is evidence that perceived use of blended learning is strongly correlated with ease in student academic achievement in MIS. The same seems to be true for faculty use of blended learning methodologies (technology-based materials and face-to-face sessions) to present content in the teaching and learning processes. Indeed, results in Ifinedo (2006, 2007) show that students who have no difficulty finding and understanding useful information, view computers as easy to use, and may have higher regard for the system's usefulness. Thus it can then be hypothesized that:

H1: Booting a computer is positively related to the perceived impact of MIS.
H2: Operating a computer is positively related to the perceived impact of MIS.
H3: Typing skills are positively related to the perceived impact of MIS.
H4: Retrieving information from the Internet is positively related to the perceived impact of MIS.
H5: Word Processing: creating and saving a document are positively related to the perceived impact of MIS.
H6: Sending and receiving e-mail messages are positively related to the perceived impact of MIS.
H7: The ability to use search engines to source materials is positively related to the perceived impact of MIS.
H8: Operating electronic devices such as overhead projectors and video is positively related to the perceived impact of MIS.
H9: Interacting with others via the Internet is positively related to the perceived impact of MIS.
H10: Knowing how to use a database is positively related to the perceived impact of MIS.
H11: Using a computer to draw a picture or diagram is positively related to the perceived impact of MIS.
H12: Presenting information using Power Point is positively related to the perceived impact of MIS.
H13: Using computer programs is positively related to the perceived impact of MIS.
H14: Using statistical packages for data analysis is positively related to the perceived impact of MIS.
H15: Knowing when information is useful or useless is positively related to the perceived impact of MIS.
H16: Having an e-mail account or address is positively related to the perceived impact of MIS.
H17: Downloading material from the Internet is positively related to the perceived impact of MIS.
H18: Competence and attitudes towards the computer are positively related to the perceived impact of MIS.
H19: The ability to effectively use an online library is positively related to the perceived impact of MIS.
H20: A positive overall assessment of oneself in the use of computer is positively related to the perceived impact of MIS.
H21: No significant relationships exists in respondents opinion based on there demographic information.

CONTEXTUALIZATION

NOVENA University is dedicated to excellence in teaching. Excellence means the state or quality of excelling. In an educational context it can mean effectively providing learning experiences that prepare students for the challenges of the multifaceted, ever varying, and diverse workplace in society. NOVENA University is one of several private universities in Nigeria. It is composed of seven colleges including Natural and Applied Sciences, Health Sciences, Management and Social Sciences, and Environmental Sciences.

The colleges of Information and Communication, Agriculture, and Science Education are still in development. The Department of Business Administration is a foundational department within the university. The guiding philosophy of the department is to produce scholars with sharp intellectual minds capable of further critical intellectual inquiry.

Management Information System (MIS) or BUS 224 is a core course for those in the Department of Business Administration and Accounting both as part of a four-year program and as a part of a major in the college of Management and Social Sciences. The teaching of MIS is ideally executed in an applied fashion and aims to produce graduates who are scientifically and technically skilled and who possess business report writing skills. Development areas such as information, data collection and analyses, and communication are all set in a problem-solving context where students learn about the planning and management processes involved in decision making. The course also involves teaching the information needs of management, the design of management information systems, the principles of systems design, decision support systems, database system architecture, database management systems, stand alone systems, bureau and consultancy, evaluation systems and budgeting control.

The successful completion of an introductory MIS course is a critical step for undergraduate students who may one day be at the helm of decision making in their place of work. This course is equally important for students who are planning to further their studies in the future as graduates will need to make informed MIS decisions as part of their professional development. Consequently, MIS courses are an essential requirement of many undergraduate programs in management, and the social and natural sciences.

MIS courses are challenging classes to teach because the technical complexity of the course material is quite high while student interest in this material can, unfortunately, be quite low. Throughout the instructional processes, take home assignments are given to students with basic instructions and sources for materials on the Internet. Assignments are submitted to faculty via e-mail and feedback is provided to students two days after the deadline for submission. Students are advised to print the feedback for presentation and discussion in class.

THE CONCEPT OF BLENDED LEARNING

The blending of different learning experiences has occurred naturally inside and outside of the classroom for hundred of years. In the context of this paper (and contemporary university learning) blended learning is often defined as the combination of face-to-face and online learning (Mortera-Gutiérrez, 2006). The blended learning model emphasizes active learning and a reduction of classroom time and is based on the concept of hybridization: the bringing together of two dissimilar parts to produce a third result. In the case of an effective blended learning course, these two dissimilar parts are the online and face-to-face classroom components. When successfully integrated, the result is an educational environment that is highly conducive to faculty teaching and student learning (Vaughan, 2007). Newhouse (2002a) made clear that a good balance between discovery learning and personal exploration on one hand, and systematic instruction and guidance on the other characterizes a powerful ICT learning environment.

According to Iloanusi and Osuagwu (2009), blended learning is a flexible form of learning that constitutes a proper amalgamation of the components of technological enabled learning and face-to-face teaching and interaction. At its best it incorporates models that enhance the delivery of e-learning for the students and faculty involved in the teaching and learning processes. Well blended e-learning easily adapts to the needs of students eliminates forced student adaptation to tools and methods that are more inconvenient than convenient.

In higher education, this type of blended learning is often referred to as a hybrid model. Hybrids are courses in which a significant portion of the learning activities have been moved online, and time traditionally spent in the classroom is reduced, but not eliminated. The goal of these hybrid courses is to join the best features of in-class teaching with the best features of online learning to promote active and self-directed learning opportunities for students with the added advantage of flexibility. Students have long indicated that this blended learning model provides them with the ability to better allot their own time and improved learning outcomes; however, they initially may encounter issues around time management, taking greater responsibility for their own learning, and using sophisticated technologies. Faculty have suggested that blended courses create enhanced opportunities for teacher-student interaction, increased student engagement in learning, added flexibility in the teaching and learning environment, and opportunities for continuous improvement (Vaughan, 2007). In terms of the concrete success of this delivery model, improved performance has been detected in those who learned through blended strategies when compared to those learning through a single method. According to Bonk, Kim and Zeng (2005), the majority of teachers with experience using web technologies in their teaching have indicated that blended learning has significantly improved student academic achievement. Despite these very positive outcomes, the use of blended learning is still new or self-effacing for most students and faculty in Nigerian.

Early results of the application of blended learning in higher education reinforces the need to: integrate blended learning principles in Nigerian schools so as to create an enabling environment where teaching and learning can be advanced, explain the professional competency issues essential to the implementation of blended learning designs, and present illustrative scenarios of blended learning designs, which would contain practical guidelines for further blended learning design and describe the tools and techniques for actively engaging students in the process (Garrison & Vaughan, 2007).

STUDENT READINESS TO LEARN MIS

Unfortunately, as children grow their passion for learning often fades as learning becomes associated with hard work instead of reward and delight. Consequently, teachers find that a large number of students are physically present in the classroom but mentally absent and many more fail to invest themselves in the experience of learning at all (Ololube, 2009). The main purpose of education is to improve the reasoning process as it is applied to solving problems. As such, students need to know why they are learning something. Students also need to be encouraged towards self-directed learning as they can flourish when they take control of how they learn. Students often also prefer a problem solving approach to learning. They learn best when the knowledge is presented in a real-life setting. For students to be motivated to learn, the new knowledge must help them solve problems they perceive as important (Miller, 2005).

Faculty must encourage students to fully participate in the teaching and learning processes. Faculty who create warm and accepting, yet professional, atmospheres will promote persistent effort and favourable attitudes towards learning. Students must find satisfaction in learning based on the understanding that the goals are useful to them or, less commonly, based on the pure enjoyment of exploring new things (Austin, Dwyer & Freebody, 2003).

Most often, a student's readiness to learn comes with time, and the role of the teacher is to support its development. Another major key to motivation is the active involvement of students in their own learning. Assigning homework that involves helping faculty determine learning objectives and activities is a step in the right direction of bringing out students' inner selves who are ready to learn. None of these methods, however, will create continual inspiration unless the goals are realistic for the learner. Thus effective faculty are those who enlist students in goal setting. To have learners assist in defining goals increases the probability that they will understand them and want to reach them. Nevertheless, students sometimes have unrealistic notions about what they can accomplish. Possibly they do not understand the precision with which a skill must be carried out or have the deepness of understanding needed to master certain instructional materials. To identify realistic goals in any case is an essential part of the profession and so faculty must be skilled in assessing student's readiness or improvement in the direction of the stated objectives (Ololube, 2009; Ololube & Egbezor, 2009).

COMPETENCIES IN TEACHING MIS

Teaching MIS is a daunting task among professionals and non-professionals alike. However, new MIS teaching methods, often taught in an Internet environment for non-computer professionals, are capable of overcoming the insufficiencies and non-systemic tendencies of the existing methods and can consequently enhancing learning. Zhongjun and Lijuan (2009) argue that adopting improved methods will strengthen teaching effects on a large scale, especially teacher-student communication.

Competencies in teaching MIS involve inspiring students to compete against themselves, to take on tasks that seem to exceed their grasp, and to discover and develop their real mettle as thinkers. In order to affect these ends, faculty need to be curious, imaginative, empathetic, interesting, friendly, and hardworking, thereby creating an environment that enhances and strengthens the learning disposition of students. Mohanan (2005) and Ololube (2011) clarify a catalogue of the principles of learning aimed at guiding faculty to improve their methodological competencies in teaching MIS. According to them:

- Students learn best by being actively involved. If students are made to participate in learning activities, rather than read about such activities, they will learn better.
- A situation which offers fresh and stimulating experiences is a kind of reward that enhances learning.
- Learning is transferred to the extent that the learner sees possibilities for transfer and has opportunities to apply the knowledge.
- Meaningful material is easiest learned and best retained.
- Learning is enhanced by a wide variety of experiences which are organized around purposes accepted by the students, hence teachers are advised to teach in-depth.
- Learning is increased when it occurs in a rich and varied environment. The richer the classroom (in terms of instructional materials) and laboratory and school surroundings in offering opportunities for learning, the greater the level of students' achievement.
- Details must be placed in a structured pattern or they are forgotten.

Competence in teaching means getting most students to use the higher cognitive level processes that the more academic students use spontaneously. Teaching works by getting students to engage in learning-related activity that helps them attain the particular objectives set for the unit or course, such as theorizing, generating new ideas, reflecting, applying and problem-solving (Ololube, 2009).

BLENDED LEARNING PROBLEMS IN NIGERIA

Almost all Sub-Saharan African countries' basic ICT infrastructures are inadequate. This as a result of a lack of electricity to power the ICT materials, poor telecommunication facilities, and insufficient funds in general as Nigeria, for example, spends less than 12% of its annual budget on education. In Nigeria, more than 85% of the population lives below the poverty line and as a result even an average middle-income earner cannot afford basic technological and communication gadgets. The cost of computer related gadgets in Nigeria is three times the monthly wage of an average worker. Thus, computer related telecommunication facilities remain less than useful for most Nigerians, as computers are still a luxury in universities, offices and homes, and many people have not had the chance to develop the skills to use them. This has made the integration of necessary on-line resources (e-mail and the world-wide-web) into education in Nigeria most difficult (Ololube & Egbezor, 2009).

The goal of educational technology is to provide as complete an education as possible. ICT knowledge and skills are essential for today's student because they allow students to stay current with the computer and telecommunications technologies used beyond the confines of the school. In places like Nigeria this is often impossible as there are limited efforts supporting the integration of ICTs in education. The term digital divide is used to refer to differing standards or imbalances between those countries who fully poised to reap the benefits of the information age and those that are unable to do so (Ifinedo, 2005). African countries tend not to have the same infrastructural facilities and support as the developed West. Several cities and rural areas in Nigeria have yet to access electricity or still experience fluctuations in its supply. Additionally, most Nigerians (82%) do not have regular access to ICT facilities including computers, e-mail, and Internet connectivity. The digital divide influences and includes ICT products and outputs (Internet access, e-mail, cell-phones, etc) as well as inputs (engineers, scientists, etc). This is a divide that increasingly makes other development gaps impossible to bridge (Haddad & Jurich, [n.d]).

RESEARCH METHODOLOGY

Research Design

This research employed a quantitative assessment design aimed at improving the best available practices, processes and performances of blended learning in a university setting, These practices and processes are increasingly central to the creation and development of excellence and the discovery of new ideas.

This chapter assessed students' readiness and faculty role in employing blended learning as a method of effective teaching. It also sought to determine the blended learning successes recorded to date and its effects on student academic achievements/performances. It is hoped that this research offers insights that may be useful for education planners and administrators and policy development.

This study used a combination of observation and text-based materials, with the latter being valuable sources of records about educational research. For the observational component, I participated as an adjunct lecturer in teaching Management Information Systems (MIS) to year two and three Business Administration and Accounting students in the College of Management and Social Science of NOVENA University. The type of observation used in this study did not imply a research strategy of immersion. Nonetheless, observations were made of the competencies of students using computer applications and software to tackle MIS problems and the quality and skills of the students in completing their assignments and participating in the classroom. Prior to the commencement of

MIS lecture, it was observed that majority of the students do no have email accounts intended to facilitate the submission of assignments and communication between faculty and students.

The sampling for this study was purposive, which is characterized by the use of judgment and deliberate effort to obtain representative samples that include the groups most likely to be found in society. This technique is usually used to overcome problems associated with geographically dispersed populations where it is time and resource-intensive to construct a sampling frame for a large geographical area, such as the higher education institutions in Delta State of Nigeria. Purposive sampling was chosen over a random cross-section of the population, because it offered specific characteristics, behaviors and experiences that would facilitate broad comparisons between groups that the researcher identified as important.

Data Sources and Method of Collection

Materials

The materials for this study included theoretical sources (textbooks, articles and reports). These categories of documents provided insight into what has been written on the topic of study. These sources were used extensively in the course of the analysis. To be able to make full use of the theoretical sources that were located, there was a need to assess their validity and importance. Four overlapping validity criteria were used in this study: authenticity, credibility, representativeness and meaning. These served as a framework for a systemic selection of documents in a fashion that mimicked a randomized sampling procedure and helped inject more robust ideas, colour and rigor into this work. The acceptance or otherwise of the retrieved information was dependent on the selection of information following a review and interpretation of it. It is hoped that the representation gleamed here is a relatively balanced and logically precise one. Though no researcher is independent of his or her own normative evaluation of a research problem, if any part of this analysis should bear the hallmark of the researchers' stance, it should be overlooked and considered as part of the researchers own over-sight (Ololube, Ubogu & Egbezor, 2007).

Questionnaire

For the purpose of gathering data, the researcher designed a two-page questionnaire. It was important that the questionnaire be as simple as possible as different categories of students were chosen as respondents. The questionnaire was designed to gather information on both the overall performance of the blended learning system as well as its specific components. Since the questionnaire also includes demographic questions, it was used to correlate performance and satisfaction with the blended learning system among students. The questionnaire was guided by the characteristics of a good questionnaire as developed by Dillman, Smyth and Christain (2008) and Fowler (2008). Assistance from professional colleagues made the development of such a questionnaire for this study possible. Feedback from colleagues helped assure that the measures reflected the content of the concept in the questions and so the face validity was determined to be intact.

This study focused on competencies, effectiveness and academic achievement in MIS, all of which are a part of the determinants of the professional development and competencies of students. As a result, statistically appraising the reliability of responses in the research questionnaire was regarded as appropriate because respondents may have answered the questions randomly given that they were directly affected by the study. A quantitative analysis was performed to statistically test the reliability of the research instrument. In research statistics, when the reliability of a research instrument has been established, it provides a basis for continuity. The instrument was tested with the Cronbach alpha coefficient and a reliability coefficient of .934 was obtained. Thus, the research instrument was accepted as very reliable in that it allowed for the consistency or repeatability of what we set out to measure (Render, Stair & Hannan, 2005).

The participants (N-59) for this study responded to a questionnaire that employed a six-point Likert-type scale (summated) (6 = excellence: nothing to improve; 5 = good: only a little to improve; 4 = fairly good: some to improve; 3 = decent: fairly much to improve; 2 = weak: much to improve; and 1 = poor: very much to improve). The questionnaire included two major sections: "A" and "B". Section A focused on participants' demographic information: gender, age, marital status, level/year of study, and department of study (see Table 1). In section "B" respondents were asked to determine the value of the impact and their perceptions of the research variables (see Table 2). The rating scale was considered to be of approximately equal "attitude value" to which participants responded to ascertain the impact of using blended learning as an instructional method in the teaching of MIS and how it has affected their mode of study (intensity) (Fink, 2008).

Data Analysis Techniques

To satisfy this investigation, a number of statistical analyses were conducted using SPSS Version 17.0: mean point value, standard deviation, ANOVA and the Chi-square (X^2) of significance. One-way-analysis of variance (ANOVA) was employed to test the relationship between variables and respondents' demographic information. The Chi-square (X^2) was used to find statistically significant differences among the variables. Statistical significance was set at $p < 0.05$ to assess if the researcher's level of confidence observed in the sample also existed in the general population (Okeke & Kpolovie, 2006; Render, Stair & Hannan, 2005).

RESULTS AND DISCUSSION

The statistical analysis for this study reveals the extent to which students perceive instructional process competencies in the teaching of MIS. All respondents agreed that the faculty teaching of MIS is effective and has a positive impact on their academic achievement. An overwhelming number of respondents (students) felt that MIS is highly beneficial for students, especially students pursuing a professional degree in accounting and business administration.

Chi-square (X^2) analysis was used to determine whether relationships existed between students' readiness and use of computer in MIS classes. Respondents showed a significant relationship between the students' readiness, use, and competencies variables and effectiveness in learning of MIS. Fifteen of the twenty students competency variables depicted positive relationships at *($p < .001$ - $p < .005$)*. The overall computer use self-assessments of students showed a positive impact at *($p < .001$)*. Thus, students were satisfied with faculty pedagogical competencies in getting them actively involved and were convinced of both the benefit of studying MIS and their effectiveness in learning MIS. (See Table 3).

Table 1. Demographic profiles of participants

Demographic variables	Groups	Freq.	%
Gender	Male	24	40.7
	Female	35	59.3
Age	Below 25 years	53	89.8
	26-35 years	6	10.2
Marital status	Single	59	100
	Married	0	0
Level/year of study	200 level	54	91.5
	300 level	5	8.5
Department of study	Accounting	35	59.3
	Business administration	24	40.7

Table 2. Research variables

1. Boot a computer	1	2	3	4	5	6
2. Operate a computer	1	2	3	4	5	6
3. Typing skills	1	2	3	4	5	6
4. Retrieving information from the Internet	1	2	3	4	5	6
5. Word processing: create a document and save it	1	2	3	4	5	6
6. Send and receive e-mail messages	1	2	3	4	5	6
7. Able to use search engines to source for materials	1	2	3	4	5	6
8. Operate electronic devices like: overhead projector, video	1	2	3	4	5	6
9. Interact with others via the Internet	1	2	3	4	5	6
10. Know how to use a database	1	2	3	4	5	6
11. Use computer to draw a picture or diagram	1	2	3	4	5	6
12. Present information using power point	1	2	3	4	5	6
13. Use computer programs	1	2	3	4	5	6
14. Use Statistical Packages for data analysis	1	2	3	4	5	6
15. Know when information is useful or useless	1	2	3	4	5	6
16. Have e-mail account/address	1	2	3	4	5	6
17. Download materials from the Internet	1	2	3	4	5	6
18. Competence and attitude towards computer	1	2	3	4	5	6
19. Use online library	1	2	3	4	5	6
20. Overall assessment of yourself in the use of computer	1	2	3	4	5	6

This study has revealed the need for faculty to be effective in the classroom. Faculty need to be curious, imaginative, empathetic, interesting, friendly and hardworking, thereby creating an environment that enhances and strengthens the learning disposition of the students (c.f., Mohanan, 2005; Ololube, 2011). Faculty competencies in teaching MIS show that students are inspired to learn when they are actively involved, see the possibility and have the opportunity to apply the knowledge they are acquiring, are pushed to comprehend concepts that seem at first to exceed their grasp and are provided with fresh and stimulating experiences. Students discover and develop their real mettle as thinkers when they have a wide variety of experiences organized around purposes accepted by them as a result of in-depth teaching.

To test hypothesis 21, ANOVA analysis was employed, and the results (see Table 4) show that significant relationships were found between the competency variables and the perception of respondents based on their gender, age, marital status, level/year of study and department of study at $F = .053$, $p > .166$, $F = 2.182$, $p > .324$, $F = .590$, respectively.

The overall ANOVA analysis of all respondents, irrespective of gender, age, marital status, level/year of study and department showed unwavering support for the teaching of MIS for professional development. In the analysis of variance, the observed variability in the sample was divided into two parts: variability of observations within group mean and variability of observations between group means. These two estimates differ in a very important way: the between-groups variance will be correct only if the hypothesis is true. If the hypothesis is false, the between-groups estimates of variance will be too large. The within-group estimates of variability do not depend

Table 3. Chi-square analysis of the impact of MIS on students' academic achievements

Competency Variables	Df	Chi-square	Sig. 2-tailed	Results
1. Boot a computer	1	31.339	P =.000 < α=.001	Impact
2. Operate a computer	4	21.085	P =.000 < α=.001	Impact
3. Typing skills	5	16.966	P =.005 < α=.001	Impact
4. Retrieving information from the Internet	5	38.525	P =.000 < α=.001	Impact
5. Word processing: create a document and save it	5	11.864	P =.024 < α=.005	Impact
6. Send and receive e-mail messages	5	19.407	P =.002 < α=.005	Impact
7. Able to use search engines to source for materials	5	12.051	P =.014 < α=.005	impact
8. Operate electronic devices like: overhead projector, video	5	5.576	P =.350 > α=.005	No impact
9. Interact with others via the Internet	5	10.864	P =.054 > α=.005	No impact
10. Know how to use a database	4	9.220	P =.056 > α=.005	No impact
11. Use computer to draw a picture or diagram	5	25.102	P =.000 < α=.001	Impact
12. Present information using power point	5	25.508	P =.000 < α=.001	Impact
13. Use computer programs	5	8.831	P =.116 > α=.005	No impact
14. Use Statistical Packages for data analysis	5	50.322	P =.000 < α=.001	Impact
15. Know when information is useful or useless	5	5.576	P =.350 > α=.005	No impact
16. Have e-mail account/address	4	55.497	P =.000 < α=.001	Impact
17. Download materials from the Internet	5	24.153	P =.000 < α=.001	Impact
18. Competence and attitude towards computer	5	14.932	P =.011 < α=.005	Impact
19. Use online library	5	12.492	P =.029 < α=.005	Impact
20. Overall assessment of yourself in the use of computer	5	31.407	P =.000 < α=.001	Impact

N=59

Table 4. ANOVA analysis of respondents' perceived opinion

Demographic variables	Groups	Freq.	%	Mean	SD	F	Sig.
Gender	Male	24	40.7	5.8579	.34	.053	P =.818 > α=.005
	Female	35	59.3	5.8333	.40		
Age	Below 25 years	53	89.8	4.0189	1.06	.166	P =.685 > α=.005
	26-35 years	6	10.2	3.8333	.98		
Marital status	Single	59	100	3.1509	1.729	2.182	P =.145 > α=.005
	Married	0	0	2.3333	1.36		
Level/year of study	200 level	54	91.5	4.0755	1.07	.324	P =.571 > α=.005
	300 level	5	8.5	4.3333	.81		
Department of study	Accounting	35	59.3	4.0943	1.81	.590	P =.446 > α=.005
	Business Administraion	24	40.7	3.5000	1.64		

N = 59
Df. = n-1

on the hypothesis being true. The observed sample means compared the between-group and within-group estimates of variability since the between-group estimates were not sufficiently larger than the within-groups estimates. Given that the hypothesis is true, one expects the ratio of the between-group mean square to within-group mean square to be close to 1 as both are estimates of the population variance.

CONCLUSION AND RECOMMENDATIONS

Despite the findings in this study, the existing curriculum designed for teaching and learning in Nigerian universities does not include the practical usage of ICT materials such as computers, software, slides, overhead projectors, and video equipment. When it is included, it is based mainly merely on theoretical paradigms, however, majority of students especially those in private universities tend to be more conversant with ICT usage than those in the public universities.

Students rarely come into contact with ICT instructional materials, including those in the department of educational technology. Universities responsible for the provision of quality education programs provide programs within the confines of the mandate given to them by federal and state governments through various bodies that coordinate their activities including the National Commission for Colleges of Education (NCCE), the National Universities Commission (NUC), and the National Board for Vocational Colleges and Technical Education (NABTECH). The ability of these bodies to be effective in prescribing increased interaction with ICT instructional materials is largely dependent on the availability of funds to purchase the needed ICT instructional equipments.

Quality education is regarded as the main instrument for the social, political and economic development of a nation. Education has continued to be a great asset to many as well as a steady source of human capital for national economies, especially in the west where education is seen and accepted as a necessary instrument for success. Thus, the strength, security and well being of Nigeria rest squarely on the quality of education provided to its citizens. It is essential that we recognize that successfully getting students and faculty ready are indispensable to successful learning about ICTs and learning, and teaching through ICTs to improve the standard of education in Nigeria.

Providing access to quality education for every university student is a significant task that must be accomplished so that they can achieve their full potential. Consequently, African universities must follow the prevailing global trend by applying new technologies to enhance their educational materials and resources. While universities are indeed struggling to meet the demands of increasing student growth, in that they lack the ability to expand educational resources to accommodate new students, they need educational environments that make them more responsive to learning and workforce challenges. Electronic learning offers one way to foster more responsive educational environments. Such learning provides students with the opportunity to access available experts, best resources and up- to-date information. It is thus not surprising that e-learning is fast becoming an accepted and indispensable part of the mainstream of educational systems especially in the developed world (Akhahowa & Osubor, 2006).

Blended learning is beginning to play a more significant role in the lives and futures of students and faculty in Nigeria. Emerging technologies have enabled teaching and learning in university education to evolve from an emphasis on teacher-centred and lecture-centred instruction to student-centred interactive learning environments (Newhouse, 2002a & 2002b).

Designing and implementing successful ICT-enabled educational programs are the key to fundamental, wide-ranging educational reforms. Universities in Nigeria will have to assume a leadership role in the transformation of education or be left behind in the swirl of rapid technological changes. For Nigerian university education to take a leadership role and reap the full benefits of ICTs in learning, it is essential that students and faculty are able to effectively use these tools for learning. Leadership in university education must be visionary in terms of conceiving a desired future state, which includes picturing where and what the university education should be in the future, without being constrained by such factors as funding and resources, and then working backward to develop action plan to get to the desired point.

A successful and effective strategic plan also depends on the extent to which proper implementation and monitoring are carried out. This relies heavily on governments, which must ensure that all universities receive ICT infrastructure to aid teaching and learning. There is an urgent need to increase the number of computers available to the students and faculty and access to the Internet needs to be improved for blended learning education to spread in Nigerian universities. National policies on distance education and e-learning initiatives (in the Nigerian national IT policy) need to be reinvigorated and the commitment of governments in this area should be unequivocal. Universal access should be encouraged so that certain parts of the society are not sidelined. Likewise, those with limited skills and knowledge at present may require additional training to enable them to reap the benefits of using ICT for and in education (Ololube & Egbezor, 2009b).

Implications for Research and Practice

This groundbreaking research functions as a realistic resource for the practical application of blended learning in university education. It offers a comprehensive view of the benefits and problems of the applicability of blended learning. Finally, this research demonstrates the ways in which the blended learning approach integrates the benefits of both traditional face-to-face teaching and online learning. Such a blended learning approach has proven to both enhance and expand the effectiveness and efficiency of teaching and learning in a university setting.

This study suggests several possible implications for future research and practice. These implications pertain most directly to higher education institutions, faculty, students and researchers. At a management level, this case study calls for policies to ensure balanced investments in, and increase funding for, higher education that will allow for the effective use, integration and diffusion of ICTs. Following this investigation, which was based on a small sample, the researcher recommends larger studies based on a more broadly administered survey. Limitations, such as the small sample size, need to be considered when evaluating the findings of this study as they raise the possibility that some differences in opinion may be more a function of research design and contextual factors than any real differences in higher education studies. As with other studies, the findings should not be regarded as definitive but as offering students, faculty, educators, researchers, planners and administrators a view of the author's' reality.

REFERENCES

Akhahowa, A. E., & Osubor, V. I. (2006). E-learning: A technology-based teaching method for providing access to sustainable quality education. *The African Symposium, 6*(3&4), 17-25.

Aladejana, F. (2007). Blended learning and improved biology teaching in the Nigerian secondary schools. *Proceedings of the World Congress on Engineering and Computer Science 2008 WCECS 2008*, October 22 - 24, 2008, San Francisco, USA.

Austin, H., Dwyer, B., & Freebody, P. (2003). *Schooling the child: The making of students in classrooms*. London, UK / New York, NY: Routledge Falmer.

Bonk, C. J., Kim, K., & Zeng, T. (2005). Future directions of blended learning in higher education and workplace learning settings. In Bonk, C. J., & Graham, C. R. (Eds.), *Handbook of blended learning: Global Perspectives, local designs*. San Francisco, CA: Pfeiffer Publishing.

Dillman, D. A., Smyth, J. D., & Christain, L. M. (2008). *Internet, mail, and mixed-mode surveys: The tailored design method* (3rd ed.). New York, NY: Wiley.

Fink, A. G. (2008). *How to conduct surveys: A step-by-step guide* (4th ed.). London, UK: Sage Publications.

Fowler, F. J. (2008). *Survey research methods: Applied social research methods*. London, UK: Sage Publications.

Garrison, D. R., & Vaughan, N. D. (2007). *Blended learning in higher education: Framework, principles, and guidelines*. Hoboken, NJ: John Wiley & Sons.

Graham, C. R. (2005). Blended learning systems: Definition, current trends, and future directions. In C. J. Bonk & C. R. Graham (Eds). *Handbook of blended learning: Global perspectives, local designs*. (pp. 3-21). San Francisco, CA: Pfeiffer. Haddad, W. D., & Jurich, S. (n.d). *ICT for education: Potential and potency*. Retrieved March 3 2010, from http://cbdd.wsu.edu/edev/Nigeria_ToT/tr510/documents/ICTforeducation_potential.pdf

Husu, J. (2006). *Analyzing teachers' rule-based competencies in practice*. Paper presented at the European conference on educational research (ECER). Geneva, Switzerland. September 13-16, 2006.

Ifinedo, P. (2005). Measuring Africa's e-readiness in the global networked economy: A nine-country data analysis. *International Journal of Education and Development using Information and Communication Technology, 1*(1), 53-71.

Ifinedo, P. (2006). Accpetance and continuance intention of Web-based learning technology (WLT) use among university students in a Baltic country. *Electrinic Journal of Information Systems in Developing Countries, 23*(6), 1–20.

Ifinedo, P. (2007). Investigating the antecedents of continuance intention of course management system use among Estonian undergraduates. *International Journal of Communication Technology Education, 3*(4), 76–92. doi:10.4018/jicte.2007100107

Ifinedo, P., & Ololube, N. P. (2007). A discourse on the problems, prospects, and progress of distance education in a developing country. In Bailey, E. P. (Ed.), *Focus on distance education developments* (pp. 183–194). New York, NY: Nova Science Publishers.

Igwe, U. O. (2005). Harnessing Information Technology for the 21st century: Library education in Nigeria. *Library Philosophy and Practice, 7*(2)

Iloanusi, N. O., & Osuagwu, C. C. (2009). ICT in education: Achievements so far in Nigeria. In A. Méndez-Vilas, A. Solano Martín, J. A. Mesa González, & J. Mesa González (Eds.), *Research, reflections and innovations in integrating ICT in education*. (pp.1331-1335). Badajoz, Spain: FORMATEX. Retrieved February 10, 2010, from http://www.formatex.org/micte2009/book/1331-1335.pdf

Miller, R. P. (2005). *Listen to the students: A qualitative study investigating adult student readiness for online learning*. Retrieved March 11, 2010, from www.agclassroom.org/consortium/pdf/.../2005/online_learning.doc

Mohanan, K. P. (2005). *Assessing qualities of teaching in higher education*. Centre for Development of Teaching and Learning(CDTL). Retrieved 13th June, 2009, from http://www.cdtl.nus.edu.sg/publications/assess/who.htm

Mortera-Gutiérrez, F. (2006). Faculty best practices using blended learning in e-learning and face-to-face instruction. *International Journal on E-Learning*, *5*(3), 313–337.

Newhouse, C. P. (2002a). *The impact of ICT on learning and teaching*. Perth, Australia: Special Educational Service.

Newhouse, C. P. (2002b). *A framework to articulate the impact of ICT on learning in schools*. Perth, Australia: Special Educational Service.

Ololube, N. P. (2006a). The impact of professional and non-professional teachers' ICT competencies in secondary schools in Nigeria. *Journal of Information Technology Impact*, *6*(2), 101–118.

Ololube, N. P. (2006b). Appraising the relationship between ICT usage and integration and the standard of teacher education programs in a developing economy. *International Journal of Education and Development Using ICT*, *2*(3), 70–85.

Ololube, N. P. (2009). *Understanding teacher professional competencies for education effectiveness*. Owerri, Nigeria: SpringField Publishers.

Ololube, N. P. (2011). *Education and society: An interactive approach*. Owerri, Nigeria: SpringField Publishers.

Ololube, N. P., & Egbezor, D. E. (2009). Educational technology and flexible education in Nigeria: Meeting the need for effective teacher education. In S. Marshall, W. Kinuthia & W. Taylor (Eds.), *Bridging the knowledge divide: Educational technology for development*. Charlotte NC: Information Age Publishing.

Ololube, N. P., & Egbezor, D. E. (2009a). Measuring the extent to which teachers interpret their role in educational terms. In Parameswaran, G., & Kader, T. (Eds.), *Educational access and social justice* (pp. 87–97). Lanham, MD: University Press of America.

Ololube, N. P., & Egbezor, D. E. (2009b). Competencies exhibited by professionally qualified teachers in Nigerian secondary schools: A research study. In James, V., & Etim, J. S. (Eds.), *Educational reform in Africa: Essays in curriculum, libraries, counseling and grade levels*. Lanham, MD: Edwin Mellen Press.

Ololube, N. P., Eke, P., Uzorka, M. C., Ekpenyong, S. U., & Nte, N. D. (2009). Instructional technology in higher education: A case of selected universities in the Niger delta. *Asia-Pacific Forum on Science Learning and Teaching, 10*(2), Article 7.

Ololube, N. P., Ubogu, A. E., & Egbezor, D. E. (2007). ICT and distance education programs in a sub-Saharan African country: A theoretical perspective. *Journal of Information Technology Impact*, *7*(3), 181–194.

Render, B., Stair, R. M., & Hannan, M. E. (2005). *Quantitative analysis for management with CD* (9th ed.). London, UK: Prentice Hall.

UNESCO. (2008). UNESCO'S ICT competency standards for teachers: Towards ICT skills for teachers. Retrieved March 5, 2010, from http://cst.unesco-ci.org/sites/projects/cst/default.aspx

Vaughan, N. (2007). Perspectives on blended learning in higher education. *International Journal on E-Learning*, *6*(1), 81–94.

Zhongjun, L., & Lijuan, H. (2009). Research on new MIS teaching and learning methods. (pp. 745-748). Pacific-Asia Conference on Circuits, Communications and Systems, 2009.

ADDITIONAL READING

Beetham, H., McGill, L., & Littlejohn, A. (2009). Thriving in the 21st Century: Final report of Learning Literacies for the Digital Age (LLiDA) project. Retrieved December 11, 2010, from http://www.academy.gcal.ac.uk/llida/

Boyd, D., & Ellison, N. (2007) (Eds). Special issue on social network sites. *Journal of Computer-Mediated Communication (JCMC), 13*(1). Retrieved January 24, 2010, from http://jcmc.indiana.edu/vol13/issue1/

Carmichael, E. Miller., K., & Smith, J. (2007). Researching literacy for learning in the vocational curriculum. In Osborne, M., Houston, M., & Toman, N. (Eds), *The pedagogy of lifelong learning: Understanding effective teaching and learning in diverse contexts*. London: Routledge.

Conole, G., de Laat, M., Dillon, T., & Darby, J. (2006). *Student experiences of technologies.* JISC LXP Final report. Retrieved August 03, 2007, from http://www.jisc.ac.uk/media/documents/programmes/elearning_pedagogy/lxp%20project%20final%20report%20dec%2006.pdf#

Creanor, L., Trinder, K., Gowan, D., & Howells, C. (2006). *LEX – The Learner Experience of E-Learning*. JISC report. Retrieved February 10, 2007 from http://www.jisc.ac.uk/uploaded_documents/LEX%20Final%20Report_August06.pdf

Douar, A., S. Harous, M. Djoudi & Djamila Mechta (2009). An Interactive 3D Distributed Environment for Distance Practical Works. *6th International Conference on Innovations in Information Technology (Innovations'09), Al Ain, UAE, December 15-17.*

Douidi, L., Djoudi, M., & Khentout, C. (2006). Learner Evaluation Tool for AVUNET Environment. *Asian Journal of Information Technology, 5*(3), 258–262.

Douidi, L., Djoudi, M., & Khentout, C. (2007). Users Assistants for Elearning Environment Over the Web. *Journal of Computer Science, 3*(3), 122–129. doi:10.3844/jcssp.2007.122.129

Douidi, L., Harous, S., Khentout, C., & Djoudi, M. (2008). An Authoring System for Pedagogical Content Creation and Management. *International Journal of Instructional Media, 35*(1).

Harbouche, K., & Djoudi, M. (2007). Agent-based design for e-learning environment. *Journal of Computer Science, 3*(6), 383–389. doi:10.3844/jcssp.2007.383.389

Herron, J. F., & Wright, V. H. (2006). Assessment in online learning: Are students really learning? In Wright, H. V., Syzmanski Sunal, C., & Wilson, E. K. (Eds.), *Research on enhancing the interactivity of online learning*. Greenwich, CT: Information Age Publishing.

Information Policy. (2009). Digital economy can lift Europe out of crisis, say Commission report. *Information Policy*, Retroeved march 11 2010, from http://www.ipolicy.org/2009/08/digital-economy-can-lift-europe-out-of-crisis sayscommission-report.html

Khentout, C., Djoudi, M., & Douidi, L. (2006). Evaluation Tool for Distance Learning Platform. *Asian Journal of Information Technology, 5*(2), 225–231.

Liang, X., & Creasy, K. (2004) 'Classroom assessment in web-based instructional environment: Instructors' experience', [Online], *Practical Assessment, Research & Evaluation,* 9(7), Retrieved March 1 2010, from http://PAREonline.net/getvn.asp?v=9&n=7

Norton, P., & Wiburg, K. M. (2003). *Teaching with technology: Designing opportunities to learn* (2nd ed.). Belmont, CA: Wadsworth/Thomson Learning.

Reeves, R. (2000). Alternative approaches for online learning environments in higher education'. *Journal of Educational Computing Research, 23*(1), 101–111. doi:10.2190/GYMQ-78FA-WMTX-J06C

Robles, M., & Braathen, S. (2002). Online assessment techniques. *Delta Pi Epsilon Journal, 44*(1), 39–49.

Rovai, A. P. (2001). Building and sustaining community in asynchronous learning networks. *The Internet and Higher Education*, *3*(4), 285–297. doi:10.1016/S1096-7516(01)00037-9

Talhi, S., Djoudi, M., & Batouche, M. (2006). A Cooperative Authoring for Intelligent Tutoring System. *Asian Journal of Information Technology*, *5*(5), 497–503.

UNESCO. (2006), The very real success of the Avicenna Virtual Campus, *A World of SCIENCE,* 4(4), *October-December 2006,* Retrieved March 19 2010, from http://unesdoc.unesco.org/images/0014/001473/147357E.pdf

Vonderwell, S. (2003). An examination of asynchronous communication experiences and perspectives of students in an online course: A case study. *The Internet and Higher Education*, *6*(1), 77–90. doi:10.1016/S1096-7516(02)00164-1

Vonderwell, S., Liang, X., & Alderman, K. (2007). Asynchronous discussions and assessment in online learning. *Journal of Research on Technology in Education*, *39*(3), 309–328.

Zhao, Y., & Frank, K. A. (2003). Factors affecting technology uses in schools: An ecological perspective. *American Educational Research Journal*, *40*(4), 807–840. doi:10.3102/00028312040004807

Zidat, S., & Djoudi, M. (2006). Task Collaborative Resolution Tool for Elearning Environment. *Journal of Computer Science*, *2*(7), 558–564. doi:10.3844/jcssp.2006.558.564

KEY TERMS AND DEFINITIONS

Advancing Technology: Includes concerted effort towards contributing to technological evolution, future innovation, fostering knowledge and maintaining academic excellence in an environment that embraces modern technology.

Blended Learning: Involves a combination of face-to-face and technology-based learning, distinct from other learning strategies that is highly conducive to faculty teaching and increased students learning.

Competencies in Teaching MIS: Refers to the mastering of theoretical knowledge and applying such knowledge to practice. It is the ability to create knowledge as well as possess it with the aim of solving MIS problems with great enthusiasm and commitment.

Digital Divide: Differences exist between the educated and uneducated, privileged and underprivileged, between developed nations and developing nations, and those living in rural urban areas. This term is used to explain the divergences between people who have and people who do not have the skills, knowledge, experiences, abilities and access needed to effectively use and deploy ICT devices.

ICT Infrastructures: This includes ICT components and resources such as computer/Internet access, power supply, and telecommunication facilities as well as ICT libraries, operations, personnel, and funds, among others.

ICT Knowledge: The knowledge, skills, experiences and abilities needed to stay informed of current technological developments. It is a collective knowledge that effectively uses and is interested in contributing to further ICT knowledge that will, in turn, lead to individual, national and global development.

Management Information System: Otherwise known as MIS is a subset of the overall internal control of a business (private or public). It covers the application of people, documents, technologies, and procedures by management and is aimed at solving business problems and ensuring effective decision making across business communities. MIS is the process that intersects technology and business management.

Specialized Training: Specialized training organized to promote and produce cutting edge professionals for high quality service. These experts possess subject matter command, skills, and abilities combined with exceptional know-how in meeting MIS learning experiences.

Chapter 12
Blending In:
Moving Beyond Categories in Digitally-Mediated Learning

Marvin D. LeNoue
North Dakota State University, USA

Ronald Stammen
North Dakota State University, USA

ABSTRACT

This chapter comprises an outline of the prototype concept referred to as Second-Wave Enabled Technology Enhanced (SWETE) instruction. SWETE is positioned to subsume the blended learning concept, critiqued as a categorization that will fade to ubiquity as second-generation e-learning paradigms predominate in digitally-mediated education and training. In this chapter, the operational attributes of the SWETE model are presented via description of second-wave technologies, delineation of recent changes in educational cultures and contexts, and discussion of the principles of effective digitally-mediated education. The authors highlight the benefits of social media-driven instructional designs and introduce the use of Blackboard LMS/social network site mashups as core tools for online teaching and learning. The chapter ends with a look at the future of mobile and blended learning, and a call for research into the use of social network technology in the delivery of learning opportunities.

INTRODUCTION

Work on the design and delivery of digitally-mediated (DM) instruction for the Educational Leadership graduate programs offered by the North Dakota State University School of Education has led to the development of an approach that we refer to as Second Wave Enabled Technology Enhanced instruction (SWETE). The SWETE model is founded upon the combination of Web 2.0 technologies applied as e-learning tools and a reconceived blended learning paradigm. SWETE utilizes many of the intuitive, interactive applications associated with the social media revolution.

DOI: 10.4018/978-1-60960-479-0.ch012

The model also includes approaches to instructional design and delivery that embody what Bonk (2009) describes as blurred distinctions between classifications such as fully online or supplemental, face-to-face or distance, synchronous or asynchronous.

Our objectives in developing the SWETE model include (a) movement beyond previous e-learning and blended-learning categories, (b) accomplishment of seamless interplay among delivery styles and tool sets, and (c) development of instructional designs oriented toward adaptation to the demands of a variety of contexts, contents, and learning objectives. A primary feature of SWETE is the employment of flexible combinations of delivery modes in the service of (a) maximizing efficiency and effectiveness at the institutional and program level, and (b) facilitating optimal course-level learning outcomes by supporting higher levels of engagement, social contact, interaction, relevance, and context in online education delivery. This is achieved by the use of Blackboard LMS/Ning social network site mashups as the core of our online delivery platform (LeNoue & Stammen, 2009). This combination affords the creation of virtual classrooms that are low-demand in terms of necessary hardware, tech support, bandwidth, and user technical proficiency. These spaces support necessary administrative functions while providing easy access to flexible, modular suites of simple-to-use content delivery and communication tools. Many of these are Web 2.0-style social media tools that allow the projection of enhanced personal presence in digitally-mediated environments, enable range and intensity in individual expression, afford multimodal interaction, and empower collaboration and co-creation on the part of course participants.

In this chapter, we will construct a rationale for adoption of the SWETE model, and offer an experiential viewpoint on this new approach to DM education. Our chapter objectives include the following:

- discussion of blended learning as a graded cognitive model
- delineation of the second-wave e-learning paradigm
- explication of the SWETE model
- description of an instructional approach that makes use of a thick tool set and a fluid delivery style
- prediction of future directions in mobile blended learning
- suggestion of future research directions

We present an overall vision of the way a broad, versatile, and readily-available set of interactive technology tools can be deployed to provide multi-modal content support, dense participant interaction, and optimized learning outcomes. SWETE is an instructional design methodology that is adaptable to tight budgetary constraints, suitable for contexts that call for rapid updating and flexible configuration, and amenable to the efficient use of open educational resources.

BACKGROUND

Beyond Blended Learning

Blended learning (BL) is a term that has entered widespread use as a description of a particular form of teaching with technology. BL has risen in profile over the past three decades, yet remains difficult to define clearly (Oliver & Trigwell, 2005). A practical descriptor that has gained some currency proposes BL to include learning environments in which face-to-face (F2F) instruction is combined with digitally-mediated instruction (Graham, 2006; Graham, Allen, & Ure, 2005; Oliver & Trigwell, 2005). As part of efforts to enrich students' learning experience, maximize efficiencies in time and facilities use, and enhance program marketability, many higher education institutions are expanding their blended course offerings (Mossavar-Rahmani & Larson-Daugherty,

2007). BL is also becoming the delivery method of choice in corporate and governmental training settings (Bonk, Kim, & Zeng, 2005).

By 2013, forty percent or more of course offerings in higher education and corporate training are likely to be characterized by blended formats (Bonk et al., 2005). In higher education, blended offerings are expected to receive more emphasis than fully online courses, and it is possible that a majority of courses will have some Web component by the end of the decade (Kim & Bonk, 2006). A future is visible in which schooling is dominated by delivery models that feature multiple instructional modes fluidly combined within the affordances of technology-enhanced delivery (Bonk, 2009; Kim & Bonk, 2006).

The scalability of these delivery models allows for the design of courses that can accommodate larger numbers of participants than has ever been possible in the past (Siemens & Downes, 2008). As experience with mega-universities such as UK's Open University, the Shanghai TVU, and others demonstrates, BL models combine human, technological, and organizational aspects in a powerful way (Daniel, 2003). These new delivery paradigms may revolutionize education by offering greatly expanded access to quality educational resources (Daniel, 2003; Jung, 2005). Moreover, a growing body of research into DM education is producing indications that individual learning outcomes may improve when instruction is enhanced by technology use. In a meta-analysis comparing web-based and offline instruction, U.S. Department of Education researchers found that students in online learning conditions performed better on average than those receiving F2F instruction. BL approaches in turn produced a larger advantage than purely online instruction (Means, Toyama, Murphy, Bakia, & Jones, 2009). These findings are limited by a lack of published studies comparing online and F2F learning, and uncontrolled effects arising from differences in design between the technology-enabled and F2F instruction. However, the results indicate the potential of technology-enhanced instruction and support the use of BL paradigms.

With the spread of broadband internet and rapid popularization of online learning worldwide, traditional F2F educational environments are converging with new, widely-distributed learning environments afforded by the online spaces referred to as networked publics (boyd, 2008). This blurring of boundaries (Bonk, 2009; Graham et al., 2005) is occurring on top of historical confusion over the exact definition of blended learning (Oliver & Trigwell, 2005). The BL concept has thus far manifested as a graded cognitive model (Lakoff, 1987) in that it is characterized in part by a scale with gradations. Examples of this can be seen in definitions of BL that go from specifying an exact percentage of technology use vs. F2F instruction (Mossavar-Rahmani & Larson-Daugherty, 2007), through descriptions that refer only to mixes of pedagogical approaches, with no mention of technology (Driscoll, 2002), to mixings of nearly any of the material or methodological aspects of instruction (Driscoll, 2002; Singh, 2003). Another aspect of the difficulty surrounding the term concerns practical levels of concept application. Graham et al. used BL in specific reference to blending that occurs as part of course level instructional designs. Others (Bonk, 2009; Rovai, Ponton, & Baker, 2008) have offered definitions that include blending at the program or institutional level, as in the case of degree programs offered online but requiring some period of on-campus residency, or dual-mode universities comprised of both on-campus and distributed education branches.

This wide range of variation leaves potential examples resistant to identification via clear and useful prototyping and categorization (Bowker & Star, 1999; Lakoff, 1987), and this leads to difficulties in communication concerning the topic. Oliver and Trigwell (2005) critiqued the blended learning label, suggesting an amorphous nature and lack of real utility as causes for either abandonment or reconception. Although we agree with their analysis, there is another reason to move beyond this term: as per Bowker and Star (1999), "classification systems in general reflect the conflicting, contradictory motives of the sociotechnical situations that gave rise to them" (p. 64). We propose the erasure of boundaries that is occurring in tandem with changes in the technological environment as characterizing a movement beyond current blended learning categories. The blended learning concept is yielding to the simple rule that increasing ubiquity inevitably leads to a lack of comparative forms which renders distinguishing terminologies unnecessary.

Digital mediation and the machines that enable it are becoming omnipresent and completely transparent to generations born into the presence of networked digital technology (Tapscott, 2009). Consider the once-common electric light, rubber tire, or color television. These are now examples of obsolete cognitive categories. Digital technology-enabled delivery modes may soon become part of every educational experience (Bonk et al., 2005). This would render BL effectively invisible as a concept, and therefore useless. While this may seem a strange idea to promote in a book like this one, it is set forth here to highlight an ontological cornerstone of the SWETE model: the movement toward ubiquity in the use of digital technology for teaching and learning.

The Social Media Revolution and Second-Wave E-Learning

Early experiences with various models of what is now referred to as first wave e-learning (Singh, 2003; Taylor, 2002) were instructive in highlighting some of the disadvantages of the use of computers in education and training (Singh, 2003). Poorly designed software, difficult and unreliable hardware, and repetitive, predictable instructional designs that provided few constructive learning opportunities were some of the initial downsides encountered by instructors and students alike (Taylor, 2002). Moreover, the increased student isolation, decreased interpersonal interaction, and loss of social connectivity that were traditional disadvantages of distance education became associated with learning delivered via computer (Anderson, 2005; Simpson, 2003; Singh, 2003). In fact, computer mediated learning can be a lonely experience, particularly in formats that feature continuous enrollment and individual pacing in an effort to maximize freedom and flexibility for participants (Anderson, 2005).

To counter this effect, guiding principles and practices for developing quality online education offerings suggest that an effective learning environment will provide a network of meaningful interactions among learners, materials, and the instructor. As a foundation for such interaction, learners must be enabled in the establishment of a social presence in the virtual environment and empowered to express themselves in multiple modalities (Garrison & Anderson, 2003; Haythornthwaite & Bregman, 2004; Haythornthwaite, Kazmer, Robins, & Shoemaker, 2004; Palloff & Pratt, 2003, 2007; Ragan, 1999). To this end, the expansion of broadband internet service and proliferation of Web 2.0 interactive *social media* tools usher in a second-wave e-learning paradigm by offering capabilities that practitioners of first wave e-learning could only dream about.

Social media can be generally understood as an umbrella term referring to the tools, services, and applications that allow people to interact via the medium of network technologies (boyd, 2008). Social media supports fluid interaction among people, and between people and data, and the potential for creation of user-generated online content in support of this interaction (boyd, 2007). Social media takes many forms, encompassing but not limited to (a) groupware, (b) internet forums, (c) online communities, (d) RSS feeds, (e) wikis, (f) tag-based folksonomies, (g) podcasts, (h) e-mail, (i) weblogs, (j) virtual worlds, (k) social network sites, (l) instant messaging, texting, and microblogging; (m) peer-to-peer media-sharing technologies, and (n) networked gaming (boyd, 2008; Greenhow, Robelia, & Hughes, 2009;

McLoughlin & Lee, 2007). Well-known examples of social media applications include Wikipedia, MySpace, Facebook, YouTube, Second Life, Flickr, and Twitter. Social media applications give Internet users the capability to create, contribute, communicate, and collaborate in the online environment without need for specialized programming knowledge.

Social software tools have swept over the online world, coming into use by hundreds of millions of people world-wide in the span of a few years. The power of social media is concisely reflected in boyd's (2008) comment that it "has affected how people interact with one another and, thus, it has the potential to alter how society is organized" (p. 93). According to Shirky (2008), "The centrality of group effort to human life means that anything that changes the way groups function will have profound ramifications for everything from commerce and government to media and religion" (p. 17). In net-infused societies, new communities are being created that are native to social software technologies. Serving the residents of these communities requires a new form of distance education. Educators are now challenged to create and sustain learning opportunities that leverage the affordances specific to the technologies upon which digitally-mediated communities are built (Anderson, 2008). McLoughlin & Lee (2007) list several examples of the educational affordances of social software tools:

- connectivity and social rapport,
- collaborative information discovery and sharing,
- knowledge and information aggregation,
- content creation and modification (p. 667).

Anderson refers to social software technology as a new genre of distance education software emerging from the intersection between earlier technologies that generally support delivery and engagement with content, and new interactive technologies that support multimodal human communication. Social software can "create opportunities for radically new conceptions of independence and collaboration in distance education" (Anderson, 2008, p. 169).

As online education delivery has developed, the emphasis has been on constructivist pedagogies that focus on knowledge construction, critical thinking, problem-solving, collaboration, and autonomous learning – all skills considered to be essential in a knowledge-based economy (Bates, 2008; Sanchez, 2003). The constructivist model is comprised by the conception of learning as a self-governed, problem-based, and collaborative process (Dalsgaard, 2006). This process ideally takes place in open-ended learning environments that enable a student-centered approach to e-learning by

1. using a management system for administrative issues,
2. offering students personal tools for construction, presentation, reflection, and collaboration,
3. facilitating networks between students within the same course, and
4. facilitating networks between students and other people working within the field. (Dalsgaard, 2006, "Towards a Student-Centered Approach," para. 1)

Comprised of a suite of tools that can support learner choice and self-direction (McLoughlin & Lee, 2007), social software can be used to create an open-ended learning environment that provides multiple possibilities for activities, and surrounds the student with tools and resources that support the problem-solving process (Dalsgaard, 2006; Land & Hannafin, 1996). These attributes align well with the general precepts of a constructivist educational philosophy (Dalsgaard, 2006).

Social software technology is still very new, but it is likely to change the way learning systems, groupware, and other project-oriented digital collaboration tools work (Marenzi, Demidova,

Nejdl, Olmedilla, & Zerr, 2008). This change is embodied in the movement toward what Bonk (2009) describes as "a new culture of learning where we assume radically new perspectives of ourselves as learners and what it means to participate in the learning process. The culture is one of personalization and participation." (p. 327). In our view, this is the culture of second-wave e-learning.

SECOND-WAVE ENABLED TECHNOLOGY ENHANCED LEARNING

Working with the affordances of social software tools and within the second-wave e-learning paradigm, we developed SWETE as a conceptual metaphor (Lakoff & Johnson, 1999) that can take the place of what is currently conceived of as hybrid or blended learning. SWETE is intended to function as an ungraded cognitive model (Lakoff, 1987), a concept comprised of attributes flexible enough to adapt to local needs, yet stable enough to define category boundaries as per Star and Griesemer's (1989) description of abstract boundary objects. SWETE as a boundary object is an "ideal type" (Star & Griesemer, 1989) in that it does not describe the exact details of any particular instance of educational opportunity delivery but instead functions as a symbol that enables communication and understanding regarding an emerging approach to education.

SWETE can serve as a stable prototype for a particular class of teaching and learning. Prototype theory delineates the manner in which classifications can blur until people may agree to categorize a number of things under the same label even though they have no binary features in common (Bowker & Star, 1999; Lakoff, 1987). This is what has occurred in the case of the blended learning meme. We position the SWETE metaphor to counter this effect by drawing on Lakoff's (1987) assertion that

> *The properties that are relevant for the characterization of human categories are not objectively existing properties that are "out there" in the world. Rather they are "interactional properties," what we understand as properties by virtue of our interactive functioning in our environment. (p. 64)*

This implies that all applications of the SWETE model will necessarily exhibit particular and constant interactional properties. For example, all instances of SWETE instruction must move from an acceptance of what Tapscott (2009) identifies as a permanent alteration of the power dynamic between students and teachers. In SWETE, students and instructors are removed from traditional hierarchies of educational information delivery and placed within a flat and multi-nodal interaction network, positioned as co-participants in the learning process and co-creators of the instruction. Another unvarying aspect of SWETE is the use of second-wave digital technology to afford participants movement beyond simple delivery and passive reception of content to interaction, collaboration, and creation. At the same time, technology is not pre-eminent over pedagogy. Rather, it is positioned as a transparent aspect of the teaching and learning experience: ubiquitous, and appearing as a diverse toolset ready to be deployed in solution to challenges that arise as part of social constructivist learning processes. These fixed attributes allow the SWETE model to serve as a category prototype for education delivery while retaining enough plasticity (Star & Griesemer, 1989) to allow for adaptation to local needs. As a model for the delivery of learning opportunities, SWETE is intended to embody flexibility while representing a common identity and structure that will be recognizable across different contexts of application.

Components of the SWETE Model

Second-wave e-learning is the first of two component concepts that comprise the SWETE model. To support second-wave paradigms, there is need for delivery systems that maximize learner independence and freedom by enabling open-enrollment and self-paced learning while providing the capabilities for communication and collaboration demanded by constructivist pedagogies (Anderson, 2005). Learning management systems (LMS) that integrate geographically dispersed learners into online asynchronous educational interactions have been available for several years. However, they tend to be institution- and content-centric and lacking in support for the affordances that lead to the establishment of flattened communication networks and collaborative information flows (Dalsgaard, 2006; Siemens, 2004). An LMS is well suited for managing student enrolment, exams, assignments, course descriptions, lesson plans, messages, syllabi, and basic course materials. However, these systems were not developed for supporting self-governed and problem-based activities and do not easily support a social constructivist approach to DM learning. It is necessary to move beyond learning management systems to engage students in self-governed, problem-based, collaborative activities that make active use of the Web itself as a resource (Dalsgaard, 2006). Social software tools can facilitate this move.

Among these tools, we find social network sites (SNS) to be particularly useful. Boyd and Ellison (2007) define these sites as web-based services that allow individuals to (a) construct a public or semi-public profile within a bounded system, (b) articulate a list (network) of other users with whom they share a connection, and (c) view and traverse their list of connections and those made by others within the system. In considering these sites, many people inaccurately conflate social networks with social networking. While SNS users may be able meet strangers and make connections that would not have been made otherwise, this networking function is not the primary feature of these sites. The unique aspect of an SNS is that it allows users to articulate and make visible their social networks (Boyd & Ellison, 2007). This may be an important and useful feature in some educational contexts, while receding in importance in others. For example, in our experience, the value of network articulation gives way to the utility of (a) hosting for customizable personal profile pages that support the establishment and maintenance of individual presence in the online learning environment, (b) provisions for the storage and display of materials including audio and video media, and (c) easy access to a suite of social media tools.

A well-designed educational SNS offers multi-modal and multi-media communication and content delivery capabilities and provides a virtual space where course participants can meet and take part in various formal and informal interactions centered on shared learning objectives. This social space can be a positive component of an online course (Palloff & Pratt, 2003), and can encourage the development of the object-centered social structures (Engstrom, 2005) that arise naturally around the content, activities, and learning objectives that constitute commonalities shared by course participants. We create second-wave DM learning environments by combining the administrative capacities of the Blackboard LMS with the suite of social media applications offered by a Ning SNS to produce *educational social software* (ESS) (Anderson, 2005). These mashups offer all of the functions and features cited by Anderson as being potentially useful in online education delivery:

- presence tools that allow learners to make their presence known synchronously and asynchronously,
- notification tools that provide learners with notification when new content or communication is entered into a learning space,
- filtering tools that remove illegitimate information while bringing legitimate and potentially useful information to the attention of users,
- support for cooperative and collaborative learning,

- referral systems that track student activities and record outcomes,
- profiling systems that record and present information about students (p. 5).

These home-made ESS tools enable our second-wave e-learning model. This model is comprised of (a) constructivist learning approaches in which students engage in self-governed, problem-based work while surrounded by tools and resources that support collaboration, construction, presentation, and reflection (Dalsgaard, 2006); and (b) instructional designs that leverage the inherent abilities of social software to encourage and facilitate multi-channel, flat-network interaction, and position students as contributors to the learning experience.

Second-wave enabled learning environments should support diverse learning styles and encourage dense interaction and the constructive co-creation of learning experiences. The establishment of online presence must be afforded by the availability of varied modes for personal expression. Our tools offer choice in the design of personal pages or spaces, the ability to display digital photographs, art forms, slideshows, and graphics, the capability to play and share music, and support for synchronous and asynchronous text-based chats and discussions, face-to-face meetings, and real-time screen sharing. Providing learners with a diverse toolset that empowers rich self-expression and authentic communication in a digitally-mediated environment is a primary aspect of SWETE.

The second component of SWETE is the concept of technology as an enhancement to teaching and learning in the sense of being an added subtle improvement. The presence of technology is constant but de-centered, lending to movement through ubiquity toward invisibility. The goal is to deploy technology to support and intensify sound pedagogy rather than in ways that allow tools and techniques to become the focus of the teaching/learning experience (Stammen & Schmidt, 2001). An array of technological media can be an ideal educational tool when correctly deployed within effective instructional designs, but it will never replace good teaching methodologies.

The high digital connectivity and need for life-long, demand-driven learning that characterize the modern world call for the development of andragogies (Knowles, 1980) and pedagogies specialized to DM environments. The effective online instructor will operate simultaneously as content expert and facilitator of both dialogue and change in learner perspective (Guilar & Loring, 2008). Palloff and Pratt (2007) note that "In effective online learning, the instructor acts as a facilitator, encouraging students to take charge of their own learning process" (p. 125). Instructors take on the role of guides, context providers, and quality controllers while simultaneously helping students make their own contributions to content and evaluations of the learning experience (Prensky, 2009). Such methods must include learners as active participants or co-producers rather than passive consumers of content, and frame learning as a participatory, social process intended to support personal life goals and needs (McLoughlin & Lee, 2007; Tapscott & Williams, 2010).

McLoughlin and Lee (2007) present a pedagogy that makes use of the affordances of social software tools. What they refer to as *Pedagogy 2.0* is defined by a number of dimensions:

- **content:** micro units of content that augment thinking and cognition; learner-generated content that accrues from students creating, sharing and revising ideas;
- **curriculum:** dynamic not fixed, open to negotiation and learner input, consisting of "bite-sized" modules, inter-disciplinary in focus, and blending formal and informal learning;
- **communication:** open, peer-to-peer and multi-faceted; supported by multiple media types;

- **process:** situated, reflective, integrated thinking processes; iterative, dynamic and inquiry-based learning;
- **resources:** multiple informal and formal sources that are media rich and global in reach;
- **scaffolds:** support from a network of peers, teachers, experts, and communities;
- **learning tasks:** authentic, personalized, learner-driven and designed; experiential and enabling multiple perspectives (p. 207).

Pedagogy 2.0 embodies the social constructivist educational paradigm. It empowers learners to move well beyond traditional teacher-centered learning and toward the possibility of heutagogy, "a new set of principles and practices that may have application across the whole spectrum of the education and learning lifespan" (Hase & Kenyon, 2000, p. 2). A principle of teaching based on fully self-determined learning, heutagogy takes into account the capabilities and motivation of the learner, the need for flexibility and student-centeredness in the design and negotiation of the learning process, and the fact that much learning occurs independently and/or informally (Hase & Kenyon, 2000). Heutagogy ties into the personal learning environment (PLE) concept. These environments are digitally-mediated front-ends, or what may be thought of as dash-boards or homepages, that serve as organizers and access points through which students interact with the information cloud for the purpose of knowledge-building of all sorts. The principles of heutagogy along with the PLE concept place the student at the center of a self-designed instructional process.

Student-centeredness is an important concept in working with cohorts of learners who have come of age in the presence of the internet. They make up what Tapscott (1999) termed as the *net generation,* and are "forcing a change in the model of pedagogy, from a teacher-focused approach based on instruction to a student-focused model based on collaboration" (p. 11). Students today want to participate in the learning process; they look for greater autonomy, connectivity and socio-experiential learning, have a need to control their environments, and are used to instant connectivity and easy access to the staggering amount of content and knowledge available at their fingertips (Johnson, Levine, & Smith, 2009; McLoughlin & Lee, 2007; Oblinger, 2008; Tapscott, 2009). These *digital natives* (Prensky, 2001a) have quantifiably different personalities than members of preceding generations. They belong to a "culture of self", often placing primary emphasis on the demands of self-actualization, and expecting that attention and resources will be dedicated to satisfying their personal wants and needs (Twenge, 2006). Indeed, mounting evidence indicates that Net Geners worldwide are developing measurable, physical changes in brain function that lead them to process information and behave differently that their parents did (Prensky, 2001b; Tapscott, 2009). Meanwhile, "the learning clientele is becoming more and more diverse each day.... This diversification stems from many factors, including increased access to learning, lifelong learning pursuits, recertification needs, immigration, longer life spans, better course marketing, and so on" (Bonk, 2009, p. 92).

To be effective, today's instructors must accommodate the needs of this changing student population and the demands of teaching in an age when "the Internet is, inexorably, becoming the dominant infrastructure for knowledge - both as a container and as a global platform for knowledge exchange between people" (Tapscott & Williams, 2010, para. 6). In a time of increasing individuation and personalization, approaches to DM instruction must be founded on the provision of opportunities for the establishment social presence by individuals working within communities that feature little or no face-to-face contact. Social presence, comprised of the co-presence of students and teacher in the learning space, and their ability to project themselves socially and emotionally in that space, is a sense of "being there" in the online environment (Garrison & Anderson, 2003). It is important to building the communication and community in the virtual classroom (Garrison & Anderson, 2003; Rovai, et al., 2008) that are associated with involvement in the online learning environment, and contribute positively to both learning outcomes and learner satisfaction with online courses (Kazmer, 2000). Three dimensions of social presence (a) social context, (b) online communication, and (c) interaction have been identified (Tu & Corry, 2002) and linked with student perceptions of learning (Picciano, 2002), and satisfaction with online courses (Gunawardena & Zittle, 1997). In the online learning environment, the three aspects of social presence are not supported by scheduled, physical proximity. Instead, the online instructor must rely on tools that can aid in the ongoing assessment and support of presence within the learning community.

SNS software offers many features that are well-suited to this task. Blogs and discussion forums can be used as collaborative work spaces to support the type of asynchronous online collaboration that is associated with "increased learner interaction, satisfaction, and learning" (Murphy, Drabier, & Epps, 1998, p. 2). However, these tools are not components unique to SNS software. It is the personal profile page that sets the SNS environment apart from other tools. The page owner can alter the look and function of the page, add text, pictures, media, and software applications, and update the profile that presents personal information. The profile page represents a space for the personalization, creation, and expression that can support the establishment of individual presence in the virtual environment (Dalsgaard & Paulsen, 2009; Garrison & Anderson, 2003). As the page is shared in the public spaces of the social network site, it serves an important function as the individual's representation on the web. In contrast to blogs or discussion forums, where individuals are represented solely by their posts and are dependent on posting for visibility, on a social network site, presence is constantly maintained through the personal page, and an implicit mode of communication is thereby enabled (Dalsgaard & Paulsen, 2009). This effect constitutes an enhancement of individual social presence.

In SWETE, technology-enhanced social presence is afforded by the capacity, scalability, and multimodality of expression offered by sets of social media tools. These tools afford the establishment of authentic cognitive and emotional presence in virtual spaces, while the Web itself is used to expand these spaces into resource-rich and open-ended contexts for the application of social constructivist approaches to learning. In DM education, good teaching means leveraging the growing set of available, inexpensive, and simple social media tools and applications that can be used to develop variations on the theme represented by the SWETE instructional model.

Instructional Designs for SWETE

Instructional designs for SWETE will be based on fundamental assumptions arising from the context particular to the situation. In our own case, the following are primary: (a) course participants will be adult learners from a diversity of professional backgrounds, (b) participants will present a range of technical proficiency levels and have varying degrees of access to technical support, (c) participants will be scattered across a wide geographic area, (d) participants will require a comprehensive range of course access options to allow for variation in local and personal technology facilities, (e) participant access and content delivery support requirements may vary from class session to session, or even within a single session, as well as from course to course; (f) designs and content should be rapidly updatable.

We meet these requirements by employing a broad selection of delivery modes, building flexibility, multimodality, and redundancy into course materials and instructional plans, using the Web as a major course content resource base, and deploying adapted or created learning activities that take full advantage of the affordances of our tool set. In our program, instructors and students alike become accustomed to combining technologies in the classroom. At the class level, it is common to witness in a single session the use of live video, web-based resources, the institutional LAN, email, phone, and FAX, and live instructor-to-student and student-to-student interaction. An example scenario might capture a portion of the class participants interacting with an instructor in an F2F classroom, while other classmates attend via a digital interactive video network (IVN). Some IVN students watch in groups at designated centers; others view the stream on their own computers at independent locations. All participants are logged into the class educational social network site on their mobile or desktop computers, operating a back-channel via the site's chat function while viewing and discussing video presentations students have created and posted on the SNS. Some students have an extra window open and surreptitiously scroll belatedly through the assigned reading for the session, a chapter in an electronic textbook. After completing an online quiz on the video content, students might engage in closing synchronous discussions, then go home to blog reflections on the class session. A few students log into the course wiki from home and make contributions to the collection of annotated video titles/URLs that is being developed there. Others multitask, chatting online casually while checking email, and listening to music posted on the SNS. Later, students can use their phones or computers to check their quiz results.

In this scenario, technology is integrated in and necessary to the purposes of the course and the context. It is deployed smoothly and seamlessly, in a manner that embodies efficiency and individual convenience for students and instructors alike. With smart instructional design and ongoing practice, the technology fades into the background, invaluable yet invisible, taken for granted and useful rather than demanding, obtrusive, and of questionable utility in terms of effort/benefit trade-off. This is the SWETE learning paradigm fully realized.

Going (Beyond) Mobile Blended Learning

The future of blended and mobile learning will be shaped by: (a) development in the realm of cloud computing, (b) creation in the area of Web 2.0-type software tools and the programming languages associated with them, (c) advances in wired and wireless networks and associated mobile technologies, and (d) convergence and extension of the PLE and life-long learning paradigms. Heutagogy as supported by the PLE concept will take precedence as technological and social change drive ongoing transformation in the way people live and work. The contemporary "information age" is characterized by the diffusion of information and communications technologies and an increasing demand for content delivery methods and educational approaches that foster lifelong learning (Fischer & Konomi, 2005; McLoughlin & Lee, 2007). Social trends such as the diversification of life trajectories, the need for multiple career paths and ongoing re-skilling, and the necessity of flexible working hours are drivers of the need for learning on demand (Punie & Cabrera, 2006), and digital modalities will rise to primacy in the effort to efficiently deliver demand-driven learning (McLoughlin & Lee, 2007).

As nearly all educational courses and training implementations come to have online components, learning and learners will become increasingly mobile. Smartphone technology will exploit networks offering ever more bandwidth and increasing Wi-Fi speeds. These networks will use heterogeneous wireless technologies that will enable seamless mobility on a global basis (Hwang, Consulta, & Yoon, 2007). High data transmission capabilities will make it possible for instructors to broadcast wireless video from a desktop or laptop computer, and students will watch from anywhere they want, using a range of technologies including MP3 music players and mobile phones (Hwang, Consulta, & Yoon; van 't Hooft, 2008). Synchronous interaction will be possible, and high definition video capabilities will allow instructors to carry out demonstrations or experiments involving very small items or manipulations. High definition graphics and high bandwidth will also open the doors to virtual worlds, where students who have grown up participating in virtual life through video games will easily adjust to studying in fully virtual school environments (Oblinger & Oblinger, 2005; Tapscott, 2009).

During this advance, the mobile learning concept will undergo the same transition that blended learning has now begun. Mobile learning will move through ubiquity to invisibility as boundaries blur, and today's revolution becomes tomorrow's standard operating procedure. At NDSU, we proactively reach for that time by deploying second-wave interactive technology enhancements across the full range of course delivery modes including full online, online/F2F, "tribrid" IVN/online/F2F, and full F2F. The features and activities that enable and avail of mobile accessibility are not necessarily associated with any particular course delivery configuration, but constitute a broad background to operations at the class, course, and program level.

FUTURE RESEARCH DIRECTIONS

The use of SNS technology in education is a new phenomenon. These sites are clearly popular among youth of student age as well as many adults (Lenhart, 2009; Lenhart & Madden, 2007; Lenhart, Madden, Smith, & Macgill, 2007). They have the potential to contribute to sound pedagogical approaches (Dron, 2006; Fitzgerald, et al., 2009; Martin & Crawford, 2008), a growing number of educators are experimenting with them (Anderson, 2008; Dalsgaard, 2006), and many faculty think SNS have or will change the way students learn (Cengage Learning, 2007). Still, these sites have only recently begun to be seriously contemplated for inclusion in academia as teaching and learning tools (Vie, 2008), and the research-based literature regarding the topic of social network sites in education is still in a thin and scattered state. In 2009, Hemmi, Bayne, and Land, 2009) stated that:

Very little formal research that is focused around the application of Web 2.0 technologies in higher education pedagogy has as yet been published. The need for such research is pressing. The currently dominant modes for e-learning within higher education – those enabled by commercial virtual learning environments (VLEs) – are generally failing to engage with the rich potential of the digital environment for learning. Their tendency is to attempt to render the online learning space familiar through a conservative dependence on pre-digital metaphors, signs and practices which are increasingly anachronistic as digital modes gain in social and cultural significance. (p. 19)

There is an obvious demand for research to uncover the affordances, benefits, and drawbacks of deploying a social network site as a component of online or blended learning delivery. As a starting point, we suggest gathering general information on the current use of social networks sites in formal educational contexts, documenting the experiences and observations of teachers who are using these tools, and capturing the views of concerned technology experts and practical users alike regarding the educational utility of such sites.

CONCLUSION

The SWETE education delivery concept is founded on the use of social software applications in online teaching and learning. These applications encourage collaboration, while supporting self-direction and individuation. In contrast to standard content management systems, which are teacher/institution centric and emphasize content handling and two-way communication (Siemens, 2004), social software offers far more interactivity and a distributed web of communication paths. In this way, social software fosters interaction, community feeling, and group motivation. The capability for personalization that is a primary feature of social software allows for flexibility and adaptation, empowering learners to effectively manage a life-long constructivist educational process as time passes and their needs change.

Social software is going to play an indefinitely ongoing part in the lives of millions of people. For better or worse, many of the young people who live in modernized societies today have been generalized as members of the *Net Generation* (Oblinger & Oblinger, 2005; Tapscott, 1999, 2009), or *Digital Natives* (Prensky, 2001a). Others, qualified by their age as *Digital Immigrants* (Prensky, 2001a), may be relative newcomers to the digitally-mediated lifestyle. Regardless of age, few people today live wholly independently of networked technology, and there is a large subset that relies on being able to live a digitally-mediated existence. Modern societies are generating a realm of communicative action and social integration that takes place in the interactive digital spaces of networked publics:

Networked publics are publics that are restructured by networked technologies. As such, they are simultaneously (1) the space constructed through networked technologies and (2) the imagined community that emerges as a result of the intersection of people, technology, and practice. (boyd, 2008, p. 15)

Networked publics are born of the enhanced communication capabilities afforded by modern digital technologies. Theories in social semiotics suggest that communication is always multimodal, implying that no sign or message ever exists in a single mode such as language or writing (Kress, 2003). Although the Internet originated primarily as a genre of linear text-based media, it has now moved far beyond that to encompass a complex universe of multi-media and multi-modal communicative transmission and meaning-making. "The old web was something you surfed for content. The new Web is a communications medium .... It has become a tool for self-organization" (Tapscott, 2009, p. 18).

For members of the networked public, the utility of the Internet as both a form and realm of communication is taken for granted, as are the social media tools that enable the digitally-mediated interaction that takes place online. Without social media tools at their disposal, many people today would likely have difficulty fully comprehending and interacting with their social and physical worlds. Accordingly, to serve the networked public most effectively, learning delivery must be digitally-mediated in part or whole, and must be facilitated by social software tools. As Mimi Ito remarked in an opening plenary for the New Media Consortium 2010 summer conference "If we're to grasp the amazing promise of this networked world, we must organize learning around the networks, not around the models that preserve the boundaries of our current educational practices" (Campbell, 2010, para. 4).

REFERENCES

Anderson, T. (2005). *Distance learning–social software's killer app?* Retrieved from http://auspace.athabascau.ca:8080/dspace/

Anderson, T. (2008). Social software technologies in distance education: Maximizing learning freedoms. In Evans, T., Haughey, M., & Murphy, D. (Eds.), *International handbook of distance education* (pp. 167–184). West Anglia, UK: Emerald Group Publishing.

Bates, T. (2008). Transforming distance education through new technologies. In Evans, T., Haughey, M., & Murphy, D. (Eds.), *International handbook of distance education* (pp. 217–235). West Anglia, UK: Emerald Group Publishing.

Bonk, C., Kim, K., & Zeng, T. (2005). Future directions of blended learning in higher education and workplace learning settings. In P. Kommers & G. Richards (Eds.), *Proceedings of World Conference on Educational Multimedia, Hypermedia and Telecommunications 2005* (pp. 3644-3649). Chesapeake, VA: AACE. Retrieved from http://www.editlib.org/p/20646

Bonk, C. J. (2009). *The world is open: How technology is revolutionizing education*. San Francisco, CA: Jossey-Bass.

Bowker, G. C., & Star, S. L. (1999). *Sorting things out: Classification and its consequences*. Boston, MA: MIT Press.

Boyd, D. (2007). *The significance of social software*. Retrieved from http://www.danah.org/papers/

Boyd, D. (2008). *Taken out of context: American teen sociality in networked publics*. Unpublished doctoral dissertation, University of California-Berkeley, School of Information. Retrieved from http://www.danah.org/papers/

Boyd, D. M., & Ellison, N. B. (2007). Social network sites: Definition, history, and scholarship. *Journal of Computer-Mediated Communication, 13*(1), 11. Retrieved from http://jcmc.indiana.edu/vol13/issue1/boyd.ellison.html.

Campbell, G. (2010). *Mimi Ito: Opening plenary at NMC 2010*. Retrieved June 13, 2010, from http://www.gardnercampbell.net/blog1/

Cengage Learning. (2007). *Many college professors see podcasts, blogs and social networking sites as a potential teaching tool*. Retrieved from http://www.cengage.com/press/release/20070507.html

Dalsgaard, C. (2006). Social software: E-learning beyond learning management systems. *European Journal of Open, Distance and E-Learning*. Retrieved from http://www.eurodl.org

Dalsgaard, C., & Paulsen, M. (2009). Transparency in cooperative online education. *International Review of Research in Open and Distance Learning, 10*(3). Retrieved from http://www.irrodl.org.

Daniel, J. S. (2003). *Mega-universities=mega-impact on access, cost and quality*. Keynote address presented at the First Summit of Mega-universities, Shanghai, PRC. Retrieved from http://portal.unesco.org

Driscoll, M. (2002) *Blended learning: Let's get beyond the hype*. Retrieved June 12, 2010, from http://www-07.ibm.com/services/pdf/blended_learning.pdf

Dron, J. (2006). Social software and the emergence of control. *Proceedings of the Sixth IEEE International Conference on Advanced Learning Technologies* (pp. 904-908). Washington, DC: IEEE Computer Society. Retrieved from http://portal.acm.org/ citation.cfm?id=1156266

Engstrom, J. (2005). *Why some social network services work and others don't- or: The case for object-centered sociality*. Retrieved from http://www.zengestrom.com/blog/2005/04/why_some_social.html

Fischer, G., & Konomi, S. (2005). Innovative media in support of distributed intelligence and lifelong learning. *Proceedings of the Third IEEE International Workshop on Wireless and Mobile Technologies in Education* (pp. 3-10). Retrieved from http://doi.ieeecomputersociety.org/10.1109/WMTE.2005.35

Fitzgerald, R., Barrass, S., Campbell, J., Hinton, S., Ryan, Y., & Whitelaw, M. … McGinness, N. (2009). *Digital Learning Communities (DLC): Investigating the application of social software to support networked learning* (Project Report CG6-36). Retrieved from http://www.digitalrepository.qut.edu.au/

Garrison, D. R., & Anderson, T. (2003). *E-learning in the 21st century*. Retrieved from http://www.questia.com

Graham, C. R. (2006). Blended learning systems: Definition, current trends, and future directions. In Bonk, C. J., & Graham, C. R. (Eds.), *Handbook of blended learning: Global perspectives, local designs* (pp. 3–21). San Francisco, CA: Pfeiffer Publishing.

Graham, C. R., Allen, S., & Ure, D. (2005). Benefits and challenges of blended learning environments. In M. Khosrow-Pour (Ed.), *Encyclopedia of information science and technology* (pp. 253–259). Retrieved from http://www.netlibrary.com

Greenhow, C., Robelia, B., & Hughes, J. E. (2009). Learning, teaching, and scholarship in a digital age: Web 2.0 and classroom research: What path should we take now? *Educational Researcher*, *38*(4), 246–259. .doi:10.3102/0013189X09336671

Guilar, J. D., & Loring, A. (2008). Dialogue and community in online learning: Lessons from Royal Roads University. *Journal of Distance Education*, *22*(3), 19–40. Retrieved from http://www.jofde.ca.

Gunawardena, C., & Zittle, F. (1997). Social presence as a predictor of satisfaction within a computer mediated conferencing environment. *American Journal of Distance Education*, *11*(3), 8–26. Retrieved from http://www.ajde.com. doi:10.1080/08923649709526970

Hase, S., & Kenyon, C. (2000). *From andragogy to heutagogy*. Retrieved from http://ultibase.rmit.edu.au/index.htm

Haythornthwaite, C., & Bregman, A. (2004). Affordances of persistent conversation: Promoting communities that work. In Haythornthwaite, C., & Kazmer, M. M. (Eds.), *Learning, culture, and community in online education: Research and practice* (pp. 129–143). New York, NY: Peter Lang Publishing, Inc.

Haythornthwaite, C., Kazmer, M. M., Robins, J., & Shoemaker, S. (2004). Community development among distance learners: Temporal and technological dimensions. In Haythornthwaite, C., & Kazmer, M. M. (Eds.), *Learning, culture, and community in online education: Research and practice* (pp. 35–57). New York, NY: Peter Lang Publishing.

Hemmi, A., Bayne, S., & Land, R. (2009). The appropriation and repurposing of social technologies in higher education. *Journal of Computer Assisted Learning*, *25*(1), 19–30. .doi:10.1111/j.1365-2729.2008.00306.x

Hwang, J., Consulta, R. R., & Yoon, H. (2007). 4G mobile networks: Technology beyond 2.5G and 3G. *Proceedings of the 2007 Pacific Telecommunications Council Conference*. Retrieved from http://www.ptc.org/past_events/ptc07/program/papers/ T24_RoyConsulta.pdf

Johnson, L., Levine, A., & Smith, R. (2009). *The 2009 horizon report*. Retrieved from http://www.nmc.org/publications/2009-horizon-report

Jung, I. (2005). Quality assurance survey of megauniversities. In C. McIntosh (Ed.), *Perspectives on distance education: Lifelong learning and distance higher education* (pp. 79-95). Retrieved from http://unesdoc.unesco.org/images/0014/001412/141218e.pdf

Kazmer, M. M. (2000). Coping in a distance environment: Sitcoms, chocolate cake, and dinner with a friend. *First Monday*, *5*(9). Retrieved from http://firstmonday.org/.

Kim, K. J., & Bonk, C. J. (2006). The future of online teaching and learning in higher education: The survey says. *EDUCAUSE Quarterly*, *29*(4). Retrieved from http://www.educause.edu.

Knowles, M. S. (1980). *The modern practice of adult education: From pedagogy to andragogy* (2nd ed.). New York, NY: Cambridge Books.

Kress, G. (2003). *Literacy in the new media age.* Retrieved from http://www.questia.com

Lakoff, G. (1987). Cognitive models and prototype theory. In Neisser, U. (Ed.), *Concepts and conceptual development: Ecological and intellectual factors in categorization*. Cambridge, UK: University of Cambridge.

Lakoff, G., & Johnson, M. (1999). *Philosophy in the flesh: The embodied mind and its challenge to western thought*. New York, NY: Basic Books.

Land, S. M., & Hannafin, M. J. (1996). A conceptual framework for the development of theories-in-action with open-ended learning environments. *Educational Technology Research and Development, 44*(3), 37–53. Retrieved from http://www.aect.org. doi:10.1007/BF02300424

Lenhart, A. (2009). *Adults and social network websites*. Retrieved from http://www.pewinternet.org

Lenhart, A., & Madden, M. (2007). *55% of online teens use social networks and 55% have created online profiles, older girls predominate*. Retrieved from http://www.pewinternet.org/

Lenhart, A., Madden, M., Smith, A., & Macgill, A. R. (2007). *Teens and social media.* Retrieved from http://www.pewinternet.org

LeNoue, M., & Stammen, R. (2009). Building online learning communities with Web 2.0 tools. In T. Bastiaens, et al. (Eds.), *Proceedings of World Conference on E-Learning in Corporate, Government, Healthcare, and Higher Education 2009* (pp. 1751-1755). Retrieved from http://www.editlib.org/p/32713

Marenzi, I., Demidova, E., Nejdl, W., Olmedilla, D., & Zerr, S. (2008). Social software for lifelong competence development: Challenges and infrastructure. *International Journal of Emerging Technologies in Learning, 3*, 18–23. Retrieved from http://online-journals.org/i-jet/issue/view/30.

Martin, S., & Crawford, C. (2008). Multiple streams of social media: Using social software to create information connections and conversations in learning environments. In K. McFerrin, R. Weber, R. Carlsen, & D. A. Willis (Eds.), *Proceedings of Society for Information Technology and Teacher Education International Conference 2008* (pp. 541-548). Chesapeake, VA: AACE.

McLoughlin, C., & Lee, M. J. W. (2007). Social software and participatory learning: Pedagogical choices with technology affordances in the Web 2.0 era. In R. J. Atkinson, C. McBeath, S. K. A. Soong, & C. C. Cheers (Eds.), *ICT: Providing choices for learners and learning. Proceedings of ASCILITE Singapore 2007* (pp. 664-675). Retrieved from http://www.ascilite.org.au/conferences/singapore07/procs/mcloughlin.pdf

Means, B., Toyama, Y., Murphy, R., Bakia, M., & Jones, K. (2009). *Evaluation of evidence-based practices in online learning: A meta-analysis and review of online learning studies*. Retrieved from http://www.ed.gov/rschstat/eval/tech/evidence-based-practices/finalreport.pdf

Mossavar-Rahmani, F., & Larson-Daugherty, C. (2007). Supporting the hybrid learning model: A new proposition. *MERLOT Journal of Online Learning and Teaching, 3*(1), 67-78. Retrieved from http://jolt.merlot.org/

Murphy, K., Drabier, R., & Epps, M. (1998). Interaction and collaboration via computer conferencing. *Proceedings of the National Convention for Education Communication and Technology.* Retrieved from ERIC database. (ED 423852).

Oblinger, D. G. (2008). Growing up with Google: What it means to education. In *Emerging technologies for learning* (BECTA Report, Vol. 3), (pp. 11-29). Retrieved from the http://www.becta.org.uk/

Oblinger, D. G., & Oblinger, J. L. (Eds.). (2005). *Educating the net generation*. Retrieved from www.educause.edu

Oliver, M., & Trigwell, K. (2005). Can blended learning be redeemed? *E-learning, 2*(1), 17–26. Retrieved from http://www.wwwords.co.uk/elea/.

Pallof, R. M., & Pratt, K. (2007). *Building online learning communities: Effective strategies for the virtual classroom*. San Francisco, CA: Jossey-Bass.

Palloff, R. M., & Pratt, K. (2003). *The virtual student: A profile and guide to working with online learners*. San Francisco, CA: Jossey-Bass.

Picciano, A. G. (2002). Beyond student perception: Issues of interaction, presence, and performance in an online course. *Journal of Asynchronous Learning Networks, 6*(1), 21–40. Retrieved from http://www.sloan-c.org/publications/jaln_main.

Prensky, M. (2001a). Digital natives, digital immigrants. *Horizon, 9*(5), 1–6. Retrieved from http://www.marcprensky.com. doi:10.1108/10748120110424816

Prensky, M. (2001b). Digital natives, digital immigrants, part II: Do they really think differently? *Horizon, 9*(6), 1–9. Retrieved from http://www.marcprensky.com. doi:10.1108/10748120110424843

Prensky, M. (2009). H. Sapiens digital: From digital immigrants and digital natives to digital wisdom. *Innovate Journal of Online Education, 5*(3). Retrieved from http://innovateonline.info/

Punie, Y., & Cabrera, M. (2006). *The future of ICT and learning in the knowledge society.* (EUR 22218 EN). European Commission Joint Research Center, Institute for Prospective Technological Studies. Retrieved from http://www.epractice.eu/en/library/281771

Ragan, L. C. (1999). Good teaching is good teaching: An emerging set of guiding principles and practices for the design and development of distance education. *Cause/Effect, 22*(1). Retrieved from http://net.educause.edu/ir/library/html/cem/cem99/cem9915.html

Rovai, A. P., Ponton, M. K., & Baker, J. D. (2008). *Distance learning in higher education: A programmatic approach to planning, design, instruction, evaluation, and accreditation*. New York, NY: Teachers College Press.

Sanchez, F. (2003). Skills for a knowledge-based economy. *Leadership, 33*(2), 30–33. Retrieved from http://www.bnet.com/.

Shirky, C. (2008). *Here comes everybody: The power of organizing without organizations*. New York, NY: Penguin Press.

Siemens, G. (2004). *Connectivism: A learning theory for the digital age*. Retrieved from http://www.elearnspace.org/Articles/connectivism.htm

Siemens, G., & Downes, S. (2008). *Connectivism and connective knowledge: A rather large open online course*. Retrieved from http://ltc.umanitoba.ca/connectivism/

Simpson, O. (2003). *Student retention in online, open, and distance learning*. Retrieved from http://www.questia.com/Index.jsp

Singh, H. (2003). Building effective blended learning programs. *Educational Technology, 433*(6), 51–54. Retrieved from http://asianvu.com/digital-library/ elearning/blended-learning-by_Singh.pdf.

Stammen, R. M., & Schmidt, M. A. (2001). Basic understanding for developing distance education for online instruction. *NASSP Bulletin, 85*(628), 47–50. doi:10.1177/019263650108562805

Star, S. L., & Griesemer, J. R. (1989). Institutional ecology, translations, and boundary objects: Amateurs and professionals in Berkeley's Museum of Vertebrate Zoology, 1907-39. *Social Studies of Science, 19*, 387–420. .doi:10.1177/030631289019003001

Tapscott, D. (1999). *Growing up digital*. New York, NY: McGraw-Hill.

Tapscott, D. (2009). *Grown up digital* (2nd ed.). New York, NY: McGraw-Hill.

Tapscott, D., & Williams, A. D. (2010). Innovating the 21st-century university: It's time! *EDUCAUSE Review*, *45*(1), 16–29. Retrieved from http://www.educause.edu/er.

Taylor, C. R. (2002). *E-learning: The second wave*. Retrieved from http://www.providersedge.com/docs/km_articles/E-Learning_-_The_Second_Wave.pdf

Tu, C., & Corry, M. (2002). *Research in online learning community*. Retrieved from http://www.usq.edu.au/electpub/e-jist/docs/html2002/chtu.html

Twenge, J. M. (2006). *Generation me: Why today's young Americans are more confident, assertive, entitled, and more miserable than ever before*. New York, NY: Simon & Schuster, Inc.

van 't Hooft, M. (2008). Mobile, wireless, connected: Information clouds and learning. In *Emerging technologies for learning* (BECTA Research Report, Vol. 3), (pp. 30-46). Coventry, UK: BECTA. Retrieved from http://www.becta.org.uk

Vie, S. (2008). Digital divide 2.0: Generation M and online social networking sites in the composition classroom. *Computers and Composition*, *25*, 9–23. Retrieved from www.elsevier.com/locate/compcom. doi:10.1016/j.compcom.2007.09.004

ADDITIONAL READING

Alexander, B. (2006). Web 2.0: A new wave of innovation for teaching and learning. *EDUCAUSE Review, 41*(2), 32–44. Retrieved from EDUCAUSE website: http://www.educause.edu/apps/er/erm06/erm0621.asp

Anderson, T. (2004). Toward a theory of online learning. In T. Anderson & F. Elloumi (Eds), *Theory and practice of online learning* (45-74). Athabasca, AB: Athabasca University. Retrieved from Athabasca University website: http://cde.athabascau.ca/online_book/index.html

Bush, V. (1945, July). As we may think. *Atlantic Monthly*. Retrieved from http://www.theatlantic.com/doc/194507/bush

Cormode, G., & Krishnamurthy, B. (2008). Key differences between Web 1.0 and Web 2.0. *First Monday*, *13*(6). Retrieved from http://www.uic.edu/htbin/cgiwrap/bin/ojs/index.php /fm/index.

DiNucci, D. (1999, July). *Fragmented future*. Retrieved from http://cdinucci.com/Darcy2/ articles/articlesindex.html

Downes, S. (2005, October 17). E-learning 2.0. *ELearn Magazine*. Retrieved from http://www.elearnmag.org/subpage.cfm?section=articles&article=29-1

Downes, S. (2005, December 22). An introduction to connective knowledge [Blog post]. *Stephen's Web*. Retrieved from http://www.downes.ca/cgi-bin/page.cgi?post=33034

Ewbank, A., Carter, H., & Foulger, T. (2008). MySpace dilemmas: Ethical choices for teachers using social networking. In K. McFerrin, R. Weber, R. Carlsen, & D. A. Willis (Eds.), *Proceedings of Society for Information Technology and Teacher Education International Conference 2008* (pp. 2580-2584). Retrieved from http://www.editlib.org/p/27606

Friedman, T. (2005). *The World Is Flat: A Brief History of the Twenty-First Century*. New York, NY: Farrar, Straus, and Giroux.

Greenhow, C., & Robelia, B. (2009). Old communication, new literacies: Social network sites as social learning resources. *Journal of Computer-Mediated Communication*, *14*(4), 1130–1161. .doi:10.1111/j.1083-6101.2009.01484.x

Hargadon, S. (2009). *Educational networking: The important role Web 2.0 will play in education* [Elluminate White Paper]. Pleasanton, CA: Elluminate USA. Retrieved from http://www.elluminate.com/whitepapers/

Hewitt, A., & Forte, A. (2006, November). *Crossing boundaries: Identity management. Student/faculty relationships on the Facebook.* Paper presented at the Computer-supported Cooperative Work Conference, Banff, Alberta, Canada. Retrieved from http://www.cc.gatech.edu/~aforte/HewittForteCSCWPoster2006.pdf

Hill, R. J., Wiley, D., Nelson, L. M., & Han, S. (2004). Exploring research on internet-based learning: From infrastructure to interactions. In D. H. Jonassen (Ed.), *Handbook of research on educational communications and technology* [Questia Media online version] (pp. 433-460). Retrieved from http://www.questia.com

Hogan, B. J. (2009). *Networking in everyday life*. Unpublished doctoral dissertation, University of Toronto. Retrieved from http://individual.utoronto.ca/berniehogan/Hogan_ NIEL_10-29-2008_FINAL.pdf

Horrigan, J. B. (2009, June). *Home broadband adoption 2009* [Research Report No. 202-419-4500]. Retrieved from Pew Internet & American Life Project website: http://www.pewinternet.org

Iiyoshi, T., & Vijay Kumar, M. S. (2008). Introduction. In T. Iiyoshi & M. S. Vijay Kumar (Eds.), *Opening up education: The collective advancement of education through open technology, open content, and open knowledge*. Retrieved from: http://mitpress.mit.edu/ catalog/item/default.asp?ttype=2&tid=11309

Kvavik, R. (2005). Convenience, communications, and control: How students use technology. In D. G. Oblinger & J. L. Oblinger (Eds.), *Educating the net generation*. Boulder, CO: EDUCAUSE. Retrieved from www.educause.edu/educatingthenetgen/

Mazer, J. P., Murphy, R. E., & Simonds, C. J. (2007). I'll see you on "Facebook:" The effects of computer-mediated teacher self-disclosure on student motivation, affective learning, and classroom climate. *Communication Education*, *56*(1), 1–17. doi:10.1080/03634520601009710

Miller, R. (2007). *A new culture needs a new education*. Retrieved from Paths of Learning website: http://www.pathsoflearning.net/articles.php

Nielsen Company. (2010, January 22). *Led by Facebook, Twitter, global time spent on social media sites up 82% year over year* [Web log post]. Nielsen Wire. Retrieved from Nielsen website: http://en-us.nielsen.com/

O'Reilly, T., & Battelle, J. (2009). *Web squared: Web 2.0 five years on*. Retrieved from http://www.web2summit.com/web2009/public/schedule/detail/10194

Oblinger, D. G. (Ed.). (2006). *Learning spaces*. Boulder, CO: EDUCAUSE. Retrieved from http://www.educause.edu/LearningSpaces

Shea, P., & Bidjerano, T. (2008, January). Measures of quality in online education: An investigation of the community of inquiry model and the Net Generation. *Journal of Educational Computing Research*, *39*(4), 339–361. .doi:10.2190/EC.39.4.b

Siemens, G. (2006). *Knowing knowledge* [Creative Commons online version]. Retrieved from http://www.elearnspace.org/KnowingKnowledge_LowRes.pdf

Wesch, M. (2008). Anti-teaching: Confronting the crisis of significance. *Education Canada*, *48*(2), 4–7. Retrieved from http://www.cea-ace.ca/media/en/AntiTeaching_Spring08.pdf.

Wesch, M. (2009, January). From knowledgeable to knowledge-able: Learning in new media environments. Academic Commons. Retrieved July 10, 2009 from http://www.academiccommons.org/commons/essay/knowledgable-knowledge-able

KEY TERMS AND DEFINITIONS

Affordance: A capability that a particular tool offers to individuals who have access to it.

Digitally-Mediated Learning: Education delivery in which interaction among participants, and between participants and learning materials is carried out through the medium of electronic technologies of various types and configurations.

Networked Publics: Virtual and conceptual spaces constructed from networked technologies, and the aggregations of people and activities that occupy these spaces.

Second-Wave E-Learning: Digitally-mediated learning that is characterized by the use of a broad range of user-friendly networked software tools that support multi-modality in expression, communication, and interaction.

Second-Wave Enabled Technology-Enhanced Learning: Learning delivered in and by environments that support second-wave e-learning paradigms and provide multiple means for the enhancement of digitally-mediated individual presence.

Social Media/Social Software: These two terms are used interchangeably in the literature, with the former coming to the forefront in recent years. They refer to networked tools, services, and applications that allow people to participate in digitally-mediated interaction with others, and offer the capability for online creation, contribution, communication, and collaboration on the part of internet users.

Social Network Sites: Web-based services that allow individuals to construct and maintain public or semi-private personal online spaces that present information about themselves, as well as about other people with whom they share a connection.

Chapter 13
Short Message Services for Supporting Student Learning:
A Blended Approach

Dick Ng'ambi
University of Cape Town, South Africa

ABSTRACT

This chapter discusses the blending of anonymous short message services (SMS) with a learning management system (LMS) to support non-traditional postgraduate learners in a block release programme at a higher education institution. The personal ownership of the mobile phone, coupled with its consistent presence and connectivity, was enhanced through the provision of anonymous communication via SMS. The seamless integration allowed for optimal use by learners who had limited access to the LMS but greater access to the mobile device. The mobile phone enhanced with anonymity created a safe learning environment based on andragogical principles. The postgraduate programme made extensive use of the learning management system (LMS). In block release programmes, learners may be distributed in developing countries and have one contact week per module. During both pre and post-contact sessions, learners are located in contexts where mobile connectivity is more guaranteed than Internet access. Most resources are downloaded during the contact week for reading offline. As learners interact with resources they engage in internal dialogue and mobile phones can facilitate a way to artefact internal dialogues through blogging. The use of anonymous communication using SMS creates a safe and equal socially networked knowledge production environment.

INTRODUCTION

Blended learning is an integration (not a layering of one on top of the other) of face-to-face and online learning experiences (Garrison & Kanuka, 2004). It is the combination of conventional teaching approaches and e-learning elements within a single course or programme (Littlejohn & Pegler, 2007).

Among other reasons, the increasing popularity of blended learning can be attributed to the manner in which it opens up educational opportunities to people excluded from accessing

DOI: 10.4018/978-1-60960-479-0.ch013

education. These exclusions are often due to an inflexible academic calendar or time constraints affecting attendance at full-time contact sessions. Ross and Gage (2006) pointed out that combining course and curriculum design with blended models (e.g., technology-supported courses, alternating face-to-face and online class meetings, videoconferencing to multiple class sites, or use of webcams) could increase the number of student enrolments in university programmes. While a focus on increasing enrolment numbers is desirable, the additional challenge of ensuring that learners successfully complete their study programmes within the prescribed time frame has to be considered. These issues and challenges require rethinking both the provision of learner support and design of learning activities in blended programmes particularly in cases where learners are distributed in developing countries that has limited access to Internet but have ubiquitous access to mobile networks. Without Internet access the educational affordances of blended learning cannot be realized. However, mobile learning is providing a new learning experience that is neither face-to-face nor online and is potentially changing the traditional notions of contact education.

The notion of contact education, as opposed to distance education, presupposes increased face-to-face interaction between learners and educators. Traditionally, attendance at a contact learning institution demands that learners physically attend prescribed and pre-registered courses in allocated buildings at specified times. This suggests that traditional contact education is defined in terms of purpose, time, space and distance. The purpose is the underlying agenda set for a particular meeting for example a seminar on teaching with Twitter to be held on Friday 19 November at 12h45-14h00 in the Centre for Educational Technology meeting room. The purpose, date, time and venue are set in advance and the attendees notified. The people go to attend meetings/seminars and meetings/seminars do not go to the people. Contact education is often inflexible, a person can only be at one meeting at a time, a venue can only hold one meeting at a time, and failure to converge and synchronize the date, time and venue could result in a person missing the event. Any change to purpose, date, time and venue needs to be communicated in advance. It is at the convergence of purpose, time, space and distance that face-to-face interaction happens in contact education. Whereas a blended approach based on an integration of mobile phones with LMS seeks to provide flexibility on purpose, time, space and distance. The teaching and learning challenges of non-traditional learners enrolling at a traditional contact institution cannot be addressed using traditional teaching approaches.

In this chapter, non-traditional learners, defined as adult learners not straight from undergraduate degree, who juggle work, family, and education. For these learners work and family is so imbedded that it is not practical to take leave from either to focus on education. These learners work and study full-time and have family responsibilities. Since 2007, the author has convened a postgraduate programme in Educational Technology for non-traditional learners at a contact institution. The programme, which attracts diverse international learners, makes extensive use of a learning management system (LMS) with high differentials of access but all learners had mobile phones for which educational uses were extremely minimal. It was this background that created opportunities to explore ways of blending anonymous short message services (SMS) with LMS to support non-traditional postgraduate learners. Mobile learning has potential to not only enable seamless learning across contexts, but also to mitigate some of the pedagogical challenges of blended courses through its ability to blend formal and informal learning as well as ubiquitous and institutional technologies. This argument is premised on the fact that nearly all students, regardless of their country of residence, either own a mobile phone or have access to one. Henschke (2010) observed that one of the challenges facing higher education institutions in the 21st century is serving the educational needs of a non-traditional population (older than the traditional college age of 18-22) that requires different approaches for fulfilling their educational needs.

In the next section, the educational context in terms of the contact institution, the programme students enrolled in, and the background of learners is described.

EDUCATIONAL CONTEXT

The University of Cape Town (UCT) is a research-led contact university located in Cape Town South Africa. UCT is recognized internationally as Africa's leading research university with more than 21000 students, of which 15000 are undergraduates, 6000 postgraduates and 4000 international students. The university has learners from diverse socio-economic and historical backgrounds with varying degrees of preparedness prior to enrolling to the university. The learning management system, Sakai (locally branded as Vula) was deployed at UCT in 2006. Vula is supported and maintained by the Centre for Educational Technologies (CET) located in the Centre for Higher Education Development (CHED). Vula has an email help desk that supports both staff and students.

The postgraduate programme, co-convened by the School of Education, in the Faculty of Humanities and CET, is geared specifically at people who work, who are intending to move into a work setting where technology is used for teaching and learning. The target market is not limited to educators, but also to those at the fringes of the discipline of Education. The programme also attracts learners with an interest in technical IT skills that work with the end user aspects of software design and the human-machine interface. Such people may already be designing educational software and would be interested in learning about what underlies effective engagement within a software domain. Thus, the programme is aimed at non-traditional learners. While the current offerings in the School of Education specifically target educators in general, this programme is for those who have a specific interest in learning/teaching with ICTs. In order to meet the varying needs of potential learners, prospective learners may enroll for a one-year postgraduate diploma in education (PGDE), which also serves as masters' course work. The second part of the masters' programme involves writing a proposal and conducting an independent study leading to a minor dissertation.

In the last three years (2008, 2009 and 2010), the programme enrolled students from South Africa, Congo DRC, Botswana, Sudan, Zimbabwe, Zambia, Malawi, Nigeria, Mozambique, Uganda and Kenya. The students not only come from geographically diverse countries but also have varied access to Internet and bandwidth. Although reading materials and assignments were delivered via a LMS, lack of bandwidth and intermittent access experienced by some learners made this delivery mode less than ideal. For example, most non-traditional learners work during the week and conduct their studies on the weekend. However access to certain university systems over weekends can be problematic since the ICTS helpdesk only operates during working hours or the server could experience problems over the weekend resulting in limited or unavailable Internet access. These challenges call for a rethink on the realistic delivery modes especially when learners are distributed and technological access is unpredictable.

The challenge therefore lies in how to manage and meet learner expectations driven by diverse reasons for which non-traditional students decide to pursue studies.

LEARNING NEEDS

At the start of the first module, students were assigned a preliminary task to introduce themselves and to explain why they decided to enrol on the programme. The latter was particularly important for gauging student's educational needs. Below are statements from seven of the sixteen learners. The seven statements are chosen because they represent the diversity in the intentions that learners had for undertaking to study.

Student 1: …I chose this course because I am very interested in trying to understand how people use technology and to discover how ICT is used / can be used in the context of education.

Student 2: …I am interested particularly in the psychology of learning in an e-environment and the pedagogy and learner psychosis in an e-learning environment.

Student 3: …I'm interested in finding out why multimedia students - who help create the web - don't use it for learning.

Student 4: …to help sharpen my skills to effectively participate in the on-going e-learning debates that is confronting the Gauteng/ National Department of Education and the rest of the African continent.

Student 5: …I will be fully equipped to teach my colleagues and my subordinates what I have learnt especially as regards the application of technology in processing information.

Student 6: …I would like to apply learned techniques and knowledge to contribute to the development and implementation of ICTs in the education sector.

Student 7: ...I hope that this course will answer most of my questions about online course design, when to use e-learning alone in a course, when to use both and when to use face – to – face method.

The learning needs ascertained from the responses above suggest that students were intentional and had specific learning objectives for enrolling in the programme. These expressions of intent are informed by experience and embedded in context. Ensuring that each student achieved his or her learning intentions was just as important as achieving the learning outcomes of specific modules. This suggests a need for a balance between the autonomy of an adult learner and the teaching to award qualifications. One way of addressing this challenge was to ensure that students created evidence of learning by critically reflecting and maintaining a record of their reflection (artefact).

ARTEFACTING INTERNAL DIALOGUE

While andragogy is premised on increased open learner-educator dialogue, it does not take into account internal dialogue. According to Merriam (2001) andragogy describes the adult learner as someone who (1) has an independent self-concept and who can direct his or her own learning, (2) has accumulated a reservoir of life experiences that is a rich resource for learning, (3) has learning needs closely related to changing social roles, (4) is problem-centered and interested in immediate application of knowledge, and (5) is motivated to learn by internal rather than external factors. It therefore follows that self-directed learning is key in adult learning. However, when the adult learners enroll at traditional institutions, self-directed learning becomes a means to an end as they are expected to follows a pre-defined curriculum with pre-defined learning outcomes. One of the challenges of teaching adult learners in traditional learning settings is the potential for issues of power and control in the class. This is particularly evident when the class is composed of learners holding high and key positions in organizations. These issues of power and control in class tends to have a silencing effect on some voices and a privileging of dominate voices hence making uneven the production of knowledge through unbalanced class participation.

In andragogy, learners rather than a teacher take responsibility for making decisions about what, how, when learning happens and for assessing the extent to which learning has happened. It is in the decision making process that internal dialogue happens. Access to internal dialogue would provide a window to the kind of learning that is taking place and how it can be scaffolded without interfering with self-directed learning. There is therefore a need to create spaces where internal dialogue can be produced as artefacts thereby creating a learning resource based on plethora of internal dialogue. The challenge however, is that an environment for thinking-aloud needs to be safe for adult learners. To this end, anonymity could be used to provide this safety. Anonymity is employed here cautiously, as an effective learning environment need to provide anonymity confined within the bounds of a class. In other words, although anonymous, a user knows that a posting is from a member of the same class but would not know which member sent the message. It follows that adult learners can be empowered to reflect on the meaning making process of their learning, receive feedback on artefacts of internal dialogue without feeling vulnerable and get stimulated to continue learning. Henschke (2010) identified seven key factors in learning programmes that stimulated adult development:

- An environment where students feel safe and supported, where individual needs and uniqueness are honoured, and where abilities and life achievements are acknowledged and respected.
- An environment that fosters intellectual freedom and encourages experimentation and creativity.
- An environment where a faculty treats adult students as peers - where they are accepted and respected as intelligent experienced adults, whose opinions are listened to, honored, and appreciated.
- Self-directed learning, where students take responsibility for their own learning.
- Pacing or intellectual challenge. Optimal pacing challenges people just beyond their present level of ability. If challenged too far beyond, people give up. If challenged too little, they become bored and learn little.
- Active involvement in learning, as opposed to passively listening to lectures.
- Regular feedback mechanism for students to tell faculty what works best for them, what they want and need to learn – and a faculty who hear and make changes based on student input.

The above factors point to the use of andragogy rather than pedagogical approaches to teaching adult learners. Moore (1997) argues that learners are always engaged in internal or silent interaction or virtual dialogue with either an author or presenter. According to Moore, a dialogue is purposeful, constructive and valued by each party. Each party in a dialogue is a respectful and active listener; each is a contributor, and builds on the contributions of the other party or parties. It follows that there are two types of dialogue: the internal 'virtual' dialogue and external 'expressive' dialogue. The two dialogues ought to converse with each other for learning for happen as Sharples et. al., (2007) explain, in order to constitute a 'conversation'; the learner must be able to formulate a description of himself and his actions, explore and extend that description and carry forward the understanding to future activity. They add that, in order to learn, a person or system must be able to converse with itself and others about what it knows. It can be inferred that unless the internal dialogue is artefacted it is difficult for others to engage with it and to track growth in internal conversation over time. Writing is a form of communication that encourages reflection and precision of expression, and when writing is integrated with the rich dynamic of fast-paced, spontaneous verbal communication in a face-to-face learning environment, the educational possibilities increase (Garrison & Kanuka, 2004). Students were required to write a blog daily on their cognitive process. The challenge was how to create a mobile learning environment that exploited the devices that students had access to, provide stimuli for interaction while keeping a trail of the learning process.

MOBILE LEARNING ENVIRONMENT

In Africa, mobile phones are not a status symbol. Mobile phones bridge the digital divide between the technology-haves and the have-nots. Traxler (2009) observes that less privileged individuals are able to access information of their choice using their own devices without needing to accept constraints and conditions historically imposed on them. I infer from Traxler that mobile technologies have an emancipatory effect on less privileged communities and if well exploited could have a transformative effect on learning. To the extent that blended learning could be viewed as empowering learners by widening access to education, the integration of blended and mobile learning has potential of both widening access and enhancing the learning experience. According to Van 'T Hooft (2009), mobility expands learning across space and time and opens many opportunities for learning that is neither sequential nor consistent. This suggests that the blending of sequential with non-sequential, formal with informal, in space with across space, fixed-time with anytime creates new learning opportunities and impacts pedagogical designs. These new learning opportunities must take into account the challenges of having international students attending blended programmes. Biggs (1999) identified three challenges involved in teaching international students:

- **Social-cultural adjustment:** this is the stress that is associated with adjusting to a new culture. Although this is not the responsibility of a teacher, there is an obligation on the university to put in place necessary support.
- **Language:** it is difficult to learn if one is not fluent in the language medium of instruction.
- **Learning/teaching problems due to 'culture':** the cultural background of many international students make it difficult to adapt to the style of tertiary teaching adopted in the host country.

It can be inferred from Biggs that these challenges might affect students' socialization with peers and engagement online. To this end, a mobile learning environment was conceptualized to exploit the affordances of mobile phones owned and used by learners regardless of country with which they move across different contexts. Guided by Henschke's (2010) principles for stimulating learning, anonymity was used to create a mobile learning environment that blends short message services with the learning management system.

- An environment in which learners felt safe to express themselves, to ask and respond to peers' questions without feeling oppressed, domesticated or silenced.
- An environment that encouraged intellectual freedom to 'think-aloud', 'try-out' new things and reflect on lessons learnt.
- An environment in which the psychological distance between knowledgeable others (peers and experts) is reduced.
- An environment in which learners are equal partners in knowledge production

These characteristics augment curricula, andragogical approaches, and Henschke's seven principles that stimulate adult learning. Mobile learning has potential for interconnecting learning spaces; work, home, face-to-face, personal workspaces and learning management systems. It was therefore imperative that connectivity be used for interaction while supporting mobility of learners.

BLENDING CONNECTIVITY, INTERACTIVITY AND MOBILITY

Internal dialogue is both a cognitive activity and an outcome of reflection. Through internal dialogue, knowledge is constructed and deconstructed. The inputs to internal dialogue are not limited to external stimuli such as reading, listening and observing but also interaction with others. Internal dialogue is therefore more than knowledge acquisition or knowledge creation. In blending mobile phones with LMS, a learning environment that exploits connectivity and interactivity is created. In such an environment, members both support and sustain, elicit from, expand on each other's learning inputs, contributions, and products (Davidson & Goldberg, 2009). Hakkarainen (2009) identified three generations of technology-enhanced learning, the knowledge-acquisition generation, the participation generation and the knowledge-creation generation. According to Hakkarainen, the first generation is based on cognitive (knowledge acquisition) perspective; the second on social-cultural (participation) and the newer generation (the third) is aimed at overcoming the dichotomy between the cognitive and social-cultural perspectives. The portability and versatility of mobile devices, if exploited, has the potential to cause a pedagogical shift from didactic teacher-centered (knowledge acquisition – first generation) to participatory student-centered learning (encompassing both second and third generation) (Looi et. al., 2010) in an embedded learning context. Embedded learning argues that the closer a person is to needing to know something so that they can perform a task, the higher the motivation to learn. Technology and new delivery options provide access to information in the context of an individual's role, task and time available (DeViney & Lewis, 2006). It then follows that, the newer generation of technology-enhanced learning will exploit learner connectivity, interactivity and mobility to create seamless and safe embedded learning spaces across diverse contexts (Biggs, 1999; Davidson & Goldberg, 2009; DeViney & Lewis, 2006; Hakkarainen, 2009; Henschke, 2010; Looi, 2010; Sharples et. al., 2007; Traxler, 2009). The challenge with creating seamless learning spaces is that private and public spaces become blurred.

SEAMLESS INTEGRATION OF PRIVATE & PUBLIC SPACES

The seamless integration of individual learning that happens in private learning spaces (mobile learning), collaborative learning that happens in public learning spaces (learning management systems) and cognitive artefacts created across time in both physical and virtual spaces (Looi et. al., 2010) are an effective implementation model. The environment becomes seamless when the contributions from both private and public learning spaces are anonymised. In private learning spaces, conversation is with self (internal), mediated either podcasts or learning resources and expressed through interaction with a mobile phone. In public learning spaces, conversation takes the form of interacting with peers and educator expressed verbally and artefacted through blog entries and/or podcast. However, rather than create environments where students feel invaded in their private spaces, the mobile phone could be used as an option extension of the LMS. However, the term option presupposes freedom of choice, but for most of our students the choice was limited because they had more access to mobile phones than Internet.

INTERFACING MOBILITY WITH LMS

One of the criticisms of LMS is that it is generally used to prescribe the pace and sequence by which materials are accessed. The web environment or LMS encourages teachers to place the content into a weekly reading list or modules, moving in a linear pattern through a semester (Herrington et. al., 2005). The resources were structured in sessions e.g. Session #1: Introduction; Section #2: Disruptive Technologies, etc. The effect of this structure was that the products (i.e. artefacts) from each session, in particular podcasts, were associated with particular sessions. A day had an average of three sessions sandwiched with group work or discussion groups. The report back sessions from group work and discussions generated podcasts. Learners reflected on each day and podcasts served as a useful tool for scaffolding the making of a blog entry. There were three ways that learners used podcasts; (i) downloaded to a portable device for subsequent playback at a time and place of learner's convenience; (ii) downloaded to a flash drive for playback on a standalone machine; (iii) used a headset to listen directly at a point of access to the LMS.

In the next section, a blended approach for using SMS to support student learning is discussed followed by examples of how the model has been used.

IMPLEMENTATION MODEL OF BLENDED MOBILE LEARNING WITH LMS

The blended implementation model of mobile learning with LMS is located at the convergence of public and private space; mobile phone and LMS; and andragogy and pedagogy. A model for blending mobile learning with a learning management system for postgraduate non-traditional learners incorporates andragogical principles for creating a safe discursive environment with the pedagogy. The augmentation of mobility, connectivity and privacy of a mobile phone with anonymity creates a safe discursive environment in which interactivity is increased and internal dialogue artefacted. The LMS was a key pedagogical tool as it served both as a channel for disseminating learning resources and as a space for interaction with resources and knowledgeable peers. The meaning making process involved internal dialogue whose outcome was captured in a blog tool provided in the LMS. The resources placed in the LMS and the subsequent lectures were generated as podcasts which saw the LMS acting as a podcast server. Learners either subscribed to the podcasts via an RSS feed or downloaded podcasts directly from the LMS onto their mobile devices. While the LMS is an institutional tool, hence a public space, mobile devices are owned by students and therefore located in the private space. The mobile phones provide an anywhere anytime connectedness. Some students may also use mobile phones to connect to a public space (i.e. LMS) to interact with peers, educators and content. Figure 1 depicts the implementation model.

The learning resources are uploaded onto a LMS that serves as both a public as well as a private learning space. When a course site is created in the LMS, students registered for the course are automatically imported from the university's student administration system and become participants of the course site. An email account is automatically created for all registered students and it is this email that is used as default email for the LMS. All correspondence from the LMS to students is sent to the institutional student email address. When resources are posted on the LMS, an email notification is generated and sent to students' institutional email addresses. Most adult students have a minimum of two email addresses already; a work email and a private email addresses. This means that students already separate business from private work. Thus, the institutional email that is associated with the LMS becomes a third or fourth email address. As a consequence of this, students do not often access the LMS prior to attending the first contact session because they would not have seen or be aware of an institutional email address. It follows that the pre-session interaction with resources and peers through the LMS is limited before the first contact session. This challenge can be resolved through texting/SMSing to students through the LMS. In

Figure 1. Blended approach for using SMS for learning

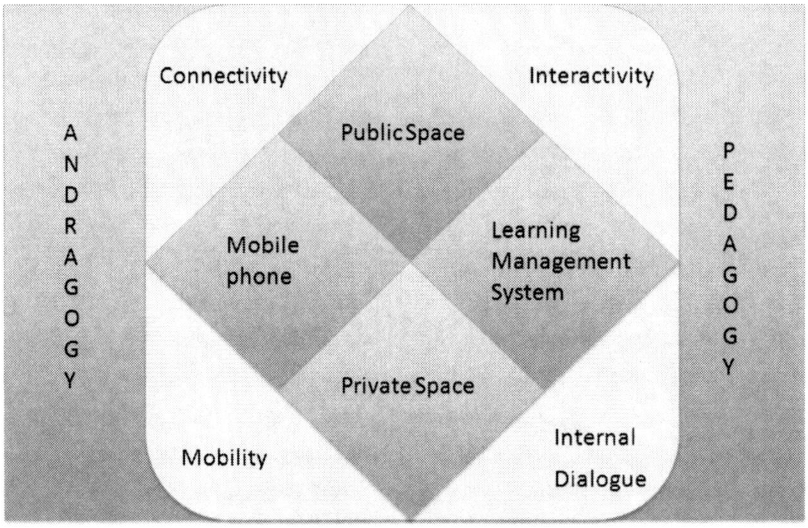

this case, the mobile phone, which is a student's private space, is used to invite students to interact in a public space. The mobility of students, and the extent to which mobile phones accompanied students all the time, meant that messages sent to the mobile phone were more likely to be seen than an email (unless the emails are received on a mobile phone, a service only available on expensive phones). When students finally access the LMS, learning tasks are designed such that students are expected to reflect (internal dialogue). Although students are expected to be self-directed learners, learning tasks are designed with specific learning outcomes (pedagogy). The LMS tools such as blogs are used to artefact students' internal dialogues. Students engaged with two types of blogs: public blogs (visible to the whole class) and private blog (visible only to the site owner – the course convener). The class comments on public blogs while private blogs provide a safe space for students to comment on their learning and anything course related.

Interactivity is conceptualized to include student engagement with reading resources in the LMS, attending lecture presentations, engagement in class discussions, group tasks and student seminars. These activities generate podcasts that are uploaded onto the LMS. Like all resources, the LMS has an option to trigger an email notification to participants about the newly uploaded resource. Due to the varying degrees of access to the Internet when away from the institutional campus, students download the podcasts to mobile devices and/or mobile phones. These class podcasts are examples of resources generated and available in the closed public space and used in a private space. Some podcasts are downloaded from the Internet (public space), remixed and uploaded in the LMS or downloaded to mobile devices. Students then choose a convenient time and space to listen to the podcast. Listening to podcasts triggers internal dialogue or reflection, which is further blogged on. In order for reflections to be effective, listening to podcasts is often done when students are in isolation and in quiet environments. During this time, questions that arise from listening to podcasts are texted/SMSed to the Q&A tool in the LMS. The value of this is that students who might be in the LMS at the time, could respond to the question in the LMS and the Q&A tool sends the response to the author of the question. In this way, the mobile phone is blended in the LMS. To the extent that the Q&A tool does not publish name nor the mobile number of the origin of the contribution, the interaction is anonymised and safe for both the author and the respondent. While interaction with a Q&A tool is one way of artefacting internal dialogue, another is through collaborative memos. These memos, short study notes, are generated either when a student is listening to podcast or engaging with other resources in the LMS. Students use mobile phones to send notes to a shared number for subsequent searching and retrieval via SMS.

The "always" connectedness of the mobile phones sandwiched between student mobility and interactivity is an indispensible environment for encouraging reflective learning through internal dialogue. When augmented with LMS, and careful rethinking of pedagogy, the affordances of this blended mobile learning environment could be enormous. The fact that students own mobile phones, use of the device in this manner by educators requires consent from the student. To this end, rather than sending messages to students' handsets, the virtual noticeboard provides a way of placing important notices on this board for students to retrieve using their mobile phones on demand. The advantage of the virtual noticeboard is that students with access to the LMS do not need to use a mobile phone to read the announcement especially when the virtual noticeboard is integrated with the LMS.

In the next section, examples of SMS uses to support student learning are discussed.

SHORT MESSAGE SERVICES (SMS) IN LMS

The SMS tool of the LMS allows students to send text messages to a mobile phone from the LMS. The sender has an option to restrict the message to users with particular roles e.g. site owners, participants or support. Alternatively a sender may paste a list of mobile numbers into the tool. The messages can also be scheduled to go out at a later date and time. Mobile phones are personal devices owned by learners and it is therefore important to give learners a choice to unsubscribe should they no longer wish to receive messages on their handsets. The LMS provided an option for users to unsubscribe. Another important consideration is that the mobile numbers are not matched to the user's name. The purpose of the SMS tool is to push messages from the LMS to students' handset. Messages sent from the SMS tool cannot be responded to.

Unlike the SMS tool, the Question & Answer tool (Q&A tool) is a bidirectional tool (sends out messages and receives messages). The Q&A tool allows users to send questions to the course site anonymously (the message is published and not the author's name or the mobile phone number). The purpose of anonymity is to ensure a safe environment for learners to express themselves without feeling suppressed or silenced. The context of work and education were so intertwined for most learners that learning had to make sense in the context of their work. The following posting in the Q&A tool illustrates this:

I don't want to sound ignorant, but I am when it comes to cell phones (don't like them, sorry Dr Dick ;-)). How does one get a gmail account - the gmail website is not very informative. Should we choose the webmail option?

The question shows the learner was not afraid to expose his/her ignorance or to think-aloud. The statement suggests that the learner was engaged in internal dialogue with self. Typical of adult learners, they would not want to publicly sound 'stupid' and ridicule themselves. The question was posted after a presentation on mobile learning and which demonstrated various possibilities of mobile technologies in education. The first response came from another learner who was an educator by profession:

An interesting thought:-) I agree that cellphones are not likable by everyone. The irony is that students like them a lot and also find them as indispensible. For interests sake, how did you start disliking cellphones? what happened?

In providing this response, the respondent seems to have been careful to ensure that the views of the author of the question were respected. It was comforting to know that not everyone liked cellphones but found it ironic that someone should dislike a device that is likable by many. However, the response ended with a question, which suggested that external dialogue was being encouraged. The author responded:

Thanks for the reply...I don't like cellphones because of the interference factor and because it's very time consuming in my line of work. I deal with about 100 companies and that many students in one year. Getting up to 9 missed calls in one hour from one student (especially over weekends) or countless SMS's is not fun. Fortunately more and more students have gmail, so I can use my e-mail and ten fingers to respond to their messages ;-)

The advantages of cellphones is the always connectedness regardless of the changing context of users. This connectedness provides a user with freedom to choose when to use the device. In making a voice call, for example, the caller and the one being called (the callee) should both have their mobile phones switched on. This means there is a convergence of time though space and distance of both the caller and the callee is theoretically immaterial. The absence of a way of knowing whether the 'callee' is available to receive a call such as is the case with social presence indicators in Instant Messaging software; there is no guarantee that the calls will always be successful. However, to the extent that SMS is asynchronous, the receiver does not need to have the device switched to receive a message as messages that find a mobile device off is held in a queue at the Short Message Control Centre (SMCC). The SMCC is responsible for delivery of the message as soon as the device is switched on. SMS is more likely to reach the intended target audience (students) than email. Needless to say, an increasing number of young people rarely read emails and should an email be sent to them, the sender is expected to send a follow-up SMS alerting them to check their email boxes. As the response below suggests, cellphones are ubiquitous and convenient devices:

Cell phones are interesting devices but I could understand your lack of interest. Even with your line of business I think they are great companions and for educators they are helpful in promoting and management of students learning and evaluation. Because they are handy learners of today prefer them as it could provide on the go information and opportunities for sharing even in 'difficulty places'. I think the trend in our technology driven society is very compelling and we could only need to re-adjust to the changing times.

While taking cognizance of expressed misgivings, the above statement focuses on the positive uses of cellphones and observes that rather than fighting the technology, it must be embraced because we are living in a technology driven society. It is becoming a common practice for people to either have two or more cellphones or sim cards, one for private use and the other for business.

I actually have 2 cellphones ;-)! One work, one private. Can't do without it when I need to contact students to organise interviews and to remind them of important classes. And I use it for photo's and video's. So yes, they can be useful...

It can be inferred that learners seek to be autonomous and to be in control of both the information they receive and the devices they use.

The anonymous Q&A can also be used for obtaining feedback from learners. The integration of anonymity with the privacy of a mobile device allows users to feel safe and confident to be expressive on both content and administrative issues of the course. Teaching adult learners is like teaching colleagues and it is sometimes difficult to give honest feedback especially if such feedback in negative. The use of anonymous SMS empowers learners to give honest feedback. It is no longer necessary to wait until the end of the programme to get feedback from learners and because feedback is timely it can be used to benefit the current cohort of learners. This is particularly important in block release modules because the contact time with learners is short and there is no time to defer decisions. Learners spend most of the time studying in isolation during the pre and post contact week so the time spent together with learners needs to be optimized. Mobile phones are used to capture the views of the learners about course content and can also be used to reinforce important points of the learning activity.

VIRTUAL NOTICEBOARD

Mobile phones have changed the notions of being online and offline. When learners are offline, they are still connected on mobile phones and therefore rarely go offline. The seamless integration of the mobile phones with the web, is an effective way of blending 'being online' and being 'connected'. Unless the site is cached, LMS, is inaccessible when offline. In contexts where Internet access is intermittent and electricity is unstable, dependence on the LMS for delivery of notices to students does not work. The use of a virtual noticeboard provides a ways of ensuring that messages such as important announcement are placed in both the LMS and on a virtual noticeboard. Messages posted on the virtual noticeboard can be retrieved using a mobile phone regardless of whether a user in online or offline. For example, to retieve a message from a course site, a user sends the message: *Edn6099-news*. The Q&A, a tool within an LMS, allows users to SMS questions and online users are able to read the postings through LMS. When offline, users with WAP enabled mobile phones and Smartphones, are able to access the LMS on the mobile handset. However, the majority of users do not have Smartphones, and the integration with the web could be through text messaging. A virtual noticeboard is not a tool in Vula but is implemented in a tool called the Dynamic Frequently Asked Questions (DFAQ), developed by the author and allows authorized users to post messages to the noticeboard using SMS and other users retrieve latest messages by sending an SMS to the noticeboard. Another example of this integration is the microblogging. In microblogging, users can send an image or video clip to a blog. The user, if desired can later edit the mobile blog entries.

COLLABORATIVE MOBILE MEMOS

Collaborative mobile memos is a shared repository where learners post brief study notes for subsequent retrieval when needed. As students study, the study notes are continuously sent to the repository. The memos in the collaborative mobile repository can be searched and retrieved by sending a keyword a short code. Example: *Edn6099-memo heart...an important body organ*. By posting memos a knowledge resources is created which is searchable. Example: *Edn6099-memo heart? OR Edn6099-memo important body?*

A related use of collaborative mobile memos is building a resource of acronyms. In technical fields such as computer science or information systems, students are overwhelmed by the number of acroynms that they need to know. Collaborative mobile memos provide a shared space for learners to deposit meanings to various acroynms and be able to retrieve them via SMS. It follows that not understanding an acronym could stand in the way of a student mastering the learning material and this problem is compounded when learners study in isolation as is the case in block release programmes. In order to address these problems, learners write down descriptions of acronyms as they study. Thus, collaborative mobile memos exploit connectivity to both post and retrieve, interactivity by way of searching the repository and mobility which allows use on demand regardless of changing context. The mobile memos feature supports dynamic creation and spontaneous acronym look-ups. Learners use their mobile phones to create shared glossaries that are searchable using keywords in the description.

COLLABORATIVE-NETWORKED LEARNING

Mobile phones enable socially networked collaborative learning. This type of learning involves creating a task that encourages cooperation, interactivity and social engagement. The task, which requires use of mobile phones, is pedagogically grounded in teaching critical reading skills, interrogation of a reading or collaborative thinking. For example, in the EDN6099 course, a task or reading is assigned a number e.g. 111. The users are required to contribute either in the form of a response to a question or a comment on a presented idea. Working independently, each learner is asked to use their mobile phones and text their contribution. In practice, the educator will create a topic by texting a short code e.g. prefix a message with a course code, edn6099 followed by a text. *Edn6099 Welcome 2 mobile learning.* The tool assigns the task a number, for example, 111. Learners are given the number 111 and asked to post their comments to that specified code. Learners might post: *Edn6099-111 + we r explorn & pushn boundries*

Edn6099-111 + g8 but y don't we c this? The '+' tells that tool to append the message to task 111. This tool extends the limitations of the 160 characters of the SMS as it allows a user to add to the message. It is an effective way of gathering student opinions on an issue or contribution or feedback etc. In one of the uses of the tool in a postgraduate class, a task was created which required students to decide how they wanted the class to spend a Friday afternoon and to motive why. In a space of 10 minutes, student views were gathered beamed to the class for all to see. All contributions were anonymised though students could see their individual views. A decision was immediately reached and the contributions served as a record of the process. In a health sciences first year class, the class was asked whether it was morally right for doctors to charge patients for their services. In order to ensure that every student's voice was heard, a task was created, assigned a number and invited contributions from the students. Other uses included use of the tool to get feedback from students on their learning.

PODCAST-MEDIATED REFLECTION

Learning is a reflective process and without reflection, learning cannot take place. However, reflecting on an article is a process of interrogation of text through questions. In essence, the reader 'interacts' with a distant author and attempts to make meaning. The context of a reader is influenced by the task at hand and the social structures on a readers mind. It means that reflection does not happen in a vacuum, the reader brings what they know, to understand what they need to know. Both when reading an article and listening to a presentation, a learner is in a continuous state of linking between the known with the need to know. An event such as listening to a lecture is a useful trigger for reflection. However, there is no time for reflection during a lecture. Learners take notes to help them reflect on a lecture later. Thus facilitating reflection through podcasts has potential for enhancing the learning experience.

Guest lecture podcasts were designed for reuse and involved a single session. Student seminars were recorded as single sessions with multiple presentations. Although the student seminars had an informal feel so as to help students relax, discussions were serious and podcasted.

A lecture is recorded and the audio files are converted to common formats such as mp3 and uploaded on to the LMS. Using tools like iTunes, learners subscribe to the LMS podcast feed, sync the iPod or mp3 player and they have the podcast on a handheld device. Once on a handheld device, learners are able to re-live a lecture at their convenience and reflect. During such reflection, learners are isolated from both peers and teaching staff. Should a need arise where they need to ask questions, the mobile phone is used to SMS the Q&A tool. In addition, learners use blogs to keep an online reflection journal.

During the contact week, several podcasts were generated from guest lecturers, student seminars, group discussions and group task report back sessions. Although there were other artefacts, such as notes, mindmaps and power points, podcasts were the only media that captured narrative details. The LMS served as a podcast server on which the audio files were uploaded to generate podcasts. With the use of different aggregators, learners subscribed to the course RSS feed and received podcasts as soon as they were published. Through listening to podcasts students were able to re-live the face-to-face engagement, reflect on issues of the day, and post their reflections in a blog. To this end, podcasts served this mediation role to support reflection. Another value for podcasts arose during the post-contact week when learners work independently on a scholarly essay, which was a deliverable for the course.

DISCUSSION

Although adult learners enrolling on the postgraduate programme can direct his or her own learning, has life-round experiences with learning needs closely related to their changing social roles and are intrinsically motivated to learn, they need more structure to ensure that effective learning happens. The extent to which the programme is offered in block format, which is deliberately planned to take place during vacations make access to higher education possible to non-traditional students. The block release format is planned such that pre-contact week interaction is mediated via the LMS but access to the LMS at this point is uneven. Accessing the LMS from some parts of Africa is difficult. Learners may experience either power failures or unreliable Internet service providers that may take hours and sometimes days to restore. LMS tend to be teacher-centric while mobile learning is learner-centric. Thus the blending of LMS with mobile learning is the blending of teacher-centric and learner-centric perspectives. In both environments, internal dialogue maybe triggered differently.

As students get more distributed in different parts of Africa, the challenges of access to the Internet and hence the LMS increases. This is further compounded by the lack of a single mobile network in Africa and therefore there are no standardized connectivity rates for the continent. The Internet access in many parts of Africa is expensive and most students cannot afford it. Even when students are in the same country (for example two of the students are based in Nigeria), interactivity between them is a challenge.

The contact week becomes an opportunity for socialization, engagement with learning resources, creation of 'take-away' resources such as podcasts, downloading of resources for offline reading, artefacting internal dialogues (blogging) and building of trust between one another. Once trust is built, the public and private spaces begin to collapse and students become 'friends'. Despite the convergence of these spaces, students respect their privacy. This is manifested through their decisions on when to use a private or public space. The use of mobile phone as a learning tool is enhanced through trust. It is this trust that is drawn upon during anonymous interaction. For example, students were selective as to whom they shared their private phone numbers, and their Skype id.

This suggests that student private spaces may be unavailable for teaching and learning unless by mutual consent.

The internal dialogue is a cognitive process that happens in a private space (cognitive mental space). In the absence of a 'window' into the cognitive space, it is difficult to gauge what is being learnt and how it is being learnt. While embracing the principles of andragogy, the incorporation of a learning requirement for daily blogging in a private space (an area visible only to the educator/site owner) of the LMS provides access to the internal dialogue in safe environment. The use of microblogging, where mobile phones are used to write to a blog in the LMS ensures that artefacting of internal dialogue is also mediated by the mobile phone. To the extent that microblogging provides a way of transforming a cognitive activity into an artefact accessible by many in the LMS, microblogging is an example where a mobility-connectivity-interactivity-internal dialogue cycle is completed. Microblogs presupposes that a user will revisit the blog post and potentially edit it to make it more meaningful. This means that for students who do not have access to the Internet this refinement of the microblog post may not happen in time.

For example, the use of a forum to post self-introductions, allowed learners to carefully consider the type of information that they were prepared to share with the 'unknown' audience and what that audience would think about them. Learners were therefore isolated both physically and epistemologically despite access to the LMS. The educator pre-selected the readings and posted them in the LMS. Learners were expected to engage with the resources. It follows that access to the LMS alone was an insufficient precondition for internal dialogue. An internal dialogue is an outcome of active listening or reading. The contact-week was a socialization phase, learners engaged with the LMS, with peers and teaching staff. The lecture presentations and group discussions generated podcasts that were downloaded to handheld devices for listening offline. Through listening to podcasts internal dialogue is triggered, and resulting questions are reflective, and when a mobile phone is used to SMS a question, internal dialogue is artefacted. Until internal dialogue is artefacted it is difficult to know whether it has occurred, and what form it takes. The post-contact phase involves researching and writing a scholarly article. During this phase learners continue socializing using instant messaging (IM), looking up the virtual noticeboard for course news, and re-live some lectures by listening to podcasts. Internal dialogue is not time and space dependent and can also happen with a trigger.

CONCLUSION

The chapter has discussed how anonymous SMS were seamlessly integrated with an institutional learning management system to create a blended mobile environment based on andragogical principles. Using a postgraduate programme at a contact higher educational institution that is grappling with an increasing demand of access to higher education by non-traditional students, the limitations of current structures and the affordances of emerging technologies to alleviate the challenges has been explored. Due to the always-connectedness of mobile phones, and the availability of the resources through the LMS, learners engage with the resources with an awareness that contact with knowledgeable others is possible via a mobile phone should a need arise. The LMS serves as an intermediary communication proxy for the class. The LMS is a public learning space, a socialization space, and a communication space. The mobile phone is a private learning space, a socialization space and a communication space. The value of blending mobile learning with LMS is that these spaces converge thereby optimising connectivity, interactivity, mobility and internal dialogue. To this end, the following is recommended:

Interactivity: via Learning Management System

LMS is an institutional public space with potential for use as a learning space, social space and a communication space. As a learning space, the use of the LMS should not be limited to it being used as a resource distribution channel. The resources placed on the LMS must be accompanied by tasks that trigger internal dialogue. As a consequence of the rich work experience that adult learners bring to the class, tasks should be designed to require students to draw from their experiences and these tend to trigger internal dialogue. As tools for interaction, it bridges the public with private tools (such as mobile phones) to maximize interaction.

Connectivity: Mobile Phone Interface to LMS

Access to the LMS presupposes access to the Internet. Do not assume that students access and read emails. Mobile phone connectivity is more guaranteed in many parts of the continent than Internet connectivity. On the first instance, obtain students mobile phone numbers and seek permission to use the students private device for educational purposes (this is usually not denied). Let students know the class short code number (a mobile phone number that links to the LMS). This number is required for Q&A, virtual noticeboard, collaborative memos etc. Assign students a small test task to ensure that the class is on the same page.

Mobility: Mobile Phone for Artifacting Internal Dialogue

Assume that students are mobile and always have their mobile phones with them. Create ways that students can post thoughts/ ideas anytime anywhere. Ensure that a safe think-aloud environment is created where students are stimulated to post ideas, questions, give and receive feedback. Adult learners welcome opportunities to comment on peers' work and this must be encouraged. Ensure that an artifact of such engagement becomes a resource for the class.

Internal Dialogue: Access to a Cognitive Process

Encourage discursive engagement that facilitates artifacting of cognitive processes. Despite the always connectedness of the mobile phone, interactivity mediated by the LMS and availability of tools such as the Q&A, virtual noticeboards etc there is no guarantee that students will blog about their cognitive processes daily. Ensure that maintaining a daily online journal is part of the course. This brings the activity to the centre rather than as a peripheral optional activity.

REFERENCES

Biggs, J. (1999). *Teaching for quality learning at university. Society for Research into Higher Education (SRHE)*. Buckingham, UK: Open University Press, State.

Davidson, N. C., & Goldberg, T. D. (2009). *The future of learning institutions in a digital age*. Cambridge, MA: MIT Press.

DeViney, N., & Lewis, J. N. (2006). On-demand learning. In Bonk, J. C., & Graham, R. C. (Eds.), *The handbook of blended learning* (pp. 491–501). John Wiley & Sons.

Garrison, R. D., & Kanuka, H. (2004). Blended learning: Uncovering its transformative potential in higher education. *The Internet and Higher Education*, *7*, 95–105. doi:10.1016/j.iheduc.2004.02.001

Hakkarainen, K. (2010). Three generations of technology-enhanced learning. *British Journal of Educational Technology*, *40*(5), 879–888. doi:10.1111/j.1467-8535.2008.00873.x

Henschke, J. A. (2010). Bringing together personal learning, higher education institutions elements, and global support for a re-orientation towards a focus on lifelong learning and education. In Wang, V. (Ed.), *Encyclopedia for using technology in adult and career education*. Hershey, PA: IGI Global. doi:10.4018/9781616929060.ch063

Herrington, J., Reeves, C. T., & Oliver, R. (2005). Online learning as information delivery: Digital myopia. *Journal of Interactive Learning Research*, *16*(4), 353–367.

Littlejohn, A., & Pegler, C. (2007). *Preparing for blended e-learning*. London, UK: Routledge.

Looi, C., Seow, P., Zhang, B., So, H., Chen, W., & Wong, L. (2010). Leveraging mobile technology for sustainable seamless learning: A research agenda. *British Journal of Educational Technology*, *41*(2), 154–169. doi:10.1111/j.1467-8535.2008.00912.x

Merriam, B. S. (2001). Andragogy and self-directed learning: Pillars of adult learning theory. Retrieved 17 June, 2010, from www.fsu.edu/~elps/ae/download/ade5385/Merriam.pdf

Mezirow, J. (2000). *Learning as transformation: Critical perspectives on a theory in progress*. Jossey-Bass.

Ross, B., & Gage, K. (2006). Global perspectives on blending learning. In Bonk, J. C., & Graham, R. C. (Eds.), *The handbook of blended learning* (pp. 155–168). John Wiley & Sons.

Sharples, M., Taylor, J., & Vavoula, G. (2007). A theory of learning for the mobile age. In Andrews, R., & Haythornthwaite, C. (Eds.), *The SAGE handbook of e-learning research* (pp. 122–138). London, UK: SAGE Publications.

Traxler, J. (2009). Mobile learning evaluation: The challenge of mobile societies. In Vavoula, G., Pachler, N., & Kukulska-Hulme, A. (Eds.), *Researching mobile learning* (pp. 151–165). International Academic Publishers.

Van 'T Hooft. M. (2009). Researching informal and mobile learning: Leveraging the right resources. In G. Vavoula, N. Pachler & A. Kukulska-Hulme (Eds.), *Researching mobile learning* (pp. 170-180). International Academic Publishers.

ADDITIONAL READING

Ng'ambi, D. (2006a). Collaborative Questioning: a case of Short Message Services (SMS) for knowledge sharing. In Kinshuk., R. Koper., P. Kommers., P. Kirrchner., D. G. Sampson., & W. Didderen. (Eds.), *Sixth International Conference on Advanced Learning Technologies* (pp. 350-351). IEEE Computer Society.

Ng'ambi, D. (2006b). SMS Collaborative Questioning: convergence of task, interactivity and outcomes. In P. Isaias., P. Kommers., & I. A. Sanchez. (Eds.), *IADIS International Conference on Mobile Learning* (pp. 26-33). International Association for Development of the Information Society (IADIS).

Ng'ambi, D. (2008). Podcasts for reflective learning. In Salmon, G., & Edirisingha, P. (Eds.), *Podcasting for Learning in Universities* (pp. 132–145). Open University Press.

KEY TERMS AND DEFINITIONS

Artefact: A persistent evidence of students' work which include an online journal, or a podcast or anything that can serve as evidence of work.

Artefacting: A verb used to describe the process of creating an artefact.

Non-Traditional Student: An adult learner not straight from undergraduate who juggles work, family and education at the same time.

Short Message Service (SMS): Also known as texting all mobile phones have this feature and is the most widely used mobile facility in the world including students.

Compilation of References

AAMC Institute for Improving Medical Education. (2007). *Effective use of educational technology in medical education* (p. 3). Washington, DC: Association of American Medical Colleges.

Ackay, H., Durmaz, A., Tuysuz, C., & Feyzioglu, B. (2006). Effects of computer based learning on students' attitudes and achievements towards analytical chemistry. *The Turkish Online Journal of Educational Technology*, *5*(6), 44–48.

Adams, J. (2008). Understanding the factors limiting the acceptability of online courses and degrees. *International Journal on ELearning, 7*(4), 573-587. (Document ID: 1580113111).

Aderinoye, R. A., Ojokheta, K. O., & Olojede, A. A. (2007). Integrating mobile learning into nomadic education programmes in Nigeria: Issues and perspectives. *The International Review of Research in Open and Distance Learning, 8*(2). Retrieved May 5, 2010, from http://www.irrodl.org/index.php/irrodl/article/view/347

Adler, M. (1984). *The Paideia program: An educational syllabus*. New York, NY: MacMillan.

Akhahowa, A. E., & Osubor, V. I. (2006). E-learning: A technology-based teaching method for providing access to sustainable quality education. *The African Symposium, 6*(3&4), 17-25.

Aladejana, F. (2007). Blended learning and improved biology teaching in the Nigerian secondary schools. *Proceedings of the World Congress on Engineering and Computer Science 2008 WCECS 2008*, October 22 - 24, 2008, San Francisco, USA.

Albrecht, B. (2006). Enriching student experience through blended learning. *Educause Center for Applied Research, 12*, 1–12.

Allen, I. E., & Seaman, J. (2010). *Learning on demand: Online education in the United States, 2009*. Retrieved January 26, 2010 from http://www.sloan-c.org/publications/survey/pdf/learningondemand.pdf

Ambivalence. (2010, May 14). In *Wikipedia, the free encyclopedia*. Retrieved May 24, 2010, from http://en.wikipedia.org/wiki/Ambivalence

Aminifar, E., Porter, A., Caladine, R., & Nelson, M. I. (2007). Creating mathematical learning resources-combining audio and visual components. *Australian and New Zealand Industrial and Applied Mathematical Journal*, *47*, C934–C955.

Anderson, T. (2008). Social software technologies in distance education: Maximizing learning freedoms. In Evans, T., Haughey, M., & Murphy, D. (Eds.), *International handbook of distance education* (pp. 167–184). West Anglia, UK: Emerald Group Publishing.

Anderson, T. (2005). *Distance learning–social software's killer app?* Retrieved from http://auspace.athabascau.ca:8080/dspace/

Anglogold, A. (2004) *Report to society*. Retrieved August 2009, from http://www.anglogoldashanti.co.za/subwebs/InformationForInvestors/ReportToSoceity04/values b us principles/community/c cs sa 7 9.htm

Arcos, F., Amilburu, A., & Ortega, P. (2008). *The language blend*. INTED2008. International Technology, Education and Development Conference, (pp. 1-10).

Ariadurai, S., & Manohantha, R. (2008). Reasons for student discontinuation in engineering degree courses offered at a distance. *The Turkish Online Journal of Educational Technology*, *9*(3), 74–86.

ARIS. (2008). *About ARIS. ARIS – Mobile learning experiences*. Retrieved from http://arisgames.org/

Aronson, E., & Patnoe, S. (1997). *The jigsaw classroom: Building cooperation in the classroom* (2nd ed.). New York, NY: Longman.

Asian Development Bank. (2008). *Education and skills: Strategies for accelerated development in Asia and the Pacific*. (pp. 1-134). ISBN: 978-971-561-702-4. Retrieved on April 15, 2010 from http://www.adb.org/Documents/Studies/Education-Skills-Strategies-Development/

Association of Faculties of Medicine of Canada. (2010). *Future of medical education in Canada*. AFMC.

Atkinson, R. C., & Shiffrin, R. M. (1968). Human memory: A proposed system and its control processes. In Spence, K. W., & Spence, J. T. (Eds.), *The psychology of learning and motivation* (*Vol. 2*, pp. 89–195). New York, NY: Academic Press.

Austin, H., Dwyer, B., & Freebody, P. (2003). *Schooling the child: The making of students in classrooms*. London, UK / New York, NY: Routledge Falmer.

Ayo, C. K., Akinyemi, I. O., Adebiyi, A. A., & Ekong, U. O. (2006). The prospects of e-commerce implementation in Nigeria. *Turkish Online Journal of Distance Education*, *8*(4), 125–134.

Azuma, R. (1997). A survey of augmented reality. *Presence (Cambridge, Mass.)*, *6*(4), 355–385.

Badat, S. (2005). South Africa: Distance higher education policies for access, social equity, quality, and social and economic responsiveness in a context of the diversity of provision. *Distance Education*, *26*(2), 183–204. doi:10.1080/01587910500168843

Baddeley, A. (2003). Working memory: Looking back and looking forward. *Nature Reviews. Neuroscience*, *4*, 829–839. doi:10.1038/nrn1201

Badenhorst, J. J. C., & de Beer, K. J. (2004). Blended learning at the Central University of Technology, Free State. *Emerge 2004 Proceedings*. (pp. 1-11) Retrieved February 2010, from http://emerge2004.net/connect/site/UploadWSC/emerge2004/file20/emerge2004article.doc

Barrows, H. S., & Tambyln, R. M. (1980). *Problem-based learning: An approach to medical education*. New York, NY: Springer.

Bass, E. B., Fortin, A. H., Morrison, G., Wills, S., Mumford, L. M., & Goroll, A. H. (1997). National survey of clerkship directors in internal medicine on the competencies that should be addressed in Medicine core clerkship. *The American Journal of Medicine*, *102*, 564–571. doi:10.1016/S0002-9343(97)00054-5

Bates, T. (2008). Transforming distance education through new technologies. In Evans, T., Haughey, M., & Murphy, D. (Eds.), *International handbook of distance education* (pp. 217–235). West Anglia, UK: Emerald Group Publishing.

Bates, T. (2010). *Strategic thinking about e-learning*. Paper presented at BC Educational Technology Users Group, Victoria, BC.

Bayrak, C. (2008). Effects of computer simulations programs on university students' achievements in physics. *Turkish Online Journal of Distance Education*, *9*(4), 53–62.

Beckwith, D. (1988). The future of educational technology. *Canadian Journal of Educational Communication*, *17*(1), 3–20.

Benford, S., Crabtree, A., Flintham, M., Drozd, A., Anastasi, R., & Paxton, M. (2006). Can you see me now? *ACM Transactions on Computer-Human Interaction*, *13*(1), 100–133. doi:10.1145/1143518.1143522

Benford, S., Flintham, M., Drozd, A., Anastasi, R., Rowland, D., & Tandavanitj, N. … Adams, M. (2004). Uncle Roy all around you: Implicating the city in a location-based performance. In *Proceedings of Advanced Computer Entertainment 2004*, Singapore. ACM Press.

Bengu, S. M. E. (1997). *Foreword in Curriculum 2005: Lifelong learning for the 21*st *century*. Pretoria, South Africa: Department of Education.

Bersin, J. (2004). *The blended learning book: Best practices, proven methodologies, and lessons learned.* Hoboken, NJ: John Wiley and Sons.

Bielawski, L., & Metcalf, D. (2002). *Blended e-learning: Integrating knowledge, performance support, and online learning* (2nd ed.). Amherst, MA: HRD Press, Inc.

Biggs, J. (1999). *Teaching for quality learning at university. Society for Research into Higher Education (SRHE).* Buckingham, UK: Open University Press, State.

Biklen, S. K., & Casella, R. (2007). *A practical guide to the qualitative dissertation.* Teachers College Press, Columbia University.

Black, S. (1996). The truth about homework. *The American School Board Journal, 183*(10), 48–51.

Bleed, R. (2001). A hybrid campus for a new millennium. *EDUCAUSE Review, 36*(1), 16–24.

Blumenstyk, G. (2003). Companies' graduate programs challenge colleges of education. For-profit institutions find a new market: School teachers. *The Chronicle of Higher Education, 50*(2), A30.

Blunt, R. (2007). *Do serious games work? Results from three recent studies.* Presented at the The Interservice/Industry Training, Simulation & Education Conference (I/ITSEC), Orlando, FL.

Bonk, C. J., & Graham, C. R. (Eds.). (2006). *The handbook of blended learning: Global perspectives, local designs.* San Francisco, CA: Pfeiffer.

Bonk, C. J. (2009). *The world is open: How technology is revolutionizing education.* San Francisco, CA: Jossey-Bass.

Bonk, C. J., Kim, K., & Zeng, T. (2005). Future directions of blended learning in higher education and workplace learning settings. In Bonk, C. J., & Graham, C. R. (Eds.), *Handbook of blended learning: Global Perspectives, local designs.* San Francisco, CA: Pfeiffer Publishing.

Bostock, S., & Wu, L. (2005). Gender in student online discussions. *Innovations in Education and Teaching International, 42*(1), 73–85. .doi:10.1080/14703290500048978

Bowker, G. C., & Star, S. L. (1999). *Sorting things out: Classification and its consequences.* Boston, MA: MIT Press.

Boyd, D. M., & Ellison, N. B. (2007). Social network sites: Definition, history, and scholarship. *Journal of Computer-Mediated Communication, 13*(1), 11. Retrieved from http://jcmc.indiana.edu/vol13/issue1/boyd.ellison.html.

Boyd, D. (2007). *The significance of social software.* Retrieved from http://www.danah.org/papers/

Boyd, D. (2008). *Taken out of context: American teen sociality in networked publics.* Unpublished doctoral dissertation, University of California-Berkeley, School of Information. Retrieved from http://www.danah.org/papers/

Brieman, L., Friedman, J. H., Olshen, R. A., & Stone, C. J. (1984). *Classification and regression trees.* New York, NY: Chapman & Hall.

Broll, W., Lindt, I., Herbst, I., Ohlenburg, J., Braun, A., & Wetzel, R. (2008). Toward next-gen mobile AR games. *Computer Graphics and Applications, IEEE, 28*(4), 40–48. doi:10.1109/MCG.2008.85

Brown, A. L., & Palincsar, A. (1989). Guided, cooperative learning and individual knowledge acquisition. In *Knowing, learning, and instruction: essays in honor of Robert Glaser, Psychology of Education and Instruction Series* (pp. 393–452). Hillsdale, NJ: Erlbaum.

Bruner, J. A. (1966). *Towards a theory of instruction.* Cambridge, MA: Harvard University Press.

Bruner, J. (1990). *Acts of meaning: Four lectures on mind and culture.* Cambridge, MA: Harvard University Press.

Bruner, J. S. (1967). *On knowing: Essays for the left hand.* Cambridge, MA: Harvard University Press.

Burbules, N. C., & Torres, C. A. (Eds.). (2000). *Globalization and education: Critical perspectives.* New York, NY: Routledge.

Burby, L. (2006, September 17). The great homework debate. *Newsday.*

Butler, D. L., & Sellbom, M. (2002). Barriers to adopting technology for teaching and learning. *EDUCAUSE Quarterly, 2,* 22–28.

Caldwell, J. E. (2007). Clickers in the large classroom: Current research and best practice tips. *CBE Life Sciences Education, 6*(1), 9–20. doi:10.1187/cbe.06-12-0205

Calldo, F., & du Plooy, T. (2008). *Researcher's solidarity. Eskom: Skills Facts*. Retrieved 20 October, 2009, from http://www.solidariteitinstituut.co.za/docs/skills_fact.pdf

Campbell, G. (2009). Personal cyberinfrastructure. *EDUCAUSE Review, 44*(5), 58–59. Retrieved from http://www.educause.edu/EDUCAUSE+Review/EDUCAUSEReviewMagazineVolume44/APersonalCyberinfrastructure/178431.

Campbell, G. (2010). *Mimi Ito: Opening plenary at NMC 2010*. Retrieved June 13, 2010, from http://www.gardnercampbell.net/blog1/

Carbonaro, M., King, S., Taylor, E., Satzinger, F., Snart, F., & Drummond, J. (2008). Integration of e-learning technologies in an intraprofessional health science course. *Medical Teacher, 30*, 25–33. doi:10.1080/01421590701753450

Cengage Learning. (2007). *Many college professors see podcasts, blogs and social networking sites as a potential teaching tool*. Retrieved from http://www.cengage.com/press/release/20070507.html

Cercone, K. (2008). Characteristics of adult learners with implications for online learning design. *AACE Journal, 16*(2), 137–159.

Chen, J. (2007). Flow in games (and everything else). *Communications of the ACM, 50*(4), 31–34. doi:10.1145/1232743.1232769

Chen, S., & Michael, D. (2006). Proof of learning: Assessment in serious games. *Gamasutra: The Art & Business of Making Games*. Retrieved March 28, 2008, from http://www.gamasutra.com/view/feature/2433/proof_of_learning_assessment_in_.php

Cheok, A. D., Fong, S. W., Goh, K. H., Yang, X., Liu, W., & Farzbiz, F. (2003). *Human Pacman: A sensing-based mobile entertainment system with ubiquitous computing and tangible interaction* (pp. 106–117). Redwood City, CA: ACM.

Chickering, A. W., & Gamson, Z. F. (1987). Seven principles for good practice in undergraduate education. *AAHE Bulletin, 39*(7), 3–7.

Christensen, L., & Menzel, K. (1998). The linear relationship between student reports of teacher immediacy behaviors and perceptions of state motivation, and of cognitive, affective, and behavioral learning. *Communication Education, 47*(1), 82–90. doi:10.1080/03634529809379112

Christophel, D. M. (1990). The relationship among teacher immediacy behaviors, student motivation, and learning. *Communication Education, 39*(4), 323–340. doi:10.1080/03634529009378813

Christophel, D. M., & Gorham, J. (1995). A test-retest analysis of student motivation, teacher immediacy, and perceived sources of motivation and demotivation in college classes. *Communication Education, 44*(4), 292–306. doi:10.1080/03634529509379020

Clark, D. (2003). *Blend it like Beckham*. Retrieved January 25, 2010, from http://www.epic.co.uk/content/resources/white_papers/blended.htm

Clark, R., & Feldon, D. (2008). *GEL, adaptable expertise and transfer of training*.

Coady, Y., & Gibbs, C. (2009). *The virtual learning lodge: A framework under construction*. Paper presented at the Canadian e-Learning Conference, Vancouver, BC.

Cohen, M. L., Grady, M., & Springer, S. (2007). Centering on learning at Penn. *Talk About Teaching and Learning - Almanac, 50*(9). Retrieved December, 2009, from http://www.upenn.edu/almanac/v50/n09/teaching.html

Collis, B., & Moonen, J. (2001). *Flexible learning in a digital world*. London, UK: Kogan Page.

Cone, J. D., & Foster, S. L. (2006). *Dissertations and theses from start to finish: Psychology and related fields*. Washington, DC: American Psychological Association.

Connolly, T., Stansfield, M., Josephson, J., Lázaro, N., Rubio, G., & Ortiz, C. R. … Tsvetkova, N. (2008). Using alternate reality games to support language learning. In *Proceedings of the Seventh IASTED International Conference on Web-Based Education*. Innsbruck, Austria: ACTA Press.

Cook, R., Ley, K., Crawford, C., & Warner, A. (2009). Motivators and inhibitors for university faculty in distance and e-learning. *British Journal of Educational Technology, 40*(1), 149–163. .doi:10.1111/j.1467-8535.2008.00845.x

Corbel, J. R., & Valdez-Corbel, M. E. (2007). Are you ready for mobile learning? Frequent use of mobile devices does not mean that students or instructors are ready for mobile learning and teaching. *Educause Quarterly, 30*(2), 51-58.Retrieved on June 13, 2010 from http://net.educause.edu/ir/library/pdf/eqm0726.pdf

Craig, S. C., & Martinez, M. D. (Eds.). (2005). *Ambivalence and the structure of political opinion*. New York, NY: Palgrave Macmillan. doi:10.1057/9781403979094

Creswell, J. D. (2009). *Research design: Qualitative, quantitative, and mixed methods approaches*. Thousand Oaks, CA: Sage Publications.

Crichton, S., & Childs, E. (2008). Looking forward-stories of practice. In S. Hirtz (Ed). *Education for a digital world*. BC Campus and Commonwealth of Learning. Retrieved from http://www.col.org/resources/crsMaterials/Pages/edDigitalWorld.aspx

Csikszentmihalyi, M. (1991). *Flow: The psychology of optimal experience*. New York, NY: Harper Perennial.

Daft, R. L., & Lengel, R. H. (1986). Organizational information requirements, media richness and structural design. *Management Science, 32*(5), 554–571. doi:10.1287/mnsc.32.5.554

Dalsgaard, C., & Paulsen, M. (2009). Transparency in cooperative online education. *International Review of Research in Open and Distance Learning, 10*(3). Retrieved from http://www.irrodl.org.

Dalsgaard, C. (2006). Social software: E-learning beyond learning management systems. *European Journal of Open, Distance and E-Learning*. Retrieved from http://www.eurodl.org

Daniel, J. S. (2003). *Mega-universities=mega-impact on access, cost and quality*. Keynote address presented at the First Summit of Mega-universities, Shanghai, PRC. Retrieved from http://portal.unesco.org

Daniels, G. (2007). SA – maths = crisis. *Mail and Guardian Online*. Accessed March 16, 2008, from http://www.mg.co.za/articlePage.aspx.articleid=300522&area=/ the_teacher/teacher_features

Davidson, N. C., & Goldberg, T. D. (2009). *The future of learning institutions in a digital age*. Cambridge, MA: MIT Press.

Davis, S. M., & Batkin, J. W. (1994). *The monster under the bed: How business is mastering the opportunity for knowledge for profit*. New York, NY: Simon & Shuster.

Davis, M. H., & Harden, R. M. (1999). AMEE medical education guide no 15: Problem-based learning, a practical guide. *Medical Teacher, 21*(2), 130–140. doi:10.1080/01421599979743

Davis, S., Moar, M., Jacobs, R., Watkins, M., Riddoch, C., & Cooke, K. (2006). Ere be dragons: Heartfelt gaming. *Digital Creativity, 17*(3), 157–162. doi:10.1080/14626260600882430

Dawson, T., & Keenan, L. (2009). *Universal instructional design: Creating an accessible curriculum at UVic*. Victoria, BC: University of Victoria.

de Freitas, S. I. (2006). Using games and simulations for supporting learning. *Learning, Media and Technology, 31*(4), 343–358. doi:10.1080/17439880601021967

DeFleur, M., & Adams, J. (2004). Acceptability of online bachelor's degrees as criteria for admission to graduate programs. *Journal of Computing in Higher Education, 16*(1), 150–161. doi:10.1007/BF02960287

Denscombe, M. (2007). *The good research guide for small-scale social research projects. New York, NY: McGraw-Hill Education Department of Education. (2000). Instructional leadership. School management teams*. Pretoria, South Africa: Department of Education.

Department of Education. (2002). *Report on some of the key programmes of the department of education presented at the parliamentary media briefing on 15 August 2002*. Retrieved August 2008, from http://www.search.gov.za/info/previewDocument.jsp?dk=%2Fdata%2Fstatic%2Finfo%2Fspeeches%2F2002%2F02081610461001.htm%40Gov&q=%3Cphrase%3E+(project+management)&t=Asmal%3A+Parliamentary+Media+Briefing+(Education+progress+report)%2C+August+2002

DeViney, N., & Lewis, J. N. (2006). On-demand learning. In Bonk, J. C., & Graham, R. C. (Eds.), *The handbook of blended learning* (pp. 491–501). John Wiley & Sons.

Dewey, J. (1938). *Experience and education*. New York, NY: Macmillan.

Dillman, D. A., Smyth, J. D., & Christain, L. M. (2008). *Internet, mail, and mixed-mode surveys: The tailored design method* (3rd ed.). New York, NY: Wiley.

Driscoll, M., & Carliner, S. (2005). *Advanced Web-based training strategies: Unlocking instructionally sound online learning*. San Francisco, CA: Pfeiffer Publishing.

Driscoll, M. (2002) *Blended learning: Let's get beyond the hype*. Retrieved June 12, 2010, from http://www-07.ibm.com/services/pdf/blended_learning.pdf

Dron, J. (2006). Social software and the emergence of control. *Proceedings of the Sixth IEEE International Conference on Advanced Learning Technologies* (pp. 904-908). Washington, DC: IEEE Computer Society. Retrieved from http://portal.acm.org/

Duderstadt, J. J. (2000). *A university for the 21st century*. Ann Arbor, MI: Michigan University Press.

Dunleavy, M., Dede, C., & Mitchell, R. (2009). Affordances and limitations of immersive participatory augmented reality simulations for teaching and learning. *Journal of Science Education and Technology, 18*(1), 7–22. doi:10.1007/s10956-008-9119-1

Duque, G., Roberts, A., Hui, J., Posel, N., Fleiszer, D., & Chui, Q. (2006). From the facts to the screen: A blended model of teaching basic hospital skills to 2nd year medical students. *Medical Teacher, 28*(8), 729–733. doi:10.1080/01421590601032450

Dziuban, C. D., Hartman, J. L., & Moskal, P. D. (2007). Blended learning. *Educause Centre for Applied Research, 7*, 1–12.

Dziuban, C., Hartman, J., Moskal, P., Sorg, S., & Truman, B. (2004). Three ALN modalities: An institutional perspective. In Bourne, J., & Moore, J. C. (Eds.), *Elements of quality online education: Into the mainstream* (pp. 127–148). Needham, MA: Sloan Center for Online Education.

Edmundson, A. (2007). Using level 1 e-learning to support socio-economic development. *Educational Media International, 44*(2), 99–111. .doi:10.1080/09523980701295109

Edutech Wiki. (2010). *5e learning cycle*. Retrieved February 2010, from http://edutechwiki.unige.ch/en/5e_Learning_cycle

Egenfeldt-Nielsen, S. (2005). *Beyond edutainment: Exploring the educational potential of computer games*. IT University of Copenhagen, Department of Innovation.

Engelbrecht, J., & Harding, A. (2008). The impact of the transition to outcomes-based teaching on university preparedness in mathematics in South Africa. *Mathematics Education Research Journal, 20*(2), 57–70.

Engstrom, J. (2005). *Why some social network services work and others don't- or: The case for object-centered sociality*. Retrieved from http://www.zengestrom.com/blog/2005/04/why_some_social.html

Facer, K., Joiner, R., Stanton, D., Reid, J., Hull, R., & Kirk, D. (2004). Savannah: Mobile gaming and learning? *Journal of Computer Assisted Learning, 20*, 399–409. doi:10.1111/j.1365-2729.2004.00105.x

Feldman, S. (1995). Answering survey questions. In Lodge, M., & McGraw, K. (Eds.), *Political judgment: Structure and process* (pp. 249–270). Ann Arbor, MI: University of Michigan Press.

Fink, A. G. (2008). *How to conduct surveys: A step-by-step guide* (4th ed.). London, UK: Sage Publications.

Fischer, G., & Konomi, S. (2005). Innovative media in support of distributed intelligence and lifelong learning. *Proceedings of the Third IEEE International Workshop on Wireless and Mobile Technologies in Education* (pp. 3-10). Retrieved from http://doi.ieeecomputersociety.org/10.1109/WMTE.2005.35

Fitzgerald, R., Barrass, S., Campbell, J., Hinton, S., Ryan, Y., & Whitelaw, M. … McGinness, N. (2009). *Digital Learning Communities (DLC): Investigating the application of social software to support networked learning* (Project Report CG6-36). Retrieved from http://www.digitalrepository.qut.edu.au/

Fowler, F. J. (2008). *Survey research methods: Applied social research methods*. London, UK: Sage Publications.

Fozdar, B. I., & Kumar, L. S. (2006). Teaching chemistry at Indira Gandhi National Open University. *Turkish Online Journal of Distance Education, 7*(2), 80-89. ISSN 1302-6488

Fraas, J. W. (1982). The influence of student characteristics on the effectiveness of simulations in the principles course. *The Journal of Economic Education, 13*(1), 56–61. doi:10.2307/1182871

Freire, P. (1970). *Pedagogy of the oppressed.*

Garnham, C., & Kaleta, R. (2002). Introduction to hybrid courses. *Teaching with Technology Today, 8*(6). Retrieved June 14, 2010, from http://www.uwsa.edu/ttt/articles/garnham.htm

Garrison, R. D., & Vaughn, N. D. (2008). *Blended learning in higher education: Framework, principles, and guidelines*. San Francisco, CA: Jossey Bass.

Garrison, D. R., Anderson, T., & Archer, W. (2000). Critical inquiry in a text-based environment: Computer conferencing in higher education. *The Internet and Higher Education, 2*(2-3), 87–105. doi:10.1016/S1096-7516(00)00016-6

Garrison, D. R., & Vaughan, N. D. (2008). *Blended learning in higher education: Framework, principles, and guidelines*. San Francisco, CA: Jossey-Bass.

Garrison, R. D., & Kanuka, H. (2004). Blended learning: Uncovering its transformative potential in higher education. *The Internet and Higher Education, 7*, 95–105. doi:10.1016/j.iheduc.2004.02.001

Garrison, D. R., & Anderson, T. (2003). *E-learning in the 21st century*. Retrieved from http://www.questia.com

Gaskell, A. (2007). Open and distance learning on the move: Mobile learning, crossing borders, rethinking roles. *Open Learning, 22*(3), 197–200. doi:. doi:10.1080/02680510701619778

Gee, J. (2004). *Situated language and learning: A critique of traditional schooling*. New York, NY: Routledge.

General Medical Council. (1993). *Tomorrow's doctors: Recommendation on undergraduate medical education.* London, UK: General Medical Council.

Gibbins, M. L., Hadibi, R., Urbaczewski, A., & Vivian, C. (2007). Technology-enhanced learning in blended learning environments: A report on standard practices. *Communications of the Association for Information Systems, 20*(46), 741–759.

Gladwell, M. (2008). *Outliers: The story of success*. New York, NY: Penguin Press. ISSN.

Glass, G. V., & Hopkins, K. D. (1995). *Statistical methods in education and psychology* (3rd ed.). Boston, MA: Allyn & Bacon.

Gorham, J. (1988). The relationship between verbal teacher immediacy behaviors and student learning. *Communication Education, 37*(1), 40–53. doi:10.1080/03634528809378702

Graber, M. A. (2005). Does stimulation training for medical students change patient opinions and attitudes towards medical student procedures in the emergency department. *Academic Emergency Medicine, 12*, 635–639. doi:10.1111/j.1553-2712.2005.tb00920.x

Graham, C. R. (2004). *Blended learning systems*. San Francisco, CA: Wiley Press.

Graham, C. R. (2006). Blended learning systems: Definition, current trends, and future directions. In Bonk, C. J., & Graham, C. R. (Eds.), *Handbook of blended learning: Global perspectives, local designs* (pp. 3–21). San Francisco, CA: Pfeiffer.

Graham, C. R. (2008). Blended learning models. In Khosrow-Pour, M. (Ed.), *Encyclopedia of Information Science and Technology* (*Vol. 2*, pp. 375–382). Hershey, PA: Idea Group Inc.

Graham, C. R., Allen, S., & Ure, D. (2005). Benefits and challenges of blended learning environments. In M. Khosrow-Pour (Ed.), *Encyclopedia of information science and technology* (pp. 253–259). Retrieved from http://www.netlibrary.com

Graven, M. (2002). Coping with new mathematics teacher roles in a contradictory context of curriculum change. *The Mathematics Educator, 12*(2), 21–27.

Greenhow, C., Robelia, B., & Hughes, J. E. (2009). Learning, teaching, and scholarship in a digital age: Web 2.0 and classroom research: What path should we take now? *Educational Researcher, 38*(4), 246–259. .doi:10.3102/0013189X09336671

Gremmen, H., & Potters, J. (1997). Assessing the efficacy of gaming in economic education. *The Journal of Economic Education, 28*(4), 291–303.

Griffiths, M. E., & Graham, C. R. (2009a). The potential of asynchronous video in online education. *Distance Learning*, *6*(2), 13–22.

Griffiths, M. E., & Graham, C. R. (2009b). Using asynchronous video in online classes: Results from a pilot study. *Instructional Technology & Distance Education*, *6*(3), 65–76.

Griffiths, M. E., & Graham, C. R. (2010. (in press). Using asynchronous video to achieve instructor immediacy and closeness in online classes: Experiences from three cases. *International Journal on E-Learning*.

Griffiths, M. (2010). *Improving the asynchronous video learning model*. Unpublished doctoral dissertation, Brigham Young University, Provo, UT.

Guilar, J. D., & Loring, A. (2008). Dialogue and community in online learning: Lessons from Royal Roads University. *Journal of Distance Education*, *22*(3), 19–40. Retrieved from http://www.jofde.ca.

Gunawardena, C., & Zittle, F. (1997). Social presence as a predictor of satisfaction within a computer mediated conferencing environment. *American Journal of Distance Education*, *11*(3), 8–26. Retrieved from http://www.ajde.com. doi:10.1080/08923649709526970

Gunter, G. A. (2007). The effects of the impact of instructional immediacy on cognition and learning in online classes. *International Journal of Social Sciences*, *2*(3), 196–202.

Hainey, T., Connolly, T., Stansfield, M., Boyle, L., Josephson, J., & O'Donovan, A. …Ortiz, C. R. (2009). Arguing for multilingual motivation in Web 2.0: An evaluation of a large-scale European pilot. In *Proceedings of ECGBL 2009 The 3rd European Conference on Games Based Learning* (pp. 110-119). Graz, Austria.

Hakkarainen, K. (2010). Three generations of technology-enhanced learning. *British Journal of Educational Technology*, *40*(5), 879–888. doi:10.1111/j.1467-8535.2008.00873.x

Harden, R. M. (2000). Evolution or revolution and the future of medical education: Replacing the oak tree. *Medical Teacher*, *22*(5), 435–442. doi:10.1080/01421590050110669

Harden, R. M. (2000). The integration ladder: A tool for curriculum planning and evaluation. *Medical Education*, *34*, 551–557. doi:10.1046/j.1365-2923.2000.00697.x

Harden, R. M. (2001). AMEE guide no 21: Curriculum mapping: A tool for transparent and authentic teaching and learning. *Medical Teacher*, *23*(2), 123–137. doi:10.1080/01421590120036547

Harden, R. M., Crosby, J. R., & Davis, M. H. (1999). AMEE guide no. 14: Outcome-based education: Part-1-an introduction to outcome-based education. *Medical Teacher*, *21*(1), 7–14. doi:10.1080/01421599979969

Harden, R. M., & Davis, M. H. (1995). AMEE medical education guide no 5: The core curriculum with options or special study modules. *Medical Teacher*, *17*(2), 125–148. doi:10.3109/01421599509008301

Harden, R. M., Laidlaw, J. M., Ker, J. S., & Mitchell, H. E. (1996). AMEE medical education booklet no 7, part 1: Task-based learning: An educational strategy for undergraduate, post-graduate and continuing medical education. *Medical Teacher*, *18*, 7–13. doi:10.3109/01421599609040254

Harden, R. M., Snowden, S., & Dunn, W. R. (1984). ASME medical education booklet no 18: Some educational strategies in curriculum development: The SPICES model. *Medical Education*, *18*, 284–297. doi:10.1111/j.1365-2923.1984.tb01024.x

Harden, R. M. (2000). Independent learning. In Dent, J. A., & Harden, R. M. (Eds.), *A practical guide for medical teachers* (pp. 147–157). Edinburgh, UK: Churchill Livingstone.

Harden, R. M., & Hart, I. R. (2002). An international virtual medical school (IVIMEDS): The future for medical education. *Medical Teacher*.

Harding, A., Engelbrecht, J., Lazenby, K., & le Roux, I. (2006). Blended learning in undergraduate mathematics at the University of Pretoria. In Bonk, C. J., & Graham, C. R. (Eds.), *Handbook of blended learning: Global perspectives, local designs* (pp. 400–418). San Francisco, CA: Pfeiffer.

Harding, A., Kaczynski, D., & Wood, L. (2005). Evaluation of blended learning: Analysis of qualitative data. *Uniserve Science Blended Learning Symposium Proceedings* (pp. 56-62). University of Sydney, Australia.

Harrison, C., & Killion, J. (2008). Ten roles for teacher leaders. *Educational Leadership*, *65*(1), 74–77.

Hartman, J. L. (2010). *The promise and practice of blended learning*. Presented at the meeting of the Sloan-C Blended Learning Conference, Chicago, IL.

Hase, S., & Kenyon, C. (2000). *From andragogy to heutagogy*. Retrieved from http://ultibase.rmit.edu.au/index.htm

Hays, W. L. (1963). *Statistics for psychologists*. New York, NY: Holt, Rinehart, and Winston, Inc.

Hays, W. L. (1973). *Statistics for the social sciences* (2nd ed.). New York, NY: Holt, Rinehart, and Winston, Inc.

Hays, R. T. (2005). *The effectiveness of instructional games: A literature review and discussion*. (Technical Report No. 2005-004). Naval Air Warfare Center Training Systems Division. Retrieved from http://stinet.dtic.mil/oai/oai?&verb=getRecord&metadataPrefix=html&identifier=ADA441935

Haythornthwaite, C., & Bregman, A. (2004). Affordances of persistent conversation: Promoting communities that work. In Haythornthwaite, C., & Kazmer, M. M. (Eds.), *Learning, culture, and community in online education: Research and practice* (pp. 129–143). New York, NY: Peter Lang Publishing, Inc.

Haythornthwaite, C., Kazmer, M. M., Robins, J., & Shoemaker, S. (2004). Community development among distance learners: Temporal and technological dimensions. In Haythornthwaite, C., & Kazmer, M. M. (Eds.), *Learning, culture, and community in online education: Research and practice* (pp. 35–57). New York, NY: Peter Lang Publishing.

Hemmi, A., Bayne, S., & Land, R. (2009). The appropriation and repurposing of social technologies in higher education. *Journal of Computer Assisted Learning*, *25*(1), 19–30. .doi:10.1111/j.1365-2729.2008.00306.x

Henschke, J. A. (2010). Bringing together personal learning, higher education institutions elements, and global support for a re-orientation towards a focus on lifelong learning and education. In Wang, V. (Ed.), *Encyclopedia for using technology in adult and career education*. Hershey, PA: IGI Global. doi:10.4018/9781616929060.ch063

Herrington, J., Reeves, C. T., & Oliver, R. (2005). Online learning as information delivery: Digital myopia. *Journal of Interactive Learning Research*, *16*(4), 353–367.

Hitt, J. C., & Hartman, J. L. (2010). Two views of alignment. *EDUCAUSE Review*, *45*(2), 8–9.

Hogan, R. (2009). Societal issues, legal standards, & international realities universities face in the distance-learning market. In Song, H. (Ed.), *Distance learning technology, current instruction, and the future of education: Applications of today, practices of tomorrow* (pp. 284–301). Hershey, PA: IGI Global.

Hogan, R. (2009). Attitudes of indigenous peoples toward distance learning in the South Pacific: An empirical study. In G. Siemens & C. Fulford (Eds.), *Proceedings of World Conference on Educational Multimedia, Hypermedia and Telecommunications 2009* (pp. 1064-1072). Chesapeake, VA: AACE. Retrieved from http://www.editlib.org/p/31621

Holly, D., & Oliver, M. (2010). Student engagement and blended learning: Portraits of risk. *Computers & Education*, *54*, 693–700. doi:10.1016/j.compedu.2009.08.035

Holosko, M. J. (2006). *Primer for critiquing social research: A student guide*. Thomson Brooks / Cole.

Hopper, T., & Sanford, K. (2010). Program-wide e-portfolios: Creating new spaces for an inside-out approach to teacher education. *Teacher Education Quarterly*. Retrieved June 14, 2010 from http://teqjournal.org/hopper.html

Horton, W. (2001). *Leading e-learning*. Alexandria, VA: ASTD.

Hughes, C., Toohey, S., & Velan, G. (2008). eMED teamwork: A self moderating system to gather peer feedback for developing and assessing teamwork skills. *Medical Teacher*, *30*, 5–9. doi:10.1080/01421590701758632

Husu, J. (2006). *Analyzing teachers' rule-based competencies in practice*. Paper presented at the European conference on educational research (ECER). Geneva, Switzerland. September 13-16, 2006.

Hwang, J., Consulta, R. R., & Yoon, H. (2007). 4G mobile networks: Technology beyond 2.5G and 3G. *Proceedings of the 2007 Pacific Telecommunications Council Conference*. Retrieved from http://www.ptc.org/past_events/ptc07/program/papers/ T24_RoyConsulta.pdf

Ice, P., Curtis, R., Philips, P., & Wells, J. (2007). Using asynchronous audio feedback to enhance teaching presence and students' sense of community. *Journal of Asynchronous Learning Networks*, *11*(2), 3–25.

Ifinedo, P. (2006). Accpetance and continuance intention of Web-based learning technology (WLT) use among university students in a Baltic country. *Electrinic Journal of Information Systems in Developing Countries*, *23*(6), 1–20.

Ifinedo, P. (2007). Investigating the antecedents of continuance intention of course management system use among Estonian undergraduates. *International Journal of Communication Technology Education*, *3*(4), 76–92. doi:10.4018/jicte.2007100107

Ifinedo, P., & Ololube, N. P. (2007). A discourse on the problems, prospects, and progress of distance education in a developing country. In Bailey, E. P. (Ed.), *Focus on distance education developments* (pp. 183–194). New York, NY: Nova Science Publishers.

Ifinedo, P. (2005). Measuring Africa's e-readiness in the global networked economy: A nine-country data analysis. *International Journal of Education and Development using Information and Communication Technology*, *1*(1), 53-71.

Igwe, U. O. (2005). Harnessing Information Technology for the 21st century: Library education in Nigeria. *Library Philosophy and Practice*, *7*(2)

Iloanusi, N. O., & Osuagwu, C. C. (2009). ICT in education: Achievements so far in Nigeria. In A. Méndez-Vilas, A. Solano Martín, J. A. Mesa González, & J. Mesa González (Eds.), *Research, reflections and innovations in integrating ICT in education*. (pp.1331-1335). Badajoz, Spain: FORMATEX. Retrieved February 10, 2010, from http://www.formatex.org/micte2009/book/1331-1335.pdf

Insung, J. (2009). The emergence of for-profit e-learning providers in Asia. *TechTrends: Linking Research & Practice to Improve Learning*, *53*(2), 18–21. doi:.doi:10.1007/s11528-009-0262-1

Jacobsen, M., & Kopp, G. (2008). Female tenure tracks in educational technology. In Beaudin, L. (Ed.), *Hard and soft technologies: Stories of women and technology*.

Jakobson, R. (1960). Concluding statements: Linguistics and poetics. In Sebeok, T. A. (Ed.), *Style in language*. Cambridge, MA: MIT Press.

Jansen, J. D. (1998). Curriculum reform in South Africa: A critical analysis of outcomes-based education. *Cambridge Journal of Education*, *28*(3), 321–331. doi:10.1080/0305764980280305

Januszewski, A., & Molenda, M. (Eds.). (2008). *Educational technology: A definition with commentary*. New York, NY: Lawrence Erlbaum Associates.

Jasinski, M. (2007). *Innovate and integrate: Embedding innovative practices*. Brisbane, Australia: Commonwealth of Australia. Retrieved June 14, 2010 from http://innovateandintegrate.flexiblelearning.net.au/docs/Innovate_and_Integrate_Final_26Jun07.pdf

Jeffrey, L. M., Atkins, C., Laurs, A., & Mann, S. (2006). *E-learner profiles: Identifying trends and diversity in student needs, orientations and aspirations*. Education counts, New Zealand.

Jenkins, H. (2006). *Convergence culture*. NYU Press.

Jenkins, H. (2002, March 29). Game theory. *Technology Review*. Retrieved February 11, 2010, from http://www.technologyreview.com/energy/12784/

Johnson, L., Levine, A., Smith, R., & Stone, S. (2010). *The 2010 horizon report*. Austin, TX: The New Media Consortium. Retrieved January 29, 2010, from http://www.nmc.org/pdf/2010-Horizon-Report.pdf

Johnson, L., Levine, A., & Smith, R. (2009). *The 2009 horizon report*. Retrieved from http://www.nmc.org/publications/2009-horizon-report

Johnston, J., Massey, A., & Sheldon, L. (2009). *Using alternate reality games to influence physical activity in the college population*. Presented at the Games for Health Conference 2009, Boston, MA.

Jonassen, D. H. (Ed.). (2004). *The handbook of research for educational communications and technology* (2nd ed.). Mahwah, NJ: Lawrence Erlbaum Associates.

Jung, I. (2005). Quality assurance survey of megauniversities. In C. McIntosh (Ed.), *Perspectives on distance education: Lifelong learning and distance higher education* (pp. 79-95). Retrieved from http://unesdoc.unesco.org/images/0014/001412/141218e.pdf

Kazmer, M. M. (2000). Coping in a distance environment: Sitcoms, chocolate cake, and dinner with a friend. *First Monday*, *5*(9). Retrieved from http://firstmonday.org/.

Ke, F. (2008). A case study of computer gaming for math: Engaged learning from gameplay? *Computers & Education*, *51*(4), 1609–1620. doi:10.1016/j.compedu.2008.03.003

Kim, K. J., & Bonk, C. J. (2006). The future of online teaching and learning in higher education: The survey says. *EDUCAUSE Quarterly*, *29*(4). Retrieved from http://www.educause.edu.

King, K. P. (2003). *Keeping pace with technology: Educational technology that transforms. Vol. two: The challenge and promise for higher education faculty*. Cresskill, NJ: Hampton Press.

Klopfer, E. (2008). *Augmented learning: Research and design of mobile educational games*. Boston, MA: The MIT Press.

Knowles, M. (1984). *Androgogy in action*. San Francisco, CA: Jossey-Bass.

Knowles, M. (1990). *The adult learner: A neglected species* (4th ed.). Houston, TX: Gulf.

Knowles, M. S. (1980). *The modern practice of adult education: From pedagogy to andragogy* (2nd ed.). New York, NY: Cambridge Books.

Koepke, W. (1990). Epistolary fiction and its impact on readers: Reality and illusion. In Burwick, F., & Pape, W. (Eds.), *Aesthetic illusion: Theoretical and historical approaches*. Berlin, Germany: Walter de Gruyter.

Kovalic, S. (1993). *ITI: The model: Integrated thematic instruction*. Books for Educators.

Kramsch, C. (1998). *Language and culture*. New York, NY: Oxford University Press.

Kress, G. (2003). *Literacy in the new media age*. Retrieved from http://www.questia.com

Kuh, G. D., Kinzie, J., Schuh, J. H., & Whitt, J. E. (2005). *Student success in college: Creating conditions that matter*. San Francisco, CA: Jossey Bass.

Lakoff, G., & Johnson, M. (1999). *Philosophy in the flesh: The embodied mind and its challenge to western thought*. New York, NY: Basic Books.

Lakoff, G. (1987). Cognitive models and prototype theory. In Neisser, U. (Ed.), *Concepts and conceptual development: Ecological and intellectual factors in categorization*. Cambridge, UK: University of Cambridge.

Land, S. M., & Hannafin, M. J. (1996). A conceptual framework for the development of theories-in-action with open-ended learning environments. *Educational Technology Research and Development*, *44*(3), 37–53. Retrieved from http://www.aect.org. doi:10.1007/BF02300424

LaRose, R., & Whitten, P. (2000). Re-thinking instructional immediacy for web courses: A social cognitive exploration. *Communication Education*, *49*(4), 320–338. doi:10.1080/03634520009379221

Lattuca, L. R. (2001). *Creating interdisciplinarity*. Nashville, TN: Vanderbilt University Press.

Lau, F., & Bates, J. (2004). A review of e-learning practices for undergraduate medical education. *Journal of Medical Systems*, *28*(1), 71–87. doi:10.1023/B:JOMS.0000021522.30587.ff

Lave, J., & Wenger, E. (1991). *Situated learning: Legitimate peripheral participation* (1st ed.). Cambridge, UK: Cambridge University Press.

Lenhart, A. (2009). *Adults and social network websites*. Retrieved from http://www.pewinternet.org

Lenhart, A., & Madden, M. (2007). *55% of online teens use social networks and 55% have created online profiles, older girls predominate*. Retrieved from http://www.pewinternet.org/

Lenhart, A., Madden, M., Smith, A., & Macgill, A. R. (2007). *Teens and social media*. Retrieved from http://www.pewinternet.org

LeNoue, M., & Stammen, R. (2009). Building online learning communities with Web 2.0 tools. In T. Bastiaens, et al. (Eds.), *Proceedings of World Conference on E-Learning in Corporate, Government, Healthcare, and Higher Education 2009* (pp. 1751-1755). Retrieved from http://www.editlib.org/p/32713

Leutner, D. (1993). Guided discovery learning with computer-based simulation games: Effects of adaptive and non-adaptive instructional support. *Learning and Instruction, 3*(2), 113–132. doi:10.1016/0959-4752(93)90011-N

Lim, K. F. (2006). Use of spreadsheet simulations in university chemistry education. *Journal of Computer Chemistry, Japan, 5*(3), 139–146. doi:10.2477/jccj.5.139

Littlejohn, A., & Pegler, C. (2007). *Preparing for blended e-learning*. London, UK: Routledge.

Locke, L. F., Spirduso, W. W., & Silverman, S. J. (2000). *Proposals that work: A guide for planning dissertations and grant proposals*. Thousand Oaks, CA: Sage Publications.

Long, J. S. (1997). *Regression models for categorical and limited dependant variables*. Thousand Oaks, CA: Sage Publications.

Long, W. A. (1985). The practitioner and adolescent medicine. *Seminars in Adolescent Medicine, 1*(1), 85–90.

Looi, C., Seow, P., Zhang, B., So, H., Chen, W., & Wong, L. (2010). Leveraging mobile technology for sustainable seamless learning: A research agenda. *British Journal of Educational Technology, 41*(2), 154–169. doi:10.1111/j.1467-8535.2008.00912.x

Lorenzo, G., & Moore, J. (2002). *The Sloan Consortium report to the nation: Five pillars of quality online education*. Retrieved July 8, 2008 from http://www.sloanconsortium.org

Luca, J. (2006). Using blended learning to enhance teaching and learning. In D. Tolhurst & S. Mann (Eds.), *Proceedings of the 8th Australian Conference on Computing Education* (pp. 3-4). Hobart, Australia.

Maguire, C., & Zhang, J. (2006). *Effective blended learning for development.* Workshop on Designing and Delivering Blended Distance Learning Programs through GDLN. World Bank Tokyo Development Learning Center and DGHE Indonesia, Jakarta.

Maher, F. A., & Tetreault, M. K. T. (2007). *Privilege and diversity in the academy*. New York, NY: Routledge.

Mail & Guardian online. (2009). *Mantashe: Education struggles with apartheid legacy*. Retrieved February 2010, from http://www.mg.co.za/article/2009-10-08-mantashe-education-struggles-with-apartheid-legacy.

Manchester, H., Ralph, S., & Shipova, O. (2005). The teacher's role in using WebCT as a communication tool with postgraduate students. *The International Journal of Learning, 12*(4), 101–107.

Mapuva, J. (2009). Confronting challenges to e-learning in higher education institutions. *International Journal of Education and Development using Information and Communication Technology, 5*(3), J1-J14. (Document ID: 1881793981).

Marenzi, I., Demidova, E., Nejdl, W., Olmedilla, D., & Zerr, S. (2008). Social software for lifelong competence development: Challenges and infrastructure. *International Journal of Emerging Technologies in Learning, 3*, 18–23. Retrieved from http://online-journals.org/i-jet/issue/view/30.

Marshall, S., Kinutia, W., & Taylor, W. (2009). *Bridging the knowledge divide: Educational technology for development*. Charlotte, NC: Information Age Publishing, Inc.

Martin, S., & Crawford, C. (2008). Multiple streams of social media: Using social software to create information connections and conversations in learning environments. In K. McFerrin, R. Weber, R. Carlsen, & D. A. Willis (Eds.), *Proceedings of Society for Information Technology and Teacher Education International Conference 2008* (pp. 541-548). Chesapeake, VA: AACE.

Martinez, M. D., Craig, S. C., & Kane, J. G. (2005). Pros and cons: Ambivalence and public opinion. In Craig, S., & Martinez, M. (Eds.), *Ambivalence and the structure of public opinion* (pp. 1–14). New York, NY: Palgrave Macmillian.

Marzano, R. J., Pickering, D. J., & Pollock, J. E. (2001). *Classroom instruction that works*. Alexandria, VA: Association for Supervision and Curriculum Development.

Massachusetts Institute of Technology. (n.d.). *MITAR software download. Scheller Teacher Educational Program: Augmented reality games.* Retrieved from http://education.mit.edu/drupal/MITARSoftware

Mathematics Education Community. (2000). *Submission to the Council of Education Ministers* (CEM). Retrieved February 2010, from http://academic.sun.ac.za/mathed/AMESA/NGO.htm

May, S. (2009). *Hangaia te matapuna o te mohio: Learning foundations for Maori adults*. New Zealand: Education Counts.

Mazur, E. (1997). *Peer instruction: A user's manual*. Upper Saddle River, NJ: Prentice Hall.

McGonigal, J. (2007). Why I love bees: A case study in collective intelligence gaming. In *The ecology of games: Connecting youth, games, and learning* (pp. 199–227). The John D. and Catherine T. MacArthur Foundation Series on Digital Media and Learning.

McGonigal, J. (2005). *Alternate reality learning*. Presented at the Creative Design Panel, E3 Education Arcade, Los Angeles, CA. Retrieved from http://avantgame.com/McGonigal_ILOVEBEES_education%20arcade_May%20 2005.pdf

McGonigal, J. (2009). *Superstruct: How to invent the future by playing a game*. Presented at the ETech 2009, San Jose, CA. Retrieved from http://assets.en.oreilly.com/1/event/20/Superstruct_%20How%20to%20Invent%20 the%20Future%20by%20Playing%20a%20Game%20 Presentation.ppt

McGonigal, J. (2010a). *TED 2010: Reality is broken. Game designers must fix it*. Retrieved from http://www.wired.com/epicenter/2010/02/jane-mcgonigal/

McGonigal, J. (2010b). *Fixing the world with online games*. Retrieved from http://www.cnn.com/video/?/video/tech/2010/02/15/jane.mcgonigal.ted2010.cnn

McLoughlin, C., & Lee, M. J. W. (2007). Social software and participatory learning: Pedagogical choices with technology affordances in the Web 2.0 era. In R. J. Atkinson, C. McBeath, S. K. A. Soong, & C. C. Cheers (Eds.), *ICT: Providing choices for learners and learning. Proceedings of ASCILITE Singapore 2007* (pp. 664-675). Retrieved from http://www.ascilite.org.au/conferences/singapore07/procs/mcloughlin.pdf

McNiff, J. (2008). *Planning, designing and doing action research*. Retrieved June 2010, from http://www.action-research.net/writings/jack/jmplanar.pdf

Means, B., Toyama, Y., Murphy, R., Bakia, M., & Jones, K. (2009). *Evaluation of evidence-based practices in online learning: A meta-analysis and review of online learning studies*. Retrieved from http://www.ed.gov/rschstat/eval/tech/evidence-based-practices/finalreport.pdf

Meheabian, A. (1969). Some referents and measures of non-verbal behavior. *Behavior Research Methods and Instrumentation, 1*, 213–217.

Merriam, B. S. (2001). Andragogy and self-directed learning: Pillars of adult learning theory. Retrieved 17 June, 2010, from www.fsu.edu/~elps/ae/download/ade5385/Merriam.pdf

Metcalf, D., Milrad, M., Cheek, D., Raasch, S., & Hamilton, A. (2008). My sports pulse: Increasing student interest in STEM disciplines through sports themes, games and mobile technologies. In *Proceedings of the Fifth IEEE International Conference on Wireless, Mobile, and Ubiquitous Technology in Education* (pp. 23-30). IEEE Computer Society.

Meyer, K. (2006). When topics are controversial: Is it better to discuss them face-to-face or online? *Innovative Higher Education, 31*(3), 175–186. .doi:10.1007/s10755-006-9019-3

Meyles, S., & Woo, S. (2007). *ACIT/COMP 2101 Portfolio development*. Retrieved June 10, 2010, from http://whileone.ca/download/ePortfolio-intro/ePortfolio-introduction.html

Mezirow, J. (2000). *Learning as transformation: Critical perspectives on a theory in progress*. Jossey-Bass.

Milgram, P., & Kishino, F. (1994). A taxonomy of mixed reality visual displays. *IEICE Transactions on Information and Systems, 77*(12), 1321–1329.

Miller, R. P. (2005). *Listen to the students: A qualitative study investigating adult student readiness for online learning*. Retrieved March 11, 2010, from www.agclassroom.org/consortium/pdf/.../2005/online_learning.doc

Milne, J. K. (2006). Designing blended learning space to the student experience. In D. Oblinger (Ed.), *Learning spaces* (pp. 11.1 – 11.12). Retrieved June 14, 2010, from http://www.educause.edu/LearningSpaces

Mohanan, K. P. (2005). *Assessing qualities of teaching in higher education*. Centre for Development of Teaching and Learning(CDTL). Retrieved 13th June, 2009, from http://www.cdtl.nus.edu.sg/publications/assess/who.htm

Moller, L., Wellesley, R. F., & Huett, J. (2008). The evolution of distance education design on the potential of the Web. *TechTrends, 52*(4), 66–70. doi:10.1007/s11528-008-0179-0

Montola, M. (2005). Exploring the edge of the magic circle: Defining pervasive games. In *Proceedings of the 2005 Digital Arts and Culture* (pp. 1--3). Copenhagen, Denmark: IT University. Retrieved from http://citeseerx.ist.psu.edu/viewdoc/summary?doi=10.1.1.125.8421

Morris, D. (2008). Economies of scale and scope in e-learning. *Studies in Higher Education*, *33*(3), 331–343. .doi:10.1080/03075070802066164

Mortera-Gutiérrez, F. (2006). Faculty best practices using blended learning in e-learning and face-to-face instruction. *International Journal on E-Learning*, *5*(3), 313–337.

Moseley, A. (2008). *Great history conundrum: An alternative reality for research skills teaching*. Presented at the ARGs in Charity and Education Conference, London, England.

Moser, F. Z. (2007). Faculty adoption of educational technology. *Educause Quarterly*, *30*. Retrieved on September 14, 2007, from http://connect.educause.edu/library/abstract/FacultyAdoptionofEdu/40010

Moskal, P. D., & Dziuban, C. D. (2001). Present and future directions for assessing cyber-education: The changing research paradigm. In Vandervert, L., Shavinina, L., & Cornell, R. (Eds.), *CyberEducation: The future of long distance learning* (pp. 157–184). Larchmont, NY: Mary Ann Liebert Publishers.

Mossavar-Rahmani, F., & Larson-Daugherty, C. (2007). Supporting the hybrid learning model: A new proposition. *MERLOT Journal of Online Learning and Teaching*, *3*(1), 67-78. Retrieved from http://jolt.merlot.org/

Mphala, D., & Tshishonge, N. (2008). Khanya project. *Innovation insights 10, Case study 2*. Public Services Innovation CPSI. Retrieved February 2010, from http://www.cpsi.co.za/documents/Innovation%20Insight/Insight%2010,%20march%202008.pdf

Murphy, K., Drabier, R., & Epps, M. (1998). Interaction and collaboration via computer conferencing. *Proceedings of the National Convention for Education Communication and Technology*. Retrieved from ERIC database. (ED 423852).

Newhouse, C. P. (2002a). *The impact of ICT on learning and teaching*. Perth, Australia: Special Educational Service.

Newhouse, C. P. (2002b). *A framework to articulate the impact of ICT on learning in schools*. Perth, Australia: Special Educational Service.

Ngosana, C. (2008). *SA needs teachers*. Retrieved December 2009, from http://www.news24.com/Content/SouthAfrica/News/1059/6920a322b4e44e9ba7ff6e68f209b623/01-06-2008-02-30/SA_needs_teachers

Nicholson, Z. (2009). Matric maths crisis looms. *Weekend Argus*. Retrieved February 2010, from http://www.iol.co.za/index.php?set_id=1&click_id=13&art_id=vn20090726064117725C376939&singlepage=1

Nieuwdorp, E. (2005). The pervasive interface: Tracing the magic circle. In *Proceedings of DiGRA Conference*. Vancouver, Canada: Changing Views - Worlds in Play.

Nieuwoudt, S., Nieuwoudt, H., & Monteith, J. (2007). Influence of a video class system on learners' study and learning strategies band their achievement in mathematics. *African Journal of Research in Mathematics. Science and Technology Education*, *11*(1), 29–35.

Novak, G. M., Patterson, E. T., Gavrin, A. D., & Christian, W. (1999). *Just in time teaching: Blending active learning with web technology*. New Jersey: Prentice Hall Series in Educational Innovation.

Oblinger, D. G. (2008). Growing up with Google: What it means to education. In *Emerging technologies for learning* (BECTA Report, Vol. 3), (pp. 11-29). Retrieved from the http://www.becta.org.uk/

Oblinger, D. G., & Oblinger, J. L. (Eds.). (2005). *Educating the net generation*. Retrieved from www.educause.edu

Ocampo, M. L. (2004). *A brief history of educational inequality from apartheid to the present*. Seminar paper from Global Perspectives on Human Language: The South African Context. Retrieved November 2009, from http://www.stanford.edu/~jbaugh/saw/Lizet_Education_Inequity.html

Office of Community-Based Research. (n.d.). Retrieved June 14, 2010, from http://web.uvic.ca/ocbr/

Okuda, Y. (2009). The utility of simulation in medical education: What is the evidence? *The Mount Sinai Journal of Medicine, New York*, *76*, 330–343. doi:10.1002/msj.20127

Okuda, Y., & Quinones, J. (2008). The use of simulation in the education of emergency care providers for cardiac emergencies. *International Journal of Medicine*, *1*, 73–77.

Oliver, M., & Trigwell, K. (2005). Can blended learning be redeemed? *E-learning*, *2*(1), 17–26. Retrieved from http://www.wwwords.co.uk/elea/.

Ololube, N. P. (2006a). The impact of professional and non-professional teachers' ICT competencies in secondary schools in Nigeria. *Journal of Information Technology Impact*, *6*(2), 101–118.

Ololube, N. P. (2006b). Appraising the relationship between ICT usage and integration and the standard of teacher education programs in a developing economy. *International Journal of Education and Development Using ICT*, *2*(3), 70–85.

Ololube, N. P., Ubogu, A. E., & Egbezor, D. E. (2007). ICT and distance education programs in a sub-Saharan African country: A theoretical perspective. *Journal of Information Technology Impact*, *7*(3), 181–194.

Ololube, N. P., & Egbezor, D. E. (2009b). Competencies exhibited by professionally qualified teachers in Nigerian secondary schools: A research study. In James, V., & Etim, J. S. (Eds.), *Educational reform in Africa: Essays in curriculum, libraries, counseling and grade levels*. Lanham, MD: Edwin Mellen Press.

Ololube, N. P., & Egbezor, D. E. (2009a). Measuring the extent to which teachers interpret their role in educational terms. In Parameswaran, G., & Kader, T. (Eds.), *Educational access and social justice* (pp. 87–97). Lanham, MD: University Press of America.

Ololube, N. P. (2009). *Understanding teacher professional competencies for education effectiveness*. Owerri, Nigeria: SpringField Publishers.

Ololube, N. P. (2011). *Education and society: An interactive approach*. Owerri, Nigeria: SpringField Publishers.

Ololube, N. P., & Egbezor, D. E. (2009). Educational technology and flexible education in Nigeria: Meeting the need for effective teacher education. In S. Marshall, W. Kinuthia & W. Taylor (Eds.), *Bridging the knowledge divide: Educational technology for development*. Charlotte NC: Information Age Publishing.

Ololube, N. P., Eke, P., Uzorka, M. C., Ekpenyong, S. U., & Nte, N. D. (2009). Instructional technology in higher education: A case of selected universities in the Niger delta. *Asia-Pacific Forum on Science Learning and Teaching, 10*(2), Article 7.

Orey, M., McClendon, V. J., & Branch, R. M. (2009). *Educational media and technology yearbook* (*Vol. 34*). Springer.

Orey, M., McClendon, V. J., & Branch, R. M. (2008). *Educational media and technology yearbook: Vol. 33*. Libraries Unlimited: Greenwood Publishing Group.

Ortega, P., & Arcos, F. (2009e). Zeroing in on truancy: The use of blended learning to keep truants in the classroom. *IATED, 2009*, 288–291.

Ortega, P., & Arcos, F. (2008). *How e-homework can solve the homework debate in primary schools*. ENMA2008. International Conference on Engineering and Mathematics. pp. 5-10. Bilbao, Spain: Kopiak.

Ortega, P., & Arcos, F. (2009a). *How can Moodle help struggling students?* EDULEARN2009. International Conference on Education and New Learning Technologies, (pp. 2337-2340).

Ortega, P., & Arcos, F. (2009b). *Blended learning: An efficient response to some of the problems raised by youths at risk*. INTED2009. International Technology, Education and Development Conference, (pp. 637-642).

Ortega, P., & Arcos, F. (2009c). *CLIL enhanced through digital storytelling*. ENMA2009. International Conference on Engineering and Mathematics. (pp. 228-231). Bilbao, Spain: Kopiak.

Ortega, P., & Arcos, F. (2009d). *Moodle applied within a special needs classroom*. IASE 2009, 11th Biennial Conference. (pp. 204-207).

Osguthorpe, R. T., & Graham, C. R. (2003). Blended learning environments: Definitions and directions. *The Quarterly Review of Distance Education*, *4*(3), 227–233.

Overbaugh, R. C., & Casiello, A. R. (2008). Distributed collaborative problem-based graduate-level learning: Student's perspectives on communication tool selection and efficacy. *Computers in Human Behavior*, *24*(2), 497–515. doi:10.1016/j.chb.2007.02.017

Pallof, R. M., & Pratt, K. (2007). *Building online learning communities: Effective strategies for the virtual classroom*. San Francisco, CA: Jossey-Bass.

Palloff, R. M., & Pratt, K. (2003). *The virtual student: A profile and guide to working with online learners*. San Francisco, CA: Jossey-Bass.

Pandor, N. (2007). *Statement by Naledi Pandor MP, Minister of Education, on the release of the 2007 senior certificate examination results*. Sol Plaatje, Pretoria. Retrieved July 2008, from: http://www.gov.za

Parsad, B., & Lewis, L. (2008). *Distance education at degree-granting postsecondary institutions: 2006-2007*. Washington, D.C.: National Center for Education Statistics, Institute of Education Sciences, U.S. Department of Education. Retrieved from http://nces.ed.gov/pubs2009/2009044.pdf

Pedersen, S., & Liu, M. (2003). Teachers' beliefs about issues in the implementation of a student-centered learning environment. *Educational Technology, Research and Development, 51*(2), 57-76. (Document ID: 358280011).

Petro, S. A's Maths, Science Academy. (2008). *South Africa information*. Retrieved February 2010 from: http://www.southafrica.info/business/economy/development/petrosa-291008.htm

Piatt, K. (2009, May 11). Studentquest 2006. Who is Herring Hale? *Katie Piatt*. Retrieved February 23, 2010, from http://katiepiatt.blogspot.com/2009/05/studentquest-2006-aka-who-is-herring.html

Picciano, A. G. (2009). Blending with purpose: The multimodal model. *Journal of Asynchronous Learning Networks, 13*(1), 7–18.

Picciano, A. G., & Dziuban, C. D. (Eds.). (2007). *Blended learning: Research perspectives*. Needham, MA: Sloan Consortium.

Picciano, A. G. (2002). Beyond student perception: Issues of interaction, presence, and performance in an online course. *Journal of Asynchronous Learning Networks, 6*(1), 21–40. Retrieved from http://www.sloan-c.org/publications/jaln_main.

Picciano, A., & Seaman, J. (2007). *K-12 online learning: A survey of U.S. district administrators*. The Sloan Consortium. Retrieved on April 15, 2010 from http://www.sloan-c.org/ publications/survey/pdf/K-12_Online_Learning.pdf

Piekarski, W., & Thomas, B. (2002). ARQuake: The outdoor augmented reality gaming system. *Communications of the ACM, 45*(1), 36–38. doi:10.1145/502269.502291

Power, M. (2008). The emergence of a blended online learning environment. *MERLOT Journal of Online Learning and Teaching, 4*(4), 503-514. Retrieved from http://jolt.merlot.org/vol4no4/power_1208.pdf

Pratt, D. D. (2005) Communication skills online three years down the line: Reflecting on design principles in blended learning. *Proceedings of 7th Annual Conference on World Wide Web Applications*. Cape Technikon, Cape Town, 29-31 August 2005. Retrieved June 2008, from http://www.uj.ac.za/www2005/documents/Pratt,%20DD.pdf

Prensky, M. (2008). Turning on the lights. *Educational Leadership, 65*(6), 40–45.

Prensky, M. (2000). *Digital game-based learning* (1st ed.). Columbus, OH: McGraw-Hill.

Prensky, M. (2001a). Digital natives, digital immigrants. *Horizon, 9*(5), 1–6. Retrieved from http://www.marcprensky.com. doi:10.1108/10748120110424816

Prensky, M. (2001b). Digital natives, digital immigrants, part II: Do they really think differently? *Horizon, 9*(6), 1–9. Retrieved from http://www.marcprensky.com. doi:10.1108/10748120110424843

Prensky, M. (2001). Digital natives, digital immigrants. *On the Horizon, 9*(5). NCB University Press.

Prensky, M. (2009). H. Sapiens digital: From digital immigrants and digital natives to digital wisdom. *Innovate Journal of Online Education, 5*(3). Retrieved from http://innovateonline.info/

Punie, Y., & Cabrera, M. (2006). *The future of ICT and learning in the knowledge society*. (EUR 22218 EN). European Commission Joint Research Center, Institute for Prospective Technological Studies. Retrieved from http://www.epractice.eu/en/library/281771

Puzzle Cards. (2007). *Perplex City wiki*. Retrieved February 22, 2010, from http://perplexcitywiki.com/wiki/Puzzle_Cards

Ragan, L. C. (1999). Good teaching is good teaching: An emerging set of guiding principles and practices for the design and development of distance education. *Cause/Effect, 22*(1). Retrieved from http://net.educause.edu/ir/library/html/cem/cem99/cem9915.html

Randel, J. M., Morris, B. A., Wetzel, C. D., & Whitehill, B. V. (1992). The effectiveness of games for educational purposes: A review of recent research. *Simulation & Gaming, 23*(3), 261–276. doi:10.1177/1046878192233001

Rao, K. (2007). Distance learning in Micronesia: Participants' experiences in a virtual classroom using synchronous technologies. *Innovate, 4*(1), 1-6. Retrieved on February 1, 2010 from http://www.innovateonline.info/index.php?view=article@id=437

Rapp Young, B., & Dziuban, E. (2000). Understanding dependency and passivity: Reactive behavior patterns in writing centers. *The Writing Center Journal, 21*(1), 67–87.

Reddy, V., Van der Berg, S., Lebani, L., & Berkowitz, R. (2006). A trend analysis of matric maths performance. In Reddy, V. (Ed.), *Marking matric: Colloquium proceedings* (pp. 139–160). Cape Town, South Africa: HSRC Press.

Reid, K. (2008). The causes of non-attendance: An empirical study. *Educational Review, 60*(4), 345–357. doi:10.1080/00131910802393381

Reinhold, S. (2006). WikiTrails: Augmenting wiki structure for collaborative, interdisciplinary learning. In D. Riehle & J. Noble (Eds.), *WikiSym '06 Proceedings of the 2006 Annual Symposium on Wikis* (pp. 47-58).

Render, B., Stair, R. M., & Hannan, M. E. (2005). *Quantitative analysis for management with CD* (9th ed.). London, UK: Prentice Hall.

Resnick, M. (2002). Rethinking learning in the digital age. In Kirkman, G. (Ed.), *The global Information Technology report: Readiness for the networked world*. Oxford University Press.

Rice, R. E., Hiltz, S. R., & Spencer, D. H. (2005). Media mixes and learning networks. In Hiltz, S. R., & Goldman, R. (Eds.), *Learning together online: Research on asynchronous learning networks* (pp. 215–237). Mahwah, NJ: Lawrence Erlbaum Associates, Inc.

Robinson, R. S. (2009). Using the definition in foundation building. *TechTrends, 53*(5), 34–40. doi:10.1007/s11528-009-0322-6

Rockwell, K., Schauer, J., Fritz, S., & Marx, D. (1999). Incentives and obstacles influencing higher education faculty and administrators to teach via distance. *Online Journal of Distance Learning Administration, 2*(4), 1-8. Retrieved December 26, 2008, from http://www.westga.edu/~distance/ojdla/winter24/rockwell24.html

Rogers, C. (1969). *Freedom to learn*. Columbus, OH: Merrill.

Ross, B., & Gage, K. (2006). Global perspectives on blending learning. In Bonk, J. C., & Graham, R. C. (Eds.), *The handbook of blended learning* (pp. 155–168). John Wiley & Sons.

Rosset, A., Douglis, F., & Frazee, R. V. (2003). Strategies for building blended learning. *Learning Circuits*. Retrieved December 2008, from http://www.learningcircuits.org/2003/jul2003/rossett.htm

Rourke, L., Anderson, T., Garrison, D. R., & Archer, W. (1999). Assessing social presence in asynchronous, text-based computer conferencing. *Journal of Distance Education, 14*(2), 50–71.

Rovai, A. (2002). Building sense of community at a distance. *International Review of Research in Open and Distance Learning, 3*(1).

Rovai, A. P., Ponton, M. K., & Baker, J. D. (2008). *Distance learning in higher education: A programmatic approach to planning, design, instruction, evaluation, and accreditation*. New York, NY: Teachers College Press.

Sanchez, F. (2003). Skills for a knowledge-based economy. *Leadership, 33*(2), 30–33. Retrieved from http://www.bnet.com/.

Shah, I. M., Walters, M. R., & McKillop, J. H. (2007). Acute medicine teaching in undergraduate medical curriculum: A blended learning approach. *Emergency Medicine Journal, 28*, 354–357.

Sharples, M., Taylor, J., & Vavoula, G. (2007). A theory of learning for the mobile age. In Andrews, R., & Haythornthwaite, C. (Eds.), *The SAGE handbook of e-learning research* (pp. 122–138). London, UK: SAGE Publications.

Shepherd, J. (2009, October 20). Truancy rates on the rise. *The Guardian*.

Shirky, C. (2008). *Here comes everybody: The power of organizing without organizations*. New York, NY: Penguin Press.

Shotter, J. (1993). *Conversational realities: Constructing life through language*. London, UK: Sage.

Shulman, L. S., Golde, C. M., Bueschel, A. C., & Garabedian, K. J. (2006). Reclaiming education's doctorates: A critique and a proposal. *Educational Researcher*, *35*(3), 25–32. doi:10.3102/0013189X035003025

Siemens, G. (2004). *Connectivism: A learning theory for the digital age*. Retrieved from http://www.elearnspace.org/Articles/connectivism.htm

Siemens, G. (2004). *E-portfolios. E-learn space: Everything e-learning*. Retrieved March 23, 2010, from http://www.elearnspace.org/Articles/eportfolios.htm

Siemens, G., & Downes, S. (2008). *Connectivism and connective knowledge: A rather large open online course*. Retrieved from http://ltc.umanitoba.ca/connectivism/

Simkins, C., Rule, S., & Beinstein, A. (2007). *Doubling for growth. Addressing the maths and science challenge in South Africa's schools: A report for Centre for Development and Enterprise*.

Simpson, O. (2003). *Student retention in online, open, and distance learning*. Retrieved from http://www.questia.com/Index.jsp

Singh, H. (2003). Building effective blended learning programs. *Educational Technology*, *43*(6), 51–54.

Singh, H. (2003). Building effective blended learning programs. *Educational Technology*, *433*(6), 51–54. Retrieved from http://asianvu.com/digital-library/ elearning/blended-learning-by_Singh.pdf.

Singh, H., & Reed, C. (2001). *A White Paper: Achieving success with blended learning*. ASTD State of the Industry Report, American Society for Training and Development, March 2001.

Sirotnik, K. (2001). *Renewing schools and teacher education: An odyssey in educational change*. Washington, DC: American Association of Colleges for Teacher Education.

Sloan Consortium. (n.d.). *Blended learning Chemistry course*. Retrieved January 25, 2010, from http://www.sloanconsortium.org/node/262

Sloan Consortium. (n.d.). *The Babson Strategy: Blended online education enables localness and geo-localness*. Retrieved January 25, 2010, from http://www.sloanconsortium.org/node/441

Sloan Consortium. (n.d.). *Definition: What is online learning?* Retrieved January 25, 2010 from http://www.fldlc.org/taskforce/pdf/sloan_definition.pdf

Smith, C. M., Perkins, C. D., & Bullock, I. (2007). Undergraduate training in the care of the acutely ill patient: A literature review. *Intensive Care Medicine*, *33*, 901–907. doi:10.1007/s00134-007-0564-8

Snadden, D. (2009). From medicine's margins-why all the interest in rural and remote education? *Medical Teacher*, *11*, 967–968. doi:10.3109/01421590903307857

Snadden, D., & Bates, J. (2005). Expanding undergraduate medical education in British Columbia: A distributed campus model. *Canadian Medical Association Journal*, *173*(6), 589–590. doi:10.1503/cmaj.050439

Spector, J. M., Merrill, M. D., Merrienboer, J. V., & Driscoll, M. P. (2007). *The handbook of research for educational communications and technology* (3rd ed.). Routledge/Taylor & Francis Group.

Spiliotopoulos, V., & Beers, M. (Producers), & Dekkers, P. (Director). (2007). *Teaching, learning, and working with e-portfolios*. Vancouver, BC: British Columbia Institute of Technology.

Squire, K., & Jan, M. (2007). Mad City Mystery: Developing scientific argumentation skills with a place-based augmented reality game on handheld computers. *Journal of Science Education and Technology*, *16*(1), 5–29. doi:10.1007/s10956-006-9037-z

Squire, K. D. (2004). *Replaying history: Learning world history through playing Civilization 3*. Indiana University. Retrieved from http://portal.acm.org/citation.cfm?id=1087093

Stammen, R. M., & Schmidt, M. A. (2001). Basic understanding for developing distance education for online instruction. *NASSP Bulletin*, *85*(628), 47–50. doi:10.1177/019263650108562805

Star, S. L., & Griesemer, J. R. (1989). Institutional ecology, translations, and boundary objects: Amateurs and professionals in Berkeley's Museum of Vertebrate Zoology, 1907-39. *Social Studies of Science*, *19*, 387–420. .doi:10.1177/030631289019003001

Steinkuehler, C. A. (2004). Learning in massively multiplayer online games. In *Proceedings of the 6th International Conference on Learning Sciences* (pp. 521-528). Santa Monica, CA: International Society of the Learning Sciences.

Stenros, J., Montola, M., & Mäyrä, F. (2007). Pervasive games in Ludic society. In *Proceedings of the 2007 Conference on Future Play* (pp. 30-37). Toronto, Canada: ACM.

Stewart, S. (2006, June 11). Alternate reality games. *seanstewart.org*. Retrieved March 18, 2008, from http://www.seanstewart.org/interactive/args/

Story, M., & Truede, C. (2009). *Wikis? Twittering? Facebook? The implications and challenges of Web 2.0 technologies in teaching and learning.* Presented for Learning and Teaching Centre Instructional Technology Series, University of Victoria, B.C.

Tapscott, D. (2009). *Grown up digital* (2nd ed.). New York, NY: McGraw-Hill.

Tapscott, D., & Williams, A. D. (2010). Innovating the 21st-century university: It's time! *EDUCAUSE Review*, *45*(1), 16–29. Retrieved from http://www.educause.edu/er.

Taylor, C. R. (2002). *E-learning: The second wave*. Retrieved from http://www.providersedge.com/docs/km_articles/E-Learning_-_The_Second_Wave.pdf

Teltscher, S. (2009). *The world in 2009: ICT facts and figures*. Presented at the ITU Telecom World, Geneva, Switzerland. Retrieved from http://www.itu.int/ITU-D/ict/papers/2009/Press%20briefing_Telecom09.pdf

Thompson, W. R. (2009). *Overcoming doubts about online learning*. Southern Region Education Board, Southern Region Education Board. Retrieved on April 15, 2010, from http://publications.sreb.org/2009/09T02_Overcoming_Doubts.pdf

Traxler, J. (2009). Mobile learning evaluation: The challenge of mobile societies. In Vavoula, G., Pachler, N., & Kukulska-Hulme, A. (Eds.), *Researching mobile learning* (pp. 151–165). International Academic Publishers.

Traxler, J. (2007). Defining, discussing, and evaluating mobile learning: The moving finger writes and having writ. *International Review of Research in Open and Distance Learning, 8*(1). Retrieved on April 29, 2010, from www.irrodl.org/index.php/irrodl/article/ view/346/875

Tsou, W., Wang, W., & Tzeng, Y. (2006). Applying a multimedia storytelling website in foreign language learning. *Computers & Education*, *47*, 17–28. doi:10.1016/j.compedu.2004.08.013

Tu, C., & Corry, M. (2002). *Research in online learning community*. Retrieved from http://www.usq.edu.au/electpub/e-jist/docs/html2002/chtu.html

Twenge, J. M. (2009). Generational changes and their impact in the classroom: Teaching generation me. *Medical Education*, *43*, 398–405. doi:10.1111/j.1365-2923.2009.03310.x

Twenge, J. M. (2006). *Generation me: Why today's young Americans are more confident, assertive, entitled, and more miserable than ever before*. New York, NY: Simon & Schuster, Inc.

Twigg, C. A. (2003). *Program in course redesign*. National Centre for Academic Transformation. Retrieved June 14, 2010, from http://thencat.org/PCR.htm

Umalusi (2008). Improving the quality of teaching: Making a difference in public schooling. Retrieved October 2009, from http://www.umalusi.org.za/ur/publications/20080910Improvingthequalityofteaching.pdf

UNESCO. (2008). UNESCO'S ICT competency standards for teachers: Towards ICT skills for teachers. Retrieved March 5, 2010, from http://cst.unesco-ci.org/sites/projects/cst/default.aspx

Valiathan, P. (2002). *Blended learning models*. American Society for Training and Development. Retrieved from http://www.astd.org/LC/2002/0802_valiathan.htm

Van 'T Hooft. M. (2009). Researching informal and mobile learning: Leveraging the right resources. In G. Vavoula, N. Pachler & A. Kukulska-Hulme (Eds.), *Researching mobile learning* (pp. 170-180). International Academic Publishers.

Van Eck, R. (2006). Digital game-based learning: It's not just the digital natives who are restless. *EDUCAUSE Review*, *41*(2), 16–30.

van 't Hooft, M. (2008). Mobile, wireless, connected: Information clouds and learning. In *Emerging technologies for learning* (BECTA Research Report, Vol. 3), (pp. 30-46). Coventry, UK: BECTA. Retrieved from http://www.becta.org.uk

Vaughan, N. (2007). Perspectives on blended learning in higher education. *International Journal on E-Learning*, *6*(1), 81–94.

Vaughan, N., & Garrison, D. R. (2008). *Blended faculty community of inquiry: Linking leadership, course design, and evaluation*. EDUCAUSE Learning Initiative (ELI) Annual Meeting, San Antonio, TX.

Velasquez, A., Graham, C., & McCollum, K. (2009). Online social networking used to enhance face-to-face and online pre-service teacher education courses. In I. Gibson, et al. (Eds.), *Proceedings of Society for Information Technology & Teacher Education International Conference 2009*. Chesapeake, VA: AACE.

Vie, S. (2008). Digital divide 2.0: Generation M and online social networking sites in the composition classroom. *Computers and Composition*, *25*, 9–23. Retrieved from www.elsevier.com/locate/compcom. doi:10.1016/j.compcom.2007.09.004

Vogel, J. J., Vogel, D. S., Cannon-Bowers, J., Bowers, C. A., Muse, K., & Wright, M. (2006). Computer gaming and interactive simulations for learning: A meta-analysis. *Journal of Educational Computing Research*, *34*(3), 229–243. doi:10.2190/FLHV-K4WA-WPVQ-H0YM

Vovides, Y., Sanchez-Alonso, S., Mitropoulou, V., & Nickmans, G. (2007). The use of e-learning course management systems to support learning strategies and to improve self-regulated learning. *Educational Research Review*, *2*, 64–74. doi:10.1016/j.edurev.2007.02.004

Vygotsky, L. S. (1986). *Language and thought*. Cambridge, MA: MIT Press.

Vygotsky, L. S. (1978). *Mind in society*. Cambridge, MA: Harvard University Press.

Waite, J. (2007, July 13). World without oil: The post-game press release. *ARGNet: Alternate Reality Gaming Network*. Retrieved from http://www.argn.com/2007/07/world_without_oil_the_post-game_press_release/

Walker, G., Golde, C. M., Jones, L., Bueschel, A., & Hutchings, P. (2008). *The formation of scholars: Rethinking doctoral education for the twenty-first century*. Stanford, CA: Carnegie Foundation for the Advancement of Teaching.

Walther, B. K. (2005). Atomic actions-molecular experience: Theory of pervasive gaming. *ACM Computers in Entertainment*, *3*(3), 4. doi:10.1145/1077246.1077258

Wang, L. (2009). Learning chemistry online. *Chemical and Engineering News*, *87*(36), 97–99. doi:10.1021/cen-v087n036.p097

Wang, M. C., Dziuban, C. D., Cook, I. J., & Moskal, P. D. (2009). Dr. Fox rocks: Using data-mining techniques to examine student ratings of instruction. In M. C. Shelley, L. D. Yore, & B. Hand (Eds.), *Quality research in the literary and science education: International perspectives and gold standards* (pp. 383-398). New York, NY: Springer Science +Business Media.

Weber, L. E. (2010). *University research for innovation*. Paris, France: Economica.

Weigert, A. J. (1991). *Mixed emotions: Certain steps toward understanding ambivalence*. Albany, NY: State University of New York Press.

Whitton, N. (2008). Alternate reality games for developing student autonomy and peer learning. In *Proceedings of Lick 2008*, Edinburgh, UK.

Wiggins, G., & McTighe, J. (2007). *Schooling by design*. Alexandria, VA: ASCD.

Wiggins, G., & McTighe, J. (2008). Put understanding first. *Educational Leadership*, *65*(8), 36–41.

Williams, C. (2002). Learning online: A review of recent literature in a rapidly expanding field. *Journal of Further and Higher Education*, *26*(3), 263–272. doi:10.1080/03098770220149620

Williams, J. (2003). Blending into the background. *E-Learning Age Magazine, 1*.

Willis, J. (2008). *Qualitative research methods in education and education technology*. Charlotte, NC: Information Age Publishing.

Wolcott, L., & Betts, K. S. (1999). What's in it for me? Incentives for faculty participation in distance education. *Journal of Distance Education, 14*(2), 34-39. Retrieved December 25, 2008, from http://cade.athabascau.ca/vol14.2/Wolcott_et_al.html

Worley, P., Prideaux, D., Strasser, R., Magarey, A., & March, R. (2006). Empirical evidence for symbolic medical education: A comparative analysis of the community and tertiary-based programmes. *Medical Education, 40*(2), 109–116. doi:10.1111/j.1365-2929.2005.02366.x

Wormelli, R. (2006). Differentiating for tweens. *Educational Leadership, 63*(7), 14–19.

Zenex Foundation. (2007). *The Zenex Foundation's ten-year strategy 2006-2015*. Retrieved August 2009, from http://www.zenexfoundation.org.za/strategy.php

Zhongjun, L., & Lijuan, H. (2009). Research on new MIS teaching and learning methods. (pp. 745-748). Pacific-Asia Conference on Circuits, Communications and Systems, 2009.

About the Contributors

Andrew Kitchenham is an Associate Professor in Educational Technology in the School of Education at the University of Northern British Columbia. Dr. Kitchenham's research examines teacher transformation through the use, integration, and teaching of technology. He has published numerous articles, conference papers, technical reports, and book chapters on diverse topics from technology to special education to rural professionals to gender differences. This book is one of two dealing with e-learning.

* * *

Francisco Arcos García is a part-time professor at the University of Alicante and full-time Teacher Consultant / Trainer at the Teacher's Centre in Alicante. Currently he is in charge of setting up courses for teachers which require the use of a Learning Management Systems. His main areas of interest are in the fields of pedagogy, translation and computer mediated instruction. Now, he is mainly interested in the pedagogic design and pedagogic strategies to carry out blended learning. He graduated in English Philology – from the University of Valencia in 1982 and read his doctoral thesis in 1993. He started working in the field of distance learning and blended learning some 8 years ago when Moodle appeared. He has published a score of articles related with e-learning and blended learning for the teaching of English. For 5 years running he has been implementing blended learning in his university classes.

Jered Borup is a doctoral student of Instructional Psychology and Technology at Brigham Young University. Jered is currently a blended learning instructor for a technology integration course taught to pre-service teachers. Jered previously earned a Master's degree from Idaho State University and was a public school ninth-grade social studies teacher for six years. His current research interests include building relationships in online learning environments and the effects those relationships have on course outcomes in university and K12 settings.

Thomas B. Cavanagh is Assistant Vice President of Distributed Learning at the University of Central Florida (UCF). In this role he oversees the university's distance learning strategy, policies, and practices, including program and course design, development, and assessment. In his career, he has administered e-learning development for both academic (public and private) and industrial (Fortune 500, government/military) audiences. A frequent presenter at academic and industry conferences, he is an award-winning instructional designer, program manager, faculty member, and administrator. His research interests include e-learning, technical communication, and the societal influence of technology on education, training, culture, and commerce. He is also a published author of several mystery novels.

Charles (Chuck) D. Dziuban is Director of the Research Initiative for Teaching Effectiveness at the University of Central Florida (UCF) where he has been a faculty member since 1970 teaching research design and statistics. He received his Ph.D. from the University of Wisconsin. Since 1996, he has directed the impact evaluation of UCF's distributed learning initiative examining student and faculty outcomes as well as gauging the impact of online courses on the university. He was named UCF's first ever *Pegasus Professor* for extraordinary research, teaching, and service and in 2005 received the honor or *Professor Emeritus*. In 2005, Chuck received the Sloan Consortium award for *Most Outstanding Achievement in Online Learning by an Individual*. In 2007, he was appointed to the National Information and Communication Technology (ICT) Literacy Policy Council.

Clarissa Graffeo is a faculty research associate at the University of Central Florida's Institute for Simulation and Training (UCF IST), and is pursuing a graduate degree in UCF's Literary, Cultural, and Textual Studies program. She has been a member of the Mixed Emerging Technology Integration Lab at UCF IST since the tail end of her undergraduate degree in Digital Media. During her undergraduate program, Clarissa developed an interest in game design, and currently works as part of a team both designing and researching games for learning, ranging from traditional and collectible card games to pervasive game models. She is currently interested in the relationship between game mechanics and content, and how they work together to make meaning and facilitate learning.

Charles R. Graham is an Associate Professor of Instructional Psychology and Technology at Brigham Young University with interest in technology-mediated teaching and learning. Charles studies the design and evaluation of blended learning environments and the use of technology to enhance teaching and learning. Charles has published work related to online and blended learning environments in edited books including *Online Collaborative Learning: Theory and Practice*, *Blended Learning: Research Perspectives*, *The Encyclopedia of Distance Learning*, and the *AECT Handbook of Research on Educational Communications and Technology*. Charles also co-edited the *Handbook of Blended Learning: Global Perspectives, Local Designs* which contains thirty-nine chapters with examples of blended learning in higher education, corporate, and military contexts from around the world.

Ansie Harding is an associate professor in the Department of Mathematics and Applied Mathematics at the University of Pretoria. Her field of interest is mathematics education and especially the use of technology in teaching undergraduate mathematics, on which she has published extensively. She considers herself as an offbeat mathematician and feels herself fortunate to be part of the technology generation and being able to contribute to the exciting new options in teaching. She is also interested in creativity in mathematics and ways of developing this skill. She is an after-dinner speaker on a variety of popular mathematics topics. Her recent discovery of an innovative way of visualising complex roots of functions is a source of great pleasure.

Joel L. Hartman is Vice Provost for Information Technologies and Resources at the University of Central Florida. As the university's CIO, he has overall responsibility for library, computing, networking, telecommunications, media services, and distributed learning activities. Hartman has been an active author, and presenter at industry conferences. He currently serves on the Microsoft Higher Education Advisory Group (co-chair), the Oracle Education & Research Industry Strategy Council, the Sloan Consortium Board of Directors, the Blackboard Client Strategy Council, the EDUCAUSE

Recognition Committee (chair), the *Change* magazine board of editors, the Lake Nona Medical City IT Council (Chair), and is Chairman of the Board of Directors of Florida LambdaRail, Florida's research and education network. Hartman graduated from the University of Illinois, Urbana-Champaign, with bachelor's and master's degrees in Journalism and Communications, and received his doctorate from the University of Central Florida.

Robert Hogan is associate professor in the School of Education at the University of the South Pacific. His areas of research and teaching are science education and online learning. With a service area covering five time zones and campuses in 12 member countries, USP is an ideal site for conducting blended learning research in developing countries. His most recent research was a $250,000 grant supported by the World Health Organization to develop a blended and mobile learning chemistry course. Previously, Bob completed an AusAid research grant to study the effectiveness of distance learning in the South Pacific. Prior to join USP seven years ago, Bob created the online college at Florence-Darlington Technical College in the US where he received a $450K FIPSE grant to develop online partnerships among eight colleges in France, Germany, Spain, the United States, and England. He received his M.S. from New York University and his doctorate from the University of Central Florida. Bob has also worked as a systems engineer and a science editor for Harcourt Brace. He has taught online for the University of Phoenix for 12 years.

Michele Jacobsen is an Associate Professor in Educational Technology in the Faculty of Education at the University of Calgary. Dr. Jacobsen's research focuses on inquiry-based learning with technology; currently, she is collaborating on an Alberta-wide investigation of technology and high school success that involves 24 school jurisdictions. Dr. Jacobsen is also conducting long-term research on one-to-one laptop initiatives in three school districts. For more than a decade, Dr. Jacobsen has taught and supervised Masters and doctoral students in Educational Technology, and she teaches graduate courses on media development, usability and user-centered design, and examines the impact of social networking in higher education teaching. Dr. Jacobsen teaches in the Master of Teaching program, an innovative teacher preparation program characterized by inquiry-based learning, and mentors student teachers in their classroom practica. Dr. Jacobsen has edited the Canadian Journal of Learning and Technology (www.cjlt.ca) since 2005, and started the EGallery (www.ucalgary.ca/~egallery), an online celebration of exemplary student teacher scholarship, in 1999.

Marvin LeNoue (MA-ESL University of Hawaii) has taught ESL/EFL in a wide range of contexts both in the USA and internationally. He is currently an instructor in the North Dakota State University Intensive English Language Program, an Instructional Designer and online instructor for the NDSU Department of Distance and Continuing Education, and a Doctoral Candidate in the NDSU School of Education Doctorate Program in Occupational and Adult Education. His research interests include adult education and andragogy, the use of social media in teaching and learning, and the development of new models for the delivery of digitally-mediated education and training.

David Metcalf, with a 15-year history in Web-based and mobile learning as a Senior Researcher, combines an academic grounding and continued University involvement with a strong history of industry-centered training and simulation, providing learning innovations for 3Com, Fujitsu, FedEx Ground, Tyco, and many others. As a research faculty member with the University of Central Florida's Institute for Simulation and Training (UCF IST), Dr. Metcalf continues to bridge the gap between corporate learning and simulation techniques and non-profit and social entrepreneurship with the foundation of the Mixed Emerging Technology Integration Lab (METIL). Simulation, mobilization, outsourcing, visualization systems, and operational excellence are current research topics. Dr. Metcalf frequently presents at industry and research events shaping business strategy and use of technology to improve learning and human performance.

Patsy D. Moskal is the Associate Director for the Research Initiative for Teaching Effectiveness at the University of Central Florida (UCF) where she has been a faculty member since 1989. Since 1996, she has served as the liaison for faculty research of distributed learning and teaching effectiveness at UCF. Patsy specializes in statistics, graphics, program evaluation, and applied data analysis. She has extensive experience in research methods including survey development, interviewing, and conducting focus groups, and frequently serves as an evaluation consultant to school districts, and industry and government organizations. She has also received funding from several government and industrial agencies including the National Science Foundation and the Alfred P. Sloan Foundation. She has authored or co-authored numerous articles and chapters on blended and online learning and is a frequent presenter on research involving Web courses.

Dick Ng'ambi is a leading researcher in mobile learning for developing world contexts. He has designed and developed mobile learning tools ideal for resource constrained environments. As part of the Teaching and Research team at the Centre for Educational Technology at the University of Cape Town in South Africa, he co-ordinates a postgraduate programme in ICTs in Education. As a researcher, he lives with one question: in what ways can inequalities in knowledge production be addressed? His work on anonymous knowledge sharing, use of ubiquitous technologies, podcasting and open educational resources is influenced by his search for answers to the question. His work has been published widely in reputable journals and at peer-reviewed conferences. He has presented at several conferences both locally and internationally. His work is widely acknowledged and is a National Research Foundation (NRF) rated Researcher. He holds a PhD in Information Systems (University of Cape Town).

Nwachukwu Prince Ololube earned a PhD in Education and Teacher Education with focus in Educational Management and Planning from the University of Helsinki, Finland. In addition, he holds a Post graduate Diploma in Human Resources Management, M.Ed. in Educational Management and Planning, and BSc in Political Science. He is currently a Senior Lecturer in the Department of Educational Foundations and Management, Faculty of Education, University of Education, Port Harcourt, Nigeria. His research focuses on institutional management and leadership, education effectiveness, teacher effectiveness and quality improvement, ICT in education, and research methodology. Ololube has published in various international journals, chapters in books and leading international conference proceedings.

Pablo Ortega worked as a teacher of English for some years before becoming a principal, a post he held at several secondary schools. Presently, he works full time as an inspector of education, giving initial training to future teachers and supervising the teaching practice of tenured teachers. He wrote a doctoral dissertation on discourse analysis, and has published several articles on that field. Later on, he shifted his focus of attention to the teaching of languages, especially through ICT means. He has presented communications at many ICT conferences. He has been working as an assistant professor at the University of Alicante for the last ten years.

Pragashni Padayachee is a lecturer in the Department of Mathematics and Applied Mathematics at the Nelson Mandela Metropolitan University in Port Elizabeth. Her research interests include the study of blended learning environments and the use of technology to enhance the teaching and learning of Mathematics. She is currently studying for a PhD. Her dissertation focuses on exploring the blended learning approach supported by DVD technology to identify elements that provide a supportive and encouraging learning environment. She feels strongly about promoting a passion for increasing participation and improving performance in mathematics in secondary school learners. She has been involved in Mathematics outreach projects for secondary school learners in disadvantaged communities since 1995.

Geoff Payne is currently the Assistant Dean for the Northern Medical Program, one of the sites for the UBC distributed MD program. He is also an Associate Professor in the field of vascular physiology and Director of the Northern Health Sciences Research Facility at the University of Northern BC (UNBC). Dr. Payne came to UNBC in June 2004 as founding faculty of the medical school following a post-doctoral fellowship at Yale University in the Department of Cellular and Molecular Physiology and John B. Pierce Laboratory. Dr. Payne holds a PhD from Memorial University of Newfoundland in the field of cardiovascular and renal physiology. Dr. Payne's current research interests include use of in vivo imaging to understand microvascular regulation in inflammation and immune signaling in multiple disease processes. In addition to his biomedical research, Dr. Payne has an active research program in medical education in which his interest include curriculum and assessment.

Luke Read is the Technical Coordinator for the Mixed Emerging Technology Integration Lab at the University of Central Florida's Institute for Simulation and Training (UCF IST). He graduated from UCF with a Bachelor's Degree in Digital Media (specializing in Internet and Interactive Systems) and joined the METIL team in 2007. As a technology coordinator, he has worked on continued development of the Moving Knowledge content delivery system, which integrates emerging mobile technologies with existing Web languages. Luke plays a major role in the design and development of back end systems and websites for various software and Web projects.

Valia Spiliotopoulos, PhD, is the Associate Director of the Learning and Teaching Centre and Associate Professor in the Dept. of Educational Psychology and Leadership Studies at the University of Victoria, Canada. Valia's interests include faculty development in educational technologies, the impact of learning technologies on student engagement and performance, innovation in curriculum and program development, internationalization, graduate student professional development, and language and literacy education. Valia has a background in Modern Languages (teaching English and French as a Second Language), and her PhD is in Education from the University of British Columbia (UBC) in the area of technology use for academic writing improvement.

Ronald. M. Stammen is a Professor Emeritus in the North Dakota State University School of Education. He has been a pioneering leader in the development of educational technology use in the North Dakota K-12 and higher education systems and the implementation of technology-enabled distance education in the state. Dr. Stammen has ninety publications and 27 national and 6 international presentations. His recent research interests include the use of blended learning strategies and multimodal delivery strategies in distance education delivery, and the design of learning environments to foster cultural awareness and intercultural competence. Dr. Stammen has been the major advisor for

17 completed PhD dissertations and 24 specialist degree disquisitions, and has received many awards and honors for his innovative approaches to instruction and dedication to education in North Dakota.

Sue Tappenden moved back to New Zealand in 2001 after ten years as a senior lecturer at the Anglia University in England, to take up a position with Te Piringa – Faculty of Law at the University of Waikato. She teaches property subjects, land law, and equity, and has published in those areas, but she has a strong research interest in jurisprudence. During the course of her academic career, she has enjoyed numerous opportunities for developing papers and academic courses making the best use of available technology for blended learning.

Andrea Velasquez is a graduate student of Instructional Psychology and Technology at Brigham Young University. Andrea is interested in the study of how technology can improve teaching and learning. She teaches a course for undergraduate pre-service teachers that helps pre-service teachers teach more effectively with technology. In addition, she has conducted an evaluation in Mozambique, Africa and studies cultural competence in indigenous and cross-cultural evaluation. More recently, her main interests have been directed towards the improvement of the teacher-student relationship through understanding nurturing pedagogies and theories of care to improve this relation in technology mediated contexts.

Index

C

D

E

F

K

L

M

N

O

P

Q

R

S

T

U

V

W

Y

Z

Breinigsville, PA USA
24 March 2011
258340BV00002B/1-80/P

9 781609 604790